Andrew Arnold Lambing

A history of the Catholic church in the dioceses of Pittsburg and Allegheny from its establishment to the present time

Andrew Arnold Lambing

A history of the Catholic church in the dioceses of Pittsburg and Allegheny from its establishment to the present time

ISBN/EAN: 9783742858993

Manufactured in Europe, USA, Canada, Australia, Japa

Cover: Foto ©ninafisch / pixelio.de

Manufactured and distributed by brebook publishing software (www.brebook.com)

Andrew Arnold Lambing

A history of the Catholic church in the dioceses of Pittsburg and Allegheny from its establishment to the present time

CONTENTS.

	PAGE
PREFACE	iii

CHAPTER I.—THE INTRODUCTION OF CATHOLICITY INTO WESTERN PENNSYLVANIA.
  First settlers, Dutch, Swedes, Finns — The territory of Pennsylvania granted to William Penn—His treaty with the Indians—Irish and German immigration—The Jesuits in Maryland—Early Catholic settlements in Eastern Pennsylvania—The Catholics suspected of disloyalty —and persecuted—Catholics in Western Pennsylvania—The nationality and character of the settlers................................... 17

CHAPTER II.—PITTSBURG.
  Early history of Pittsburg—French and English claims—Indians—Major Washington's mission to the French — English occupation — Fort Duquesne and its capture by the English—Baptismal register of Fort Duquesne—Fort Pitt—The town laid out—The Whiskey Insurrection —First Catholic settlers—Rev. B. J Flaget—Rev. F. X. O'Brien—First Catholic church—Very Rev. F. De Andreis—Rev. Ch. B. M'Guire—The Church enlarged—St. Paul's Church begun—The Nuns of St. Clare— Visit of Bishops Kenrick and Conwell—Death of Father M'Guire— Biographical notice.................................... 29

CHAPTER III.—ST. PAUL'S CHURCH.
  Rev. John O'Reilly, pastor of St. Paul's—The church finished and dedicated —A description of it—The Germans take possession of St. Patrick's— The nuns of St. Clare withdraw—The Sisters of Charity arrive—An orphan asylum opened—New congregations formed—Withdrawal of Father O'Reilly—His death—Sketch of his life—Arrival of Very Rev. Michael O'Connor—His works—He visits Rome..................... 49

CHAPTER IV —HISTORY OF ST. PAUL'S CATHEDRAL FROM THE ERECTION OF THE SEE OF PITTSBURG TO ITS DIVISION AND THE ERECTION OF THE SEE OF ERIE.
  The manner in which the Church was first governed in the United States— Pittsburg an episcopal see—Very Rev. M. O'Connor consecrated first Bishop—Sketch of his early life—Condition of the Church on his arrival —The first ordination—The first synod—The colored chapel—*The Catholic* published—St Michael's Diocesan Seminary—The Bishop visits Europe—The first visitation of the diocese—The Cathedral in danger— Statistics—The Cathedral destroyed by fire—A new Cathedral commenced —The Bishop visits Rome—Erection of the See of Erie—Bishop O'Connor transferred thither—Statistics................................ 55

CHAPTER V.—History of St. Paul's Cathedral from the Erection of the See of Erie to the Resignation of Bishop O'Connor.
Visit of Cardinal Bedini—Know-Nothingism—Bishop O'Connor returns to Pittsburg—He visits Rome—Consecration of the Cathedral—A description of the building—Decline of the Bishop's health—He travels in Europe and the Holy Land—Petitions for a coadjutor—Travels in Mexico—Thinks of resigning—Visits Rome—Resigns—His episcopate—Death—Biographical notice... 71

CHAPTER VI.—History of St Paul's Cathedral from 1860 to 1873.
Statistics of the diocese—Appointment and consecration of Rt. Rev. Michael Domenec—Biographical notice—He visits Rome and Madrid—Rev. J. Hickey, rector of the Cathedral—Father McMahon retires to Philadelphia—The new organ—The Bishop again visits Rome—The towers built—Consecration of Bishop Mullen of Erie—The Golden Age of Pittsburg—The Bishop again visits Rome to attend the Vatican Council—Death of Dr. Keogh, and biographical notice—The Sisters of Charity and the Ursuline Nuns—Death and sketch of Rev. D. Devlin—Little Sisters of the Poor—Sisters of the Good Shepherd—The Catholic Institute... 85

CHAPTER VII.—History of St. Paul's Cathedral from 1873 to the Present Time.
The new episcopal residence—Death of Father McMahon, with sketch of his life—The Italians—The Bishop visits Rome—Division of the diocese—Statistics—Consecration of Rt. Rev. John Tuigg, with sketch of his life—State of the diocese—The Cathedral on fire—Death of Rev. P. Cassidy, with sketch of his life—Bishop Domenec visits Rome—Resigns his see—Returns to Spain—His death—Closing scenes of his life—Reunion of the two dioceses—Improvements................................ 96

CHAPTER VIII.—Congregations formed from St. Paul's Cathedral.
St. Patrick's Church—Death and sketch of Rev. Jas. Byrnes—St. Mary's Church—Church of the Sacred Heart—St. John the Baptist's Church—St. Peter's Pro-Cathedral, Allegheny City................................. 106

CHAPTER IX.—Congregations formed from St. Paul's Cathedral (*Concluded*)
St. Andrew's Church, Allegheny—Death and sketch of Rev. Denis O'Brien—St. Bridget's Church, Pittsburg—St. Joseph's (colored) Church—St. James' Church—St. John's Church—St. Stephen's Church—Death and sketch of Rev. P. M. Ward—St. Agnes' Church—Death and sketch of Rev. P. Kerr—St. Mary of Mercy's Church—Death and sketch of Rev. J. A. O'Rourke—and of Rev M. F. Devlin—St. Malachy's Church—St. Mary of the Mount.. 121

CHAPTER X.—German Churches of Pittsburg and Allegheny.
The advent of German Catholics in Pittsburg—Formation of a German congregation—St. Patrick's a German church—St. Mary's Chapel—Establishment of the Redemptorist Fathers in Pittsburg—St. Philomena's Church—Formation of new congregations—St. Michael's Church—The

Passionist Fathers—St. Joseph's Church, Mount Oliver—St. Martin's Church—St. Peter's Church.. 145

CHAPTER XI.—GERMAN CHURCHES OF PITTSBURG AND ALLEGHENY (*Concluded*).
St. Mary's Church, Allegheny—Death and sketch of Rev. John Stiebel—St. Joseph's Church—Church of the Holy Name of Jesus—St. Winceslaus' Bohemian Church—Holy Trinity Church, Pittsburg—Death and sketch of Rev. Fr. Grimmer—and of Rev. Charles Schuler—The Carmelite Fathers—Sts. Peter and Paul's Church—Death and sketch of Rev. A. Hune, D.D.—St. Augustine's Church—Death and sketch of Rev. Philip Schmidt—The Capuchin Friars—St. Joseph's Church—St. Stanislaus' Polish Church... 165

CHAPTER XII.—CHURCHES IN ALLEGHENY COUNTY.
St. Joseph's Church, Verona—Chapel of the Sacred Heart, Plumb Creek—St. James' Church, Wilkinsburg—Braddock's Field—Chapel at Tarra Hill—St. Thomas' Church—Death and sketch of Rev. P. Hughes—St. Joseph's German Church—M'Keesport—St. Peter's Church—Death and sketch of Rev. N. Hœres—and of Rev. Cajetan Klocker—St. Agnes' Church, Bull's Run—St. Patrick's Church, Alpsville—St. Michael's Church, Elizabeth—Death and sketch of Rev. M. J. Brazill—Transfiguration Church, Monongahela City, Washington County................. 186

CHAPTER XIII.—CHURCHES OF ALLEGHENY COUNTY (*Concluded*).
St. Philip's Church, Broadhead—St. Luke's Church, Mansfield—Death and sketch of Rev. J. O'G. Scanlon—St. Joseph's German Church, Mansfield—St. Patrick's Church, Noblestown—St. Mary's German Church, Chartier's Creek—St. James' Church, Sewickley—St. Mary's German Church, Glenfield—St. Alphonsus' Church, Wexford—St. Teresa's Church, Perrysville—St. Mary's Church, Pine Creek—Death and sketch of Rev. M. Eigner—St. Joseph's Church, Sharpsburg—St. Mary's German Church—St. Anne's Church, Millvale 205

CHAPTER XIV.—CATHOLICITY IN SOUTH-WESTERN PENNSYLVANIA.
General remarks—St. Anne's Church, Waynesburg—St. James' Church, West Alexander—Death and sketch of Rev. D. Hickey—Church of the Immaculate Conception, Washington—St. James' Church, Claysville—Other stations in Green and Washington counties—Fayette and Somerset counties—Scenery, aborigines, Indian paths—First settlers—Brownsville—First Catholic settlers—Pittsburg visited as a station from Brownsville—St. Peter's Church, Brownsville—Uniontown—St. John's Church—Farmington Mission—General Braddock's grave—Church of the Immaculate Conception, Connellsville—St. Aloysius' Church, Dunbar—Le Mont Furnace Mission—St. John the Baptist's Church, Scottdale—St. John the Baptist's Church, New Baltimore—St. Matthew's Church, Meyersdale—Death and sketch of Rev. Thos. Fitzgerald—Stations: Ursina, Sand Patch, Wellsburg, etc.. 225

CHAPTER XV.—BEDFORD AND HUNTINGDON COUNTIES.
General remarks on the early Catholic settlements—Bedford—St. Thomas'

Church—Death and sketch of Very Rev. Thos. Heyden—St. John's Church, Clearville—St. Mary's Church, Shade Valley—Huntingdon—Early Catholic settlement—Holy Trinity Church—Death and sketch of Rev. P. B. Halloran—Mount Union—Church of the Immaculate Conception, Broad Top........ 253

CHAPTER XVI.—BLAIR COUNTY.
General remarks—St. Patrick's Church, Newry—Rev. Jas. Bradley—St. Luke's Church, Sinking Valley—Hollidaysburg—Early Catholic settlers—St. Mary's Church—Conversion of Heyden Smith—St. Michael's German Church—Williamsburg—St. Joseph's Church—Altoona—St. John's Church—Lloydsville Mission—German Church of the Immaculate Conception—St. Matthew's Church, Tyrone............................. 265

CHAPTER XVII.—CAMBRIA COUNTY.
General features of the county—First settlers Catholics—Captain M'Guire—First visit of a priest—First appearance of Dr. Gallitzin—His parentage and early life—He visits America—Resolves to become a priest—Is ordained—His first missions—M'Guire's settlement—He takes up his residence in the future Loretto—St. Michael's Church—His estates—Loretto... 282

CHAPTER XVIII.—CAMBRIA COUNTY (*Continued*).
Dr. Gallitzin as a land agent—As a pastor—Regulations for Mass, etc.—Sermons—Troubles—Death of the Princess Gallitzin—Wolves in sheep's clothing—Settlement of the litigations regarding his estate—Gradual extension of the colony—Bishop Egan visits Loretto—Dr. Gallitzin as a writer—A new church—Scanty remittances from his estate—He asks aid from his friends—The crisis—Relief—The little chapel—Bishop Kenrick of Philadelphia—Rev. Henry Lemcke arrives at Loretto—Fr. Lemcke at Ebensburg—Other writings of Dr. Gallitzin—The end approaching—Last illness—Death of Dr. Gallitzin—Remarks on the Loretto settlement—Church property—Dr. Gallitzin's successors......... 299

CHAPTER XIX.—CAMBRIA COUNTY (*Continued*)—CONGREGATIONS FORMED FROM LORETTO.
St. Bartholomew's Church, Wilmore—German Church of the Immaculate Conception, New Germany—St. Aloysius' Church, Summitville—Death and sketch of Rev. Thos. M'Cullagh—and of Rev. John Hackett—St. Patrick's Church, Gallitzin—St. Augustine's Church, St. Augustine—Death and sketch of Rev. Ed. Burns—St. Monica's Church, Chest Springs 328

CHAPTER XX.—CAMBRIA COUNTY (*Concluded*).
Church of the Holy Name of Jesus, Ebensburg—Carrolltown—St. Joseph's Church, Hart's Sleeping Place—St. Benedict's Church, Carrolltown—St. Laurence's Church, Glen Connell—St. Boniface's Church, St. Boniface—St. Nicholas' Church, St. Nicholas—Johnstown—St. John Gualbert's Church—Death and sketch of Rev. P. Brown—St. Joseph's German Church—German Church of the Immaculate Conception, Cambria City.. 343

CHAPTER XXI.—WESTMORELAND COUNTY.

The place it occupies in our history—First Catholic settlement in Western Pennsylvania—The first Mass—The first priest—The first church—Death of Rev. Theodore Browers—Troubles—Rev. P. Heilbron—New settlements—Death of Father Heilbron—Rev. Ch. B. M'Guire—Trustees—Rev. Terence M'Girr—Arrival of Rev. J. A. Stillenger—The Bishop and the trustees—The new church.. 359

CHAPTER XXII.—WESTMORELAND COUNTY (*Continued*)—THE BENEDICTINE ORDER AT ST. VINCENT'S.

Departure of the Benedictines from Germany and their arrival at St. Vincent's—Condition of the place—Taking possession—The first ordination—Spread of the order—St. Vincent's an independent priory—Improvements—A seminary and college opened—St. Vincent's an exempt abbey—Further improvements—The congregation—Present state of the order—Church of the Most Holy Sacrament, Greensburg—St. Boniface's Chapel, Chestnut Ridge—St. Vincent's Chapel, Youngstown—Ligonier, Church of the Holy Family—Bolivar Station—St. Mary's Church, New Florence... 373

CHAPTER XXIII.—WESTMORELAND COUNTY (*Concluded*)—INDIANA COUNTY.

Church of Our Lady of Mount Carmel—St. Martin's Church, New Derry—Church of the Holy Family, Latrobe—St. Boniface's Church, Penn.—Church of St. Mary of the Assumption, Irwin—Sutersville Mission—Smithton Mission—Indiana County—St. Patrick's Church, Cameron Bottom—Church of the Seven Dolors, Strongstown—St. Bernard's Church, Indiana—Blairesville—Sts. Simon and Jude's Church—Death and sketch of Very Rev. J. A. Stillenger—St. Matthew's Church, Saltzburg 387

CHAPTER XXIV.—THE DONEGAL SETTLEMENT—ARMSTRONG COUNTY.

Character and nationality of the colonists—Crossing the ocean and coming West—Settlement—The first visit of a priest—Armstrong County—St. Patrick's Church, Sugar Creek—A resident priest—The church farm—Death and sketch of Rev. P. O'Neil—and of Rev. P. Rafferty—and of Rev. Jos. Cody—and of Rev. P. M. Doyle—Church of St. Mary of the Nativity, Freeport—St. Joseph's Church, Natrona, Allegheny County—St. Patrick's Church, Brady's Bend—St. Mary's German Church—Kittanning, St. Mary's Church—Holy Guardian Angel's Church, Easly's Settlement—Parker City, an oil-country town—Church of the Immaculate Conception... 409

CHAPTER XXV.—BUTLER COUNTY.

The Indians and Moravians—Location of the Catholic inhabitants—St. Peter's German Church, Butler—St. Paul's Church—St. Bridget's Chapel, M'Neil's Settlement—St. Wendelin's Chapel—St. Mary's German Church, Summit—St. Joseph's Church, North Oakland—St. Joseph's German Church—St. John's Church, Clearfield—Church of the Mother of Sorrows, Millerstown—St. Alphonsus' Church, Murrinsville—Death and sketch of Rev. Jos. Haney—Chapel at Fairview—St. James' Church, Petrolia..... 439

CHAPTER XXVI.—BEAVER AND LAWRENCE COUNTIES.
Visit of a French missionary—Sts. Peter and Paul's Church, Beaver—Death and sketch of Rev. Jas. Reid—St. Cecilia's Church, Rochester—St. John the Baptist's Church, Baden—St. Joseph's Church, New Brighton—St. Rose's Church, Cannelton—St. Mary's German Church, Beaver Falls—St. James' Church, New Bedford—St. Mary's Church, Newcastle—St. Francis Xavier's Church, Stonerstown—St. Teresa's Church, Clinton.... 454

CHAPTER XXVII.—COLLEGES—RELIGIOUS ORDERS OF MEN.
Remarks—St. Michael's Seminary—The Brothers of the Presentation—St. Vincent's Abbey and College—The Franciscan Brothers—St. Francis' College—The Congregation of the Holy Ghost and the Immaculate Heart of Mary—The Pittsburg Catholic College—Other religious orders—The Passionists—The Oblates of St. Charles Boromeo—Death and sketch of Rev. P. M'C. Morgan... 470

CHAPTER XXVIII.—RELIGIOUS ORDERS OF WOMEN—ACADEMIES.
The Nuns of St. Clare—St. Clare's Academy—The Sisters of Charity—The Sisters of Mercy—St. Xavier's Academy—St. Aloysius' Academy—The Sisters of St. Francis—The Sisters of St. Joseph—Mount Gallitzin Seminary—The Benedictine Nuns—The Ursuline Nuns—Other religious communities... 483

CHAPTER XXIX.—CHARITABLE INSTITUTIONS—RELIGIOUS ORDERS OF WOMEN.
The Mercy Hospital, Pittsburg — St. Francis Hospital, Pittsburg — Asylum of the Little Sisters of the Poor, Allegheny—St. Paul's R. C. Orphan Asylum, Pittsburg—St. Joseph's German Asylum, Allegheny—St. Michael's German Orphan Asylum, Pittsburg—House of the Good Shepherd, Allegheny—Conclusion...................................... 496

SUPPLEMENTARY CHAPTER.—ERRORS IN OUR EARLY CATHOLIC HISTORY.
"The old priest" mentioned by Wm. Penn in 1686—The first priest to say Mass in Philadelphia—The first church in Philadelphia—Miss Elizabeth M'Gawley's Chapel near Nicetown................................... ... 521

A History of the Catholic Church

IN THE

DIOCESES OF PITTSBURG AND ALLEGHENY.

CHAPTER I.

THE INTRODUCTION OF CATHOLICITY INTO WESTERN PENNSYLVANIA.

First settlers : Dutch, Swedes, Finns—The territory of Pennsylvania granted to William Penn—His treaty with the Indians—Irish and German immigration—The Jesuits in Maryland—Early Catholic settlements in Eastern Pennsylvania—Suspicion and legislation against Catholics—Catholic settlements in Western Pennsylvania—The nationality and character of the people.

BEFORE entering upon the history of Catholicity it will be necessary to glance briefly at the civil and political history of the State, that the reader may be better prepared to form an idea of the field in which the Church labored, and the difficulties she had to encounter. The first attempt at a colonization of the territory embraced within the present State of Pennsylvania was made by the Dutch, under the auspices of the East India Company, who began a settlement in the south-eastern part of the State in the year 1609. A large body of Swedes and Finns followed about thirty years later, and settled in the same place. But the power of the latter soon predominated, and they continued to rule until 1664, when the territory passed into the hands of the English. It was granted to William Penn, a member of the Society of Quakers, or Friends, by King James II., by royal charter, dated March 4th, 1681, in payment of a debt of £16,000 due his father, Admiral Sir William Penn, from the British Government. The charter vested the perpetual proprietaryship of the vast region in him and his heirs, on the fealty of the annual payment of two beaver-skins. He designed at first to call the territory New Wales, and afterwards suggested Sylvania, but the king peremptorily ordered the name of Pennsylvania to be inserted, in honor, as he said, of his late friend the admiral. Aided by the advice of Sir William Jones, and Henry, the brother of Algerton Sydney, he drew up a liberal scheme of government and laws for the colony, by which all who believed in God were permitted to worship him according to the dictates of their own consciences. He embarked for America, and landed in October, 1681. After several meetings with the Indians he made his famous treaty with them at Shackamaxon, now Kensington, at the end of November—a treaty that was never sworn to and never broken.* There was at this time, according to the most reliable authority, a little less than 50,000 Indians within the limits of the colony, being for the most part Delawares and their descendants.† Having settled the affairs of the government, Penn returned to England in 1684, leaving a population of about 7000 Europeans in the colony.

The first large accession to the population next to the Quakers was an immigration from the north of Ireland, from 1715 to 1725, which was gradually diffused over the whole colony, but which finally settled most thickly in the western and south-western portions. They were Presbyterians of the most illiberal school, as will be seen in the sequel. The next accession was a German immigration, begun about the year 1730, which peopled several of the eastern counties, and which has given prominence to that nationality in all the subsequent history of the State.‡

The colony was governed by the provisions of Penn's constitution till the breaking out of the war of the Revolution.

The truths of our holy religion were first preached in Pennsylvania by the Jesuit fathers from Maryland. A brief sketch of the advent of the Society into that State will consequently not be out of place. As early as 1570 Father Segura,

---

* American Cyclopedia, art. William Penn. † Hist. of Allegheny County, p. 12.
‡ Amer Cycl., art. Penna.

with eight other fathers of the Society and an Indian convert whom they had educated and named Don Luis, sailed from Florida and entered the Chesapeake Bay, which they named St. Mary's. But after landing and travelling a considerable distance into the interior they were betrayed into the hands of hostile Indians by the treacherous Don Luis, and murdered. The soil thus watered by the blood of the martyrs lay uncultivated for sixty-four years until the colony under Lord Baltimore, the pioneer of religious liberty in the New World, landed and took possession of Maryland on the Feast of the Annunciation, March 25th, 1634. The date was auspicious, and the pious reader of American history cannot but observe from this and many kindred occurrences the manner in which the Immaculate Queen of Heaven claimed the New World for her own from the days of Columbus, and still claims it. Accompanying Lord Baltimore were two Jesuit fathers, Revs. Andrew White and John Altham. They were the first English-speaking missionaries who labored for the salvation of the Indians in the Western Continent. Father White justly merits the title of Apostle of Maryland.* Amid every vicissitude the Society of Jesus has since held possession of the territory purchased with so much blood.

Catholics were found at an early date in Eastern Pennsylvania. The first chapel in which Mass was offered up was a small frame building that stood south of Walnut Street and east of Fourth, near the site of the present St. Joseph's Church, Philadelphia. But after the dethronement of James II., in 1689, the penal laws began to be enforced; and Penn, who was looked upon with suspicion for his attachment to the cause of the late king, wrote from London, under date of July 29th, 1708, to James Logan, his colonial governor: "There is a complaint against your government that you suffer public Mass in a scandalous manner.† Pray send the matter of fact, for ill use of it is made against me here."‡ In a subsequent letter he returned to the same subject, and said: "It has be-

---
* Shea's Hist. of the Church in the United States, pp. 22 *et seq*.

† In a small chapel on Walnut Street.—Note of the Editor of the Memoirs.

‡ Memoirs of the Historical Society of Pennsylvania, vol. x., being the Penn and Logan Correspondence, vol. ii., p. 294.

come a reproach to me here, with the officers of the crown, that you have suffered the scandal of the Mass to be publicly celebrated."*

Nothing further is known of the condition of the Catholics there until 1730, when Rev. Josiah Greaton, S.J., was sent thither from Maryland. He at first celebrated Mass in the chapel already mentioned; but in 1733 he bought a lot on Fourth Street and built a chapel. The authorities took umbrage at the erection of a *Roman Mass-house* contrary to the statutes of William III., and opposed its being so used *in so public* a place.† It is not, however, known to what extent the opposition was carried. Father Greaton labored for twenty years in Philadelphia, and is justly regarded as the Apostle of that city.

The celebrated German mission of Goshenhoppen, Berks County, forty-five miles north-west of Philadelphia, is more interesting to us as being one of the points from which Catholic emigration set in towards the western part of the State.‡ It is said to have been founded in 1741 by Rev. Theodore Schneider, S.J., who built a church four years

* Watson's Annals of Philadelphia.
† Colonial Record, vol. iii. pp. 546, 563.
‡ The importance which this settlement played in the history of Catholicity in western Pennsylvania will add to the interest of the following curious document, signed by five justices of the peace of Berks County, and presented to the Governor of Pennsylvania during the French war, soon after Braddock's defeat :

"As all the Protestant inhabitants of Berks County are uneasy at the behavior of the Roman Catholics, who are very numerous in this county, some of whom show great joy at the bad news lately come from the army, we have thought it our duty to inform your Honor of our dangerous situation, and to beg your Honor to enable us by some legal authority to disarm or otherwise disable the Papists from doing any injury to the other people who are not of their vile principles. We know that the people in the Roman Catholic Church are bound by their principles to be the worst of neighbors, and we have reason to fear just at this time that the Roman Catholics of Cussahoppen, where they have a magnificent chapel and lately have had large processions, have bad designs ; for in the neighborhood of that chapel it is reported and generally believed that thirty Indians are lurking with guns and swords and cutlashes. The priests at Reading as well as at Cussahoppen last Sunday gave notice to their people that they could not come to them again in less than nine weeks, whereas they constantly preach once in four weeks to their congregations ; whereupon some imagine that they've gone to consult with our enemies at Fort Duquesne. It is a great unhappiness at this time to the people of this province that the Papists should keep arms in their later, and remained in the settlement for twenty years. This was from an early day a very flourishing mission. In the same year, 1741, Rev. William Wapeler, S.J., the companion of Father Schneider, founded the mission at Conewago, in York, now Adams County.* It soon rivalled Goshenhoppen, and became, like it, the parent of new western missions. Both were at first composed principally of Germans, but an Irish element was soon introduced into them. The same Father Wapeler is said to have purchased ground at Lancaster, in 1741, on which to erect a church; but it was left to his successor, Rev. Ferdinand Farmer, whose original name was Steinmeyer, and who came in 1758 or 1759, to carry his designs into execution.

But the sons of Erin, whose record is so illustrious in every part of the world, were not slow in finding their way into the wilds of Pennsylvania, to plant the faith which they had nurtured amid so many difficulties at home. In 1725 nearly 6000 of these exiles—some of whom doubtless were Catholics—landed at Philadelphia to join those of their countrymen who had preceded them.

These were the first and principal settlements in the eastern part of the State of which Catholic historians make mention.

Although umbrage was taken, as we have seen, at the few Catholics who had settled in the colony of Pennsylvania for opening chapels, or "Mass-houses" as they were called, it appears certain that no active measures were taken to curtail their liberties prior to the commencement of hostilities between the English and French in America. But during the period of this war, that is from 1753 to 1763, the Catholics were regarded with suspicion owing to an opinion, as opposed to right reason as it is to the teaching of history, that they must necessarily be disloyal subjects. And because the

houses, against which the Protestants are not prepared; who, therefore, are subject to a massacre whenever the Papists are ready. We pray your Honor would direct us in this important business.

"Heidelburg, July 23, 1755."

On examining into the matter, the Provincial Council replied, August 9th: "We apprehend there is very little foundation for that representation."—*Colonial Records*, vol. vi. pp. 503, 533.

* *Caughnawaga* is an Indian word signifying "the rapids."

French were looked upon as a Catholic people, and the English were conscious of their persecution of their Catholic subjects at home, the latter were regarded as persons ready to sell their country to her enemies.

Frequent reference to the Catholics, or Papists as they were called even in public documents, may be found at this time by any one who will be at the trouble of consulting the "Pennsylvania Archives" (Old Series) and the "Colonial Records."

Thus Dan. Clause, in a letter to Governor Morris of Pennsylvania, under date of October, 1754, warns him against a certain man who is a dangerous character because the writer is certain of his being a Roman Catholic, for he was seen making his confession to a priest in Canada.* Governor Morris of Pennsylvania, writing to Governor Dinwiddie of Virginia, August 19th, 1755, complains of the defenceless state of the country against the inroads of the French, "who," he says, "might march in and be strengthened by the German and Irish Catholics, who are numerous here" (in Philadelphia).† The latter governor replies, September 20th, 1755: "I have not omitted writing to the ministry the unaccountable conduct of your Assembly, the dangers we are in from the German Roman Catholics, and I have no doubt the next session they will seriously consider of it, and make some alteration in your constitution." ‡ They did consider it, and made alterations as we shall see. In a letter from Governor Morris to Governor Hardy of New York, of July 5th, 1756, the former writes: "The Roman Catholics in this and the neighboring provinces of Maryland are allowed the free exercise of their religion." Governor Hardy, in his reply of the 9th of the same month, commenting on the French war, thinks that certain facts regarding the colonists had transpired "through the treasonable correspondence of the Roman Catholics with the French," and adds: "I have heard you have an ingenious Jesuit in Philadelphia."§

The suspicion of Catholic loyalty which the foregoing extracts evince found its full expression in "An Act for

---

* Pa. Archives (Old Series), vol. ii. p. 176.
† Ibid., p. 390.   ‡ Ibid., p. 423.
§ Ibid., p. 694.

Regulating the Militia," passed by the Provincial Assembly, March 29th, 1757, from which the following extracts referring to the *Papists* are taken. The act provides that the local authorities shall immediately take a list of all persons in their several districts fit for military duty except "religious societies or congregations whose tenets and principles are against bearing arms, and all Papists or reputed Papists." These were to be designated by marks opposite their names in the roll-book. Again, it is "provided always that no Papist or reputed Papist shall be allowed or admitted to give his vote or be chosen an officer of the militia within any of the districts within these provinces."

"And be it enacted by the authority aforesaid that all arms, military accoutrements, gunpowder and ammunition, of what kind soever, any Papist or reputed Papist within this province hath or shall have in his house or houses, or elsewhere, one month after the publication of this act, shall be taken from such Papist or reputed Papist by warrant, etc., . . . and if any such Papist or reputed Papist shall attempt to conceal such arms, etc., . . . every such person so offending shall be imprisoned by a warrant from said justices for the space of three months without bail or main-prize.

"And whereas all Papists and reputed Papists are hereby exempted from attending and performing the military duties enjoined by this act, . . . and nevertheless will partake of and enjoy the benefit . . . thereof, . . . Be it, therefore, enacted . . . that every male Papist or reputed Papist between the age of seventeen and fifty-five years . . . pay the sum of twenty shillings."*

Other instances might be given from the same source and of the same tenor; but these are deemed sufficient. It may be added, however, that this feeling of hostility to the Catholics remained for some years after the close of the war with the French and the extinction of her claims to all land east of the Mississippi. For example, in the beginning of 1769 the colonial government refused to pass "An Act to enable John Cottringer and Joseph Cauffman to hold lands in this

---

* Pa. Archives (Old Series), vol. ii. p. 120 *et seq.*

province," because the rulers "have considered that the persons mentioned in the bill are Roman Catholics."*

As the result of the act regarding the militia and the census taken of the Catholics, we have the following interesting figures relative to the Catholic population:

"A LIST OF ALL THE ROMAN CATHOLICS IN PENNSYLVANIA, 1757—
That is, of all such as receive the sacraments, beginning from twelve years of age or thereabouts.

	Men.	Women.
Under the care of Robert Harding :		
In and about Philadelphia, being all Irish (or English)	72	78
In Chester County	18	22
Under the care of Theodore Schneider :		
In and about Philadelphia, being all Germans	107	121
Philadelphia County, but up country	15	10
Berks County	62	55
Northampton County	68	62
" " Irish	17	12
Bucks County	14	11
Chester "	13	9
" " Irish	9	6
Under the care of Father Farmer :		
In Lancaster County, Germans	108	94
" " " Irish	22	27
" Berks County, Germans	41	39
" " " Irish	5	3
" Chester "	23	17
" " " Germans	3	..
" Cumberland County, Irish	6	6
Under the care of Matthias Manners :		
In York County, Germans	54	62
" " " Irish	55	38
	692	673
Total sum	1365	

April 29, 1757."

Let us now turn to the west. Apart from the gradual encroachment of the pioneers on the domain of the red man, which must, in process of time, have subjected it to the advancing civilization, circumstances were not wanting to give an additional impetus to settlement. In 1748 the Ohio Company obtained a charter granting it 500,000 acres of land on

* Colonial Records, vol. ix. p. 596.

the southern bank of the Ohio River between the Monongahela and the Great Kanawha, with the additional privilege of occupying lands north of the first-named stream. This territory embraced a large portion of South-western Pennsylvania. Preparations were being made for taking immediate possession of it, when public attention was forcibly drawn to the west by the threatened encroachments of the French from the vicinity of Lake Erie. This subject will be treated at length in the history of Pittsburg. From that time forward "the Forks," as the site of the present city of Pittsburg was then designated, became familiarly known throughout the colonies. A dispute also arose between Virginia and Pennsylvania regarding the boundary line between the two colonies, which drew still further attention to the west. It was at length settled by arbitration, August 31st, 1779. Pioneers continued to encroach on the Indians, till at the time of the excise troubles which ended in the "Whiskey Insurrection," in 1794, that portion of the State embraced within this history, was generally, though sparsely, occupied by settlers.

Before entering upon the history of the various congregations in the two dioceses, it is proper to pause first and give the reader an idea of the manner in which Catholicity was introduced into the western part of the State. The sources of information are few and meagre, but sufficient, it is believed, to establish what follows.*

---

* Christian Frederick Post, a Moravian missionary, who had considerable influence with the Indians, and who was on several occasions employed by the English to use his influence with the former in their behalf, thus writes in his journal under date of September 1st, 1758, giving an account of an interview he had with the Indians at Logstown, twenty-two miles below Pittsburg, on the north bank of the Ohio River, and a speech that he had made to them, says: "My brothers, I know you have been wrongly persuaded by many wicked people; for you must know there are a great many Papists in the country in French interest, who appear like gentlemen and have sent many runaway Irish Papist servants among you, who have put bad notions into your heads and strengthened you against your brothers, the English." ("The Olden Time," vol. i. p. 116.) To this the editor adds the following explanatory note: "The Indian traders used to buy the transported Irish to be employed in carrying up goods among the Indians. Many of these ran away from their masters and joined the Indians."

On the fifth of the same month, in another speech, Mr. Post tells the Indians: "Those wicked people who set you at variance with the English by telling you many wicked stories are Papists in French pay; besides, there are many among

The pioneers of Catholicity appear to have penetrated the western wilds by four different routes. The first of these led from Goshenhoppen, already mentioned, through Huntingdon County to Hollidaysburg, where it crossed the main ridge of the Allegheny Mountains, and continued to the spot occupied by St. Vincent's Abbey, Unity Township, Westmoreland County. Here, in the fall of 1787, was laid the foundation of the first permanent Catholic settlement in Western Pennsylvania. It became, in the process of time, the parent of numerous other congregations; and was long a resting-place for colonists going further west. Many immigrants, leaving the direct route, settled to the north of it in the vicinity of Bellefonte and Huntingdon; others found homes to the south, in the vicinity of Newry; while a few settled on the route or near it, about Sinking Valley, Frankstown, etc. The Unity Township colony was much larger than any of the settlements along the route, and in Nov., 1799, when Rev. Peter Heilbron (or Helbron) came to take charge of it, numbered seventy-five communicants.* About two years previous to that time Rev. Father Lanigan, who had but lately arrived in the colony and who was dissatisfied with the state of affairs arising out of the conduct of the unhappy Father Fromm, led a body of the people of the same mind as himself to West Alexander, Washington County, to establish a branch colony at that place. But not finding the land which they had purchased suitable for agricultural purposes, they soon disposed of it, and proceeded south-east to Waynesburg, Greene County, where they made a permanent settlement.

The second route led from Conewago, and, entering Huntingdon County in the south-east at Shade Gap, united with the other route at a point east of Hollidaysburg. Many families, some German, some Irish, came by this route to Unity Township, Westmoreland County, and to Loretto, Cambria County.

us in the French service who appear like gentlemen, and buy Irish Papist servants and promise them great rewards to run away to you and strengthen you against the English, by making them appear as black as devils."—*Ibid.*, p. 120.

From this it would appear that at least a small number of Catholics were scattered through the western part of the State at that time.

* Rev J. A. Stillinger's MS.

The third route led from Maryland by way of Bedford along the foot of the eastern slope of the Allegheny Mountains to the point at which the first route crossed. By it came the colonies of Bedford and later of Harman Bottom, but principally that of Loretto, from which the greater part of the congregations of Cambria County were formed.

The fourth route was that opened by Gen. Braddock in his unfortunate expedition against Fort Duquesne, in 1755, which crossed the mountains from Cumberland by way of Uniontown and the Yohioghenny River to Pittsburg. This is known in history as *Nemacolin's Path*, so called from a Delaware Indian of that name.* By this route came the important Irish colony that settled at Donegal Township, Butler County, in 1795. But leaving the route near Stewart's Crossing (now Connellsville), they bore north past the Westmoreland County settlement, and from thence to the Allegheny River, which they crossed at Freeport; and proceeded from that point directly to the term of their journey. Nearly all the congregations of Armstrong and Butler counties were originally formed by members of this colony or their descendants. At the beginning of this century it was the largest settlement in the western part of the State. Brownsville and the upper Monongahela valley were peopled by the same route. Towards the close of the last century a small number of German families settled at Jacob's Creek, a tributary of the Yohioghenny River, about thirty miles south-east of Pittsburg; but the colony never attained any importance. The number of Catholics who had settled in Pittsburg before the beginning of the present century was so insignificant, it would appear, as not to have attracted the attention of the few missionaries.

As regards the nationality of the early Catholic settlers, they were almost exclusively German and Irish. The former predominated at Unity Township; at the settlements east of the mountains the two nationalities were represented from the beginning, but the Irish soon predominated; while the Donegal and Brownsville settlements were exclusively Irish.

History does not inform us that the French missionaries to

---

* The Monongahela of Old, p. 25.

the far west established any post at Presqu' Isle (Erie), or at any other place in the north-western part of the State. Nor do the missionaries appear to have done so who accompanied the French forces in their expeditions in the middle of the last century. Their labors appear to have been confined to the soldiers and the Indians within the fortifications. As to white settlers, there were none at that early day. From a manuscript of Bishop O'Connor, now before me, it would appear that a small body of Irish emigrants settled on Oil Creek about the close of the century. But the south-western part of the State was settled earlier than the north-western. It is superfluous to remark that the early colonists did not proceed in a compact body to the term of their journey; many, in fact, did not know where that would be, but that some preferred to settle at different points along the way. It may be further remarked that the first settlers being solely intent upon agriculture, took possession of such land only as was considered fertile. But as time went on and the mineral resources of the country, which constitute its principal source of wealth, were developed, and canals and railroads were opened—which, from necessity or the requirements of mining and manufacture, usually follow streams or penetrate mountain regions—the subsequent accessions to the population were principally drawn to these localities, leaving the first settlements without any considerable additions to their numbers. For this reason it is that Brownsville, Uniontown, Waynesburg, Jacob's Creek, Bedford, Sinking Valley, and Shade Gap were as important numerically sixty years ago as they are at present. Almost the same may be said of Huntingdon; while Slippery Rock is entirely forgotten.

CHAPTER II.

PITTSBURG.

Early history of Pittsburg—French and English claims—Indians—Major Washington's mission to the French—English occupation—Fort Duquesne, and its capture by the English—Baptismal Register of Fort Duquesne—Fort Pitt—A town laid out—The Whiskey Insurrection—First Catholic settlers—Rev. B. J. Flagget—Rev. F. X. O'Brien—First Catholic Church, St. Patrick's—Very Rev. F. De Andreis—Rev. Ch. B. M'Guire—St. Patrick's Church enlarged—St. Paul's Church begun—The Nuns of St. Clare—Visit of Bishops Kenrick and Conwell—Death of Father M'Guire—Biographical notice.

HAVING given the reader an idea, necessarily brief and imperfect, of the manner in which Catholicity was first introduced into the western part of the State, we shall now take up the history of the several congregations.

Pittsburg, although not the first place to receive the saving truths of Christianity, will yet be the first to claim our attention, from the fact that it has become the centre of Catholic rule and unity. And first of its civil, as a foundation for its religious, history.

The treaty of Aix-la-Chapelle, ratified October, 1748, by which a long-continued struggle between France on the one side and England and other European Powers on the other was apparently terminated, and the two leading nations left in the same condition, as regards their possessions, as before the war, was not without its effect on the relations of their respective American colonies. The Governor of Canada claimed, in the name of his royal master, extensive territory, including within its limits the western half of Pennsylvania, and prepared, with the aid of the forces at his command and the Indians who were ready to fight under the French standard, to take possession by the force of arms. The English colonial authorities prepared to oppose him in the same manner.

"At that time the country adjacent to the forks of the Ohio was occupied by various tribes, or nations. The *Shawanese*, who may scarcely be said to have had a permanent abiding-place, were settled along the Ohio and Allegheny rivers. The *Delawares* were intermingled with *Shawanese*, having removed westward from their former homes on the Delaware and Susquehanna rivers. Their king, *Shingiss*, was found by Washington in 1753, located at the mouth of Chartier's Creek, about two miles below the Forks, and their queen, *Aliquippa*, at the mouth of the Youghiogheny. The *Delawares* also had a town, called *Shanopin's Town*, on the left bank of the Allegheny, two miles above the Forks. The *Senecas* of the Six Nations were also dwelling on both the Allegheny and Ohio; and these distinct nations appear to have been living peaceably together, at the same time preserving their manners, customs, and dress." *

After referring to the warlike preparations of the representatives of the two powers, the historian continues: "The year 1753 begins the interesting history of the region around the present city of Pittsburg. The eyes of two of the most powerful European nations were upon it, each determined to occupy and hold the grand strategical point at the confluence of the Allegheny and Monongahela rivers, or rather at the mouth of the latter stream, for the Allegheny was then called the Ohio by many.†

"Here among the rugged hills of Western Pennsylvania, on the head-waters of the Ohio, began the conflict apparently

---

* History of Allegheny County, p. 18.

† In the "Baptismal Register of Fort Duquesne," to which reference will hereafter be made, the Ohio is called "Oio;" in Charlevoix's "History of New France" it is named "L'Oyo, au la Belle Rivière;" and in Kip's "Early Jesuit Missions" (Father Marest's journal) it is termed the "Ouabache" River. May not the good father have confounded this river with the Wabash? The name Ohio appears to be from the Seneca word *Ho-he-yu*, meaning *clear water*.—*Olden Time*, vol. i. p. 426.

The term *Allegheny* is derived from *Yallagawe*, or *Allegewi*, the name of a powerful tribe, which, as tradition has it, inhabited this and other parts of the country prior to the advent of the tribes found by the first white men.—*History of Allegheny County*, p. 11.

The name *Monongahela* is also of Indian origin, and signifies "Falling in Banks."—*Craig's History of Pittsburg*, p. 190.

for the control of the site where now stands one of the great manufacturing centres of the globe, but which eventually enveloped America, Europe, and Asia in the sulphur-clouds of war, precipitated the American Revolution, and, finally, broke up the ancient feudalism of Europe. The grandest character in this great drama, as the curtain arose upon the opening scene, was far in the background of the glittering throng of crowned and jewelled monarchs, and princes, and famous commanders who crowded to the front: a plain, unpretending lieutenant-colonel of colonial militia—George Washington." *

Robert Dinwiddie, Lieutenant-Governor of Virginia, was the first to take active measures for asserting the claims of the British crown. On the 31st of October, 1753, he appointed Major Washington the bearer of his despatches to the commander of the French forces in the north-western part of Pennsylvania. He set out immediately, and arrived at the Forks November 24th.† At that time no white man as yet occupied the spot. In his journal of the expedition he thus describes it: "The land in the Fork I think extremely well situated for a fort, as it has the absolute command of the two rivers. The land at the point is twenty-five feet above the common surface of the water, and has a considerable bottom of flat, well-timbered land all around it, very convenient for building." He arrived at the end of his journey, a fort on French Creek, some distance from its mouth, December 4th, delivered his letters, and took accurate notes of all he could see of the French armament. They were determined to take possession of the Ohio early in the spring, an undertaking which their armament seemed able to accomplish without much difficulty. With this intelligence Washington returned with all speed to the governor. The latter despatched Captain William Trent with about seventy-five men, January 4th, 1754, with orders to construct a fort at the Forks and prepare to defend it. Captain Trent did not, however, arrive until the 17th of February, when he reached the Forks in company with

---

* History of Allegheny County, p. 19.

† The Indian name for the site of Pittsburg is said to have been *De-un-daga*, which simply means "The Forks."

the celebrated pioneer, Christopher Gist, who lived not far from where Connellsville now stands. It was a memorable day in our history, for then was commenced the first residence of a white man in what was destined to be the greatest iron-manufacturing city of the world.

But while Ensign Ward, who had command of the place during a temporary absence of Captain Trent, was engaged on his little fortifications, the French and Indians suddenly appeared, April 16th, to the number of one thousand, with eighteen cannon, in sixty bateaux and three hundred canoes, under the command of Captain Contrecœur. Their landing was followed by a summons to Ward to surrender immediately. Nothing was left but to comply with it; and the next day he was permitted to retire with his men to Redstone, the site of the present Brownsville. The French then built a fort, to which they at first gave the name of the Assumption of the Blessed Virgin, but afterwards changed it to that of Fort Duquesne, in honor of the Marquis Duquesne, the Governor of Canada. This little fort stood in the Point, while that of Trent stood on the bank of the Monongahela, a very short distance from the Point. "It at once became the centre of all the military operations of the French in this country, and its commanding position rendered its restoration to the English a matter of the first importance. In 1755 General Braddock, at the head of the largest expedition that had ever crossed the Alleghenies, was sent to recapture it. On July 9th he was met and defeated by the French and Indians at a point on the Monongahela ten miles above the fort (since known as Braddock's Field). A force of 800 men under Major Grant was cut to pieces in a second attempt in 1758; but a third of 6000 men under General Forbes was successful, November 15th, 1758, the French, disheartened by the failure of several attacks on the advancing army, having abandoned and set fire to it on the previous day."

During their occupation of the fort the French were attended, as they were in all their expeditions, by a Catholic chaplain, and the chapel in which he offered up the holy sacrifice—the first religious service in the city of Pittsburg—was dedicated under the title of "The Assumption of the Blessed Virgin of the Beautiful River."

The French, it may be stated by way of explanation, designated the Ohio and Allegheny rivers by the common term Ohio, or rather Oio; but on account of its limpid waters and enchanting scenery it was more generally known as "the Beautiful River." This occupation by the French, though transitory, forms an interesting episode in the city's history. But for the Catholic it possesses a special interest. It shows how the August Queen of Heaven claimed what was afterwards to be the diocese of Pittsburg as she had claimed from the beginning the entire New World. Commenting on the title and dedication of this chapel, Bishop O'Connor says: "It is presumed it was dedicated under this title on the Feast of the Assumption of the Blessed Virgin after their (the French soldiers') first arrival, as it is only after that day that it is designated by that name in the Register. It would appear that this dedication was accepted by the Blessed Virgin, as at the first Synod of the new Diocese of Pittsburg the new Diocese was placed under the protection of the Holy Virgin under the title of the Assumption, though no one was aware at that time of the previous dedication under the same title, the Bishop having been led to make this selection of a patron in consequence of the bull of erection being dated a few days before that feast, and he himself having been consecrated as its first Bishop on that festival.*

Reference will again be made to this title and dedication under the head of the Church of St. Mary of Mercy.

I have before me a copy of the register of the baptisms and deaths as kept by the army chaplain, which, although professing to be of Fort Duquesne only, contains entries from the other posts, at Presqu' Isle (Erie City) and those on " La Rivière aux Beufs" (French Creek), a stream that flows into the Allegheny River from the west at Franklin, 124 miles above Pittsburg. The history of this volume is interesting, and will not be out of place here. Bishop O'Connor, who took a lively interest in all that related to the early days of the Church in his diocese, found that the register, such as we now

---

* Diocesan Register.

have it, was kept in the archives of the city of Montreal. He had an authenticated copy made from it, from which he caused a small number of copies to be printed in the original French, in the year 1859. It is an octavo volume of 52 pages, entitled "Registres des Baptêmes et Sepultures qui se sont faits au Fort Duquesne pendant les années 1753, 1754, 1755 et 1756." The register is divided into three parts, each duly authenticated by Contrecœur, and containing fifteen baptisms, of which two only are French, eight English, two Irish, and three Indians, one being that of Jean Baptiste Christiguay, "great chief of the Iroquois," who was then in the ninety-fifth year of his age. The number of interments is forty-two, all of which are French except two English and four Indians. The first entry is dated July 11th, 1753, and the last October 10th, 1756.

Whether the chaplain withdrew at that time, or, which is more probable, the register for the remaining two years was destroyed with the fort, or lost, cannot now be determined. The first entry from Fort Duquesne—there are a few at the beginning from other posts—is an interment, dated June 5th, 1754, in which there is no other title than that of "Fort Duquesne of the Beautiful River." So the other entries until August 6th, when the designation is changed to that of "Fort Duquesne under the title of the Assumption of the Blessed Virgin." But from September 12th of the same year the entries to the end of the register are made "at Fort Duquesne under the title of the Assumption of the Blessed Virgin of the Beautiful River." All entries are signed Fr. Denis Baron, P.R., Chaplain, except three at the beginning of the register, two of which bear the name of Gabriel Anheuser, Royal Chaplain, and the other his name in conjunction with that of Fr. Baron. The whole is preceded by an introduction, of which the following is the most interesting part: "As a parish register the following pages would not deserve to be printed; but they are of great importance by reason of the light they shed on the bold attempts made by the French in seizing the peninsula which commands the Ohio, after having driven out the colonists of Virginia; and these pages become the more interesting from the curious details they furnish of the battle of the Monongahela and its hero, Daniel Leonard Sieur de Beaujeux.* Before marching against Braddock he prostrated himself before the altar and prepared himself for death. He evidently did not think that he would return as the conqueror of an army so numerous and important as that of the English; yet he considered it his duty as a French nobleman to face death in so unequal a struggle. His courage and self-sacrifice inspired his soldiers with hopes greater than his own; and though a simple captain of infantry, he died in the midst of the conflict, after having gained one of the most glorious victories in the French annals— a victory so complete that English and American historians mention it by no other name than Braddock's Defeat.†

Gen. Stanwix succeeded Gen. Forbes immediately after the evacuation of the fort by the French in 1758, and built a large fortification at the point, which he named Fort Pitt, in honor of the British prime minister. From this the city takes its name. The first plan of a town was laid out by Col. John Campbell in 1764, which embraced only the four squares of the present city bounded by Water, Market, and Ferry streets and Second Avenue.

A warrant was issued January 5th, 1769, for the survey of "the manor of Pittsburg," ‡ which then embraced 5766 acres. In his third visit to the spot in 1770, Washington thus de-

---

* In the register of his interment he is called Leonard Daniel.

† I have carefully examined "The Olden Time" and "Craig's History of Pittsburg" for references to Catholicity, but all they contain beyond the remarks of Mr. Post, already quoted, is the following precious item, which, from what is known of the French, as well as from the matter-of-course manner in which it is given, goes to show that the army chaplain not only ministered to those who remained at the forts, but also followed the different expeditions and scouting parties. In the journal kept by M. de Villiers of an expedition which he led against the English, who were posted near the Great Meadows, now in Fayette County, we read: "The 28th (June, 1754) I posted myself at a short distance above the first forks of the Monongahela;" that is, a short distance above M'Keesport, on the Youghiogheny River. "The 29th. Mass was said in the camp, after which we marched," etc.— *Olden Time*, vol ii. pp. 210, 211.

That no further reference should be found is accounted for by the fact that it was not until March, 1859, that Bishop O'Connor brought the Baptismal Register of Fort Duquesne to light.

‡ The first use of the name *Pittsburg*, so far as is known with certainty at present, was in a communication dated "Fort at Pittsburg, March 21st, 1760."— *Craig's History of Pittsburg*, p. 87.

scribes the incipient town: "The houses, which are ranged in streets, are on the Monongahela, and I suppose may be about twenty in number and inhabited by Indian traders." The town was laid out on a larger scale in June, 1784, by Thomas Vickroy, of Bedford County. Arthur Lee, who visited it in December of the same year, gives a sorry picture particularly of its religious condition. He says, "There is a great deal of small trade carried on, the commodities of exchange being money, wheat, flour, and skins." There were then in the town four attorneys, two physicians, "but not a priest of any persuasion, nor church, nor chapel; so that they are likely to be damned *without the benefit of the clergy*. The place I believe will never be very considerable." *

Two years later a Calvinist minister settled in the town, for the inhabitants were principally Scotch and Irish Presbyterians; and a church was soon after built for him on the site of the present First Presbyterian Church, Wood Street. It was the first church erected in Pittsburg.

During the excise troubles Pittsburg was the scene of much violence, a circumstance by which it became still better known abroad. On the re-establishment of order settlers were drawn in numbers, and the population increased. It was incorporated as a borough, April 22d, 1794; and chartered as a city, March 18th, 1816, having then a population of about 6000. Anterior to the latter date the manufacture of glass, iron, and nails had been commenced, which was destined to play so important a part in promoting the wealth and prosperity of the city. We shall now turn to the religious history of Pittsburg.

It would appear that a very small number of Catholics, of whom a part at least were French, had settled in Pittsburg prior to the year 1792. Probably the first priest who appeared in the town was Rev. Father Whalen, who was sent by very Rev. John Carroll to the Catholics of Kentucky in 1787.† The usual mode of travel to the West in those early days was either to come overland to Pittsburg, and there embark on the Ohio in a flat-boat, or to Brownsville, on the Mo-

---

* The italics are in the original.
† Sketches of Kentucky, by Rev. M. J. Spalding, D.D., p. 42.

nongahela, and embark in the same manner. The former was the more ordinary way; and if Father Whalen adopted it, as he most probably did, he was the first priest to set foot in Pittsburg, and the first to offer up the holy Sacrifice in Western Pennsylvania after the French occupation. In 1792 Rev. B. J. Flaget, afterwards Bishop of Bardstown, Ky., also passed through, and as he was delayed in the town for several months an account of his sojourn will be interesting, and the more so as our means of obtaining information respecting those early days is very limited. Says his biographer: "He set out on his journey (from Baltimore to Vincennes) in the month of May, in a wagon destined to Pittsburg. He travelled alone with the conductor of the wagon. . . . In Pittsburg he was detained for nearly six months, in consequence of the low stage of the water in the Ohio. He carried with him letters of introduction from Bishop Carroll to Gen. Wayne, who was stationed at that point preparing for his great expedition against the Indians of the North-west. . . . During his detention in Pittsburg, Monsieur Flaget was not idle. He boarded in the family of a French Huguenot married to an American Protestant lady, by whom he was kindly and hospitably entertained. He said Mass every morning in their house; and during the day he devoted himself to the instruction of the few French inhabitants and French Catholic soldiers.

"The small-pox having broken out in the place, he was indefatigable in his attentions to those stricken with the loathsome disease. Forgetful of his own imminent danger, he generously devoted himself for their bodily and spiritual comfort. His zeal brought with it a blessing, and his heart was much consoled by these first-fruits of his ministry in America.

"An incident occurred while he was in Pittsburg which presented an occasion for the exercise of his charity and zeal. Gen. Wayne, though a humane man, was a rigid disciplinarian. Four soldiers had deserted, and on being apprehended they were promptly condemned to death by a court martial. Two of them were Irish or American Catholics, one was a Protestant, and the fourth a French infidel. Monsieur Flaget visited them in prison; and though but little acquainted with English, he had the happiness to receive the Protestant into the Church, and to administer the sacraments to the two Catholics. They were in the most happy dispositions; and he mingled his tears of joy with theirs of repentance. The Frenchman proved obdurate; and the zealous priest could make no impression on his heart.

" He accompanied the convicts to the place of execution; but his tender heart would not permit him to hear the fatal shot by which they would be launched into eternity. So much was he moved that on his hasty departure from the spot he fell into a swoon; and on recovering, he found himself lying in a ravine by the wayside. Several hours had already elapsed since the execution, and the whole appeared to him like a dream. The Frenchman was pardoned by Gen. Wayne, the moment before the order to fire, out of regard for the feelings of M. Flaget, who had exhibited the most poignant grief that his unhappy countryman was so totally unprepared to die. In November he left Pittsburg in a flat-boat bound for Louisville." *

In the autumn of the following year Rev. Stephen Badin and Rev. M. Barrieres also passed through Pittsburg, remaining for a short time, as may be gathered from the following: " The two missionaries left Baltimore on the 6th of September, 1793, and travelled like the Apostles, on foot to Pittsburg, over bad roads and a rugged wilderness country. On the 3d of November they embarked on a flat-boat which was descending the Ohio." †

A very small number of Catholics, emigrants from Ireland, for the most part, also settled in Pittsburg about the beginning of the century. But so few were they that when Rev. D. A. Gallitzin, the first priest residing in Pennsylvania who is known to have visited the place, made his appearance among them, in 1804, there are said to have been only fifteen souls to assist at his Mass. Rev. P. Heilbron and perhaps one or two other priests are thought to have visited the town at distant

---

* Sketches of the Life, etc., of the Rt. Rev. B. J. Flaget, by Rev. M. J. Spalding, D D., pp. 31-33.

† Ibid. p. 75.

intervals during the next two years. Rev. F. X. O'Brien was the first to come at regular intervals. Says Mr. Shea, on what authority I know not: " In the first years of this century the Rev. F. X. O'Brien had the centre of his mission at Brownsville, forty miles south of Pittsburg, which latter city he visited once in the month, to say Mass for the few Catholics, who gathered around him in a private house." *

I have not been able to find a confirmation of this statement, further than that Father O'Brien visited Pittsburg during a part of the years 1806 and '7. His name does not occur prior to the former year, and he left Brownsville in the latter, a considerable time before he took up his residence in Pittsburg. Be this as it may, for historical data are neither copious nor exact, he was appointed resident pastor of the little town in October, 1808. The Catholics at this time are said to have numbered only twenty souls; but the future prospects were such as to encourage the zealous missionary to undertake the erection of a church. And here an important question arises. *When was the first church erected in Pittsburg?* The date commonly given is 1808. But this is evidently erroneous. Father O'Brien, as we have seen, did not arrive until the close of that year; and he would not then commence so important a work. It may have been, and probably was, begun the following spring. But, though small, it was a great undertaking for the little, indigent flock; and Father O'Brien was obliged to go elsewhere for assistance. He visited a number of the wealthy Catholic families of Baltimore and other parts of Maryland, and was assisted by the Archbishop himself. The lot upon which the church stood was donated by Col. Jas. O'Hara. This being the first property acquired by the Church in Pittsburg, possesses a special interest to the historian. It also aids in determining the date at which the church was built. From the records in the court-house which I have examined, I learn that James O'Hara and Mary, his wife, deeded to Philip Gilland and Anthony Beelen a lot of ground 60 by 64 feet, at the corner of Liberty and Washington Streets, in consideration of one dollar, " as of divers other considerations them thereunto more especially

---

* The Catholic Church in the United States, p. 285.

moving. .... On which the Roman Catholic chapel is erected. .... IN TRUST for the Roman Catholic congregation of Pittsburg and vicinity, to and for the only proper use and behoof of the said congregation and their posterity forever, and for no other use or purpose whatever." The deed is dated November 6th, 1811, and was recorded by Lazarus Stewart, Justice of the Peace, December 8th.* The property of which the church lot formed a part had been purchased from Prestly Neville, July 15th, 1799. From this it is evident that the first church of Pittsburg was built before the close of 1811. But how long it had been in course of erection cannot be determined; for the work upon it necessarily progressed but slowly, and it was not yet finished when Bishop Egan of Philadelphia visited the city, in the latter part of the summer of 1811. This was the first visit of a Bishop to the western part of the State; for although Bishop Carroll set out on a visit in 1802, he was deterred from crossing the mountains by the condition of the roads, or, it may be, by the absence of roads. Bishop Egan administered Confirmation in a private house. There were then about fifteen families.

At length the new church was completed, and was dedicated to St. Patrick, a sufficient evidence that here, as in countless other places, the foundations of religion had been laid by emigrants from the Island of Saints. It was an unassuming brick building, perhaps fifty feet in length by thirty in width; and stood at the head of Eleventh Street, in front of the present Union Depot. To this day it is spoken of as "Old St. Patrick's."

The residence of a priest and the completion of a church, added to the erection of manufactories, which pointed out Pittsburg as a good place for laborers, stimulated the Catholic settlement. Numbers of German families came; but the Irish element always predominated in the city, and still predominates. Time wore on, and the good priest who had been thought too sanguine in erecting *so large a church* beheld it crowded with an ever-increasing congregation. But neither he nor any other of the pioneer priests confined his labors to

* Deed Book, vol. xvii. pp. 368, 369.

one congregation, or even to one county. Their mission frequently embraced a circuit of fifty, seventy-five, or even a hundred miles, which they traversed and ministered to as frequently as circumstances permitted.

The following extracts from a letter of the Very Rev. Felix De Andreis, who, passing through Pittsburg in the autumn of 1816, remained in it a short time with his eleven companions, members like himself of the Congregation of the Mission, will be read with interest, conveying as they do an idea of the means of travel afforded in those days, and the condition of religion in Pittsburg:

"Having set out in two parties from Baltimore," he writes, under date of September 16th, to Mr. Sicardi, Vicar-General of the Congregation at Rome, "we crossed, partly on foot and partly on wretched vehicles, the rugged mountains of Pennsylvania; some of us accomplished the journey in nineteen, others in ten days; but for all it was attended with great expense and inconvenience. The distance we had to go was about three hundred miles; and, not meeting with any Catholic church on our way, we could neither celebrate nor hear Mass. The worst of it was, however, that even when we reached Pittsburg, a pretty considerable town, in a commercial point of view, there was no means of obtaining this consolation. Among a population of ten thousand the Catholics scarcely number three hundred. They are all generally very poor, so that the church is almost destitute of everything; the pastor, who has under his care a parish nearly equal to ten dioceses, is constantly employed in visiting his parishioners; he was absent when we arrived, and having taken with him the chalice, our devotion, no less than that of the people, was disappointed, for all seemed most anxious to see us officiate. At last a pewter chalice was found, but there was no paten; however, yesterday, late in the evening, having gone with one of my companions to our lodging in the house of a worthy Catholic family, a paten was found most unexpectedly. I sent my companion to bear the good news to the others, and to the principal Catholics of the place, who soon spread the tidings from house to house; so that this morning we celebrated our five Masses, including one that was chanted. This afternoon we had Vespers." *

Writing in his journal, he says: "We had to remain until the 23d of October at Pittsburg, the waters of the Ohio being too low to allow us to proceed on our way. On the above-named day we started in a sort of vessel called a flat-boat, made precisely like a small house, the roof of which served as a deck. It was a moving sight to see the banks crowded with persons who came to bid us farewell; many of them gave us considerable sums of money, and exhibited lively marks of sorrow for our departure." † During their stay they were aided materially by Mr. Anthony Beelen, whose name figures prominently in the early history of the Church in Pittsburg. He was a Belgian, and his father had been the ambassador of Joseph II., Emperor of Germany. Upon the death of the emperor, in 1790, Baron De ·Beelen determined to remain in Philadelphia. His son Anthony came to Pittsburg about the beginning of this century, and, being possessed of wealth and education, he soon attained to an honorable position. He received Louis Philippe when passing through the city, also Lafayette on his visit in 1825; and he ably seconded whatever was undertaken in the interests of religion. But he at length became entangled in the meshes of Freemasonry and a mixed marriage, and died without having been reconciled to the Church.

Father O'Brien, who was naturally of a delicate constitution, soon found that his strength was not equal to his zeal. But so far from rest and repose being in store for him, his labors were destined to increase; for at this time a number of State roads, or "pikes" as they were familiarly called, were laid out and to be opened; and as they would be mainly constructed by Catholic Irishmen, a new field was opened for him. But nature, if not a motive of self-preservation, will impose a limit to zeal. Father O'Brien's strength was finally so far exhausted as no longer to permit him to continue his labors, and he retired to Maryland, his native State, early in 1820, where he remained until his death, with the exception of a

---

* Sketches of the Life of the Very Rev. Felix De Andreis, pp. 95, 96.
† Ibid p. 98.

short time spent at Conewago. Little more is known of this good priest except that, worn out more by labor than by age, he died, most probably at Annapolis, on the Feast of All Saints, 1832.

Father O'Brien was succeeded, March, 1820, by Rev. Charles B. M'Guire, O.S.F., who had been pastor of the church in the Westmoreland County settlement for some time, and who had visited Pittsburg at intervals during the previous year. "Moved by the wants of the Catholics of Pittsburg, he was transferred, or transferred himself thither," as Father Heyden remarks in one of his letters, "for there was no great order in those days. . . . He made the Church at Pittsburg what it is." But his labors, like those of his predecessor, were not confined to the city. They extended to the scattered families in the country for many miles around. Soon after his arrival he purchased a small two-story brick house on Liberty Street, Nos. 340 and 342, in which he lived, and which is yet standing as a relic of the past.

The little church at length became too small for the congregation, and Father M'Guire determined to enlarge it. Col. O'Hara had donated an addition to the original lot, about the same size as it, some time prior to 1815; and about the year 1824 or 1825 Father M'Guire built an addition to the church in the form of a transept across the rear of the existing building. It was ready for occupation about the commencement of 1826, but was not finished in the interior until later, and was as simple in its style of architecture as the original building. The congregation had now sufficient accommodation; but only for a short time. The cemetery was for many years attached to the church. Father M'Guire also purchased a farm on the hill south of the Monongahela, and a short distance east of the spot now occupied by the Passionist Monastery, but at what precise time is uncertain, upon which he contemplated the erection of a house of his order. But circumstances, and especially the death of Rev. Anthony Kenny, then his companion, prevented him from carrying out his plans.

In the early part of the summer of 1819 Bishop Flaget, of Bardstown, passed from Erie down the Allegheny River to

Pittsburg, where he remained two days and administered Confirmation.

Soon after the addition was made to St. Patrick's a fresh impulse was given to business in the city, and a more rapid increase to the population, in which the Catholics more than others were likely to be benefited. The Pennsylvania Canal, to traverse the entire length of the State from Philadelphia to Pittsburg, was laid out, and work was commenced upon it in 1826. In view of the increase of the Catholic population which must necessarily accompany and follow the construction of the canal, Father M'Guire conceived the idea of erecting a new church, which should be the greatest work of his life. His mind, schooled in the pomp with which religion is surrounded in Catholic countries, was not disposed to satisfy itself with such a church as circumstances force upon a country in its infancy. He would raise an edifice such as few dioceses, if any, in the United States could then boast, one which he could contemplate with feelings of pride and leave at his death to an admiring future.

A meeting of the Catholics of Pittsburg was called, August 27th, 1827, at which he presided, to take the matter into consideration. A committee, or board of trustees, was selected, with himself as president, who should purchase a site, and hold it in trust for the congregation. They selected the lots on the north-west corner of Fifth Avenue and Grant Street, the site of the present magnificent cathedral, which was then in the outskirts of the city. This location, for its central position and elevation, could not be excelled. The lot had an elevation of about twenty feet above the present level of the street, the latter having been cut down on two different times, as we shall hereafter have occasion to remark. It was most probably about this time that Father M'Guire received his first assistant, and Pittsburg became the residence of two priests. Work was soon after commenced on the foundation of the proposed church, the hill was graded off in view of a future grading of the street, and the corner-stone was laid without ceremony by Father M'Guire, June 24th, 1829. It appears that in the report of the proceedings by a local paper the church was styled a *cathedral*, whereupon the *U. S. Catholic Miscellany* expressed its surprise that Pittsburg should have been raised to the dignity of an episcopal see without its knowledge, and it thereupon read Father M'Guire a very orthodox lecture on his duties of submission to his ecclesiastical superiors. Poor man! Although St. Paul's did become a cathedral, it was not his fault.

In the year 1828 or 1829 a colony of Poor Clare Nuns opened a house of their order in Allegheny town.* With this colony came Rev. Vincent Raymacher, O.S.D., who was their chaplain until he was succeeded by Rev. A. F. Van de Wejer, a Belgian of the same order, some time after the fall of 1830. Both these chaplains assisted Father M'Guire, especially in ministering to the Germans. The Germans were encouraged to contribute towards the erection of the new church by the promise that upon its completion St. Patrick's would be given to them, and they would be organized into a separate congregation. During the progress of the work Bishop Kenrick visited the city, June 26th, 1830, in company with Bishop Conwell, on their way to Philadelphia after the consecration of the first-named prelate. Says the correspondent of the *U. S. Catholic Miscellany:* " They were, after their arrival, visited by Father M'Guire and his assistant, Rev. Patrick Rafferty. Shortly afterwards the prelates visited the ground whereon the new and spacious church intended to be dedicated to St. Paul is now erecting. They found the building in progress, and had occasion to admire the great increase of Catholics in the city, where, in the memory of a layman then present, only six Catholics existed, whilst now nearly 4000 are calculated to be enclosed within its precincts. They inquired the number of baptisms on record in the pastor's register during the last ten years, and learned that 1214 had received this sacrament. Emigration from Europe had partially swelled the congregation; but conversions had also contributed to its increase. Forty-three converts had been received in 1828, and twenty-seven in 1829. On Sunday, the 27th, Bishop Conwell administered Confirmation in St. Patrick's."

---

* The establishment of religious orders, opening of educational and charitable institutions, and organization of congregations mentioned in the text will be treated of at length in their proper places.

But the force of circumstances obliged Father M'Guire soon after to suspend work on the new edifice, and before it could be resumed he was called to his reward, July 17th, 1833. During his pastorate Father M'Guire had for assistants Rev. Anthony Kenny, Rev. P. Rafferty, Rev. A. F. Van de Wejer, Rev. John Grady, Rev. Thos. Gegan, and finally Rev. John O'Reilly, who came in November, 1832, and succeeded him after his death.

Father Kenny died soon after his ordination. The following notice of his death, from the *American Manufacturer*, is all we know of Father Gegan: "Rev. Thomas Gegan, late and amiable assistant of the late Ch. B. M'Guire, died at Newry, Huntingdon County, July 15th, 1833, in the 33d year of his age. He was on his way from this city (Pittsburg) to Philadelphia, when his stay with Rev. Jas. Bradley was prolonged by an aggravation of his disease, consumption, which has thus terminated his useful and disinterested labors in the ministry of the Catholic Church."

The following biographical notice of Father M'Guire is compiled principally from an article published in the *American Manufacturer* immediately after his death, and which was evidently written by one intimately acquainted with him. Many of his relations then lived in the city, and could have furnished the writer with all the particulars of his life. If space permitted, many interesting incidents could be given of his life and character; but it is necessary to omit them. The distinguished services which he rendered to religion in Pittsburg entitle him to a more extended notice than could be given to many others.

REV. CHARLES BONAVENTURE M'GUIRE was born near the town of Dungannon, in the county Tyrone, Ireland, in the year 1768. (Another account states that he was born December 16th, 1770.) From an early age he was destined for the sacred ministry, and having received the rudiments of an education at home, he went to the university of Louvain to finish his studies. Upon attaining the proper age he was ordained, and exercised the duties of the sacred ministry in various parts of the Netherlands and Germany. During this period he acquired a remarkable knowledge of the German language. Soon the fury of the French revolution extended to the Netherlands. "He was among the clergy who in defence of their own rights and the interests of religion took part with the French Government against the revolutionists. For this he, in common with the rest of the clergy, was proscribed and his life forfeited. On one occasion he was seized and dragged towards the guillotine, when a cooper, who knew him, heroically attacked with an edged instrument of his trade the persons who had him in custody, and effected his rescue. He fled and escaped, but not until he had witnessed the massacre of his noble-souled and lion-hearted deliverer, who was instantly cut to pieces by the infuriated insurgents. From Louvain he escaped to the city of Rome, where he remained for six years in the performance of his clerical duties. He left that city at the time that the armed legions of Napoleon tyrannized over the Pope and his adherents throughout Italy. He then travelled over the most of the Continent of Europe, making observations. In 1815 he was engaged by the King of Bohemia to perform a religious office towards a member of the royal family who was at Brussels. In the performance of this mission it so happened that he reached the city just at the time of the memorable battle of Waterloo. To many of the wounded and dying he administered the last rites of the Church. We have heard him speak of fragments of military equipments which he collected on the battle-field, and which he preserved as relics of the scene. Shortly after this period he started for America, and reached our shores in 1817. He was not stationed until nearly a year after his arrival, although engaged in the discharge of pastoral duties. He was then stationed as pastor of the congregation in Westmoreland County, where he remained until transferred to Pittsburg. With his appearance a new era commenced with the entire Catholic body. Religion found in him an expositor worthy of herself, and the Catholic body gradually assumed, and maintained henceforward, a dignity and respectability in the opinions of dissenting Christians which were not allowed them before his arrival. As a man, as a priest, as a scholar, none knew him but to respect and love him. He was one among those rare beings who unite the traits of liberality, urbanity, and sociableness with the qualities of a pious Christian and an eminent scholar. Master of four or five languages, well versed in classic lore, he was withal as simple, as inoffensive, as innocent as a child." In appearance he was tall and portly, of a commanding presence, and with a ruddy, good-humored countenance. His remains were interred at the convent of the Poor Clares (of whom he had been ecclesiastical superior), until the completion of the new church, when they were deposited in one of the vaults. Upon the destruction of that church by fire, in 1851, they were laid in St. Mary's Cemetery, where they yet repose with a simple stone to point them out.

CHAPTER III.

ST. PAUL'S CHURCH.

Rev. John O'Reilly pastor of St. Paul's—The church finished and dedicated—A description of it—The Germans take possession of St. Patrick's—The Nuns of St. Clare withdraw—The Sisters of Charity arrive—An orphan asylum opened—New congregations formed—Withdrawal of Father O'Reilly—His death—Sketch of his life—Arrival of Very Rev. Michael O'Connor—His works—He visits Rome.

FORTUNATE was it for the unfinished church and the congregation that Father O'Reilly succeeded Father M'Guire. His skill, energy, and administrative ability eminently fitted him for the completion of so important an undertaking. Work was immediately resumed on the unfinished church, and through his untiring exertions it was ready for dedication the following spring. Preparations were made for the ceremony, when a difficulty arose respecting the deed. Bishop Kenrick required the trustees to comply with certain regulations which he had found it necessary to enforce respecting the titles of church property; and the trustees, who were taking measures to obtain a charter, imagined that the Bishop was about to take the church from them. Matters were explained in a satisfactory manner, however, and preparations were completed for the solemn ceremony.* The dedication took place on Sunday, May 4th, 1834, and the church was placed under the invocation of St. Paul the Apostle. Bishop Kenrick performed the ceremony, Father O'Reilly sang the Mass, and Rev. John Hughes, afterwards Archbishop of New York, preached the sermon. Unlike the present cathedral, the old St. Paul's fronted on Fifth Avenue. The following description from the *American Manufacturer*, and most probably fur-

* Archbishop Kenrick and his Work: A Lecture by Rev. M. O'Connor, S.J., p. 12.

nished by the architect, Mr. Kerrins, will give an idea of the size and style of the new edifice:

"This church, which is probably the largest in the United States, occupies an area of 175 by 76 feet, vestries and vestibules included. The elevation of the side walls to the top of the embattled parapets by which they are surmounted is 25 feet. These are flanked by 26 buttresses, finished with pediment pinnacles and crocketed spires. The east end is embellished with a large ornamented Gothic window in the centre, flanked by two others of regular but diminished proportions, and finished at the top with minaret and cross, sprung from rampant arches, and occupying the highest point of the gable parapet. The tower stands on the west end, which is the front of the church, and is immensely strong, being supported by four buttresses with flying terminals. It is yet unfinished, being little higher than the comb of the roof.*

"This immense superficies is enclosed with four double Gothic doors with enriched panels, and 57 splendid ornamental windows, exhibiting in perfect symmetry the florid Gothic style throughout. The grand entrance is made by three double doors, which open into as many vestibules, from the right and left of which the galleries are ascended by sets of elliptical stairs. The nave is regulated by one central and two side aisles, and contains 240 pews, which with those in the gallery make 350 (calculated in the aggregate to seat 2500 persons). There are 16 Gothic columns, 40 feet high, which, supporting the heart of the galleries on their richly carved capitals, break round the tracery, and extend to support the corbels and soffits which form the lowest terminals of the richly grained ceiling. The ceiling is Gothic, and is neatly frescoed. The chancel, which is separated from the nave by railing arranged in open tracery, is spacious, and the most splendid of this very splendid edifice. It contains a high altar, uniform in style with the church. To the sanctuary are attached a small chapel to the rear, and two vestry rooms. . . . . One feels instinctively impelled to exclaim, 'Truly this is the house of God!' This feeling is not a little increased by the radiant glow encircling the golden cross exhibited

---

* It was never finished.

over the face of the altar canopy, and the very appropriate text underneath: 'The Lord is in his holy temple; let all the earth be silent before him.'"

This splendid edifice was erected without soliciting aid from abroad, but many non-Catholic citizens contributed liberally towards it. To add to the imposing appearance of the church, it occupied such a position as to be the first object that met the eye of a person approaching the city from any direction.

The English congregation was now transferred to St. Paul's, and St. Patrick's became for some years a German church. For this reason I shall now drop the history of the latter until coming to speak of the German congregations of the city. Father O'Reilly continued to exercise the office of pastor of St. Paul's until April 1st, 1837, when he was transferred to Philadelphia, and Rev. Thomas Heyden of Bedford succeeded him. In the mean time, May, 1835, the Poor Clare Nuns withdrew from their convent to another part of Allegheny, where they remained about two years before returning to Europe, and a colony of Sisters of Charity from Emmittsburg took up their residence in Pittsburg. When Father Heyden was promoted to the See of Natchez, November 22d, 1837, a dignity which he declined, he returned to Bedford, and was succeeded at St. Paul's by Rev. P. R. Kenrick, the present Archbishop of St. Louis. In the summer of 1838 Father O'Reilly, who was then pastor of St. Mary's Church, Philadelphia, exchanged places with Father Kenrick, and returned to Pittsburg. Here he remained until succeeded by Very Rev. Michael O'Connor, June 17th, 1841.

During his second pastorate Father O'Reilly organized a board of directors for an orphan asylum, June 6th, 1838, purchased property, and opened an asylum. In the following summer the first congregation was formed from St. Paul's—that of St. Philip's, Broadhead, about three miles south-west of the city. About the same time a disturbance arose in a portion of St. Paul's congregation out of the enforcement, by Bishop Kenrick, of certain regulations respecting the pews, by which he sought to increase the revenue of the church. The object appears to have been to have the congregation contribute, as it was unquestionably bound to do, towards the support of the diocesan seminary. Be that as it may, I have before me a printed circular of an inflammatory character, dated June 8th, 1839, addressed to the congregation, and signed "Many members of the congregation," in which their "rights" are eloquently stated, and strong appeals are made to the people to resist every encroachment of authority. This ebullition appears, however, to have soon after subsided. On the second Sunday of October, 1840, St. Patrick's Church was restored to the English, and Rev. E. F. Garland, who had been assistant at St. Paul's since his ordination, in the spring of 1838, became pastor. Previous to this, Father O Reilly, who does not appear to have entertained very flattering ideas of the future of Catholicity in Pittsburg, was disposed to sell the church. A meeting of the congregation was called to discuss the matter, when Father Garland energetically and, as the event proved, very wisely opposed the project, and prevented the sale of the venerable edifice. This was the second time Father O'Reilly wished to dispose of it. It was afterwards discovered that it could not have been sold without special legislation, as the lots upon which it stood had been donated by Mr. O'Hara, as we have seen, as a site for a church and for no other purpose whatever.

REV. JOHN O'REILLY, C.M., deserves to be ranked with Father M'Guire as one of the great benefactors of the Church in Pittsburg. Born in Ireland, he came to this country before the completion of his studies and entered Mount St. Mary's College, Emmittsburg, where he finished his course of theology and was ordained in 1826 or 1827. He was then sent to the mission in Huntingdon and the adjacent counties. He erected a church at Huntingdon, another at Bellefonte, and another at Newry; after which he was transferred to St. Paul's, Pittsburg, where we have seen his labors in the cause of religion, education, and charity. Upon the arrival of Father O'Connor he retired from the diocese and went to Rome, where he entered the Congregation of the Mission. Returning to the United States, he was made superior of the house of the fathers of his order at St. Louis. He was then transferred to La Salle, Ill., where he founded a house of which he was elected superior, and built a church. From there he was taken to the Seminary of St. Mary of the Angels, at Niagara Falls, of which he was made superior on the promotion of Father Lynch to the archiepiscopal see of Toronto. In his declining years he was elected deputy to the General Assembly of the Congregation at Paris in the summer of 1861. On his return, he retired to St. Louis, where, worn out with labors and rich in merit, he was called to his reward March 4th, 1862, in the sixty-fifth year of his age.

An event so fraught with consequences, not only to the Church of Pittsburg, but also to that of the entire western part of the State, as the arrival of Very Rev. Michael O'Connor, V.G., at St. Paul's, is thus humbly chronicled in his Notes: "June 17th, 1841. Arrived in Pittsburg on this day (Thursday), lodging at Mrs. Timmons' at $4 per week." As yet there was no pastoral residence. The congregation at this time numbered about 4000 souls, and the pastor was assisted in the discharge of his duties by Rev. Joseph F. Deane. However successfully the affairs of St. Paul's had been administered previous to that date, the arrival of Father O'Connor marked the beginning of a new era in the history of the congregation. He immediately turned his attention to the erection of a school-house, and for that purpose called a meeting of the men of the congregation, July 18th, at which a committee was appointed and a subscription opened which reached $1251 the same day. Arrangements were also made at a meeting held December 30th, 1842, for opening a reading-room. Connected with this was the Catholic Institute, a literary society organized January 6th, 1843, " which had for its object to promote literary improvement in its members, and give them a more thorough acquaintance with history and Scripture connected more especially with the development of Catholic principles."

But Father O'Connor was Vicar-General of the western part of the diocese as well as pastor of St. Paul's. In that capacity he dedicated St. Patrick's Church, Sugar Creek, Armstrong County, July 29th, 1841, and Sts. Simon and Jude, Blairsville, Indiana County, October 2d, 1842, and perhaps others. He also wrote to Bishop Kenrick recommending the division of the city into districts, a wish to which the Bishop acceded. Other matters having for their object the good of religion were noted down to be laid before a future diocesan synod.*

He had long been desirous of uniting himself to the Society of Jesus, and of thereby escaping the honors he had reason to apprehend were in store for him. He set out on a visit to Rome, May 5th, 1843, to obtain from the Holy Father the requisite permission, as a student of the Propaganda, for entering a religious order. But he was hastening towards the honors which he sought to escape. During his absence Father Hayden again became pastor of St. Paul's, who, on the return of Father O'Connor as Bishop, went back to Bedford.

* His Notes.

CHAPTER IV.

HISTORY OF ST. PAUL'S CATHEDRAL FROM THE ERECTION OF THE SEE OF PITTSBURG TO ITS DIVISION AND THE ERECTION OF THE SEE OF ERIE.

The manner in which the Church was first governed in the United States—Pittsburg an episcopal see—Very Rev. Michael O'Connor consecrated first Bishop—Sketch of his early life—Condition of the Church on his arrival—The first ordination—The first synod—The colored chapel—*The Catholic* published—St. Michael's Diocesan Seminary—The Bishop visits Europe—The first visitation of the diocese—The Cathedral in danger—Statistics—The Cathedral destroyed by fire—A new Cathedral commenced—The Bishop visits Rome—Erection of the See of Erie—Bishop O'Connor transferred thither—Statistics.

BEFORE entering upon the history of Pittsburg as a diocese, it becomes necessary to cast a glance at the manner in which the Church in this country was first governed. Reference will be made to those portions only which were subject to the crown of Great Britain. When the numbers of the clergy and laity had so far increased that organization and a form of government became expedient for the good of religion, the Vicar of London, to whose jurisdiction the Church in the English colonies pertained, appointed a Vicar-General for America. The first of these of whom history furnishes reliable information was Rev. John Hunter, an Englishman, who resided at Port Tobacco, Md. He was exercising jurisdiction as early as 1774, but was succeeded, before the breaking out of the Revolution, by Rev. Mr. Lewis, who had been Superior of the Jesuits of Maryland and Pennsylvania at the time of their suppression. After the close of the Revolution the clergy addressed a memorial to the Holy See, praying that a Vicar-General might be appointed holding immediately from Rome. In compliance with this request, Rev. John Carroll was appointed Superior of the American clergy in 1785, and received extraordinary faculties. Seeing everywhere on the visitation which he made the imperative need of a Bishop, he wrote to that effect to the Holy See; and bulls were expedited early in the spring of 1789, authorizing the American clergy to select both the priest of their own number best suited in their judgment for Bishop, and to name the city most proper for his see. The choice fell upon their Superior as the man and Baltimore as the place. Both were confirmed at Rome by bulls dated November 6th of the same year. The consecration of the Bishop-elect was performed by Rt. Rev. Charles Warmsly, Bishop of Rama *in partibus* and Vicar Apostolic of London, in the chapel of Lulworth Castle, August 15th, 1790. At the first synod, held at Baltimore, November 7th, 1791, Rev. Anthony Francis Fleming was appointed Vicar-General of Pennsylvania. But inasmuch as he and his successors resided at Philadelphia, they do not appear to have exercised jurisdiction over the western part of the State. Baltimore was easier of access at that time than Philadelphia. At length the Diocese of Baltimore was divided, and that of Philadelphia among others erected, April 8th, 1809, embracing the entire States of Pennsylvania and Delaware and a part of New Jersey. Rev. Michael Egan was named first bishop; but the troubled state of Europe prevented the bulls of his appointment from arriving until September, 1810. He was consecrated October 28th of the same year; paid one visit to the western part of the State, as we have seen; and died July 22d, 1814. The see was then governed by an administrator, under the title of Apostolic Vicar-General. Rev. Lewis de Barth and his successor, Rev. William Matthews, were administrators till the fall of 1820, at which time a candidate for the mitre was found, after much difficulty and many refusals, in the person of Very Rev. Henry Conwell, V.G., of Armagh, Ireland. One of the first acts of his episcopate was the appointment of Rev. D. A. Gallitzin, of Loretto, Vicar-General of the western part of the State. But as the limits of his jurisdiction as Vicar-General were not defined, he did not exercise his additional faculties till a few years later, when the lines were accurately drawn.* Bishop Conwell never visited the western part of the State, except on

---

* Life of Gallitzin, by S. M. Brownson, p. 366.

the occasion already mentioned. But when Dr. Kenrick was consecrated Coadjutor Bishop of Philadelphia, June 6th, 1830, he made frequent visitations in that portion of his diocese. About the same time Dr. Gallitzin* resigned the office of Vicar-General, and no one was appointed until the arrival of Rev. M. O'Connor. Having premised so much, we shall now take up the history of the erection of the new diocese.

The geographical position of Pittsburg pointed it out as a place of future importance not only in the civil but also in the ecclesiastical order. Bishop Flaget appears to have been the first to regard it as the future see of a Bishop, having entertained this idea as early as 1825. Previous to that date Dr. Gallitzin urged upon Archbishop Maréchal the propriety of establishing a bishopric in the western part of Pennsylvania, and spoke of the advantages possessed by his favorite Loretto.† Few would have agreed with him at that time, so far as the locality was concerned; none would have agreed with him twenty years later, when the see was actually established. It was not, however, until twelve years later that a motion was made in that direction by the proper authorities. "As early as 1835 Bishop Kenrick proposed to the Cardinal Prefect of the Propaganda a division of his diocese by the erection of a new see at Pittsburg, and he recommended the appointment of Rev. John Hughes as Bishop either of Philadelphia or Pittsburg, as might seem most expedient to the Holy See. The suggestion was approved, and in January, 1836, the documents erecting the new See of Pittsburg and transferring Dr. Kenrick to it, and appointing Dr. Hughes Coadjutor and Administrator of Philadelphia, were actually prepared at Rome." ‡ Bishop England, of Charleston, S. C., suggested a canonical impediment, and nothing was done until the meeting of the Third Provincial Council at Baltimore, April 16th, 1837, when the matter was discussed, but without any definite action being passed upon it. The Fourth Council did not raise the question, and in the mean time Dr. O'Connor was sent to Pittsburg as Vicar-Gen-

---

* I have everywhere used the designation "Dr. Gallitzin," as the name by which he is universally known in Western Pennsylvania.

† Life of Gallitzin, p. 346.

‡ Lives of the Deceased American Bishops, vol. i. p. 500.

eral, as we have seen, which partially supplied the want of a Bishop. The subject was taken up in the Fifth Provincial Council, which assembled May 14th, 1843, and the division was recommended to the Holy See, with the name of Dr. O'Connor, as it is believed, as the most suitable person to fill the new see. Both were confirmed at Rome. "The new diocese being detached from Philadelphia comprised, according to the bull of erection, 'Western Pennsylvania.' This designation not being so well defined as was first supposed, the Bishops of Philadelphia and Pittsburg agreed to consider the latter as comprising the counties of Bedford, Huntingdon, Clearfield, M'Kean, and Potter, and all west of them in Pennsylvania. This was afterwards confirmed by the Holy See, the two Bishops having united in an application for that purpose. . . . The new county of Fulton having been created before the issuing of this Rescript, it was considered as belonging to the Diocese of Philadelphia, inasmuch as, though previously forming part of Bedford, it was a separate county at the receipt of the Rescript, which described Bedford as the eastern boundary of the Diocese of Pittsburg." *

The new diocese consequently embraced twenty-seven of the most western counties of the State—Blair, Laurence, and Cameron having been formed at a subsequent date—and an area of about 21,300 square miles, or a little less than half that of the State, with perhaps not more than one third either of the entire or of the Catholic population.

A report of the acts of the Council reached the Holy Father soon after the arrival of Dr. O'Connor in Rome, and the confidence of the American prelates, the reputation of Fr. O'Connor at Rome, and the impression which his appearance was so well calculated to make upon those with whom he came in contact, determined the Holy Father to consult rather for the good of the Church than for the wishes of one of her members by confirming the choice of the Council. The surprise and dismay of the unsuspecting priest may well be imagined, when, upon kneeling at the feet of the venerable Pontiff to ask permission to enter the Society of Jesus, he was forbidden to rise until he should promise to become Bishop of Pittsburg.

* Diocesan Register.

"You shall be a Bishop first," said the Holy Father, "and a Jesuit afterwards." These prophetic words, as we shall see, were literally fulfilled. The bull of this appointment was dated August 7th, and he was consecrated by Cardinal Fransoni, in the church of St. Agatha, at Rome, on the 15th. Immediately the care of his diocese became the sole object of his attention. But before contemplating him as Bishop a brief sketch of his early life will be of advantage to the reader.

MICHAEL O'CONNOR was born near the city of Cork, Ireland, September 27th, 1810. He received his early education at Queenstown, and at fourteen years of age crossed over to France, where he continued his studies for a few years. He was then sent to the College of the Propaganda at Rome by the Bishop of Cloyne and Ross. To this institution came students from all parts of the world, the select youths of their respective dioceses, and to find a place among them was in itself an evidence of more than ordinary natural endowments, as well as the manifestation of a disposition to turn them to the best account in the service of religion. Here he prosecuted his course of studies, which was closed with one of the most successful and brilliant defences ever witnessed in that celebrated institution—a defence which left him a reputation for learning that few have been able to equal and perhaps none to surpass. Cardinal Wiseman, then rector of the English College, speaks in terms of high commendation of the manner in which Mr. O'Connor won the doctor's cap and ring. He was ordained a priest June 1st, 1833, and immediately appointed Professor of Sacred Scripture at the Propaganda, and soon after Vice-Rector of the Irish College. He returned to his native land, but at what precise date is not known, and was placed by the Bishop of Cloyne in the parish of Fermoy. After remaining in Ireland for some time, he accepted the invitation of Bishop Kenrick in 1839 to come to Philadelphia. Immediately after his arrival he was made a professor in the ecclesiastical seminary of St. Charles Borromeo, and soon after president. He also attended Morristown twice in the month. While still at the seminary he built St. Francis Xavier's Church, Fairmount, and was finally transferred to Pittsburg as Vicar-General and pastor of St. Paul's.

Bishop O'Connor left Rome soon after his consecration, and passed through Ireland on his way to America, with a view of providing priests and religious for his diocese; for he had not merely to govern, but, much more, to create it. Calling at Maynooth, he made an appeal to the students, which has been described by one who heard and responded to it.* Says the writer:

"On an evening in October (1843), as the students were assembled in the prayer-hall, a strange prelate was observed beside the dean on the bench usually occupied by the latter. The whole exterior of the distinguished visitor, in whom it was hard to say whether the captivating grace of natural dignity or the impressive evidence of intellectual superiority predominated, bespoke the presence of no ordinary man." Having been introduced by the dean, "the distinguished visitor arose and addressed the students; . . . and in conclusion observed he had no inducement to offer except plenty of labor and little for it." Five students whose course of studies was almost completed, and three others also far advanced, resolved to accompany the Bishop. Coming to Dublin, he obtained a colony of seven Sisters of the recently founded Order of Our Lady of Mercy, to take charge of parish schools and of the higher education of young ladies. These were the first Sisters of the order to establish a convent in the United States; and the permanent benefit they have conferred on religion not only in the Diocese of Pittsburg but throughout the country is the highest eulogium that could be pronounced on the zeal and foresight of Dr. O'Connor in introducing them. He sailed for America November 12th, and arrived at Pittsburg on the 3d of December.

"The following," he writes, "is a description of the Diocese of Pittsburg at the time of its erection:

"In *Allegheny County*: In the city of Pittsburg there was St. Paul's Cathedral, congregation estimated at 4000 souls.

---

* Rt. Rev. T. Mullen, Bishop of Erie. Reminiscences of Rev. Thos. M'Cullagh. p. 27.

The Bishop was assisted by Rev. Joseph F. Deane. St. Patrick's Church, brick, Rev. E. F. Garland pastor, congregation about 3000. St. Philomena's (German), temporary church, attended by the Redemptorist Fathers, congregation about 4000. Rev. A. P. Gibbs resided in Pittsburg to attend several small congregations outside the city. St. Philip's Church, Chartier's Creek (now Broadhead), brick, congregation 150, attended from Pittsburg. Pine Creek Church, log, congregation 400. Wexford, St. Alphonsus', brick, about 250. M'Keesport, St. Peter's, brick, 300. Making in all seven churches, six priests, and about 12,500 souls.

"*Westmoreland County:* St. Vincent's, brick, and Mt. Carmel (near Derry), log, Rev. Jas. A. Stillenger, 1350.

"*Indiana County:* Blairsville, brick, 1000. Cameron Bottom, stone, 300, Rev. J. A. Stillenger.

"*Butler County:* Butler, St. Peter's, stone. Donegal (now North Oakland), St. Joseph's, 1300. Murrinsville, St. Alphonsus', stone; and Clearfield Township (now St. Mary's, Summit), 500, Rev. H. P. Gallagher.

"*Armstrong County:* St. Patrick's, brick, formerly known as Buffalo Creek Mission, 1000; and St. Mary's, Freeport, brick, 300, Rev. J. Cody.

"*Washington County:* West Alexander, St. James', log, 107.

"*Fayette County:* Brownsville, church in course of erection, of stone, 183 souls.

"*Greene County:* Waynesburg, St. Anne's, brick, 64. Other stations in Washington, Fayette, and Greene counties, 160, Rev. M. Gallagher.

"*Beaver County:* Beaver, Sts. Peter and Paul, frame, 300.

"*Bedford County:* Bedford, St. Thomas', brick, 200; and *Somerset County:* Harman Bottom, St. John's, stone, Rev. Thos. Heyden, 400.

"*Huntingdon County:* Huntingdon, Holy Trinity, brick, 175. *Blair County:* Newry, St. Patrick's, stone; Hollidaysburg and Sinking Valley, churches in course of erection, Rev. Jas. Bradly, 1100.

"*Cambria County:* Loretto, St. Michael's, frame, 1800; Jefferson (now Wilmore), St. Bartholomew's, stone, 550; Johnstown, St. John Gualbert's, brick, 400; Ebensburg, St.

Patrick's, frame, 250; Hart's Sleeping Place, St. Joseph's, log, 300; and Summit, St. Aloysius' Church, in course of erection, frame, 500, Rev. H. Lemcke and Rev. M. Gibson." *

From this it will be seen that the Bishop had in his diocese thirty-three churches, a few of which were unfinished; fourteen priests, and a Catholic population of a little less than 25,000. There was also an orphan asylum, affording shelter to about twenty orphans. As yet there were but two religious communities in the diocese, the Redemptorist Fathers and the Sisters of Charity.

But it was not long before the influence of the Bishop's presence was everywhere felt. One of his first official acts was the ordination of Mr. Thos. M'Cullagh, one of the students who had accompanied him from Maynooth. It took place February 4th, 1844, and was the first ordination for the Diocese of Pittsburg. St. Paul's schools, already mentioned, were opened April 14th; and at the call of the Bishop the congregation met, June 14th, to take measures toward the erection of an episcopal residence. The result was a neat and commodious dwelling for the Bishop and the priests attached to the cathedral. On the 16th of the same month the first diocesan synod was held, and statutes were enacted for the government of the Church. Still another good work was inaugurated on the 30th of the same month, the opening of the Chapel of the Nativity, for the use of the colored Catholics of the city.

Later in the same year the city council passed an ordinance to grade off the streets a few feet on Grant's Hill, as that part of the city on which the cathedral stands was then called. It was feared that the foundation of St. Paul's would be thereby endangered, and a subscription was started to raise money to build walls to support the ground upon which it stood and prevent it from gradually crumbling away. But when the grading was finished all fears were dispelled, and a motion was set on foot for finishing the tower, which had not been raised above the roof of the church. This was also abandoned.

The Sisters of Mercy opened an academy for young

* Diocesan Register.

ladies in September; while one for boys was opened about the same time, with Rev. T. Mullen, the present Bishop of Erie, as principal. A circulating library came into existence about this time. There were also two temperance societies attached to St. Paul's and St. Patrick's churches, containing in the aggregate 3500 members. The only other temperance society in the city was one composed of Welshmen, and numbering 400 members.* The publication of *The Catholic* was begun in February of this year. But by far the most important work undertaken by the Bishop, and one which evinces both his zeal and his courage, was the founding of St. Michael's Ecclesiastical Seminary for the education of candidates for the sacred ministry. Its beginnings were humble, but it was notwithstanding destined to be productive of incalculable benefit to the cause of religion. A limited number of students were at first assembled in a small building at the corner of Smithfield Street and Virgin Alley, with Rev. Richard H. Wilson, D.D., as principal professor; and an effort was made to erect a seminary on a part of the lot occupied by the cathedral. For this purpose a meeting was held June 14th, 1844, at which $2000 were subscribed; but the plan was not carried into execution, and the students appear to have remained in their first building until they were transferred to Birmingham, in 1847. Thus we see that in the brief space of a single year the Bishop had succeeded in thoroughly organizing all the departments of his vast diocese.

But the scarcity of priests and teachers was sorely felt in the diocese, and it must be some years before a competent supply of either could be expected from the diocese itself. In the mean time the Bishop, like many of his colleagues in the episcopacy, must draw upon the Catholic countries of Europe for the necessary supply. Fortunately the American Church has seldom appealed in vain; and the number of priests and religious of both sexes from Germany and France, and most of all from Ireland, who devoted their energies and lives to the cause of religion in this country will in all future times be held in grateful remembrance. The Bishop set out for Rome

* Harris' Business Directory, 1844.

and other European countries in the interest of his diocese July 23d, 1845, leaving Very Rev. J. A. Stillenger Vicar-General and Administrator. Among the acquisitions which he brought with him on his return were four Presentation Brothers from the city of Cork, who were expected to found a house of their institute and take charge of the boys' schools. He arrived in Pittsburg on his return, December 13th.

Having organized his diocese, the Bishop set out on his first visitation, July, 1846, commencing at Beaver and passing north and east through the present Diocese of Erie. I have before me, in his own handwriting, a brief account of this visitation, with the number of souls in each congregation, the number confirmed, and other matters of interest. This visitation was completed the following summer. But by far the most important event of this year was the introduction of a large colony of the venerable and learned Order of St. Benedict, which came from Bavaria and settled at St. Vincent's, Westmoreland County, October 24th. Further on an occasion will be presented of speaking at great length of this foundation, and the good it has achieved in the cause of religion and religious education. This, too, was the first introduction of the Benedictine Order into the United States. Two new churches were also dedicated this year. The Catholic population of the diocese is given in the *Catholic Directory* for this year at 30,000.

The year 1847 was destined to be more eventful than any of its predecessors. The Mercy Hospital was opened by the Sisters of Mercy in January, in a temporary building, and in August the contract was let for the erection of the present spacious building. June 2d, Rev. Jos. F. Deane withdrew from the cathedral, where he had been since before the first arrival of Dr. O'Connor, to a mission in Clarion County, bearing with him a testimonial from the congregation. He was succeeded by Rev. James Madison Lancaster, late of Kentucky. Prior to this date the Bishop had purchased a large farm on the side and top of the hill south of Birmingham, known at present as Mt. Oliver, for which he paid, I believe, $16,000. It was a profitable investment; for after perhaps $100,000 worth of building lots had been sold, the balance was assessed before the panic at $162,000. St. Michael's Church, the Franciscan Convent, and the Passionist Monastery stand on a part of it. The frame house on the property, which had been occupied for a time by the Presentation Brothers, now became St. Michael's Seminary, under the presidency of Rev. Thos. M'Cullagh. In the same year was introduced a colony of Brothers of the Third Order of St. Francis, as school and college teachers, who came from Clifton and Roundstone, in the Archdiocese of Tuam, Ireland, and established themselves at Loretto. But the event of the greatest importance to St. Paul's and to the diocese was the second grading of the streets on Grant's Hill, begun in June of this year, by which the foundations of the cathedral were irreparably injured and the approach rendered extremely difficult. When the grading was completed the cathedral stood perched on a mound some twenty feet or more above the level of the street, and high flights of stairs were necessary to enable the congregation to enter it. The bank was sustained by temporary supports; but it was evident to all that the venerable edifice could not stand long, owing to the action of the frost and rain on the foundation. A suit was instituted against the city, and a verdict obtained for $4000; but an appeal was made to the Supreme Court, which on the 7th of November, 1851, confirmed the sentence of the inferior tribunal. But besides the delay and expense in obtaining redress, the award was trifling when compared with the injury inflicted on the building and the expense and inconvenience entailed on the congregation. The episcopal residence, which had been built after the first grading, did not suffer.

Four new churches were dedicated this year.

The following is the registry of baptisms at St. Paul's for the fourteen years from 1834 to 1848. The years date from May to May, because it was in that month the church was dedicated. It will also show the population to have been fluctuating; but account must be had of the new congregations formed during that time in the city and vicinity. In 1834 there were 222 baptisms; in 1835, 210; in 1836, 252; in 1837, 260; in 1838, 218; in 1839, 312; in 1840, 252; in 1841, 144; in 1842, 204; in 1843, 218; in 1844, 212; in 1845, 320;

in 1846, 234; in 1847, 304—total, 3362. These with the 1214 baptized from 1820 to 1830, and perhaps 600 between 1830 and 1834, and 400 prior to 1820, will give a grand total of 5576. In September of this year Father Lancaster returned to his native State, where he died a few years ago, Vicar-General of the Diocese of Covington. He was succeeded in the pastorate of St. Paul's by Rev. James O'Meally. The Oblate Fathers of the Blessed Virgin Mary took charge of St. Michael's Seminary November 22d, but remained only a short time.

Five new churches were erected in 1848.

The year 1848 was not so eventful as its predecessor had been. The congregation continued to augment with the increase of the population of the city. But, inasmuch as many Catholics had by this time taken up their residence in Allegheny City, the necessity of forming a congregation on that side of the river became daily more apparent. A meeting of those interested was therefore called in September, the new congregation was organized, and measures were taken for purchasing a site and erecting a church. What was then humbly commenced has since grown into St. Peter's parish, perhaps the most flourishing English congregation in the western part of the State.

The cemetery attached to St. Patrick's Church, and that on Boyd's Hill near the Mercy Hospital, in which the English Catholics were interred, became so full, and so much within the constantly extending limits of the city, that it was necessary to purchase new grounds, and these, if possible, so extensive as to serve for a general burying-ground for all the English congregations of the city for the future. To this end the present St. Mary's Cemetery, consisting originally of about fifty acres, was purchased early in 1849, at a cost of $20,000. It was chartered soon after, and has since been used and will for many years be the general cemetery of the city. In the same year the Franciscan Brothers from Loretto established a house of their order in the city, and took charge of the boys of St. Paul's school. About the same time the celebrated Joe Barker, whose name figures so prominently in the Know Nothing movements in the city, began to gain notoriety by his inflammatory street harangues against the Church and the clergy.

There were two churches enlarged and a new one built in 1849.

The condition of the cathedral became daily more precarious, on account of the injury done the foundation, and a meeting was called January 27th, 1850, to consider what was best to be done, although on this point there could be little difference of opinion. It was unanimously resolved to tear it down, grade off the lot to the level of the street, and erect a new one. It is proper to state that measures of this kind would have been taken perhaps two years before, but for the tardiness of the city officials in cutting down the streets and fixing their final grade. The necessary committees were appointed at the meeting, and a subscription for the new cathedral was opened, which the Bishop headed with $1000. Proposals for grading the lot were asked, and plans were ordered for the new edifice. The latter were accepted July 20th; but the lateness of the season made it advisable to await the coming spring before commencing work.

Father O'Meally had withdrawn from the cathedral to Cincinnati early in the spring, and was succeeded in April by Rev. Edward M'Mahon, who had lately arrived from Lexington, Ky. This zealous and laborious priest was destined to play a more important part in the history of St. Paul's, and of the diocese, than any other had done since the days of Father O'Reilly.

In 1850 two new churches were built.

The subscription for the new cathedral had reached almost, if not quite, $30,000 by the spring of 1851; and when all was in readiness for commencing to tear down the old building, and when even the insurance policies, with the exception of one of $5000, had been permitted to expire in view of that event, this noble monument of the zeal, energy, and taste of Father M'Guire took fire at the roof from sparks from a chimney of the episcopal residence, at 11 o'clock A.M., May 6th, and was entirely destroyed with the exception of such furniture as could be hastily removed. The organ, valued at $3000, was a total loss. The Bishop was absent at the time.

Nothing remained but to carry the plan of a new building into immediate execution. The remains of Fathers M'Guire, Hoy, M'Caffrey, and Kenny were removed from the vaults of the ruins to the new cemetery, where they still repose; and work was commenced on the foundation. It was prosecuted with such despatch that the foundations were ready for the laying of the corner-stone by the middle of June of the same year. In the mean time, and until the basement was finished, the people accommodated themselves as best they could in the school-rooms. The corner-stone was laid with great solemnity by the Bishop on the afternoon of Trinity Sunday, June 15th, 1851. Two inscriptions were placed in the stone, one of which referred to the old cathedral and the other to the new one. The completion of the cathedral was now the great work for the Bishop and his people. But it was not to be the work of a day. The Know Nothing excitement, under the charm of Joe Barker's popular eloquence, now began to disturb the quiet of the city and turn the tide of shallow public opinion against the Catholic portion of the population. Adverse circumstances and the breaking out of the cholera forced the Bishop to close the Seminary in June, and send his students to other institutions to complete their course of studies; and it was not reopened for five years.

Five new churches were dedicated in 1851.

Work was progressing on the cathedral when 1852 set in to mark its impress on the diocese and the world. The increase of the Catholic population, the extent of the diocese, and the want of facilities for travelling rapidly from place to place induced the Bishop to consider the propriety of having the diocese divided and a new one formed from the northern counties. He laid the matter before the Fathers of the First Plenary Council of Baltimore, which assembled May 9th; and as his reasons for the division were strong, and his voice well-nigh all-powerful, the matter was decided according to his wishes, and the formation of a new diocese, with the see at Erie, was recommended to the Holy See. The Holy Father confirmed the action of the Council by a bull, dated April 29th, 1853, of which we shall take occasion to speak further on.

Father M'Mahon was made Vicar-General of the Diocese

of Pittsburg April 26th, 1852. But the scarcity of priests still greatly perplexed the good Bishop. He was, besides, anxious to have religious established in his diocese whose duty it should be to give missions in the churches. With a view of procuring them, as well as of transacting other business of importance connected with the administration of the diocese, he set out on a trip to Europe July 23d, leaving Father M'Mahon Administrator during his absence. When in Rome he called on the Father General of the Passionist Order, and obtained the promise of a small colony of the order for his diocese. Three Fathers sailed for America, landing at Philadelphia, whence they proceeded to Pittsburg, where they established the first house of their congregation in the United States, and which is still the mother-house. Thus was Dr. O'Connor the first to introduce another order into the country, and again did the results which followed attest the wisdom of his choice. He arrived in Pittsburg on his return, November 20th.

In the spring of this year St. Bridget's congregation was organized by Father Tuigg, the present Bishop of Pittsburg, principally from St. Patrick's, but in part also from St. Paul's. St. James', Temperanceville, was also formed in autumn, partly from St. Paul's and partly from St. Philip's, Broadhead.

In 1852 there were two new churches built.

In January and February, 1853, the Bishop addressed a number of letters to the Governor of Pennsylvania on the common schools, which he published in *The Catholic*.

The bulls dividing the Diocese of Pittsburg and erecting the new See of Erie were dated, as we have said, April 29th, 1853. The dividing line ran east and west along the northern boundaries of Cambria, Indiana, Armstrong, Butler, and Laurence counties, giving thirteen counties to the new and fifteen to the old diocese. The area of the Diocese of Pittsburg was reduced from 21,300, to 11,314 square miles, or a fraction more than one fourth that of the State ; but it retained full three fourths of the Catholic population of the original diocese. Dr. O'Connor chose the new bishopric as his portion , and, the Holy See approving his choice, he was transferred thither by a Bull dated July 29th, 1853. A bull was also expedited promoting Rev. Josue M. Young, of the Archdiocese of Cincinnati, to the vacant See of Pittsburg. Bishop O'Connor, to the great grief of the Catholics and all the citizens of Pittsburg, set out for his new field of labor October 14th, bearing with him addresses from both the clergy and laity of his late diocese. Very Rev. E. M'Mahon was appointed administrator of Pittsburg until the consecration of the Bishop-elect.

A comparison of the condition of the diocese at the date of its division with what it was at the time of its erection will furnish the most convincing evidence of the zeal, prudence, and energy which characterized the Administration of Bishop O'Connor during the nine years that he filled the See of Pittsburg. At the time of the division there were seventy-eight churches, and four more in course of erection; sixty-four clergymen; and a Catholic population of 50,000.

CHAPTER V.

HISTORY OF ST. PAUL'S CATHEDRAL FROM THE ERECTION OF THE SEE OF ERIE TO THE RESIGNATION OF BISHOP O'CONNOR.

Visit of Cardinal Bedini—Know Nothingism—Bishop O'Connor returns to Pittsburg—He visits Rome—Consecration of the Cathedral—A description of the building—Decline of the Bishop's health—He travels in Europe and the Holy Land—Petitions for a coadjutor—Travels in Mexico—Thinks of resigning—Visits Rome—Resigns—His episcopate—Death—Biographical notice.

On the 10th of December, 1853, the Papal Nuncio, Cardinal Cajetan Bedini, arrived in Pittsburg, and was received in the basement of the new cathedral, which had been opened on the 8th of the preceding September. The Know Nothings were then at the zenith of their power, and during the few days His Eminence stopped in the city he could not be permitted to remain without insult. His carriage was surrounded and stopped near St. Patrick's Church, but the crowd was dispersed with little further demonstration than insulting language. It was at this time and in the following year that Joe Barker, then in the height of his glory, allowed nothing that was Catholic to escape his vituperation. The character of the Bishop and his clergy was attacked with fabricated stories, and in the excitement of the moment, when many were disposed to listen with avidity to any abuse of foreigners—which usually means Irish Catholics—they experienced no little anxiety. So well planned were some of his attacks upon character that it was with the greatest difficulty that even the Bishop could succeed in repelling them. So high did feeling run for a time that the Bishop found it necessary to require the clergy to lay aside every distinctive mark in dress, etc., the better to escape molestation and insult. Having enjoyed his triumph, the unhappy Barker was destined to feel the hand of God, whom he had insulted in his Church and its ministers. Returning from a political meeting which he had addressed, he was struck by a locomotive while walking on the railroad, and, being thrown down a steep embankment, was instantly killed, August 2d, 1862.

The enmity to the Church which the Know Nothing movement had fanned into a flame added to the difficulty of raising means for the completion of the Cathedral. The basement had been finished and opened for divine service, as we have said; and it was the intention of the Bishop to have built the entire structure of cut stone. But the magnitude of the undertaking, and the difficulty of collecting means, forced him reluctantly to abandon this design after the completion of the basement, and finish the superstructure in brick, roughly, to be afterwards coated with cement in imitation of stone. But this coating has never yet been put on, and most probably never will be.

The number of churches finished and dedicated during the course of 1853 was six.

The clergy and people of Pittsburg felt deeply the loss of their good Bishop, and united in a petition to the Holy See for his return. They felt that he who had ruled the diocese with so much zeal and prudence in the past, and who was intimately acquainted with all that related to its every department, must continue its government more successfully than any other; and that he who had planned its great Cathedral was the most fitting person to secure the execution of his plans. The reluctance of Father Young to accept the mitre of Pittsburg seconded their petition, and induced the Holy See to grant their request. A bull was issued, restoring him to his former see, February 20th, 1854. He returned soon after, and Father Young was consecrated Bishop of Erie.

The Bishop pushed forward the work on the new Cathedral amid almost insurmountable difficulties, arising in part out of the magnitude of the undertaking, in part out of the feelings of the people towards the Catholics, and in part out of the financial depression that was everywhere beginning to be felt. But Dr. O'Connor was not a prelate to be easily turned aside from his purpose, and while he realized to their full extent the difficulties by which he was surrounded, he yet entered upon the struggle with that energy which was characteristic of him, and that confidence in Divine Providence which marks the true Christian. And the people of our day who contemplate this magnificent pile have their admiration for him who planned and built it no little increased by a knowledge of the fact that it required almost superhuman efforts on the part of as great a mind as that of Bishop O'Connor to call it into existence. But he was already beginning to pay the penalty of his zeal in the impairing of his health, which began about this time to give evidence of a decline.

The summons of the Holy Father called the hierarchy of the Catholic world to the Eternal City, and Dr. O'Connor was again obliged to visit Rome. Leaving Father M'Mahon Administrator during his absence, he sailed on the 14th of October, 1854, and, having transacted business connected with the administration of the diocese in other parts of Europe, arrived in Rome a few days before the ever-memorable 8th of December. It was on this day that the dogma of the Immaculate Conception of the Blessed Virgin Mary was defined to be an article of faith; and it is believed that in promoting this important decision the influence of the Bishop of Pittsburg contributed no little. It is asserted by some, but upon what authority I know not, that certain alterations in the wording of the decree itself were due to the learning of the same prelate. Having witnessed with no ordinary spiritual consolation the promulgation of a decree at which the whole Catholic world burst forth in acclamations of joy and thanksgiving, Dr. O'Connor returned to his diocese, arriving in Pittsburg January 24th, 1855.

In 1854 there were two churches enlarged and seven new ones built.

The great work of the Bishop—his new Cathedral—was drawing toward completion, or toward the state in which it would be allowed to remain until the times should improve; and preparations were made for its solemn consecration. There it stood in majestic grandeur, on one of the most prominent sites in the city, having sprung into life in the midst of the bitterest Know Nothing times, a silent witness of the power of the Church against the spirit of Satan. At the time of its consecration it was, if not the largest church in the United States, the largest with but one or two exceptions; while in point of architectural beauty it was, and is yet, unsurpassed by any church on the American continent.

Sunday, June 24th, 1855, was the day fixed for the solemn consecration. The preparations were in keeping with the grandeur of the temple that was to be dedicated to the Most High. The Most Rev. F. P. Kenrick, Archbishop of Baltimore, was the consecrating prelate. The following prelates, and a large number of the clergy of this and other dioceses, were present: Most Rev. Archbishop Hughes, of New York; Bishops O'Connor, of Pittsburg; Poitier, of Mobile; Whelan, of Wheeling; Henni, of Milwaukee; O'Reilly, of Hartford; Spalding, of Louisville; Rappe, of Cleveland; Neumann, of Philadelphia; M'Gill, of Richmond; Loughlin, of Brooklyn; Amat, of Monterey; Young, of Erie; Reagan, of Chicago; Timon, of Buffalo; and Carroll, of Covington. The Bishops and clergy who assisted at the consecration entered the Cathedral at five o'clock, the people not being admitted, and the solemn ceremony was begun. At nine o'clock the procession of the prelates and clergy moved from the episcopal residence to the main entrance, and passing up the nave entered the sanctuary. Soon the people, who had been impatiently waiting, thronged into the sacred edifice, filling every available spot, and it is estimated that about six thousand were able to find room within its walls. Right Rev. M. Poitier, Bishop of Mobile, celebrated Mass, and Archbishop Hughes, of New York, preached the dedication sermon, taking for his text the words of St. Paul, Acts xx. 28: " Take heed to yourselves and to the whole flock, wherein the Holy Ghost hath placed you Bishops, to rule the Church of God which he hath purchased with his own blood." The sermon was one of Dr. Hughes' best efforts. Dr. Kenrick preached in the evening, at Vespers, on the character and virtues of St. John the Baptist. Thus ended one of the most memorable days witnessed by the Church in this country.

Says a writer of the day : " No artist, however skilled, can convey an adequate idea of the massive beauty of this building. It is a cathedral. Take away even the spires and crosses, and there is no fear of its being taken for anything but a Catholic church. The former Cathedral was in its day a wonder, but this is *the* wonder, and will be so for many days, years, and centuries, should not some unlucky disaster overwhelm the well-proportioned pile." But it is the material structure and not the decoration that must be considered. Frescoing would undoubtedly add to its appearance; but even under the coating of dust which attaches itself to every object in the "Smoky City," the perfect harmony of all its parts uniting to form a grand whole is such as to make it one of the most splendid architectural monuments in America. The following description was furnished by Mr. Charles Bartberger, the architect: The ground form of the building is the Roman cross; its head forms the sanctuary or chancel, its arms the south and north wings of the transept, with the dome standing over the centre. Of this dome it must be remarked that from the exterior there is nothing that could lead the spectator to look for such an object. You behold a gigantic steeple with spire and cross rising, it may indeed be said with truth, speaking of the "Smoky City,' far above the clouds. It is then an unexpected delight when you approach the chancel to look up to a very high and very large dome, through the windows of which heaven's pure light, like an emblem of its grace, beams on the sanctuary. The stem of the cross forms the nave, with the aisles attached to its sides. The outer aisles are to be closed by towers, which are connected by a corridor, or rather an arcade, into which the congregation enter by three doorways from Grant Street; and two doorways, one in each tower, from the opposite sides of the building. The arcade supports the organ-loft, and is the termination of the nave and the inner aisles. The building is capable of holding at least five thousand persons. The ground upon which the cathedral stands falls from the front, giving a basement under the rear half of the building capable of accommodating about sixteen hundred persons. It is used as the children's chapel, and for lectures, etc.

The shortness of the lot, 240 feet, prevented the full extension of the longitudinal dimensions of the building. The front, consequently, seems rather wide in proportion to the length. In the angles formed by the transept and the sanctuary are arranged the sacristies. Between these and the transept, and opening into the latter, are two chapels on each side of the high altar. The dome is supported by four massive Norman pillars. Two rows of pillars support the clerestory roof and ceiling, while two outer rows support the roof of the aisles and their ceilings, which, as all the ceilings of the church, are finished with stucco in the rich composite style of Gothic and Byzantine.

The following are the principal dimensions: Extreme length, 220 feet; extreme width, 140 feet; width of front, 116 feet. The sanctuary and both wings of the transept are 42 feet square by 75 feet high; nave, 115 feet by 42 feet wide and 75 feet high; two aisles, each 115 feet long by 15 wide and 60 high; two outer aisles, each 100 by 14 feet and 48 high. Height of side walls from floor of church, 32 feet. Height of the clerestory walls from floor of church, 66 feet. The dome covers a square of 42 feet by 130 from the upper, or 152 from the lower floor in the clear. Its full height is 272 feet. The two towers on the corners in front are not yet finished. The basement walls are faced with brown sandstone; the cornice tops, etc., are of cut stone, as are the bases of the exterior walls and of the inner pillars and columns, the shafts of which are built of hard brick laid in cement. The roofs are covered with tile.

Enter the church. The first object of attraction on the right, near the entrance, in a semicircular recess with light beaming from the top, and enclosed by a semicircular railing, is the baptistery. Look around. All the appropriate ornaments, which impart so rich a finish, are stucco work. The groined ceiling of the nave is ornamented by portraits of the twelve Apostles. The walls of the transept and sanctuary are adorned by six colossal statues representing St. Peter, St. Paul, St. Patrick, St. Bridget, St. Aloysius, and St. Rose. The windows are all of stained glass of home manufacture, not gorgeous, but in perfect keeping with the majesty of the place. The Bishop's throne, the stalls for the clergy, and the pulpit are of white oak, and, like the massive communionrail and eight confessionals, are carved in highly ornamental style. The same may be said of the ends and doors of the pews. The altars, five in number, including the main one, are of wood, but so beautifully carved and so richly gilded as to leave nothing to regret. The organ, which is but a small one, is placed not on the gallery over the main entrance, but in a small organ-loft in the right transept.

The estimated cost of the cathedral was eighty thousand dollars. But before its completion it cost much more; and although the exact amount is not known, and could not perhaps be ascertained, it is no overestimate to fix it in round numbers at three hundred thousand dollars.

Seven new churches were erected in 1855, and but two in the following year.

The study and labor connected with the building of the Cathedral and the government of the diocese proved too great a burden for the Bishop; and his health began rapidly to decline during 1855 and 1856. Toward the close of the latter year he was advised by his physician to take a trip to Europe for the benefit of his health. He accordingly sailed December 10th, accompanied by Rev. T. S. Reynolds, leaving Very Rev. E. M'Mahon Administrator during his absence. After stopping a short time at Rome and in other parts of Europe, he sailed for Alexandria, in Egypt, in April, 1857, stopping at Malta a few days on his way. Toward the latter end of May he passed into the Holy Land. The first Mass he celebrated at Jerusalem was in the grotto of the Holy Sepulchre. A month later he was at Constantinople; and having passed slowly through Europe he returned home, arriving in Pittsburg September 16th. But his health was but little improved, and fears were entertained that it would never be restored, or if at all, it would only be after a still further repose.

During his stay in Rome he procured the magnificent painting of the Crucifixion over the high altar of the Cathedral. It is from the pencil of Gagliardi, a celebrated artist, and was painted expressly for the altar of St. Paul's. It is in the style of Guido Reni, and represents our divine Redeemer hanging on the cross in the dim light of Good Friday afternoon, with Mary Magdelene clinging convulsively to the redeeming wood, while across the top of the picture is the appropriate legend which it so fittingly illustrates: "God hath so loved us." In addition to its beauty of execution is its colossal size, it being twenty-seven feet high by twelve wide. The dust of the city has dimmed the lustre of this magnificent work of art, but to the eye of the critic it will ever pay a fitting tribute to the eminent master whose work it is.

The Bishop now thought of procuring aid in the administration of the diocese, and accordingly petitioned the Holy See for a coadjutor. In compliance with his request, Rev. John B. Byrne, of St. Matthew's Church, Washington City, was appointed coadjutor May 9th, 1857. He did not arrive in Pittsburg until about the end of August, soon after which time the day of his consecration was fixed. But quite unexpectedly the bulls were returned, and he retired to Mount St. Mary's, where he died a few years later. The dignity was then offered to Very Rev. Edward Purcell, brother of the Archbishop of Cincinnati; but he declined the honor, and Bishop O'Connor was left to bear the burden unaided. His health was now so much impaired that his physician required him to seek the air of a more southern clime during the winter months; and he accordingly set sail for the West Indies and Mexico in October, 1857. But so far from reposing he spent much of his time in collecting money for the Cathedral, an undertaking in which he met with considerable success. 1857, it will be remembered, was the year of the great financial panic; and the Bishop's home resources were limited. Returning, he arrived in Pittsburg April 22d, 1858. But his desire of laboring for the good of his diocese prevented him from reposing even when he professed to do so; and his return found his health still more impaired than it was at his departure. During this year he was unable to make the visitation of his diocese; and Bishop Young, of Erie, performed it, or at least a part of it, for him.

In 1857 three new churches were added to the diocese.

Fearing that the Church would suffer from his inability to administer the affairs of the diocese, he began seriously to entertain the thought of resigning an office he felt himself no longer able to fill. He again crossed the Atlantic July 16th, 1859, and visited Rome, leaving his brother, Rev. James O'Connor, the present Vicar Apostolic of Nebraska, Administrator in his absence. He did not return, it would appear, before the beginning of the following year; and then only to bid farewell to the flock in whose behalf he had so zealously labored.

During his absence the splendid episcopal residence was destroyed by fire, November 3d, 1859. A plan of a new house was prepared which should cost $16,000 and occupy a part of the ground upon which the present palace stands; bids had been received and the contract was about concluded, when the Bishop returned; but thinking it far too expensive, he refused to ratify the contract, and determined to take up his residence in such a part of the old building as remained intact. A member of the committee, from whom I have received these particulars, then proposed that at least the front of the building should be newly faced with brick to give it the appearance of a house. To this the Bishop reluctantly gave his consent; and so it remained for sixteen years.

Three new churches were erected in 1858.

"The resignation of the Right Rev. M. O'Connor, of the See of Pittsburg, was accepted on the 23d of May, 1860, and the announcement of the same was received by him on the 15th of June following."* The moment of separation drew near, and unexpectedly to almost all both of the clergy and laity he published his valedictory in *The Catholic*, under date of June 18th, 1860, which was very brief, and stated that ill-health, as many knew, had forced this painful measure upon him. He was at this time in New York City. Very Rev. James O'Connor was named Administrator until the appointment of a successor. Meetings of the clergy and others of the laity were held, at which suitable addresses were prepared and forwarded to him July 7th, to which he replied in appropriate terms. He sailed for Europe to enter the novitiate of the Society of Jesus, October 13th. He visited Pittsburg but two or three times afterwards.

* Diocesan Register.

We cannot take leave of this illustrious prelate in a more fitting manner than by quoting the words of one who was long and intimately acquainted with him, and who was capable both of appreciating his worth and of expressing it in terms suitable to the subject :

"Any one who understands the resources of the Diocese of Pittsburg would find it difficult to comprehend how this zealous prelate contrived to accomplish so much for the good of religion. A stranger, after examining all that has been done—the various charitable and educational establishments that have been founded, and the number of churches built— would at once conclude that Bishop O'Connor to accomplish so much must have had the control of vast means, or must have been at the head of a numerous and influential Catholic body, possessed of immense wealth and unbounded munificence. Yet Bishop O'Connor enjoyed none of these advantages. The Catholics of the Diocese of Pittsburg, though ever ready to extend a generous support to their religion, cannot be said to be influential in a numerical or pecuniary sense. For sixteen years they have enjoyed the advantages of an episcopal administration, all things considered perhaps the most brilliant and most successful in the history of the American Church. At their head they beheld a prelate, young, learned, zealous, and experienced, endowed with a creative genius and a rich fertility of resources under difficulties, such as fall to the lot of few men. Sublime in his conceptions and prompt in his movements, he excited the admiration of all no less by the grandeur of his plans than by the rapidity of their execution. Conscious of his own strength and the justice of his claims on popular support, he engaged in enterprises from which common men would have recoiled ; and each bold move, as it culminated in success, inspired additional confidence in his indomitable energy, and served as a base of operations for the inception of something else, which, while it tended to bring out in bold relief the most popular features of the Church, would minister in the most practical way to the increasing wants of the community around him.

"At home, year after year, there arose splendid monuments attesting his industry and energy. Abroad, when questions of vast import to the interests of religion came up for discussion, so great was his reputation as a writer, lecturer, and theologian that all turned instinctively to Pittsburg for the light of that brilliant intellect that so long adorned its see. Accustomed not only to sketch out the outlines, but to supply the minutest details of the various measures which originated with himself for the advancement of religion, the greater part of his administration has been one of great mental activity and close application to business, sufficient to induce premature decay on the most vigorous constitution. In contemplating the improvements which on all sides mark the period over which his episcopate extends, Bishop O'Connor must be cheered with the assurance that comes from all classes of his fellow-citizens, but especially from his own flock, that he has done his duty, his whole duty, and done it well."

Justice requires us to add, with the same writer: "It would, however, be neither agreeable to him nor just to them to ignore in this brief tribute to his merits the hearty coöperation he received from a body of priests singularly unselfish and proud to emulate the zeal of their great Bishop. Encouraged by his counsel and stimulated by his example, they have, in the many religious institutions scattered throughout the diocese, left on imperishable record a glowing testimony of their generous efforts in the cause of religion from 1844 to 1860.*

RT. REV. MICHAEL O'CONNOR, S.J.

Besides the picture of Bishop O'Connor's life that has already been presented to the reader, it remains to sketch the close of his career in the illustrious Society of Jesus—the fulfilment of the prophetic words of Pope Gregory XVI.

Having resigned his see, his first care was to put in execution the desire which he had long entertained of entering the Society of Jesus. He accordingly entered one of the houses of the Society in Germany, where he hoped to make his novitiate unknown to all save the few to whom a knowl-

* Reminiscences of the Rev. Thos. M'Cullagh, by Rev. T. Mullen, pp. 30, 31.

edge of his former dignity was necessary. But it was hard for him to forget good habits, and, to his own humiliation and the surprise of all, he once saluted the community after the *Gloria* in the Mass with the *Pax vobis* of Bishops, instead of the *Dominus vobiscum* of the inferior clergy. By a special dispensation of the Father General of the Society, he was permitted to take the customary vows at the end of two years. Almost immediately after he returned to the United States, and taught theology for some time in the Society's college in Boston. "He was then appointed Socius of the Father Provincial, and until his death was a preacher, a lecturer, and director of spiritual retreats all over the country, from Maine to Louisiana ; and out of the country, for he visited Canada and at last visited Europe."* He manifested great zeal for the poor colored people, and it was through his exertions that St. Xavier's Church, Baltimore, was purchased for their accommodation.

Another evidence of his humility and desire of remaining as much as possible retired from the more attractive scenes of life was the request he made of the Holy Father when the latter accepted his resignation. It is well known that when a Bishop is permitted to retire from the government of his diocese he still possesses the power necessary for administering confirmation, if asked to do so by the Bishop in whose diocese he may be for the time. Foreseeing that he would frequently be called on to administer this sacrament, Dr. O'Connor requested the Holy Father to withdraw the faculty for exercising that power, which the Pope was pleased to do.

His health improved after his resignation, but it never attained its pristine vigor. Age, added to his incessant labors and great mental activity, gradually undermined it, and forced him at length to retire to Woodstock College, Md., where, worn out with laboring in his Master's vineyard, he was called to his reward October 18th, 1872, in the sixty-third year of his age. His remains were deposited by the side of his brethren of the Society to which his affections ever clung, and there reposes all that is mortal of one of the most bril-

---

* Funeral Discourse of Fr. Clarke, S.J.

liant lights that has ever shed its lustre on the Church in the United States.

"Father O'Connor's mind was massive, solid, and deep, expanding and embracing within its compass almost every department of science and art; and although we cannot say, 'Quid tetigit ornavit,' for neither taste nor talent fitted him for the graces of diction, ... we may say, 'Nihil tetigit quod non solidavit;' for no one who listened to him in conversation, sermon, or lecture could have failed to observe that, whether he treated a subject analytically or synthetically, he touched and sounded its every part, and always presented it in its greatest strength. And with respect to his style, I think I should add that, like his world-renowned countryman Edmund Burke, his language became more ornamental and eloquent as he advanced in age. Statesmen and lawyers with whom he conversed on ecclesiastical subjects regarding which they had attempted to legislate, and scholars who chatted with him in regard to studies which they had made specialties, were astonished at the variety, extent, and accuracy of his learning, and were frequently convinced by the clearness and the cogency of his reasoning. They found him a giant in intellect: master of every subject that he handled, whether it was the taxation of ecclesiastical property, the school question, or any other subject, a match for any antagonist; and, like a true and valiant knight of the cross, ever ready to dare and to do, and, if need had been, to die for his faith. . . .

"It may be asked why a man of zeal so ardent and of enterprise so constantly crowned with success laid down the burden of the episcopate and sought the retirement and repose of the religious life. I answer, first, that the religious life was his first choice. He had petitioned for admission into the Society of Jesus before he was consecrated. Secondly, declining health and the advice of physicians proved that it was highly proper, perhaps absolutely necessary. Thirdly, in his resignation and retirement he followed the example of some of the greatest saints whom the Church proposes not only for our admiration but for our imitation." *

---

* Funeral Discourse of Fr. Clarke, S.J.

Together with his other acquirements, Dr. O'Connor was also a linguist of considerable note. Besides the English language, he was familiar with the Latin, Greek, and Hebrew, among the dead, and with the Irish, French, German, Italian, and Spanish, among the living tongues.

In stature Dr. O'Connor was slightly above the medium height, rather heavy than slender, but not adipose; of an erect and commanding figure, but without affectation or assumption of dignity. On the contrary, he was indifferent of his dress and appearance to a degree bordering on carelessness. But notwithstanding this he could not if he wished conceal his innate superiority, and we may say with the poet:

> "His grandeur he derived from heaven alone,
> For he was great ere Fortune made him so."

Dr. O'Connor left no writings beyond a few published lectures and his contributions to *The Catholic* and perhaps to some other periodicals. His life was too active to permit the leisure necessary to commit his thoughts to writing.

CHAPTER VI.

HISTORY OF ST. PAUL'S CATHEDRAL FROM 1860 TO 1873.

Statistics of the Diocese—Appointment and consecration of Rt. Rev. Michael Domenec—Biographical notice—He visits Rome and Madrid—Rev. J. Hickey rector of the Cathedral—Father M'Mahon retires to Philadelphia—The new organ—The Bishop again visits Rome—The towers built—Consecration of Bishop Mullen, of Erie—The Golden Age of Pittsburg—The Bishop again visits Rome to attend the Vatican Council—Death of Dr. Keogh, and biographical notice—Sisters of Charity and Ursuline Nuns—Death of Rev. D. Devlin—Little Sisters of the Poor—Sisters of the Good Shepherd—The Catholic Institute.

BEFORE attempting to trace the history of the diocese under the administration of its second Bishop, it is proper to cast a retrospective glance at the condition of the Church over which he was called to rule. When Bishop O'Connor was forced by declining health to resign his see, the statistics of the diocese were as follows: Seventy-seven churches, eighty-six priests, thirty clerical students, four male and two female religious orders, one seminary, three male and two female institutions of learning, two orphan asylums, one hospital, and a Catholic population of more than 50,000.

The first intelligence that reached Pittsburg of the appointment of a successor to the late Bishop was a report that a consistory had been held on the 28th of September, 1860, in which Rev. Michael Domenec, pastor of St. Vincent of Paul's Church, Germantown, Pa., had been promoted to the vacant see. The report proved to be correct, and the appointment was officially announced in *The Catholic* of November 24th. The Bishop-elect arrived in the city early in December, and fixed the 9th of the same month as the day of his consecration. The ceremony took place in the cathedral, and was attended with unusual pomp. Most Rev. F. P. Kenrick, Archbishop of Baltimore, was consecrating prelate. The sermon was preached by Rt. Rev. J. Timon, of Buffalo. And here it is proper to pause and give a brief sketch of the early life of the newly consecrated prelate.

RT. REV. MICHAEL DOMENEC was born of wealthy parents in the city of Ruez, near Tarragona, in the north-east of Spain, in 1816. His early education was acquired in the schools of Madrid; but owing to the disturbances occasioned by the Carlist war, he was obliged at the age of fifteen to retire to France. He entered a college in the southern part of that country, and some time later came to Paris, where he entered the seminary of the Lazarists, and soon after joined their congregation. He sailed from France in company with Very Rev. John Timon, Visitor-General of the congregation in the United States, on the 15th of October, 1837, and arrived at the Barrens in Missouri on the 10th of the following February.* After remaining here and pursuing his studies, especially the study of the English language, he was raised to the sacred dignity of the priesthood, June 29th, 1839. In the following year he was sent with two other fathers of the congregation to Cape Girardeau, where he built a college, and in 1842 he returned to the seminary at the Barrens.† Not satisfied, however, with his duties as professor, he also labored on the mission in the wilds of Missouri until the year 1845, when he was sent in company with other fathers of the congregation to take charge of the diocesan seminary at Philadelphia. He was at the same time pastor of the little congregation at Nicetown, and afterwards of that at Germantown. Here he erected a handsome church, and took up his residence; and it was from here that he was called to rule the Diocese of Pittsburg.

The diocese had been so thoroughly organized by Bishop O'Connor that little was left to his successor beyond paying off a considerable debt still due on the cathedral, and providing for the wants of an increasing Catholic population. The zeal and energy which he manifested in the administration of the diocese was not long in bearing its fruits, as the sequel

---

* Life of Bishop Timon, pp. 62, 64.

† Life of Very Rev. Felix De Andreis, pp. 267 and 268. In this work his name is invariably spelled *Domenech*.

will amply testify. In 1861 he dedicated two new churches and another that had been enlarged.

At the invitation of the Holy Father he crossed the Atlantic on his first visit to Rome, sailing April 21st, 1862, to be present at the canonization of the Japanese Martyrs, and leaving Very Rev. E. M'Mahon Administrator. The Rebellion was then at its height, and it is said that the Bishop accepted a mission from the Government of the United States to that of Spain, which kingdom it was feared was about to recognize the Southern Confederacy. He visited Madrid, where he had several audiences with the queen and her ministers. Archbishop Hughes, at whose instance this important mission was entrusted to him, is reported to have said that " Bishop Domenec, of all those who had been sent by the Government of the United States to arrange these matters, is the only one who had ever really succeeded in his mission." This was certainly a high compliment when the delicate and perplexing nature of the negotiation is taken into account.* He returned to Pittsburg on the 16th of September.

During this year three new churches were built or enlarged. The demand for iron created by the war began also to be favorably felt in Pittsburg.

On the 6th of January, 1863, Rev. John Hickey, till then assistant at St. Patrick's Church and professor for a time at the diocesan seminary, was appointed rector of the cathedral in the place of Very Rev. E. M'Mahon, who had filled that important post in a very able manner for about thirteen years. Soon after this time Rev. T. Mullen, of Allegheny City, succeeded Father M'Mahon as Vicar-General of the diocese. The latter then retired to Philadelphia, where he was immediately appointed pastor of one of the leading congregations of that city. His departure was a serious loss to the Diocese of Pittsburg; for besides being a man of mature age and vast experience, he was eminently fitted for the transaction of business. Towards the close of the same year Very Rev. James O'Connor was succeeded by Dr. Keogh as president of the seminary. He too retired to Philadelphia, and

---

* The Biographical Encyclopedia of Pennsylvania for the Nineteenth Century, Art. M. Domenec.

was appointed to an honorable position. They were joined in 1865 by Dr. Keogh, and Pittsburg lost three of its most learned and valuable priests.

Ten churches were built or enlarged in different parts of the diocese in 1863 and '4.

In November, 1865, a public Catholic library and reading-room were opened principally through the exertions of Father Mullen. The Sisters of St. Francis also entered the diocese, and soon after opened a hospital; and two new churches were dedicated.

The small organ in the cathedral was replaced by a very large and powerful instrument in 1866, which at the time of its erection was, with few exceptions, the largest in the country. In the same year the Franciscan Brothers retired from Pittsburg, and the boys' school passed into the hands of the Sisters of Mercy, by whom it is still taught.

Five new or enlarged churches were also added to those already in the diocese, and eight in the following year.

On the 20th of May, 1867, Bishop Domenec again set out for Rome, to be present at the canonization of certain saints and the celebration of the centenary of the martyrdom of St. Peter. He returned September 27th of the same year.

About this time Father Hickey directed his attention to the erection of the two front towers of the cathedral At the time the sacred edifice was built one of these had been raised to the level of the roof, but nothing had been done on the other. In 1868 he finished one of them, and in the following year the other. They are built of brick, with cut-stone trimmings, and rise to the extraordinary height of 282 and 285 feet respectively. Their fine proportions excite the admiration of all who see them. In the cross of the tower, at the left front corner, is a cross of gas-jets which is lighted on the eves of certain feasts by means of electricity, and may be seen at a great distance.

That portion of the cathedral congregation lying in the vicinity of Oakland and Soho was detached in April, 1868, to form the parish of St. Agnes. The Point was also cut off in November, to form the congregation of St. Mary of Consolation, now St. Mary of Mercy. But the most important event of the year was the promotion of Very Rev. Tobias Mullen, of St. Peter's Church, Allegheny, to the vacant See of Erie. He was consecrated with imposing ceremony by Bishop Domenec in the Cathedral of Pittsburg, August 2d, 1868, in presence of a large number of prelates and of the inferior clergy, Rev. S. Wall, of the seminary, preaching the sermon. On the 30th of March, 1869, the rector of the cathedral was appointed Vicar-General of the diocese, and Rev. J. Tuigg, of Altoona, Vicar-Forane for the mountain district.

During the same year five new or enlarged churches marked the increase of the Catholic population. The years that followed the close of the Rebellion until the financial crisis of the fall of 1873 were the season of the greatest prosperity for Pittsburg. Work was abundant in the mines and manufactories, wages were high, and, although building lots commanded a fair price, houses were erected in large numbers, the limits of the city were extended, and the population increased rapidly. The laboring population, which is largely composed of natives of Ireland and Germany, swelled the city congregations especially, and forced their pastor to enlarge existing churches and form new parishes. It was the Golden Age in the history of Pittsburg. Men became infatuated with their prosperity, and precipitated the crisis that so sadly changed the face of things. The Church, tasting of the material prosperity, also caught the infatuation to some extent, and in a few instances brought upon herself embarrassments from which she will not be free until after many years of the most rigid economy. Nor need we wonder at this; for if men were deceived who had made financiering the business of their lives, much more might those be misled whose business it is to lay up and teach others to lay up their treasures rather in heaven than upon earth. The priest, like every one else, occupies a position that requires certain necessary qualifications; and it is a misfortune that in a country like ours where the Church is being built up, the collection and disbursement of money, or financiering, as it is called, should be among these qualifications. But it is taking a very erroneous, not to say, more truly, a very degrading, view of the sacred ministry to estimate a priest's worth and character by his ability to raise money and pay it out to advantage. His mission is of an infinitely higher order ; and, provided he makes a proper use of the talent which God has given him, it is no reproach that he whom St. Paul calls a " man of God " should be but an indifferent man of the world. It is pitiable enough for worldlings to worship the golden calf : but it is an abomination to give it a place in the sanctuary.

When the organ and the towers of St. Paul's were completed the magnificent edifice stood forth in all the grandeur of Bishop O'Connor's conception of it, and but for the dust that slumbered on every part it would have been one of the most splendid monuments of the faith and generosity of American and Irish Catholics in this country. It was found necessary to take down the central tower, which was of wood and too frail to be considered safe, and with it was taken away a part of the brick-work. The dome was then covered with an iron imitation of a dome, which, however useful it may be, can hardly be regarded as ornamental. But though finished, St. Paul's was burdened with considerable debt, and it is a matter of debate whether it would not have been better to have deferred its completion for a time.

In September, 1869, that portion of the cathedral congregation lying south of the Monongahela River was formed into a separate parish under the patronage of St. Malachy. Soon after this date, October 18th, the Bishop set out for Rome, to be present at the Vatican Council, and he did not return till after the close of its sessions. In the mean time Father Hickey was administrator of the diocese. In the same year seven churches were either built or enlarged.

Among the events of the following year was the death of Rev. James Keogh, D.D., a man upon whom Providence had bestowed the most extraordinary gifts. His death took place on the 10th of July, 1870, at Our Lady of Victories, East Liberty. The following sketch will afford an idea, necessarily imperfect, of his uncommon endowments.

REV. JAMES KEOGH, D.D., a man who for mental endowments has had few equals and no superior in the Church in this country, was the son of Mr. Martin Keogh, and was born at Enniscorthy, in county of Wexford, February 4th, 1834.

He came to this country with his parents in 1841, and made his home for a short time in Cleveland. But they soon after came to Pittsburg, where young James, a prodigy even in childhood, attracted the attention of Bishop O'Connor. He was afforded all the facilities of education which the limited resources of Pittsburg placed within his reach, and at twelve years of age entered the preparatory department of St. Michael's Seminary. But so brilliant were his talents and so exemplary his conduct that the Bishop determined to send him to Rome, where he should have opportunities in keeping with his natural ability. He set out for the Holy City at the age of sixteen, and on arriving entered the College of the Propaganda. No better evidence of his extraordinary talent and the use he made of it could be given than the *defence* in Philosophy which he made on the 21st of August, 1851, when he had been in the college little more than a year and a half, and when he was but seventeen and a half years of age. Commenting upon this defence, *The Catholic* says: "He sustained nobly one hundred and twenty propositions from the whole course of Philosophy and embracing the most important points of Logic, Ideology, Natural Theology, Psychology, Cosmology, as well as Ethics, general and particular. Professors from the Roman College, the Roman Seminary, and the Ecclesiastical Academy, and others, entered the lists against him. He acquitted himself most honorably, as we may learn from the fact that he received by the unanimous vote of the faculty the highest degree of the college in that department and a splendid gold medal into the bargain, and he whom many of our readers remember as a little fair-haired boy who used to serve Mass so well in St. Paul's Cathedral is now, though not yet eighteen, Doctor of Philosophy in the Propaganda at Rome."

But however brilliant his defence may have been on this occasion, it was eclipsed by that in Theology, which occurred on the 19th of November, 1855. This was the most remarkable that had taken place in the Propaganda since that of the late Cardinal Cullen, in 1828. *The Civiltà Cattolica*, the leading Catholic paper of the world, in an article translated by *The Cincinnati Catholic Telegraph*, after complimenting the

Propaganda, according to the Roman style, on its prosperity, continues:

"On the 19th of November we witnessed a proof of this prosperity in a public Defence of Theses selected from History and Dogmatic Theology, by James Keogh, of Pittsburg, in the United States of America. The theses themselves are a proof of the high grade of studies in the college; the answers of the youthful *defendant* showed an extraordinary talent, and were evidence of energetic and persevering study of his subject; and the noble assemblage of the most learned and dignified personages of Rome shows the interest felt by all ranks in this well-conducted institution.

"Of the 317 theses, 103 were from Ecclesiastical History, the remaining 214 from Dogmatic Theology.

"The Historical theses involve the great controverted points of history regarding the authority of the Holy See, questions of the *simple* or *dogmatic* facts; and they show, besides a wide comprehension of an immense subject, the depth and solidity of the study of history. The Dogmatic propositions are divided into five parts—'Of God and his Attributes, Of the Divine Trinity, Of the Chief Prophecies concerning the Messiah, Of the Incarnation of the Son of God, Of the Sacraments of the New Law'—and evince correct apprehension, a sound judgment, and vast knowledge of Theological science. This, however, is the merit of the Faculty of the Urban College. The merit of the young student (but twenty-one years of age) consists in his great advancement in these studies. In the Exhibition of the 19th, both morning and evening, he showed himself able to catch at once the most difficult objection, to grapple with it, and not only to solve it but make it a text for a brief but conclusive confirmation of his thesis. Some of the most learned and dignified persons in Rome, some by invitation, some by choice, entered the lists with the youthful champion, and were delighted with the readiness, the clearness, the profoundness shown in his answers to the well-proposed objections.

"As to the assemblage that gave such *éclat* to this exhibition, it is enough for us to say that rarely even in Rome, where they are wont to be conducted with the greatest splendor, have we witnessed one accompanied with such magnificence as this. For besides the very great number of the most learned and eminent Romans who were present, His Holiness Pope Pius IX. was pleased not only to accept the dedication of the *public act* made to himself, but also to honor it by his presence in the afternoon."

Besides the degree of Doctor of Divinity, Mr. Keogh received a large gold medal " for his talent and promptness, his extensive information and powerful reasoning," which was approved, as the programme of the exercises says, " by the Holy Father himself."

As yet he was too young to be ordained even by ordinary dispensation, and he was obliged to wait until the 5th of the following August. He was then raised to the sacred dignity of the priesthood by Cardinal Patrizi. He soon after set out for America, stopping in Ireland on his way, and arrived in November. He was assigned the chaplaincy of St. Xavier's Academy, Westmoreland County, and with it the care of the rising congregation at Latrobe, where he finished the church then in course of erection. Having remained there until October, 1857, he was transferred to the diocesan seminary then opened at Glenwood. Here he filled the chair of Dogmatic Theology and of several other branches, and was vice-president of the institution, and those who had the privilege of attending his classes can bear witness to his ability as a professor. In October, 1863, he succeeded Very Rev. James O'Connor as president; but from about this time his health began to decline, and at different times his life was believed to be in danger. He was also editor of *The Catholic*, a position which he resigned on the 7th of September, 1864.

At length in the following summer he withdrew to the Diocese of Philadelphia, whither Very Revs. E. M'Mahon and Jas. O'Connor had preceded him. His health improved, and he was appointed to the professorship of Dogmatic Theology, Hebrew, Sacred Scripture, and Rubrics in the Seminary of St. Charles Borromeo. When the Second Plenary Council opened at Baltimore, in October, 1866, he was appointed one of the secretaries, and his extensive learning was brought into requisition. When the (Philadelphia) *Catholic Standard* was first published, in the same year, he became editor, and he continued to fill the chair until 1868, when, his health continuing to decline, his physician required him to retire for a time from his active duties and seek repose in the country. He returned to the Diocese of Pittsburg, where so many of his friends and former pupils were laboring on the mission; and retired to St. Augustine's Church, Cambria County, where in quiet, and as his health permitted, he assisted the pastor, Rev. Ed. Burns. He also contributed a number of articles to the *Catholic World*, among others, as he informed me, that on "The Council of Trent" (October, 1869) and that on "The Greek Schism" (March, 1870). Besides these he has left no writings except a few printed lectures.

But the hopes that had been entertained of the re-establishment of his health were doomed to disappointment. At times he appeared to rally, but he was in reality declining. Feeling that his end was drawing near, he came to Pittsburg about the end of June, 1870, and stopped at the house of the Oblates of St. Charles Borromeo, in East Liberty. Here he terminated his career by a most edifying death on the 10th of July, in the 37th year of his age. His funeral took place from St. Mary's Church, Forty-sixth Street, and his remains were laid to rest in St. Mary's Cemetery.

In the words of the *Catholic Standard*, "Dr. Keogh was a thorough scholar, an accomplished gentleman, a great linguist. In society he was genial, and as a conversationalist he was without a superior, so great and varied was the store of his knowledge." It may be remarked, however, that he was better fitted both by nature and inclination for the chair of a professor than for the administration of the public affairs of the Church.

During the year 1870 six new churches were built, and the Sisters of Charity opened a convent in Altoona. In January of the following year a colony of French Ursuline Nuns established themselves in Pittsburg, and opened a young ladies' academy.

On the 28th of November Rev. Daniel Devlin, one of the assistant priests of the Cathedral, died somewhat suddenly at the residence of his parents, a few miles south of Pittsburg, in the 34th year of his age.

REV. DANIEL DEVLIN was born near Pittsburg; but his parents had emigrated a short time before from a place near Coleraine, in county Tyrone, Ireland. At the age of fourteen he was sent to the academy of the Franciscan Brothers at Loretto, and after remaining there for a time he was sent to another institution to pursue his course of theology. He then entered the Benedictine Order at St. Vincent's Abbey. As a member of that body he labored on the mission in different parts of Canada. Returning to the United States, he joined the ranks of the secular clergy and labored on various missions. The last years of his life, when his health was declining, were spent at the Cathedral. He was remarkable for the simplicity of his character and his gentleness of manner. His remains repose in St. Mary's Cemetery.

Ten churches were built or enlarged during the course of 1871, and the Catholic population, especially in the cities, was rapidly increasing and enjoying a high degree of temporal prosperity.

In April, 1872, a colony of Little Sisters of the Poor arrived in Pittsburg and opened a home for the aged; and in October of the same year the Sisters of the Good Shepherd also came and founded a Magdelene asylum. The Catholic Institute, a day college, was opened this year, and gave fair promise of a prosperous career. This year was also destined to surpass all previous and subsequent years in the number of churches built and enlarged. Eleven were dedicated during its course. But from this time forward a marked decline will be perceived, which results from the financial panic of 1873.

CHAPTER VII.

HISTORY OF ST. PAUL'S CATHEDRAL FROM 1873 TO THE PRESENT TIME.

The new episcopal residence—Death of Father M'Mahon, with sketch of his life—The Italians—The Bishop visits Rome—Division of the diocese—Statistics—Consecration of Rt. Rev. John Tuigg, with sketch of his life—State of the diocese—The Cathedral on fire—Death of Rev. Patrick Cassidy, with sketch of his life—Bishop Domenec visits Rome—Resigns his see—Returns to Spain—His death—Closing scenes of his life—Reunion of the two dioceses—Improvement of the Cathedral.

AFTER the burning of the episcopal residence in the fall of 1859, the committee of the Cathedral proposed to erect a new building at a cost of $16,000; and with the consent of the rector plans were prepared, subject to the approval of the Bishop, who was then absent. But upon his return, he deemed it too expensive for the times, and instead of a new residence contented himself with that part of the old that had been spared by the flames. In this small and uncomfortable home the Bishop and the clergy attached to the Cathedral had since resided. But the time, it was thought, had come for improving their condition; and in the summer of 1872 plans were prepared on a grand scale, as the present edifice amply testifies, and work was commenced on the foundation. Scarcely, however, was the first stone laid when the panic came, and business was prostrated and public confidence at an end perhaps for years. Nothing daunted, and notwithstanding the debt already on the Cathedral and the orphan asylum, the work was pushed forward, and gradually the immense edifice, a real palace, commanded the admiration of all who saw it. It was completed and occupied about the middle of December, 1875. The cost is said to have been $92,000; but it is thought to have been considerably more, for even at the present day the debt due upon it exceeds that sum. The building is ninety feet front by one hundred and ten feet deep, and three stories high besides the basement and finished attic; and it is trimmed with Massillon stone elegantly dressed. But it is much larger than the wants of the parish will ever demand.

About the year 1873 serious apprehensions were entertained for the safety of the Cathedral from the movement that was agitated for a time for cutting down the streets in that part of the city. But the proposition was finally abandoned, and it is not likely that it will again be mooted.

On the 7th of October of the same year, Very Rev. E. M'Mahon, who had for so many years been identified with the history of the Cathedral and the diocese, died in Philadelphia in the 74th year of his age.

VERY REV. EDWARD M'MAHON "was born in Milltown, a suburb of Dublin, in 1800. He made his studies and was ordained subdeacon in that city, but feeling himself called to labor for the salvation of souls in a foreign mission, he asked and obtained an *exeat* from his Ordinary, the most Rev. Dr. Murray, in 1824, with permission to become the subject of Bishop Flaget, of Bardstown, Kentucky, or of any other Bishop in the United States. He was ordained priest by Bishop Flaget July 3d, 1825. So high was the estimate formed of his piety and ability by this saintly prelate that, only a few months after his ordination, he appointed him superior of the Preparatory Seminary of St. Thomas, to which a small college was then attached." In 1830 he was appointed vice-rector of St. Mary's College. A year later he was appointed pastor of Scott County, which had several missions attached to it; and he may be said to have been the founder of all the most flourishing missions in the present Diocese of Covington. But we cannot detail his labors in Kentucky. In 1841 he visited his native land. Five years later he became president of St. Joseph's College, Ky., in which he soon restored order out of chaos. Soon after the Bishop gave the college to the Jesuits, and he came to the Diocese of Pittsburg. Here he was placed at Hollidaysburg, in the winter of 1849, for a short time, and thence transferred to St. Peter's Church, Allegheny City, which he finished. In 1850 he became pastor of St. Paul's Cathedral, and soon after Vicar-General of the diocese. We have seen his labors here in the cause of religion. On retiring to Philadelphia he was appointed pastor of St. Edward's Church, where he passed the closing years of his long and eminently useful life.[*]

About the time of the opening of the Catholic Institute, Rev. Jas. M'Tighe, who was president and at the same time professor in St. Michael's Seminary, made an attempt to form the Italians of the city into a congregation. Being a student of the Propaganda and master of the Italian language, he felt that he should attempt to better the spiritual condition of the Italian Catholics, of whom there are perhaps one hundred and fifty families, living principally in the vicinity of the Cathedral, all of whom are very poor. But after a few months he was appointed to a parish a considerable distance from the city, and the Italians have since been left as they were before without any spiritual guide, although there is always a priest at the Cathedral acquainted with their language.

During the summer of 1874 the splendid stained-glass window over the entrance of the Cathedral was put in, at a cost of about $2000; and in 1876 that in the transept facing on Fifth Avenue was put in, at a cost of about $2500. In 1874 the Capuchin Fathers entered the diocese. Three churches only were built or enlarged in 1873, and five in the following year.

On the 5th of November, 1875, the Bishop set out on a visit to Rome, leaving Father Hickey Administrator. The object of his visit was not known; and hence when, in January, 1876, it was announced that the diocese had been divided and a new one formed, with Allegheny City as its see, people were taken by surprise and found it difficult to credit the report. But further intelligence confirmed it. The Diocese of Pittsburg was divided, and Bishop Domenec was transferred to the new See of Allegheny, the bulls for both the division and the

---

[*] Compiled principally from " A Sermon by Very Rev. James O'Connor, D.D., preached at the Month's Mind."

transfer being dated January 11th, 1876. Many persons had expected that a division would take place in time, but that the panic would have the effect of deferring it for a few years. But in the event of it transpiring, Altoona, it was thought, would be the new see. By bulls dated January 16th, Very Rev. John Tuigg, of Altoona, was elevated to the vacant See of Pittsburg. The dividing line between the sees of Pittsburg and Allegheny started at the southern boundary of the State between Bedford and Somerset counties, and passed north till it reached Cambria, and thence west to Westmoreland. Passing along the eastern, southern, and western boundary of this county, it struck the Allegheny River, and passed down that stream and the Ohio to the western limits of Allegheny City. From that point it struck due north through Allegheny County to the southern boundary of Butler, and continued west and north to the line dividing Lawrence and Mercer counties. It then followed that line to the western boundary of the State. Thus the new diocese had eight counties, with about one fourth of Allegheny, or an area of about 6530 square miles; leaving the parent diocese six counties and about three fourths of Allegheny, with an area of about 4784 square miles.

The following were the principal statistics of the diocese at the time of the division, as given in the *Catholic Directory* for 1876. (During the year 1875 eleven churches had been built or enlarged.) Priests, secular and religious, 160; churches, 115; chapels, 15; male religious orders, 7; female religious orders, 12; parish schools, 70; educational institutions, 10; academies, 10; diocesan seminary; Sisters of Mercy, 178; of Charity, 22; of St. Joseph, 17; Benedictine Nuns, 40; Ursulines, 17; Sisters of Notre Dame, 25; number of children attending parochial schools, about 17,000; asylums, 4; hospitals, 2; and a Catholic population of about 200,000. Many are of opinion, however, that the population of the diocese was estimated at too high a figure, and this opinion is strengthened by a comparison of the percentage of increase in the Catholic and in the general population of that part of the State embraced within the limits of the diocese during the previous fifteen years. It is further confirmed from the fact that although in the division of the diocese the population appeared to be about equally divided between the two sees, yet when the newly consecrated Bishop Tuigg had the census of his diocese taken in May, 1876, it reached only 56,800. Although this was most probably an underestimate, yet it could not have fallen more than 10,000, if indeed so much, below the actual number. I am of opinion that it would have been a very fair estimate of the numerical strength of the Catholics in the diocese to have placed it at about 135,000. And although this statement may appear to savor of temerity in the presence of figures published, yet it is certain that the population of a large number of the congregations was only approximated for that report. I may further state that in every instance, with perhaps no more than three or four exceptions, I have found the population of congregations far less than it was generally supposed to be, and sometimes not half so much. Since the division of the diocese the population, although not increasing as rapidly as before the panic, has yet been adding slowly to its numbers, and it will reach at the present time, I am of opinion, about 140,000.

The division was not well received, particularly by those of the parent diocese; and more especially as the diocesan institutions were left heavily in debt, while their resources were greatly diminished. All the churches, with one or two exceptions, that were involved in debt were on the same side, while the educational institutions were in the new diocese, with the exception of the diocesan seminary, an institution that could not long survive the division, and the Ursuline Academy.

The 19th of March, Feast of St. Joseph, which that year fell on Sunday, was the day fixed for the solemn ceremony of the consecration of the Bishop-elect. All the ceremonies were in keeping with the solemnity of the occasion. Archbishop Wood, of Philadelphia, was the consecrating prelate; Rt. Rev. J. F. Shanahan, of Harrisburg, preached the sermon; and Very Rev. J. Hickey read the papal bulls. There were present, besides these, Bishops Mullen, of Erie; O'Hara, of Scranton; Domenec, of Allegheny; and Abbot Wimmer, of St. Vincent's, with Very Rev. F. M. Boff, Administrator of Cleveland, and about one hundred of the inferior clergy. In the evening many of those present at the ceremonies of the morning went to St. Peter's pro-Cathedral, Allegheny, to witness the installation of Bishop Domenec. The installation was attended with all the ceremonies prescribed by the ritual; and a new Bishop and a new see were added to the Church in America.

It is proper before proceeding further to say a few words regarding the new Bishop of Pittsburg. Any lengthy remarks would be out of place. Rt. Rev. John Tuigg, D.D., is a native of county Cork, Ireland, where he was born in the year 1820. Having pursued his studies for some time in All-Hallows Missionary College, he came to this country and entered St. Michael's Seminary, Pittsburg. Upon the completion of his course of Theology he was ordained by Bishop O'Connor on the 14th of May, 1850, and placed at the Cathedral as an assistant. Here he remained, sharing with the other priests in the arduous duties of that large congregation and acting as secretary to the Bishop. About the beginning of 1853 he was assigned the duty of organizing St. Bridget's congregation and building the church, although remaining at the same time at the Bishop's residence. When the church was well under way he was assigned the more important mission of Altoona, in July of the same year. His labors there in the cause of religion, the success that attended them, and the monuments that he has left to bear witness to his energy and zeal, will be seen at length in their proper place.

Immediately after his consecration he set vigorously about the affairs of his exalted position, and after expending much time and toil became fully acquainted with the difficulties by which he was surrounded.

On the morning of June 2d, 1877, the Cathedral accidentally took fire, and had it not been for the heavy wall of the transept, between the body of the church and the sacristy, where the fire originated, it would probably have been destroyed. As it was the damage amounted to about $3000.

In the latter part of the summer of the same year Rev. Patrick Cassidy, a priest of the diocese, died in Ireland, in the 27th year of his age.

REV. PATRICK CASSIDY was a native of county Derry,

Ireland. At an early age he felt an attraction for the sanctuary, and began those studies that should fit him for entering the ranks of the sacred ministry. He came to America early in the summer of 1866, and soon after entered the seminary at Pittsburg. Having finished his studies, he was ordained on the 20th of December, 1873, and placed at the Cathedral. But in the following January he was appointed chaplain of St. Paul's Orphan Asylum, where he remained until the autumn of the same year, when declining health forced him to retire from the city and seek the purer country air. He took charge of the little congregation at Cameron Bottom, where he remained a year. But his health was being slowly undermined by consumption, and he returned to the cathedral, where he performed such duties as his health permitted, or reposed from labor. Seeing that there was no hope of his recovery in this country, he determined to cross over to his native land, and accordingly set sail on the 20th of July. But scarcely had he reached the home of his childhood when his brief career in the sacred ministry was run, and God called him to his reward.

When the Bishop of Allegheny withdrew his students from the diocesan seminary it was found impossible to continue it, and it was closed at the end of December, 1876. During this year but two churches were dedicated in the Diocese of Pittsburg, both of which had been purchased from the Protestants; and one in that of Allegheny.

In January, 1877, Revs. J. Holland and F. Kittell were despatched to Rome in the interest of the Diocese of Pittsburg; and in April Bishop Domenec also crossed over, leaving Very Rev. R. Phelan Administrator during his absence. But he never returned to America. Having devoted almost seventeen years of incessant labor to the welfare of religion in the most exalted, as it is the most onerous, position that man can occupy in this world, and having everywhere left monuments of his zeal and devotedness to the flock over which he had been called by the voice of Christ's vicar to preside, he resigned the See of Allegheny on the 29th of July, 1877, and retired soon after to his native land. It was his intention, it appears, to return to America, and various reports were circulated regarding exalted positions in the Church in this country which had been offered to him; but upon this point we have no certain information. While his friends in America were daily expecting to hear of his return, they were suddenly cast into deepest sorrow by the news of his death from pneumonia putrida, on the 7th of January, 1878. Nothing could have been more unexpected; for although in the sixty-second year of his age, he yet appeared in the prime of life, and was remarkable for his extraordinary power of endurance. He seemed a stranger to fatigue, and never appeared in his proper element except when laboring to promote the interests of religion. In every part of the diocese he has left imperishable monuments of his zeal in the cause of religion; and if we were disposed to pass an opinion we should say that he was too kind-hearted, and shrank from doing or saying anything that might cause another pain. In reply to a letter of inquiry from the *Pittsburg Evening Leader* the Hon. Frederick H. Schenck, American consul at Barcelona, in Spain, wrote as follows regarding the closing scenes in the life of Bishop Domenec:

"The late Mr. Domenec came to Barcelona in the early part of the fall, and remained for several months, preaching in the different Catholic churches twice every week and many times oftener; and, being considered by the public in general a very fine speaker, and beloved by all who knew him personally, the churches were on all occasions overcrowded. He left Barcelona for his native city, Reus, about five miles from Tarragona, to once more visit the places of his youth before returning to the United States, on the 30th of December last; but on his arrival in Tarragona he took very suddenly sick, and was taken to the House of the Beneficence against the wishes of the Archbishop of Tarragona, who offered him his own residence. Failing very rapidly, the Bishop received the last sacraments; and the last words he said were in answer to renewed entreaties of the Archbishop to allow himself to be transferred to his (the Archbishop's) house: 'A thousand thanks, sir. You know my mission is not to incommode anybody.' He then did not recover his senses, and died quietly January 7th, at a quarter before 1 o'clock P.M."

A fuller account of his obsequies is found in the official journal of the Archbishop of Tarragona, a copy of which was sent to Pittsburg. We give it entire, both for the information it contains and in order to preserve it. Says the journal:

"Right Rev. Bishop Domenec, after having received the holy viaticum, on the evening of the 6th inst., from the hands of the Most Rev. Archbishop, who was accompanied by the chapter and clergy of the Cathedral, by the students of the seminary and many of the faithful, expired at a little after noon on the following day.

"After the recitation of the solemn office of the dead, the Archbishop, the chapter and clergy of the Cathedral, went in procession to the Church of Our Lady of Mercy to chant the customary responses over the corpse, which, clothed in pontifical habiliments, reclined on a grand catafalque in the centre of the church.

"On the following morning (the 8th inst.), after the conventual Mass, and according to a notice inserted in the daily papers, the illustrious deceased was buried in the cloister of the Cathedral, in the rear of the Chapel of Our Lady de la Guia. The corpse was carried to its last resting-place with the same pomp and solemnity that are observed in the funeral obsequies of the Most Rev. Archbishops. The streets through which the funeral procession passed on its way to the Cathedral were crowded with people of all classes assembled to take a last look at a prelate who in the United States had gained so many souls to Christ, erected and consecrated so many churches to the worship of the true God, and established so many schools for the Christian instruction of youth. The presence of the civil and military officers of the province, of a committee of the councils headed by the mayor, of the government employés, and many other important personages; the long line of the clergy, and the music furnished by the military bands of the garrison—all contributed more and more to the solemnity of the funeral ceremony. The Archbishop presided at the solemn functions, which, after a pontifical Mass of requiem, terminated at midday in the midst of an extraordinary concourse of people.

"During his illness, which lasted but a few days, Bishop

Domenec manifested a holy resignation in his sufferings, and a readiness to pass to eternity, there to receive the reward merited by his labors on earth. He ceased not to ask the mercy of God, and was profuse in his gratitude to the Archbishop, who frequently visited him, and to the Sisters of Charity, who ministered to his wants." Such was the death of a good Bishop whose name is indelibly written on the memory of his former spiritual children.

After mature deliberation the Holy See entrusted the administration of the vacant See of Allegheny to the Bishop of Pittsburg by official documents bearing date August 3d, 1877. Referring to it in an official letter of September 18th to the clergy and laity of the two dioceses, the Bishop says: "We have been notified that the Holy Father, by the advice of the Sacred Congregation de Propaganda Fide, had entrusted to us, though unworthy, the administration of the Diocese of Allegheny, in spirituals and temporals, promiscuously—'promiscuæ'—to be governed and administered as if both sees formed but one, 'ac si una esset diœcesis.'"

In this manner the dioceses are still governed, and no doubt will continue to be for many years to come.

During the year 1878 the interior of the Cathedral was freed from the dust that had so long been accumulating, and was appropriately painted, which adds no little to its appearance. Two new Gothic side altars of beautiful design also replaced the old ones. But the diocese being now well supplied with churches, there were but three dedicated in 1877, and one each in the two following years. The Cathedral congregation will number perhaps twelve thousand souls, and it will probably undergo but little change for many years.

CHAPTER VIII.

CONGREGATIONS FORMED FROM ST. PAUL'S CATHEDRAL.

St. Patrick's Church—Death and Sketch of Rev. Jas. Byrnes—St. Mary's Church —Church of the Sacred Heart—St. John the Baptist's Church—St. Peter's pro-Cathedral, Allegheny City.

ST. PATRICK'S CHURCH, PITTSBURG.

THE history of this church has in part been already laid before the reader. We have seen that it was built by Father O'Brien, most probably in the year 1810; that it was enlarged by Father M'Guire about the year 1825, and that upon the completion of St. Paul's, in the summer of 1834, it became the first German as it had been the first English church of the city. Having been occupied by the Germans until 1839 or '40, it was restored to the English, when the former purchased the property upon which St. Philomena's now stands. Father O'Reilly, then pastor of St. Paul's, mistaking the future prospects of Catholicity in the city, was in favor of selling St. Patrick's; but his assistant, Rev. E. F. Garland, was of a different opinion. A meeting of the congregation was called to discuss the affair, when it was found that the pastor and his assistant were the ablest advocates of the conflicting views. Fortunately for the cause of religion in the city, the opinion in favor of retaining the property prevailed, and some time later, in October, 1840, Father Garland was appointed pastor of St. Patrick's, with the care of organizing and presiding over the second English congregation in the city. This he did with but slight interruption, as we shall see, for thirty-eight years. The growth of Catholicity in the city was such that it soon became necessary to increase the accommodations of the church, and additional galleries were built in as large a part of it as possible. In the course of time an assistant also became necessary. In the spring of 1853 St. Bridget's congregation was organized, the greater part of which was taken from St. Patrick's. A little later in the same year St. Mary's Church, Laurenceville, was built, which drew away another portion. A school was also opened, but the date has not been ascertained.

But the venerable church was doomed to destruction. A fire broke out in a machine-shop near it on the morning of August 10th, 1854, and the flames being communicated to the church it was entirely consumed. Nothing remained but to replace it. But the city had extended up the Allegheny River a considerable distance, and it was deemed advisable to set the new church somewhat further in the same direction. The Bishop obtained a release from the fulfilment of the conditions upon which the original lot had been donated, and this done he sold it to the Pennsylvania Railroad Company. Lots were then purchased at the head of Fourteenth Street—the old church had stood at the head of Eleventh—and the new building was immediately undertaken. In September, 1856, Father Garland exchanged places with Rev. Thomas M'Cullagh, of Summitville, Cambria County. The latter finished the church and remained with the congregation until its dedication by the Bishop, August 15th, 1858, when he returned to the mountain and the former pastor of St. Patrick's resumed his city charge. The church was of brick, and was perhaps 90 feet in length by 45 in width, and standing with the front to the hill had a basement under a considerable part of the rear, which was used as a school. The building was without a tower, and made little pretensions to architectural style and finish.

During these years that portion of the city embraced within the limits of the congregation continued to be built up quite rapidly, and the parish was constantly adding to its numbers. In the autumn of 1862 an assistant was appointed to the pastor, who, since the formation of the parishes above referred to, had been alone. Since the latter date, however, two and later three priests have been required to minister to the spiritual necessities of the people. But at the close of the Rebellion an extraordinary impetus was given to manufactures, and Pittsburg enjoyed an unusual degree of prosperity. The common between the city and Laurenceville was rapidly built up, and St. Patrick's congregation became so large as no longer to find accommodations in the church.

Besides, the Pennsylvania Railroad Company was then contemplating the erection of the Union Depot, and wished to purchase the church lot, which lay in the route they were desirous of occupying with their tracks. Father Garland was also anxious to obtain a more central position for the church; and he readily accepted the proposition of the railroad company to purchase the old one. He had already secured a lot on the corner of Liberty and Seventeenth streets. Upon this he commenced the erection of a church, which on the event of its completion was dedicated by the Bishop, December 17th, 1865. The church, which is in the Attic-Ionic style of architecture, is 120 feet in length by 60 in width, and is surmounted by a belfry. In the front is a porch supported by columns in keeping with the style of the building. The ceiling is flat. There are three altars. The front is approached by a high flight of steps from Seventeenth Street, and a basement extends under the entire building, which is used for the accommodation of a part of the schools.

In the year 1866 a convent of the Sisters of Mercy was built in Liberty Street against the rear of the church, and a young ladies' academy was opened in connection with the school, which for some time before had been in charge of the Sisters. A pastoral residence was built beside the church about the year 1868. Additional school-rooms were built to the rear of the convent some time after its completion.

Among the assistants who shared the labors of the pastor was Rev. James Byrnes, whose health, never robust, finally gave way in the arduous duties that fell to his lot. He retired to the home of his parents, not far from the church, where he gradually sank, until death cut short his career in the sacred ministry, in the 26th year of his age, December 2d, 1874.

REV. JAMES BYRNES was a native of the county and town of Carlow, Ireland, where he was born at the end of December, 1848. His parents emigrated to this country and settled in Pittsburg while he was yet in his infancy. Here, in the home of his pious parents, James grew up and developed those good qualities of mind and heart for which he was afterwards remarkable. He entered the diocesan seminary in the spring of 1863, where he was a classmate of the writer, though younger than any other member of the class. Having finished his course, he was obliged to wait until he had attained the canonical age, when he was raised to the priesthood on the 3d day of June, 1871. He was now appointed assistant to the pastor of St. Mary's Church, Forty-sixth Street, although remaining at the seminary during the week and teaching the branches he had taught, principally dogmatic theology, prior to his ordination. In August, 1872, he was appointed assistant at St. Patrick's Church, and at the same time he left the seminary to devote his entire attention to the mission. Here his health gave way, and his career was terminated by consumption. Father Byrnes was well versed in the sacred sciences. Though brief his career, he has left a name for zeal, piety, and learning that is destined long to survive.

Worn out by forty years of active duties in the sacred ministry, Father Garland found his health at length so far impaired and his strength so much reduced as no longer to permit him to exercise his sacred calling, and in March, 1878—just forty years from his ordination, March 10th, 1838—he rested from his labors. In order to receive the best attention in the evening of his life, he retired soon after to the Mercy Hospital, where he calmly awaits the reward promised to the good and faithful servant. After his retirement the congregation was for a time under the care of his first assistant, Rev. Thos. Neville.

In the autumn of 1878 measures were taken to organize a new parish, and a church was commenced at Thirty-second Street, as will presently be noticed at length. Two priests will then be sufficient to minister to the congregation. Prior to this it was the largest English congregation in the western part of the State, with the exception of the Cathedral, and would probably number twelve hundred families. It cannot increase in the future, being surrounded as it is by other parishes, and lying in a closely built portion of the city; nor is it likely to decrease, but to pursue the even tenor of its way, independent of vicissitudes.

In April, 1879, Rev. S. Wall was appointed pastor. Father Neville had retired a short time previously to St. Xavier's, Westmoreland County, to recruit his health, which was much impaired. Upon the arrival of Father Wall he put the church and house through a much-needed course of improvements and repairs.

ST. MARY'S CHURCH, PITTSBURG.

St. Mary's Church stands on Forty-sixth Street, about half a mile east of the Allegheny River, from which the ground rises gently. Upon the first appearance of the white man an Indian village stood here; but in 1816 a town was laid out by W. B. Foster, which he named Laurenceville, in honor of Captain Laurence, of the U. S. navy.* But by an act of the legislature of April 6th, 1866, to take effect on the 1st of the following January, the city limits were extended to take in Laurenceville, East Liberty, and other eastern suburbs. But this, like the others, is more generally known by its original name.

The first Catholics who settled in the village heard Mass at St. Patrick's Church, or at St. Joseph's, Sharpsburg. But a movement was made in the summer of 1853 to erect a church and school, and a meeting was called September 1st to take the matter into consideration. A lot of about three acres was secured, which is perhaps the finest piece of church property in the diocese. The contract was immediately given for the erection of a building which should answer the twofold purpose of a church and school. It was finished at the beginning of the next year; and in the absence of a Bishop—for Dr. O'Connor had been transferred to Erie—it was dedicated, under the invocation of the Blessed Virgin, by Very Rev. E. M'Mahon, Adm., January 23d. It was an unpretending frame structure, seventy feet in length by thirty feet in width. Rev. A. P. Gibbs, who was then pastor of this and the

* Day's Historical Collections, p. 90.

church at Sharpsburg, soon after transferred his residence to the new church, where he has since remained. A brick house was built for his reception, which was afterwards enlarged when the growth of the congregation required the ministration of two priests.

In time a frame school-house was built, but was replaced by the present neat brick one. But the growth of the town increased the congregation, and additional accommodations were demanded. With a view to supplying them a transverse section was put to the end of the church, and thus enlarged it was dedicated by the Bishop August 16th, 1863. The better to minister to his congregation, the pastor resigned the care of the church at Sharpsburg at the beginning of this year, and has since confined his labors exclusively to St. Mary's.

The schools passed into the hands of the Sisters of Mercy in the autumn of 1866, who having come out daily for a year from St. Mary's Convent, Webster Street, a commodious brick convent was built for their reception, of which they took possession September 7th, 1867.

But the congregation was now increasing more rapidly than ever before, not only in numbers but in general importance, and the church was no longer able to accommodate it. A new church must be built, which, although a great undertaking, was yet within the reach of so large and able a community. Work was commenced in the spring of 1873, and the corner-stone was laid by Bishop Domenec on the 23d of June. The church was ready for dedication by the following spring, and the ceremony, which was unusually imposing, was performed April 19th by Bishop Mullen, of Erie, in the presence of Bishop Domenec, who afterwards celebrated the Holy Sacrifice. The Bishop of Erie preached an eloquent sermon on the occasion. The church, which is of brick and modelled after the Gothic style of architecture, is 146 feet in length by 56 in width. There is no steeple, but the front and rear walls are surmounted by gracefully cut stone pinnacles. The ceiling rises from the sides, ribbed towards the centre, in a fashion which has lately come into vogue in this diocese. There are three superb Gothic altars of wood, which, with the pulpit, confessionals, etc., are made to harmonize with the style of the church. On the whole, it is one of the most substantial and elegant churches in the diocese. Prior to the building of the church an assistant was required to share the labors of the pastor. The old church, or rather that part of it which had not been torn away to give place to the new one, was converted into a school for the boys. The growth of the congregation was arrested by the panic of 1873; but it must still continually add to its numbers, although not so rapidly as before that event. As it is the parish is one of the largest, and with one or two exceptions the most flourishing, English congregations in the diocese, notwithstanding that a part has been taken off to form the new congregation of St. John the Baptist.

THE CHURCH OF THE SACRED HEART, PITTSBURG.

After the annexation of the borough of East Liberty to Pittsburg it became generally known as the "East End." The first Catholic population, as will be stated further on, was German, for whom a church was erected in 1859. But an English element soon began to mingle with the German, and either heard Mass at the German church or in one of those of the city. At length the number of families became sufficiently large to form a separate congregation and require a church of its own. Rev. J. M. Bierl, then pastor of the German church, purchased a lot at the corner of College and Centre avenues, on the northern side of the Pennsylvania Railroad, in the spring of 1872. Rev. Bernard F. Ferris was appointed first pastor, and entrusted with the organization of the parish. He celebrated Mass for the first time August 4th of the same year by a special arrangement in the German church, which it was agreed the new congregation should be permitted to use until such time as it should have one of its own. But this arrangement proving unsatisfactory, he commenced the next day the erection of a temporary church; and so great was the energy displayed that he had a wooden building, 32 by 50 feet, ready for divine service on Sunday the 18th of the same month.

The congregation then numbered about seventy-five families, with very flattering future prospects.

Plans were now prepared and work commenced on a permanent church, the corner-stone of which was laid by the Bishop June 15th, 1873. A neat and comfortable brick pastoral residence was built the same year and occupied about Christmas. Although the congregation was increasing rapidly, the erection of a church such as that upon which they were now engaged was a great undertaking, and the panic which took place soon after the work was begun was calculated to dampen the ardor of both pastor and people. But the work was continued, and the church, being finished, was dedicated by the Bishop October 24th, 1875. It is a cruciform brick building fronting on Centre Avenue, and is 127 feet in length by 46 in width in the nave and 75 in the transept. The steeple, which stands at the left front, is finished to the height of the roof for the present. The style of architecture is peculiar. The ceiling both of the nave and transept follows the pitch of the roof, the greatest height being 46 feet, while that of the walls is 24. The head of the nave is formed into an apse for the sanctuary, and is furnished with a marble altar. There are, besides, two side-altars. The two confessionals, as well as the pews, are finished in a very artistic manner. The stained-glass windows are embellished with designs illustrative of the life of Christ.

A school, under the charge of lay teachers, was opened in the temporary church in January, 1873. Two years later a colony of seven Sisters of Charity from Altoona took charge of the schools, and occupied, and still occupy, the pastoral residence as a convent, while the pastor, as before its erection, went to lodge in a hotel. This, it is worthy of remark, is the first entrance of the Sisters of Charity into the city since their withdrawal about thirty years before. During the summer of 1874 a brick school-house, 44 feet square and two stories high, was built; and when the schools were transferred to it the temporary church was transformed into a pastoral residence, and so it remains. The outfit of the congregation is now complete, but a very heavy debt remains to engage the attention of both pastor and people for many years to come.

But the future prospects are more flattering than those of the other city congregations generally, and a large proportion of the people are of the wealthy and influential class. There are at present about two hundred families in the parish, and it is gradually but slowly increasing. Father Ferris was succeeded by Rev. Francis Keane, the present pastor, in February, 1878.

ST. JOHN THE BAPTIST'S CHURCH, PITTSBURG.

For several years the need of a church between St. Patrick's and St. Mary's had been apparent, but it was not until the spring of 1878 that steps were taken to erect it. Lots were then purchased at the corner of Liberty and Thirty-second streets, and work was commenced under the direction of Father Gibbs, of St. Mary's. The corner-stone was laid by the Bishop on the 20th of October of the same year, and it is worthy of remark that it is the first ceremony of the kind performed by that prelate. The building, in the erection of which St. Patrick's and St. Mary's contributed a part, was finished and ready for dedication early in the following summer. The solemn ceremony was performed by the Bishop on the 8th of June, when the church was placed under the invocation of St. John the Baptist. The building is of brick, is 80 feet in length by 40 in width, and two stories high, and is planned to answer the purposes of a church and school. The lower story, which is high and is finished with gallery, altar, confessionals, etc., is for the use of the congregation, while the upper story is divided into school-rooms.

When the church was finished Rev. C. V. Neeson was appointed pastor, and soon after he rented a house near by, as a residence has not yet been built. The congregation is formed in part each from St. Patrick's and St. Mary's, and is sufficient to fill the church at two Masses on Sunday. There must necessarily be a limit to its future growth, being surrounded as it is on all sides by other congregations; but notwithstanding this it is destined to increase considerably. At the beginning of September, 1879, the schools were placed under the care of the Sisters of Charity, who at present come daily by the cars from the convent attached to the Church of the Sacred Heart.

THE CHAPEL OF THE NATIVITY (COLORED), PITTSBURG.

Colored Catholics were found in the city from an early day. The first attempt at forming them into a separate congregation was made by Rev. R. H. Wilson, D.D., president of St. Michael's Seminary. With the consent of the Bishop he rented a hall on Smithfield Street, near Diamond, that had been previously occupied by a congregation of Methodists, and had it blessed, under the title of the Nativity of the Blessed Virgin Mary, June 30th, 1844. The zeal of the pastor was extraordinary, and amounted to enthusiasm. He would visit the homes of his sable flock, spend hours among them, and even seat himself at their table and partake of their frugal repast, so intent was he on gaining them to Christ. Soon he succeeded in collecting together a large number who were already of the faith, and others who were under instruction. But his success excited the jealousy of the sects, and a trick was resorted to in order to destroy the fruit of his labors. A minister declared from the pulpit of one of the colored churches on the hill that Dr. Wilson was a pro-slavery man who, when he had collected a sufficient number of colored people, would have them seized and carried South, to be there sold into slavery by his agents. The trick had the desired effect: the poor, simple people took the alarm, and the congregation was dispersed about a year after its formation. The chapel was closed and abandoned, and the colored people from that period until the opening of St. Joseph's Chapel, to be hereafter noticed, attended the other churches of the city.

ST. PETER'S PRO-CATHEDRAL, ALLEGHENY CITY.

Allegheny City, which lies north-west of Pittsburg, and on the opposite side of the river of the same name, was laid out under an act of the General Assembly approved September 11th, 1787. The original town was exactly square, containing one hundred lots, each sixty feet by two hundred and forty.

It was incorporated as Allegheny Town by an act of the General Assembly of April 14th, 1828, and chartered as a city April 10th, 1840, having then a population of about 10,000. The present population is about 80,000.

Catholics settled in Allegheny about the beginning of this century, but attended one of the churches of Pittsburg until the year 1848. Their number having by this time increased sufficiently to render the formation of a separate congregation both feasible and necessary, a meeting was called for that purpose on the 17th of September. Rev. James O'Connor, brother of the Bishop, was appointed pastor of the incipient congregation, and measures were taken toward the erection of a church. Lots were purchased on Anderson Street, near Washington, in the northern part of the city, at a cost of about $6000, and the erection of a church was soon after begun. Toward the end of the following year Father O'Connor was succeeded by Rev. E. M'Mahon. The church was finished the following spring at a cost of about $10,000, and dedicated, under the invocation of St. Peter the Apostle, by Bishop Whelan, of Wheeling, April 21st, 1850. On the 24th of the same month Father M'Mahon was transferred to the Cathedral, where he was appointed pastor, and was succeeded at St. Peter's by Rev. James Kearney. A school taught by the Sisters of Mercy, from St. Mary's Convent, Pittsburg, was now opened in the basement of the church. Soon the pastor resolved to establish a house of the Sisters in the parish, and accordingly St. Anne's Convent, commonly known as the House of Industry, was built on Washington Street, near the church, about the year 1854. The school-houses of the parish were built on the same lots not long after. Father Kearney was succeeded, October 24th of the same year, by Rev. T. Mullen. About this time, or a little before it, the Franciscan Brothers, from the Cathedral, took charge of the boys' school and continued to teach it until the summer of 1866.

The pastor of St. Peter's has always had charge of the Catholic inmates of the Western Penitentiary, to whom he ministers at regular and frequent intervals. Prior to the organization of St. Andrew's parish, Manchester, he performed the same office of mercy to the unfortunate protégés of the

House of Refuge, or Pennsylvania Reform School, when bigotry would condescend to permit it. The fanatical opposition of the officers of the institution to the visits of a priest occasioned quite a spirited public correspondence between Father Mullen and John L. Logan, president of the Refuge, in February, 1862. Through the influence of Father Mullen a supplement to the act of incorporation of the institution was immediately introduced into the legislature, by which the inmates were permited in time of sickness to confer with a minister of their choice, *in sight*, but if desired not *in hearing*, of an officer of the institution, as the rules previously required. The act was approved March 31st of that year; and the unfortunate children felt their condition somewhat ameliorated in being able to make their confession, a privilege from which they had before been debarred.

Another supplement, more just and reasonable, was forced upon the managers by the Catholic members of the legislature May 5th, 1876, when a large appropriation was asked from the State for the completion of the new buildings at Morganza. This act provides that "the inmates of said institution shall have the right to receive religious instruction from ministers of any denomination or belief without any obstruction or interference whatever." We shall have occasion hereafter to observe how this provision is carried out by the present board of officers.

Upon the withdrawal of Very Rev. E. M'Mahon from the diocese, in 1864, Father Mullen was appointed Vicar-General, and continued to discharge the duties of that office until his elevation to the See of Erie.

The population of Allegheny was increasing rapidly at this time, but principally in the western part of the city, the eastern being already closely built. The number of Catholics was also augmenting, and St. Peter's, even with three Masses on a Sunday, began to be inadequate to their accommodation. The borough of Manchester, which since its annexation to the city, in 1867, forms the western wards, was also becoming a place of note, and, being the site of extensive iron manufactories, contained a considerable Irish Catholic population. The distance at which these people lived from St. Peter's induced

Father Mullen to build a church for their accommodation. St. Andrew's was consequently built, and dedicated December 20th, 1863. For several years it was attended from the mother-church, a circumstance which necessitated the appointment of an assistant pastor.

The erection of the new church and the withdrawal of a part of the congregation afforded but a temporary relief. A larger church was absolutely necessary. Measures were being taken looking toward its erection, when the pastor was promoted to the See of Erie, and consecrated at St. Paul's Cathedral by Bishop Domenec August 2d, 1868. On taking leave of the congregation over which he had so long presided, Rev. R. Phelan, of Freeport, was appointed his successor, July 21st. The first care of the newly appointed pastor was the erection of the church. Additional lots were purchased adjoining those already owned by the congregation on the corner of West Ohio Street and Sherman Avenue. Plans were obtained after a little delay, and work was commenced in the fall of 1870. The corner-stone was laid with imposing ceremony by Bishop Domenec April 16th, 1871. Work was pushed forward rapidly, as the old church was already sold to the railroad company and possession was to be given upon a fixed date. But the building is large, and time was demanded in its construction. The basement was blessed by the Bishop and opened for occupation December 1st, 1872. Gradually the building rose from its foundation and began to assume those proportions which attract the attention of all and delight the eye of the critic. The solemn dedication, which was the most remarkable event as yet in the history of the congregation, was performed by Bishop Domenec Sunday, July 5th, 1874.

The church is in the Gothic style of architecture, but without a transept, and is 165 feet in length by 70 in width, consisting of a basement and main story, with a tower at the left side in front. The basement is almost wholly beneath the level of the street, but has a passage of perhaps six feet on each side the entire length, which secures ventilation and light. The walls of the basement are of stone, and those of the superstructure, including the tower, are faced with stone. All the door and window jambs, tracery, label mouldings, corbels and string-courses, turrets and pinnacles, are of cut stone, and the plane surface of the walls is chiselled. The tower, on reaching the height of the roof, is finished in a pyramidal spire, and measures 200 feet from the basement floor to the top of the cross. The basement is one single room, having a recess for the altar, with the sacristies on each side, and is thirteen feet high in the clear. There are three rows of cast-iron pillars to support the columns and floor of the main story. Here the week-day Masses are commonly celebrated.

The church proper consists of the nave and two aisles, with groined ceilings supported by beautiful clustered columns of cast iron. The aisles are 30 feet to the ceiling and the nave 55, but without a clerestory. A spacious gallery over the front supports an organ and affords accommodation to a large number of persons besides. There are three elegant marble altars, the high altar being of rare workmanship. The sanctuary is spacious, and is admirably adapted to the imposing ceremonies of the Church. To the rear of the side altars are the sacristies, which communicate with each other by a passage behind the high altar. The pulpit, which is built against one of the columns, together with the confessionals, the altar-rail, and the pews, is of exquisite workmanship. The ceilings are finished with heavy stucco mouldings, with rich corbels, which with the plane surface is of an immaculate white and will remain so as long the smoke of the cities permits. The windows are filled with stained glass of home manufacture, which for richness and beauty is not surpassed by any in the county. The entire cost of this splendid edifice was about $125,000.

The old church has entirely disappeared, and the spot where it stood can with difficulty be recognized by those who for years frequented it.

Soon after the completion of the church the attention of the congregation was turned to the erection of a pastoral residence; for, strange as it may appear, it was as yet without one, and the priest was obliged to live in a rented dwelling. It was immediately determined upon, and as a result there is the elegant residence, brick with cut-stone front, that stands to the rear of the church, on Sherman Avenue. It was finished in the spring of 1876.

Upon the formation of the Diocese of Allegheny, St. Peter's became the pro-Cathedral, and Bishop Domenec took up his abode with the pastor. When he made his last trip across the Atlantic, in the spring of 1877, he left Fr. Phelan Administrator of the diocese, an office which he continued to fill until the two dioceses were united under one administration, August 3d of the same year.

St. Peter's is one of the largest and by far the wealthiest and most flourishing English-speaking congregation in Western Pennsylvania; and in point of substantial, neat, and commodious buildings is not equalled, much less surpassed, by any other. But it is not destined to increase in numbers, being surrounded as it is on all sides by other congregations.

CHAPTER IX.

CONGREGATIONS FORMED FROM ST. PAUL'S CATHEDRAL—
(CONCLUDED).

St. Andrew's Church, Allegheny—Death and sketch of Rev. Denis O'Brien—St. Bridget's Church, Pittsburg—St. Joseph's (colored) Church—St. James' Church—St. John's Church—St. Stephen's Church—Death and sketch of Rev. P. M. Ward—St. Agnes' Church—Death and sketch of Rev. P. Kerr—St. Mary of Mercy's Church—Death and sketch of Rev. J. A. O'Rourke—and of Rev. M. F. Devlin—St. Malachy's Church—St. Mary of the Mount.

ST. ANDREW'S CHURCH, ALLEGHENY CITY.

THE borough of Manchester was laid out by John Sampson and others in 1832, and incorporated into Allegheny March 12th, 1867. It now forms the south-western portion of that city.

In treating of St. Peter's it was stated that Fr. Mullen built a church in Manchester for the accommodation of the Catholics who had there taken up their residence. The lots upon which the church stands are situated at the corner of Beaver Avenue and Brady Street. This church, a plain and neat brick building, seventy feet in length by thirty in width, but without steeple or belfry, was erected in the summer of 1863, and was dedicated, under the invocation of St. Andrew the Apostle, by Fr. Mullen December 20th of the same year. At that time this portion of the city for a considerable distance round was a common. Small as the church was, the congregation was yet insufficient to fill it; and the most sanguine could hardly have imagined that in less than eight years it would be in the heart of a closely built portion of the city, and that people would be demanding a church capable of accommodating four times as many. But no suburb of Pittsburg or Allegheny was built up more rapidly than this.

The church was attended from St. Peter's until the 1st of February, 1866, when it became independent, and Rev. M. J. Mitchell was appointed first resident pastor. One of his first undertakings was the erection of a neat and commodious brick residence by the side of the church. He was succeeded April 1st, 1868, by the late Rev. P. M'C. Morgan. During these years the common was laid out in building-lots and built up, and manufactories sprung into life on all sides. The cloud from the consumption of coal gradually grew darker overhead, and the "Smoky City" gratefully recognized the flourishing borough as one of her suburbs. The Pittsburg Locomotive Works was built on Beaver Avenue, directly opposite the church.

After ministering to the congregation until February 3d, 1870, Fr. Morgan withdrew on account of declining health, and was succeeded by the present pastor, Rev. Mathew Carroll.

The growth of the congregation was more rapid than that of the town, and St. Andrew's became daily less capable of accommodating the number that thronged to hear Mass. The erection of a larger church could no longer be deferred; and Fr. Carroll undertook it in the summer after his appointment. The corner-stone was laid, in the presence of an immense multitude, by the Bishop September 11th, 1870, the day of his return from the Vatican Council. At the end of two years it was dedicated by the same prelate, October 28th. The church is 135 feet in length by 65 in width, is of brick, and constructed after a style of architecture in which the Gothic elements predominate. The tower in the centre in front is finished at present to the comb of the roof, its completion being reserved to a future time. The heavy trusses that support the steep roof rest upon massive buttresses, a circumstance which enabled the architect to dispense with pillars in the interior to sustain the ceiling, that rises from the sides toward the centre, ribbed in a semi-Gothic style now much in vogue. There are three altars, of which the main one has a spacious sanctuary. A gallery over the entrance supports the organ. The pulpit is built against the wall, and the pews in front of it are reversible. Through the prudence and energy of Fr. Carroll the church was almost entirely free from debt at the time of its completion.

St. Andrew's is without a basement, and until recently no school-house was erected. Nor need we be surprised at this if it be remembered that the congregation built two churches and a pastoral residence in the brief space of nine years.

At the date of the completion of the new church the congregation was so large as to require an assistant to aid the pastor in the discharge of his duties. Rev. Denis O'Brien, then ordained, was appointed in the summer of 1873, and continued to fill that position until declining health forced him to retire early in the autumn of the following year. He withdrew to St. Joseph's Hospital, Philadelphia, where he remained for a short time, and afterwards came to the residence of Rev. Thos. Ryan, an uncle of his, at Gallitzin, on the summit of the Allegheny Mountains, where he breathed his last, of consumption, November 5th, 1874.

REV. DENIS O'BRIEN was born in the parish of Burgess, county Tipperary, Ireland, in the year 1849. After pursuing his studies for some time in his native land, he came to America in the spring of 1869 and entered St. Michael's Seminary at the commencement of the September session. Having finished his course of theology, he was ordained June 7th, 1873, and soon after appointed to St. Andrew's. Although he was not permitted to attain a ripe age, his career was yet sufficient to endear him to all with whom he came in contact and impress them with a high idea of his zeal and virtue. His body reposes in the cemetery of St. Patrick's Church, Gallitzin, on the summit of the montains, over the tunnel of the Pennsylvania Railroad. Soon after his interment a tasteful monument was erected by Fr. Ryan to mark the spot.

The duty of ministering to the Catholic inmates of the House of Refuge, which, until its removal in the year 1876 to Morganza, stood a short distance from the church, devolved upon the pastor of St. Andrew's. After the passage of the last act elsewhere referred to Mass was offered up every Saturday, and instruction given and confessions heard on Friday evening. About one third of the children are Catholics.

A neat and substantial brick school-house, 60 by 40 feet and three stories high, was built in the summer of 1876, consisting of four rooms, and a spacious hall on the third floor. But owing to the difficulty of obtaining religious to teach, the school was not opened until September, 1877, when the Sisters of Mercy, from the House of Industry, took charge of it.

This congregation more than any other in the cities suffered from the financial crisis of 1873. Perhaps one third of the people sought employment elsewhere, and many of those that remained were reduced to the verge of starvation. But it is gradually recovering from the shock, and must continue to do so and to increase in numbers in the future.

ST. BRIDGET'S CHURCH, PITTSBURG.

St. Bridget's Church stands on the hill about a mile from the Point and equidistant between the two rivers. Originally it was formed from St. Patrick's and the Cathedral, but the greatest part has grown up since the congregation was organized. Early in the spring of 1853 Rev. J. Tuigg, then one of the assistant priests at the Cathedral, now its Bishop, was deputed by Dr. O'Connor to organize the congregation and erect the church. A site was purchased on what is at present Wylie Avenue, above Arthur Street, and the church was undertaken. Father Tuigg lodged at the episcopal residence. The building was planned to be two stories, the lower of which should serve as a church, the upper as a school. By the time the first story was finished Father Tuigg was transferred to Altoona, and was succeeded in July, 1853, by Rev. James Treacy, then assistant at St. Patrick's. He also came to lodge at the Cathedral, and together with the care of the congregation took charge of the Mercy Hospital. The church was finished the same year, and was dedicated by Rev. Thomas Malone in December. The building, which is of brick, small, and simple in style, is yet standing. When it was completed the pastor portioned off "a suite of apartments" for himself on the second floor, and furnished them in a style not unlike that in which the Sunamitess furnished the cell she had built for the prophet Eliseus. Here he lodged for many years, laboring and studying by day and resting by night, and taking his meals at such places as were found to be most advantageous.

A school was opened in the remaining portion of the second story, which was conducted by a lay teacher until it passed into the hands of the Sisters of Mercy.

The hill portion of the city, offering no inducement to manufacturers, was built up but slowly ; and the congregation was in its infancy for about eleven years. At the end of that time residences began to spring up rapidly, and soon St. Bridget's was a flourishing parish. A new and larger church now became necessary, and measures were taken to supply the want in the spring of 1865. The corner-stone was laid by the Bishop with the imposing ceremony customary in those days, July 30th. According to the plan the building should occupy a part of the original lot, front on Enoch Street, and be 110 feet in length by 53 in width, with basement of cut stone and superstructure of brick. The basement was finished as soon as possible, and occupied by the congregation ; but work on the superstructure progressed more slowly. In the spring of 1871, when $25,000 had been spent on the building, and both pastor and people looked forward to its completion at no distant day, it took fire early on Holy Saturday morning, April 8th, and was entirely destroyed. The congregation was forced to return to the old church. The loss, though great, was not irreparable, and a meeting was called on Sunday to deliberate on what was best to be done. Forced by necessity, they determined to begin anew. The outstanding debt of $15,000 was covered by the insurance. The congregation, however, had increased since the commencement of the church, and it was necessary to make the second new building larger than the first had been. Want of space prevented its extension in length, but an addition was made to its width, making it 70 by 110 feet. The foundation walls of the ruins were used as far as they were deemed safe and the proportions of the building permitted. The corner-stone was laid by the Bishop July 16th, 1871, and the basement was occupied before the beginning of winter. About this time an assistant to the pastor was appointed. The church was finished and dedicated by the Bishop April 28th, 1872. But it was not completed without entailing a burden of debt that it will require many years to liquidate.

St. Bridget's, though differing in style from all the churches of the city, is superior to many of them. It consists of a nave and aisles separated by seven octagonal pillars on each side that support the ceiling, which is modelled after the tunnel vault of the Romanesque style. The altar-rail extends across the entire building, separating the main and two side altars from the body of the church. The pulpit is not yet erected, and the high altar is temporary. The windows, filled with stained glass, are of the Romanesque pattern. The large organ in the gallery over the entrance is perhaps richer in tone than any other in our churches. Since its completion the church has been tastefully frescoed.

Upon the completion of the new building the old church was transformed into a school-house. The erection of a pastoral residence, which was about this time in contemplation, was abandoned on account of the heavy debt on the church, and the pastor was left as before to occupy a rented dwelling. It has fallen to the lot of few priests to contend against greater difficulties, trials, and disappointments than Father Treacy has found thickly strewn on his path; and there is no one who has enlisted a larger share of public and of Catholic sympathy than he.

The financial embarrassments consequent on the panic of 1873 were felt in all their force by the pastor and congregation of St. Bridget's. With a debt which it would have been sufficiently difficult to liquidate in times of prosperity, they found themselves unequal to the task when the panic prostrated business. The payment of the interest was then a work of no ordinary magnitude. The schools were discontinued in the summer of 1876 with a view of reducing expenses, and a year later the assistant was dispensed with. In addition to these the zealous pastor, who for a quarter of a century had devoted his days and nights to the service of his flock, had other difficulties of a trying nature to disturb his brief moments of repose; and, regretted by all, he was forced to withdraw from St. Bridget's and from the diocese at the close of the year 1877. He was succeeded by Rev. Jerome Kearney, from Latrobe, the present pastor.

For several years the assistant pastor of St. Bridget's was chaplain of the Ursuline Convent, which is located but a short distance from the church. Mass is at present celebrated by one of the priests of the Catholic College.

St. Bridget's congregation must continue to increase gradually with the growth of the city until its outer portions are cut off to form new congregations. In 1879 Father Kearney built a spacious brick residence.

ST. JOSEPH'S CHURCH (COLORED), PITTSBURG.

On his return from the Second Plenary Council of Baltimore, in the fall of 1866, Bishop Domenec turned his attention to the care of the colored Catholics of Pittsburg. As they lived principally within the limits of St. Bridget's parish he committed them to Rev. Jas. Treacy, who by his advice purchased a lot for a church on Arthur Street, near St. Bridget's, toward the payment of which the Bishop donated $1000. A small church was begun; but when the first story was built a temporary roof was put on it, and so it remained. Vespers and instruction were given regularly from that time, and a school was opened by the Sisters of Mercy; but the people heard Mass at St. Bridget's. They are generally poor, many of them are not constant in their attachment to the Church, and it is difficult to effect great permanent good among them. Besides, the more influential among them did not attend the new church. For this reason St. Joseph's, although productive of good, did not fully realize the expectations of the Bishop. The poverty and inconstancy of the people rendered it impossible for them to pay the debt already contracted, much less to finish the building. The crisis came, and, every effort to save it proving unavailing, it was sold by the foreclosure of the mortgage, November, 1876. It is not probable that another effort will ever be made to erect a church for this people; nor is it necessary: they will find ample accommodations in the other churches of the city.

ST. JAMES' CHURCH, PITTSBURG, SOUTH SIDE.

The portion of the city embraced within the territory now claiming our attention was at first a part of Lower St. Clair Township. Later the village of Temperanceville sprung up at the mouth of Saw Mill Run, and in 1872, when all the boroughs south of the Monongahela River were incorporated into the city, this went to form the extreme south-western wards.

The first Catholic settlers either attended the Cathedral or St. Philip's Church, Broadhead. But when their number had sufficiently increased the Bishop recommended them to erect a church for their own accommodation. In the spring of 1853 he purchased a lot which is by no means eligible, and presented it to the incipient congregation. The church was undertaken in July, and, although not finished, was opened for divine service on Christmas Day. Work was continued on the interior with all the speed which the season of the year permitted, and Rev. Jas. M'Gowen, under whose pastoral care the congregation had been from its organization, had the pleasure of seeing the building finished early in the summer of 1854. It was dedicated, under the invocation of St. James the Apostle, by the Bishop on the 11th of June. The building is of brick, small, and with little attempt at architectural style. Fr. M'Gowen was succeeded in October by Rev. J. B. O'Connor, and he in February, 1855, by Rev. Con. M. Sheehan. November of the same year saw him give place to Rev. John Hackett, and at the end of two years he was succeeded by Rev. M. Carroll. During this time the congregation had undergone but little change beyond a very gradual increase in numbers. That portion of the city's suburbs was not naturally calculated to invite settlers, and while other parts were built up rapidly it kept the even tenor of its way.

For twelve years Fr. Carroll remained with the congregation, identifying himself with it in all that related to its spiritual and temporal prosperity. By the end of this time the mining and manufacturing interests of the place were considerably developed, and many Catholics had made their homes here and found employment. Additional accommodations were required, and Fr. Carroll planned an improvement in 1869 which consisted of a frame wing with its end resting against the side of the original edifice. The capacity of the church was in this way doubled. Scarcely had the addition been completed when Fr. Carroll was transferred to St. Andrew's, Manchester, and was succeeded, February, 1870, by the present pastor, Rev. F. L. Tobin.

The appointment of a resident pastor of St. Malachy's Church about this time drew away a number of families from the eastern portion of the congregation.

The large basement under the new portion of the church afforded rooms for a school, and one was opened with three lay teachers in December, 1870, and has since been continued. A school had been opened some years before, but it had been long discontinued. As yet the congregation was without a residence of its own for the pastor; but in September, 1871, a house and lot adjoining the church were purchased, and in the following summer the house was raised and remodelled, making of it a neat and comfortable residence.

What the congregation is destined to become in the future it would be difficult to conjecture. The locality is not favorable for a rapid or considerable growth of population; and the nature of the employments in which the greater part of the people is engaged makes their residence precarious. Still the congregation, which numbers at present about two hundred and fifty families, must gradually increase; and the time is not far distant when a larger church will be required for its accommodation. The congregation has already purchased a very eligible site for a church, and has collected a considerable sum of money towards its erection.

ST. JOHN'S CHURCH, PITTSBURG, SOUTH SIDE.

The borough of Birmingham, which forms the principal part of the South Side, was laid out by Nathaniel Bedford in the autumn of 1811, incorporated as a borough April 14th, 1828, and consolidated with the city of Pittsburg January 1st, 1873, in conjunction with the other boroughs south of the

Monongahela. Since that time the whole is known as the "South Side."

Simultaneously with the erection of St. James' Church was the formation of another parish from the eastern as that was from the western portion of the Catholic population south of the Monongahela River. As early as the year 1820 Fr. M'Guire preached, by invitation, in the house of Mr. Ihmsen to an assembly in which there was not one Catholic. Beyond this, however, nothing was done, and the few Catholics who settled there heard Mass at the Cathedral.

At length the erection of extensive iron and glass manufactories attracted a large population of laborers, among whom were sufficient Catholic families to make the erection of a church for their accommodation both practicable and necessary. Lots were purchased from Mr. Ihmsen on Fourteenth Street,* near the foot of the hill, and Rev. T. S. Reynolds was appointed pastor June 1st, 1853. At that time the Catholics numbered about twenty-five families. Fr. Reynolds addressed himself with energy and zeal to the work before him, and in the mean time offered up the Holy Sacrifice in an old storeroom near the spot where he was erecting the church. The building, which is brick, was finished early in the summer of 1854, and dedicated by Very Rev. E. M'Mahon, V.G., on the 7th of May. But the style of the church of that day cannot be conjectured from the appearance of the stately edifice in which the people now perform their devotions. It was constructed with a basement, which for several years served the purpose of a school-room, and in which a school was opened by a lay teacher immediately after the dedication of the church.

Fr. Reynolds accompanied Bishop O'Connor when he travelled in the Old World for the benefit of his health in 1855 and 1856. On his return, however, he resumed his former charge, and continued to minister to the spiritual necessities of the congregation until November 29th, 1859, when he exchanged places with Rev. W. Pollard, of Loretto.

The congregation had increased considerably, and would

---

* The numbered streets on the South Side are those that run at right angles from the river; they are numbered from west to east, the highest being Thirty-third Street.

have become still more numerous had it not been for the opening of a chapel at the Passionist Monastery, on the hill overlooking the town, and another at the seminary, which drew off a number of families near Six Mile Ferry, on the Monongahela. Still the church was too small, and it was necessary to enlarge it. As a preliminary step, additional lots were purchased adjoining the church, on which, in 1861, a commodious and substantial brick school-house was built, to permit the schools to be transferred from the basement of the church. The plane of the floor was then lowered, and the whole sacred edifice entirely remodelled. This done, it was rededicated by Bishop Domenec April 2d, 1865. Not long before this time an assistant was assigned to the pastor, an arrangement that still continues to exist.

The pastoral residence, which was too small and by no means prepossessing in appearance, was next enlarged and remodelled, and it is now a credit to the congregation and a comfortable home for the pastor. During the years immediately after the close of the rebellion the congregation increased very rapidly. But the erection of St. Malachy's Church in 1869 drew off a large number of families from the western extremity; and later St. Peter's German Church may also have taken a few from the eastern. The church was yet too small, and an enlargement became necessary. It was undertaken in 1872, when an addition was put to the front, making the church 110 feet in length by 55 in width. At the same time a tower was erected to the left of the entrance, which greatly improved the appearance of the edifice. The building is brick, with the front coated with cement, and pointed in imitation of stone, and approaches more nearly to the Gothic than to any other style of architecture. There are three beautiful altars, and a gallery over the entrance. The interior has been neatly frescoed.

The duty of ministering to the Catholic inmates of the Poor House at City Farm, a few miles up the Monongahela River, devolves upon the pastor of St. John's.

In 1856 the Sisters of Mercy took charge of the school, and continued to teach it until the erection of the new orphan asylum in 1867, when they withdrew from the South Side, and were succeeded by the Sisters of St. Francis. These in turn gave place to the Sisters of Charity, from Altoona, for whom a home was purchased adjoining the pastoral residence in June, 1876, which they took possession of on the 8th of August of the same year.

Of the English congregations of the diocese St. John's is the second in size, and will number almost, if not quite, 1000 families. It was at one time the intention to erect a church in the eastern part of the South Side, and had it not been for the financial crisis of 1873 it would have been done. It is needed, and cannot be deferred for any great length of time. St. John's congregation will continue to increase with the growth of the city.

ST. STEPHEN'S CHURCH, PITTSBURG.

When St. Michael's Ecclesiastical Seminary was transferred to Glenwood, on the eastern bank of the Monongahela River about five miles from its mouth, in September, 1857, a chapel was opened for the accommodation of the Catholics living in the neighborhood. Prior to that date they heard Mass at the Cathedral or at St. John's Church. At first one of the larger halls was fitted up for a chapel; but in 1862, when the congregation had increased, an additional wing was built to the seminary, the lower story of which became a permanent chapel. A considerable congregation was soon formed, consisting principally of laborers from the Frankstown furnaces and miners from the opposite side of the river at Six Mile Ferry. One of the priests connected with the seminary was pastor. Soon the congregation became too large for the chapel, many families having purchased lots and built in the vicinity after the construction of the railroad in 1862. Besides, it was from the beginning a temporary arrangement, and to those acquainted with the requirements of an ecclesiastical seminary by no means desirable.

To apply a remedy at once to both evils, Rev. S. Wall, president of the seminary, purchased a large lot at Grove Station, more than half a mile below the seminary, in February, 1867, as a site for a church. For the next two years nothing further was done than collecting money to pay for the lot; but at the end of that time Rev. P. M. Ward was transferred from Alpsville to the seminary, and appointed pastor of the congregation. Work was begun on the new church in the summer of 1870, and the corner-stone was laid by the Bishop on the 13th of November. The dedication did not take place, however, until May 5th, 1872, when it was performed by the same prelate with unusual pomp. The church, which is brick, is about 90 feet in length by 45 in width, and has a short tower at the left front through which the entrance is made. The church differs in style from all the others in the diocese, but is one of the most beautiful. The ceiling follows the pitch of the roof, and is finished in wood. The main altar stands in an arched recess, with the sacristies on either side. The finish of the interior, especially of the woodwork, is in a high style of art. After the completion of the building, Father Ward erected a small brick pastoral residence, and removed from the seminary, where he had held a professorship for many years; and it was not without feelings of regret on the part of all that he was seen to withdraw. But his health was so much impaired by his untiring devotion to his many duties that it became necessary for him to relinquish part of them. But in the summer of 1874 it began to decline so rapidly as to excite the liveliest apprehensions of his friends; and despite the skill and attention of his physicians he continued to decline, till, after a protracted illness, he gave up his pure soul to God on the morning of November 26th. The funeral was attended by more than fifty priests, and the remains were deposited in St. Mary's Cemetery.

REV. PATRICK MARTIN WARD was a native of Ireland, but was brought to this country by his parents, who emigrated in his infancy and settled at Hollidaysburg. Here he spent his youth and commenced his studies. At a suitable age he was sent to St. Vincent's College, Westmoreland County, where he remained until the fall of 1856, when he entered St. Michael's Seminary, then opened at Summitville. He came with it to Glenwood when the seminary was transferred thither, a year later, and in the spring of 1860 was sent to Rome to finish his course in the American College. He was ordained by Cardinal Patrizi September 19th, 1863, but did not return to America until the following June. At the opening of the September session at the seminary he was appointed Professor of Dogmatic Theology and Ecclesiastical History, which he continued to teach with but little interruption till within a short time before his death. In connection with this he was for a time assistant to Father Mullen at St. Peter's Church, Allegheny, and was afterwards appointed pastor of Alpsville, where he built a church, as we shall see further on. He was finally transferred to St. Stephen's, from which he was called to his reward in the 37th year of his age. In stature he was a little above medium, slender and erect, and in appearance and deportment, in mind and heart, he was a model priest.

Rev. John Ward, younger brother of the deceased, succeeded him at St. Stephen's, where he remained until April, 1876, when it fell to the lot of Father Wall, of the seminary. In January, 1878, he gave place to Rev. M. Ryan, and he, in July, 1879, to the present pastor, Rev. Daniel Devlin.

About the year 1866 a lot was purchased in Frankstown, about two miles below the seminary, where the greater part of the congregation resided; and a school-house was soon after built upon it. A school was opened by a lady teacher, and continued until the circumstances of the congregation forced it to be closed in the summer of 1876.

The financial crisis of 1873 fell heavily on St. Stephen's. The greater part of the people were thrown out of employment, and many of them were forced to go elsewhere; and the church, which was a great undertaking had prosperity continued, was left deeply in debt. Not without the greatest difficulty, and by means of assistance from other places, will it be able to clear itself, and this cannot be for many years. The congregation is smaller than it was when the church was built, and will number no more perhaps than one hundred and fifty families, few of which are in independent circumstances. But it must increase in time and even become large.

The territory embraced within the congregation was received into the city January 1st, 1867, and now forms the eastern wards.

ST. AGNES' CHURCH, PITTSBURG.

St. Agnes' was the first of the congregations more recently formed from that of the Cathedral. The impulse given to trade and manufacture during the war and immediately after its close accelerated the building up of all the suburbs, but of none more rapidly than of Soho and Oakland. The Catholic population being thus increased, and the distance to the Cathedral being considerable, the people requested that a church should be erected in their midst. Their request was complied with by the rector of the Cathedral, who purchased a site near Oakland in the spring of 1868. But the ground, being too steep for building purposes, was rejected. In April of the same year Rev. James Holland, then assistant at the Cathedral, was appointed pastor of the prospective congregation. His first step was to lease a small building at the corner of Fifth Avenue and Soho Street, which he fitted up for a temporary church. While organizing the congregation he lodged at the Cathedral. But failing health obliged him to seek a less arduous mission, and he was succeeded July 20th by Rev. W. A. Burke, also of the Cathedral. Adopting the plan of his predecessor, he purchased a lot on the right of Fifth Avenue, almost two miles east of the Point and about four squares from the Monongahela. Of the buildings, all of which were old and ill-looking, he fitted up one for a church, another for a school, and a third for a residence, which purpose the last still serves. The lot is not level, but is the best that could be had in a central locality.

The congregation increased not only by additions to the laboring class, which the extensive iron-works on the bank of the Monongahela invited, but also by accessions of the wealthier citizens, who, leaving the central parts of the city, built residences at Oakland east of the church. But Father Burke's health also failing, he was succeeded November, 1871, by Rev. P. Kerr, from the Cathedral. The newly appointed pastor, who had not been in good health for two or three years before, gradually sank under the burden imposed upon him, and gave evidence that his career in the sacred ministry was rapidly drawing to a close. In September, 1872, he set out for Loretto Springs, near Loretto, to perform the exercises of the annual retreat of the clergy, although hardly able to leave his room. The fatigue of travelling and the change of air proved fatal, and, surrounded by his brethren and fortified by the Sacraments of the Church, he calmly expired on the 23d of September, in the afternoon, in the 41st year of his age.

REV. PATRICK KERR was born at Donoughmore, county Donegal, Ireland, but emigrated to this country about ten years before his death, and continued the studies he had commenced in his native land. After surmounting greater difficulties than fall to the lot of most poor students, he was ordained in the seminary chapel September 5th, 1865. He was first appointed pastor of the church at Murrinsville, Butler County, where he remained until May of the following year, when he was transferred to St. Joseph's Church, Sharpsburg. In February, 1867, he came to the Cathedral, and thence, as we have seen, to St. Agnes'. His remains repose in St. Mary's Cemetery.

For several months the church was without a regular pastor, but on the 17th of January, 1873, Father Holland returned and resumed the pastoral duties. He immediately turned his attention to the erection of a new church, which the growth of the congregation imperatively demanded. But the raising of Fifth Avenue in front, and the lowering of Forbes Street to the rear of the lot, greatly increased the natural inclination of the ground; and while the congregation received but a trifling compensation for damages, it was assessed heavily for improvements, according to the principle in vogue in those days. The corner-stone of the new building was laid by the Bishop August 24th, 1873. The inclination of the ground gives the church two basements, one of which extends half the length of the building, making commodious school-rooms; while the other extends the entire length, forming a spacious hall. These basements were finished before the end of the year, and the upper one was blessed by the Bishop, December 28th. A temporary roof was put upon the building, and nothing more was or will be done until the debt shall have been paid and a pastoral residence erected, as the basement is capable of accommodating almost as many persons as the church will when finished. When completed the church will be 130 feet long by 60 wide, with a steeple, and will be, as the basements are, of frame, from the fact that the ground is not sufficiently firm to sustain a brick building.

From the date at which the congregation was organized a school was conducted by lay teachers until September, 1878, when it passed into the hands of the Sisters of Mercy, who come daily from St. Mary's Convent, Webster Avenue. The parish is as large as one priest is capable of attending. During Father Holland's absence in Rome, in the latter part of 1877, it was under the pastoral care of Rev. M. Shede. On his return, the pastor, at his request, was transferred to Latrobe with a view of improving his health, and Rev. S. Wall succeeded him. In June of the following year he gave place to the present pastor, Rev. James P. Tahaney.

St. Agnes' congregation is constantly increasing, and its prospects are more flattering than those of any other parish in the city.

ST. MARY OF MERCY'S CHURCH, PITTSBURG.

This congregation occupies the portion of land lying between the two rivers at their confluence, which has long been known by the familiar name of "the Point." It was, as the reader will remember, the site of the fortification commenced by Captain Trent in January, 1754, and also of Fort Duquesne. In the latter a chapel existed from 1754 to 1758, under the title of "The Assumption of the Blessed Virgin of the Beautiful River," and in it the first religious services of any kind in the city were held. This chapel dates from a period of more than fifty years prior to the organization of the first Catholic congregation—St. Patrick's—and twenty-eight years before that of the first Protestant congregation of Pittsburg—the German Evangelical Protestant, which claims to have been the first and dates from the year 1782. It was also the site of the first Catholic settlements in the city, and the spot where Mass was first offered up.

A tract of land situated here is owned by an Englishman, by whom it is leased in long terms of years and in small lots to persons who build their own houses upon it. It is the most densely populated section of the city, and it would not be difficult to find at least one hundred families who occupy but a single room each, and that perhaps no more than twelve by fourteen feet. The people are, with very few exceptions, Irish Catholics from county Galway, Ireland, who settled here about twenty-five years ago, and the Irish language is spoken more generally here perhaps than in any other place out of their native isle. As an evidence of this it may be said that many of the children born and raised here speak it fluently, while not a few, both men and women, who have lived here for ten or fifteen years cannot make themselves understood in any other. In their attachment to the faith of their fathers they are no less remarkable. But their practice did not on all occasions correspond with their belief; for, living but a short distance from the Cathedral, to which they belonged, they did not in all cases comply with their religious duties as the laws of the Church require. This may be attributed in a measure to poverty, which prevented them from appearing as they wished.

The rector of the Cathedral, wishing to consult their spiritual advantage and remove every excuse, purchased a large dwelling-house on First Street in September, 1868, which he fitted up for a chapel by removing the partitions, putting in pews, etc. It was dedicated by the Bishop, under the title of "Our Lady of Consolation," November 29th. But this step was taken without a full knowledge of the number and requirements of the people, and the room was soon found to be unable to accommodate one fifth of the congregation: more were hearing Mass in the alley before the door than in the chapel. A dwelling to the rear of the chapel and fronting on Fort Street was immediately purchased and treated as the first had been. The space between the two was built in, part of the work done a few weeks before was now torn away, and the whole when completed was dedicated by the Bishop April 11th, 1869. During this time the church was visited by Rev. Joseph Coffee, from the Cathedral, whose acquaintance with the Irish language eminently fitted him for the place. Irish sermons were now as frequent as English, and perhaps more frequent; and the novelty of it did not fail to attract the curious from other parts of the city, and the "Point Chapel" became famous.

Fr. Coffee was succeeded soon after the dedication by Rev. Jas. Nolan, who remained until forced by declining health to withdraw in the following March. Rev. J. A. O'Rourke was appointed pastor April 23d, 1870. Upon taking charge of the congregation he rented a house for a residence near the chapel; for prior to this the priest had lodged at the episcopal residence.

Little change took place beyond a gradual improvement in the religious tone of many of the people, until the end of November, 1871, when Fr. O'Rourke was taken sick. After lingering six weeks he died in the evening of January 8th, 1872, being in the thirty-third year of his age. At the earnest request of his parents, who reside in Cleveland, O., his remains were taken to that city and deposited in the family vault.

REV. JOHN ALOYSIUS O'ROURKE was born in county Clare, Ireland, but was brought to this country by his parents, who took up their residence at Cleveland. After prosecuting his studies in various institutions, he finally completed his course in theology at St. Michael's Seminary, where he was ordained December 4th, 1865. He was immediately appointed pastor of St. Mary's Church, Kittanning, where he remained until transferred to the Point. The lasting good which he effected in both congregations is the best tribute which can be paid to his zeal and piety.

Fr. O'Rourke was succeeded by Rev. M. F. Devlin, from the Cathedral, whose health, at all times feeble, unfitted him for so arduous a mission. He soon gave way, and was obliged during a great part of his time to commit the care of his flock to other hands. His life was terminated by a happy death December 28th, 1873, and his remains were interred in St. Mary's Cemetery.

REV. MARK FRANCIS DEVLIN was a native of Allegheny County, having been born a few miles south-east of Pittsburg, where his parents had settled some years before on their emigration from Ireland. His studies, after having been interrupted at times by ill-health, were completed at the diocesan seminary, where he was ordained February 1st, 1866. He was stationed at the Cathedral until his transfer to the Point. He was a classmate of Fr. O'Rourke and one year his senior, and was brother of Rev. Daniel Devlin, who had died a few years before at the Cathedral.

Fr. Devlin was succeeded by the writer of these pages, whose tenure of office still continues. The chapel, which was never very prepossessing in either external or internal appearance, did not improve with age. To secure a more becoming place for the offering up of the adorable Sacrifice, Bishop Tuigg bought the Ames Methodist Episcopal Church, corner of Third Avenue and Ferry Street, May 12th, 1876, at a cost of $12,975. The necessary alterations were made in the interior, and the church was dedicated by the Bishop September 24th, and from the feast of the day it was placed under the invocation of St. Mary of Mercy. The church is a very substantial brick structure, 72 feet in length by 55 in width, and is 14 feet to the ceiling, it being the first story only of the original plan. But, like the old chapel, it was much too small to accommodate the congregation at two Masses, and many were obliged to attend the Cathedral.

Wishing to perpetuate the memory of so important an event as that of the chapel of Fort Duquesne and the religious associations connected with it, the pastor of St. Mary of Mercy's had a beautiful memorial side-altar erected in the church in the summer of 1878, upon which he placed a Munich statue of the Mother of God, and which, in the absence of the Bishop, he blessed under the title of "The Assumption of the Blessed Virgin of the Beautiful River," September 24th of that year. Some relic of the old chapel would have been very desirable to place on this memorial altar, but it could not be hoped for, as the French had set fire to the fort when they abandoned it, and all that was in it was devoured by the flames. But the Bishop visited the church March 14th, 1879, and, in virtue of the faculties granted by the Holy See to prelates in this and other missionary countries, declared the memorial altar a privileged one, a favor that is granted to but few.

A brick pastoral residence was built on the lot adjoining the church in the fall and winter of 1878; for prior to this time the pastor had occupied a rented house.

From the beginning a school was conducted by lay teachers in the rooms on the second floor of the old chapel, and when the present church was purchased the former was converted into a school. The lay teachers were replaced in September, 1876, by four Sisters of Mercy from St. Mary's Convent, Webster Avenue, who continue to conduct the school. The congregation is the poorest in the city in the goods of this world, but is rich in treasures of a higher order. Since the opening of the new church the congregation has increased considerably and will now number nineteen hundred souls. The better to accommodate them, the pastor procured the services of one of the Fathers of the Holy Ghost from the Catholic College, to assist on Saturdays and to offer a third Mass on Sundays and feasts, beginning with September, 1879. The future increase of the congregation must be insignificant.

ST. MALACHY'S CHURCH, PITTSBURG, SOUTH SIDE.

The last of the congregations cut off from the Cathedral, or that can be cut off, is composed of the families residing on the South Side between St. John's and St. James' churches, and is composed almost exclusively of emigrants from Ireland, who find employment in the extensive iron and glass manufactories. The place has long been known by the familiar name of Limerick. Living at a distance from the Cathedral, and being unable on account of their poverty to dress as they wished, many of the people were not so regular in complying with their religious duties as could be desired. Seeing that a church in their midst would be productive of good, the rector of the Cathedral purchased two small houses adjoining each other near the spot now occupied by the church; and having torn out the partitions and fitted them up for a chapel, he dedicated them, under the invocation of St. Malachy, September 26th, 1869. The chapel was known as "The Shanties," and was attended by one of the priests of the Cathedral. Soon a change for the better was wrought among the people, for it is well known that Limerick had in those days a most unenviable reputation.

Rev. C. V. Neeson was appointed resident pastor late in the fall. He purchased a piece of ground on both sides of Carson Street, extending from the Pittsburg, Cincinnati and St. Louis Railroad to the river, as the site for a new church. The house on the property was used, as it still is, for the pastoral residence. The church was begun, and the corner-stone was laid by Father Hickey, V.G., May 15th, 1870. About this time Father Neeson was succeeded by Rev. Michael Murphy. While actively engaged in the erection of the church, and at the moment of its completion, he was transferred to Irwin Station, and St. Malachy's passed into the hands of Rev. M. J. Mitchell September 12th, 1871. The church was dedicated by the Bishop on the 24th of the same month. It is a frame building 100 feet in length by 45 in width, with basement under the whole, and is surmounted by a belfry. The ceiling rises from the sides toward the centre, and the whole interior with its gallery and three altars is finished in a chaste and simple style. But it stands in the midst of iron-works, and is almost constantly enveloped in a dense cloud of smoke.

On the 20th of December, 1871, Father Mitchell retired on account of ill-health, and was succeeded by the present pastor, Rev. James A. Cosgrave. Little remained for him to accomplish in the temporal order beyond liquidating the heavy debt contracted in the purchase of the property and erection of the church; and this has proved to be enough. He also built side-altars and had the church frescoed. In the summer of 1874 he enlarged and improved the pastoral residence. During the following summer he built a hall on the lots at the opposite side of Carson Street, which serves for lectures, etc.

The congregation has not increased in numbers, and indeed will never increase, for it occupies a narrow strip of ground between the river on the one side and on the other

Mount Washington, which rises almost perpendicularly about four hundred feet. It has rather decreased, and will continue to decrease in the future. It will number at present perhaps two hundred families.

After the erection of the church on Mount Washington in 1874, until it was made a separate parish three years later, Father Cosgrave had an assistant.

A school by lay teachers was begun with the organization of the congregation, but it passed into the hands of the Sisters of Mercy from St. Mary's Convent, Webster Avenue, in 1873, and continues to the present time under their charge.

CHURCH OF ST. MARY OF THE MOUNT.

Mount Washington, as the hill at the western extremity of the South Side is called, was so named because it is supposed to be the spot from which George Washington first viewed the site of the city of Pittsburg on his visit toward the close of 1753. In the season of prosperity it shared with the other suburbs of the city, and was rapidly built up for the most part by laborers and tradesmen anxious to secure homes for themselves. In this way a number of Catholic families, American, Irish, and German, came together, and, being unwilling to descend the hill to hear Mass, proposed to build themselves a church. Lots were purchased a short distance back from the brow of the mount, in the autumn of 1873, and the erection of the church was undertaken. The corner-stone was laid by the Bishop October 26th. It was not, however, until October 18th of the following year that the church was finished and ready for dedication. On that day it was dedicated by the Bishop under the appropriate title of St. Mary of the Mount. It is an unassuming frame building, 70 feet in length by 30 in width, and on account of the inclination of the ground upon which it stands has a basement. A school was opened in this, but was soon after discontinued owing to the financial difficulties of the congregation. The church was attended from St. Malachy's until April, 1877, when Rev. P. M'Mahon was appointed resident pastor. After a year he was succeeded by the present incumbent, Rev. Edward Brennan.

The congregation will number at present about one hundred and twenty-five families; but it is destined to increase more or less rapidly, according to the prosperity of the city, of which Mount Washington is one of the most beautiful suburbs. Its elevation gives it a commanding view, and its south-western position places it almost wholly out of reach of the city's smoke.

CHAPTER X.

GERMAN CHURCHES OF PITTSBURG AND ALLEGHENY.

The advent of German Catholics in Pittsburg—Formation of a German congregation—St. Patrick's a German church—St. Mary's Chapel—Establishment of the Redemptorist Fathers in Pittsburg—St. Philomena's Church—Formation of new congregations—St. Michael's Church—The Passionist Fathers—St. Joseph's Church, Mount Oliver—St. Martin's Church—St. Peter's Church.

ST. PHILOMENA'S GERMAN CHURCH, PITTSBURG.

ST. PHILOMENA'S is the mother German congregation of Pittsburg and of Western Pennsylvania. Its history is identified with that of the German Catholics of the city and vicinity, and will, for that reason, require to be treated at considerable length. German settlers were found in Pittsburg at a very early period. The first colony of which there is authentic record settled here before the year 1780; but the fact that the leader of the colony was a Moravian, Rev. David Zeisberger, would lead to the conclusion that no Catholics were among its members. Besides, the greater part of the colony did not remain, but with their leader went further west and settled in Beaver County, which also they left after a short time. It is probable that German Catholics came intermingled with others of the same faith, as they were found in all the other colonies, with perhaps one exception. They were always, however, in the minority in Pittsburg. It is equally probable that Rev. F. X. O'Brien, the first resident priest in the city, was sufficiently acquainted with their language to minister to their most pressing spiritual necessities. But when Fr. M'Guire took up his residence in the city, in the spring of 1820, they had all the advantages that could be desired; for, although an Irishman by birth, he had spent much of his life in Germany and was master of the language. The number of Germans, however, appears to have been insignificant until about 1825; and all the Catholics of the city and vicinity, of whatever nationality, heard Mass at St. Patrick's Church until the erection of St. Paul's.

The affairs of the Germans remained unchanged until the death of Fr. M'Guire in July, 1833, except that after St. Paul's was undertaken they contributed towards its erection in the hope, as they had been promised, of having St. Patrick's for themselves on the completion of the former. Rev. A. F. Van de Wejer, a Belgian monk of the Dominican Order and chaplain of the nuns of St. Clare, appears to have assisted at intervals in ministering to them; but toward the end of the year 1833 Rev. Francis Masquelet, an Alsacian, came to Pittsburg as their first regularly appointed pastor. Writing of him in a letter dated January 14th, 1834, Bishop Kenrick says: "He aids Fr. O'Reilly in the work of the ministry principally by taking the charge of the Germans, who are very numerous, and of some French who are there." From an account of a visitation by the same prelate I learn that at Easter of the same year there were 600 German communicants. But in addition to the Germans of the city, Fr. Masquelet visited many of the surrounding settlements, in some instances at fifty miles' distance.

After the dedication of St. Paul's, May 4th, 1834, the Germans took possession of St. Patrick's; for which, in accordance with an arrangement approved by the Bishop, they were to pay an annual rent of $300 to St. Paul's until it should be out of debt. They immediately set about the improvement and embellishment of the interior of the church,—for after its enlargement it had not been finished,—and also rented and furnished a house for their pastor. Rev. Fr. Stolschmidt came about this time to assist Fr. Masquelet; but he soon after departed. Seeing their energy, and being himself sorely pressed for money to make payments on St. Paul's, Fr. O'Reilly urged the Germans to purchase St. Patrick's for $6000. This they refused to do; and when he pressed the affair with no little earnestness, a division sprung up between those who were in favor of holding the church on the conditions approved by the Bishop and those who were determined to abandon it

altogether and find a place of worship independent of it.
And now begins a period in which "there was no king in
Israel," and in which, with the very meagre reliable data and
the host of conflicting traditions, it is difficult to arrive at
historic truth. Fr. Masquelet and that part of the congregation which preferred to abandon St. Patrick's sought another
place. After some time, during which they still held their
former church, they determined to occupy what was afterwards known as "the factory church." The part which this
building plays in our history entitles it to more than a passing
notice. It was originally a cotton factory with a number of
small buildings adjoining it, and stood at the corner of Liberty
and Factory (now Fourteenth) streets ;* and was owned and
operated by Messrs. Adams & Scott. The main building was
brick, and was sold in 1835 or '6 to Jacob Schneider. Fr.
Masquelet and a board of trustees composed of the leading
Germans purchased the building, fitting up the second floor
of it for a church, which they called St. Mary's. Fr. Masquelet soon after withdrew from the city and from the diocese.
The trustees were not able to meet their liabilities, as two
suspicious sheriff writs, now before me and dated December
8th, 1837, amply testify. In these the committee is styled the
"Trustees of the German Roman Catholic Church in the
Northern Liberties of Pittsburg."† The matter was finally
settled by arbitration. I have not been able to learn whether
St. Mary's had a pastor at this time or not. The tenure of
office was sometimes very short both in it and St. Patrick's ;
and the names even of some incumbents have not been handed
down to us. Feeling ran very high between the two parties
of St. Patrick's and St. Mary's, and the newspapers were frequently made the medium by which statements were circulated which, whether true, exaggerated, or false, were very
injurious to the cause of religion, as I learn from the papers
themselves and from a letter of Bishop Kenrick's.‡ Upon the

---

* The numbered streets of Pittsburg are those which run at right angles from the Allegheny River, beginning at the Point.

† This section of the city was then and is yet better known as "Bayardstown," so named in honor of Stephen Bayard, a wealthy German residing there.

‡ This and the other letters referred to in the text are now in my possession.

temporary adjustment of its difficulties, St. Mary's was provided with a pastor. By a letter of Bishop Kenrick's of March 1st, 1838, addressed to " Rev. Henry Herzog, Eiserman's Settlement, Venango Co., Pa.," he is transferred to "the town of Bayardstown, near Pittsburg," and receives the necessary faculties "for using as a public oratory a room fitted up in his house by Joseph Schneider." The Bishop further states that "Rev. N. Balleis, a most humble and pious Benedictine monk, will be pastor of St. Patrick's." The latter appears to have been preceded by Rev. Benj. Bayer, who had been sent as assistant to Fr. Masquelet shortly before his departure, but who preferred to officiate at St. Patrick's. But the date of his arrival and departure are unknown. By a letter of the same prelate, dated October 1st, 1838, Fr. Herzog is transferred to Reading, and the church is closed without ceremony as being, under existing circumstances, an unsuitable place for offering up the Holy Sacrifice. Fr. Balleis had left Pittsburg early in the summer.

Fortunately a spiritual guide was soon found in the person of Rev. Fr. Prost, C.SS.R., to whom the Bishop confided the congregation, and who was such as fully to supply its wants. He came from Norwalk, O., arriving in August, 1838, a date which marks the advent of the Fathers of the Congregation of Our Most Holy Redeemer, or Redemptorists, as they are commonly called, into Western Pennsylvania. He took possession of St. Patrick's, and no sooner had he entered upon his pastoral duties than a new era dawned for the German Catholics of Pittsburg. Gradually he gained their entire confidence and united them under himself as their spiritual head. A part of the opposition from St. Mary's joined him after the departure of Fr. Herzog, but a part still held out. The church was a burden on the shoulders of the trustees, and with the consent of the Bishop, as one of them informed me, they sought a pastor. That member went to Baltimore and Georgetown to the Jesuit fathers, and letters were also written to Lebanon, Ky., answers to which, dated February 18th, 1839, refusing the request are now before me. Finally all became united under Fr. Prost, who was joined soon after his arrival by another member of the congregation.

The propriety of abandoning St. Patrick's and erecting another church for themselves became daily more apparent. After spending considerable time in looking for a place, Fr. Prost at length determined to take "the factory" with the buildings attached to it. It was purchased in 1839. St. Patrick's was now abandoned, and was reoccupied by the English, as we have seen, in the following year.

Rev. Fathers Tschenhens and Chackert. C.SS.R., arrived in the autumn of 1840, and the former was appointed superior of the monastery of the congregation erected in the city. Father Prost withdrew from Pittsburg, and was soon after elected provincial of the order in the United States. After receiving Rev. J. H. Neuman, afterwards Bishop of Philadelphia, into the order, November 30th, Father Tschenhens also took his departure, leaving him to take his place, while Father Chackert visited the German missions in the vicinity of the city.

The original factory chapel was occupied by the congregation while preparations were being made to erect a large church. The foundations were commenced, and the corner-stone was laid on the feast of Corpus Christi, 1842. It was the first ceremony of the kind in a German congregation in the western part of the State, and was attended with that magnificent display for which the Germans are noted. To increase the effect, two companies of armed and uniformed militia took part in the procession and afterwards occupied prominent places on the grounds. Cannon were also planted on the cliff overlooking the spot, and were fired at intervals. Francis S. Shunk, then a lawyer in the city and afterwards Governor of the State, was, as we shall see, a conspicuous figure. Rev. M. Alig preached in German and Rev. Joseph F. Deane in English, and in the absence of a Bishop the corner-stone was laid by Father Carteyvels, superior of the monastery, amid the booming of cannon and firing of musketry. The ceremony took place in the forenoon, and was followed by a solemn Mass, and that by a public dinner, at both of which Mr. Shunk was present. This circumstance would be undeserving of attention were it not for the capital afterwards made of it, and the light it sheds on the political status of the times in relation to Catholicity. Two years later, when Mr. Shunk became the Democratic candidate for Governor of the State, the *Gazette*, the official organ of the opposite party, paraded it before the public with due flourish of trumpets. It was also asserted that the American flag had been spread on the ground in front of the corner-stone, and that Mr. Shunk and the clergy had trodden upon it to afford a practical illustration of the doctrine that the Church is superior to the State. I have examined the *Gazette* for 1844, and have found it teeming with references to the part played by Mr. Shunk on this occasion. As an illustration of the bigotry of the times, the following is taken from a long list of " Things to be Remembered :"

" That Francis S. Shunk, while a candidate for the nomination of Governor pandered to religious prejudice by *walking in a Catholic procession* at the laying of the corner-stone of the Catholic Cathedral (?) in Pittsburg, and that he was seen by hundreds of the citizens. He afterwards dined with the priests, and was toasted as ' Francis Shunk, the next Governor.' "

The rapid increase of the German Catholic population will be seen from the fact that Bishop O'Connor places the number of souls belonging to St. Philomena's congregation at 4000 at the time of his elevation to the See of Pittsburg.

The work on the new church was pushed forward with energy, but not after the contract system of our day. On the contrary, it carries the mind back to the ages of Faith, when money was scarce, but willing hearts and strong arms were ready to lend the assistance that money must otherwise procure. That a people so destitute of worldly means should erect so majestic an edifice is a matter of wonder to those who are unacquainted with the power of faith over the Catholic heart. St. Philomena's—for so the new church was to be named—is, more than any other in the diocese, a monument not to the wealth but to the faith of the congregation. When the work was undertaken the greater part of the congregation were unable to pay any considerable subscription in money, but offered their services to labor. Farmers from the country came, in some instances six miles, with their teams to work at the excavation or draw stone, brick, etc.; in short, to do willingly and earnestly whatever was to be done. Many a day the people swarmed like bees around the church. Not a few of those who came from the opposite side of the rivers were so poor as to be compelled to beg from the church the few cents necessary to pay their bridge toll. How different was this from the disunion that had heretofore reigned to so lamentable an extent!

Father Neuman was appointed superior of the monastery and pastor of the church—two offices which have always been united in the same person—March 5th, 1844, and remained until January 25th, 1847. He enlarged the plan of the building, giving it its present proportions. The walls were built around "the factory," leaving the people to occupy it as long as possible. The lot between Penn Avenue and the church upon which the schools now stand was leased and afterwards purchased from Mr. Scott; and a temporary church was erected when the chapel had to be torn down. A monastery of the same kind was also built for the community until the present one should be completed. At length the church, though not finished, was sufficiently advanced for dedication; and preparations were made on a grand scale for the ceremony. The dedication was performed by Bishop O'Connor November 4th, 1846. A procession of the Catholics of the city formed at St. Paul's, and moved to the new church, which they filled to overflowing, while the streets without were also thronged to a considerable distance. A sermon was preached in German by Rev. Clement Hammer, of Cincinnati, and one in English by Rt. Rev. Bishop Whelan, then of Richmond. A description of the church will be found further on.

St. Mary's congregation, Pine Creek, had already been formed from St. Philomena's, and about this time St. Michael's, South Side, was also cut off. And here it may be remarked that almost all the congregations formed from the parent church were organized and at first attended by the Redemptorist fathers.

Some time before the completion of the church Father Neuman turned his attention to the erection of the monastery; and the spacious building that stands to the rear of the church, on Liberty Street, is the result of his labors. It would appear that St. Philomena's and the Redemptorist Order in Pittsburg are more deeply indebted to him than to any other person; and we are not surprised to find that he so won the esteem of Bishop O'Connor as to cause that prelate to recommend him as a fit candidate for the See of Philadelphia. The monastery, though comfortable, breathes the spirit of poverty so dear to the heart of St. Liguori; and between this poverty and the richness of the house of God adjoining there is an evidence of faith, and the practical result of it, that is truly edifying. The temporary church and monastery were now torn down, and attention was directed to the completion of the church. During all this time, it is needless to remark, the congregation had been increasing; and although two others had already been formed from it, there were still sufficient members to fill the spacious edifice at several Masses. An addition of brick was now built upon the tower which raised it to the height of one hundred and sixty feet. About the year 1861 Rev. Joseph Wessel, then pastor of the church, caused the pyramidal spire of iron, and the cross by which it is surmounted, to be erected, bringing the top of the cross to the unusual height of two hundred and thirty-five feet. This iron spire is something unique in architecture, there being but few like it in the country. A clock was next placed in the tower, and to crown all a chime of five bells was procured and blessed by Bishop O'Connor April 29th, 1860, which was one of the last solemn functions performed by that illustrious prelate before laying aside the episcopal insignia to assume the humble habit of the Jesuit novice.

In the mean time the German Catholics residing in Allegheny had been cut off in 1848 to form St. Mary's congregation, and in 1857 those on the hill to form the congregation of Holy Trinity, and those of East Liberty to form that of Sts. Peter and Paul. St. Augustine's congregation, Thirty-seventh Street, was cut off in 1863.

St. Philomena's Church is 165 feet in length by 65 in width; is without a transept, and has the tower in the centre in front.

The ceiling of the nave is 60 feet high, and that of the aisles about 40, and the whole adheres strictly to the requisites of the Gothic style. The nave and isles are separated by two rows of pillars, of five each. When Rev. Lewis Dold was appointed pastor, in 1865, he set about the completion of the interior of the church, which had been left at first in an unfinished state. The pillars were in the beginning slender and of stone. But this material was found to imbibe so much dampness as to discolor the paint. To remedy this the pastor had them encased with lath and plastered with a fluted finish, and the tops furnished with imitation capitals —for the Gothic style has no real capitals—ornamented with cherubs and clusters of grapes. The ceiling was richly finished in stucco, and the level spaces of the walls of the clerestory enriched with sacred emblems in bas-relief. Every part, in a word, upon which a graceful and appropriate decoration could be placed was made to give evidence of the presence of a skilful master. Members of the congregation, anxious to second their zealous pastor, donated superb stained-glass windows. The gallery, supported by clustered iron pillars, contains a large and powerful organ, and the choir of the church has always been regarded as the best Catholic choir in the city.

Entering the sanctuary, Fr. Dold erected a superb high altar of wood after the best Gothic model, which in point of style and finish it would be difficult to surpass. The exquisite tracery is richly gilded, and contains twenty-seven niches in two tiers, in which as many statuettes of saints are placed. The altar-steps and communion-rail are of marble. The sanctuary also contains life-size statues of the twelve Apostles on brackets on the walls. The two side-altars are also of wood. That on the right is dedicated to Our Lady of Perpetual Help, and has placed upon it a copy of the miraculous picture at Rome which has touched the original and to which a plenary indulgence is granted on certain conditions for a fixed number of years. Over the arch that spans the sanctuary of this altar is a statue of the archangel St. Michael. The other altar is dedicated to the Holy Family, and contains the statues of its members. Over the altar at the back is a statue of St. Liguori in full pontificals, and over the arch is one of the Guardian Angel. The patroness of the church, St. Philomena, is represented in a statue of rare workmanship over the arch of triumph. A feature of this church that is deserving not only of commendation but much more of imitation is that the doors are so hinged as to open outward, which precludes the possibility of their closing and barring egress in case of a panic. A matter of so much importance should be enforced by law on all churches and halls in which large numbers of persons are accustomed to assemble. A sad experience should have taught the world enough by this time.

There are few churches in the county capable of being compared with St. Philomena's in point of purity and harmony of architectural style and appropriateness of the decorations that are added to increase the effect; and the stranger who visits the city without entering this magnificent temple has deprived himself of a treat not to be seen in half a dozen cities of the country.

If there be one trait more conspicuous than another in the character of our German coreligionists, it is their ardent devotion to the cause of religious education. With them it is second in importance only to the profession of their faith itself; and the German congregation must be very small and poor, as we shall have ample evidence in these pages, that will not be found able and willing to support a parochial school. This important accessory to the church claimed the early attention of both the pastors and people of St. Philomena's; and a school was opened in the basement of "the factory" long before the erection of the present school buildings. The lots on Penn Avenue, where the schools now stand, were purchased by Rev. Jos. Müller, and that part of the building occupied by the girls' department and the Sisters was commenced about the year 1848. In that year a colony of School Sisters of Notre Dame arrived from Baltimore and took charge of the girls, who prior to that date had been under the care of lay teachers. The boys were also taught by lay instructors until 1860, when a number of Brothers of Mary Immaculate, from Ohio, was secured as teachers. To afford them suitable lodging, as well as to accommodate the increasing number of children, Fr. Dold about the year 1864 erected that part of the school-house that stands at the corner of Penn Avenue and Fourteenth Street, thus finishing all the buildings necessary for the congregation. The school-house, which appears to be but one building, is in reality two having no communication with each other. In St. Philomena's schools, as in those of all the German congregations of the two dioceses, it may be stated once for all, the German language is taught during one half the day and the English during the other.

St. Philomena's congregation, although not of a great age, was originally the nucleus of what is now *fifteen* German congregations that were at different times cut off from it or formed from those that were cut off. Two of these are much larger than the parent congregation, and two more are about equal to it in numbers. St. Philomena's is not so large as is generally supposed, and will not count more perhaps than five hundred families. This decrease is due to the fact that while congregations are cut off from all parts there can be but little increase from purely internal sources; on the contrary, many of those who formerly resided within the limits of the parish have moved to the suburbs of the city. The congregation must for the same reason continue to decrease slowly in the future; but this diminution will be almost imperceptible.

ST. MICHAEL'S GERMAN CHURCH, PITTSBURG, SOUTH SIDE.

The nucleus of the present immense congregation was formed in a small frame building, consisting of a single room, which stood near the site of the present church, most probably in the year 1846. At that time the number of Catholics was not sufficient to fill this single room. No regular pastor was yet appointed, and no one thought that a church would be needed for years to come. But the congregation immediately increased with great rapidity; and in the spring of 1847 Rev. A. Schifferer was appointed pastor. Bishop O'Connor donated the ground for a church from the farm which he had lately purchased there, and of which mention will be made hereafter; and a church was undertaken. The corner-stone was laid by the Bishop July 16th, 1848; and the church was dedicated by the same prelate November 24th, under the invocation of the Archangel St. Michael. The original chapel is yet standing, but this church was torn down to give place to the present edifice. Suffice it then to say, by way of description, that the church was frame, was 90 feet in length by 50 in width, and chaste and simple in style and finish. Fr. Schifferer withdrew in 1851, and the congregation was ministered to at intervals by Rev. N. Hœres, of M'Keesport, till, after a few months, Rev. J. Hartman was appointed pastor. During his pastorate he built a brick residence, which having since been enlarged is still occupied. He remained until the arrival of the Passionist fathers at the close of the year 1853. Fr. Stanislaus, one of their number, was then appointed pastor, and remained for five years; and since that time the congregation has always been under the care of a member of that order. The rapid increase of the congregation soon necessitated the appointment of an assistant. But it was to little purpose. The increasing stream of emigrants from Fatherland was such as to demand more ample accommodations than such a church could afford. A larger one must be built. But the people, coming so lately into the country, were destitute of the means, notwithstanding their proverbial economy and frugality. In order to lessen the burden, Fr. Stanislaus divided the work; and having had plans of the whole prepared, erected that part of the church comprising the sanctuaries and sacristies against the rear of the existing building, about the year 1857. But the circumstances of the congregation improved so rapidly that no further delay was required, and the erection of the entire church was commenced in the following spring. The corner-stone—the first for a Passionist church in the United States—was laid with imposing ceremony by Fr. M'Mahon, V.G., and Administrator in the absence of the Bishop, July 18th, 1858. The new church was built around the old until it became necessary to tear down the latter, after which the congregation accommodated themselves as best they could. In the mean time Fr. Stanislaus was succeeded by Fr. Luke. The new church was finished in the fall of 1861, and preparations were made on the grandest scale for the dedication. The ceremony took place on September 29th, feast of St. Michael, patron of the church, and was the first dedication performed by Bishop Domenec. Rev. F. X. Weninger, S.J., preached on the occasion.

St. Michael's Church stands on Pius Street, at the head of Twelfth, and is about one and one half miles south-east of the Point. The location is commanding, and exhibits the church to great advantage. Standing at the foot of the hill, but on a terrace nearly a hundred feet higher than the plane upon which the surrounding portion of the city is built, it commands an extensive view—when the smoke permits. The church is brick, and is 160 feet in length by 65 in width, having a tower in the centre in front about 175 feet high. It is a good specimen of the Romanesque style of architecture. There is a basement under the whole building, although at the front and upper side it is wholly beneath the level of the street. The nave is 60 feet to the ceiling and the aisles 40; the former is separated from the latter by two piers and three columns on each side besides the pilasters at the front and rear. The piers and columns are placed alternately, as this style of architecture requires, and are furnished with cushioned capitals. The windows of the clerestory are arranged in pairs. The ceiling of the nave is groined from the piers, and that of the aisles from these and the columns, making the nave double the width of the aisles. There are three altars, those on the right and left being dedicated respectively to the Blessed Virgin and St. Joseph. The sanctuary of the high altar is the half of an octagon, an arrangement which requires less to be taken from the body of the church. The altar is surmounted by a well-executed statue of St. Michael. The baptismal-font occupies a recess in the wall on the left near the entrance. The tower contains a clock and a chime of bells. Since the frescoing of the church by the present pastor, Fr. Sebastian, in the summer of 1876, it is one of the most beautiful in the diocese.

From the date of its organization St. Michael's was blessed with a good Catholic school. At first it was taught in the little chapel, then in the frame church, both of which became school-houses during the week; and with the completion of the present edifice it was transferred to the basement. Here it remained until 1872, when Fr. Frederick, then pastor, erected a large brick school-house to the rear of the church, on the opposite side of Pius Street. This building contains ten large rooms, besides a spacious hall fitted with a stage, etc., and is without exception the largest and best Catholic school building in the two dioceses. The schools were under the control of lay teachers until the fall of 1867, when the Sisters of St. Francis, from Buffalo, established their motherhouse in the parish and took charge of them.

An interesting feature of St. Michael's is the number of sodalities and Catholic societies, nearly a dozen in all, connected with the church; and almost every man, woman, and child in the parish is a member of one or more of them.

Since the organization of St. Michael's congregation four others have been formed from it, yet the parent church is crowded at several Masses on Sundays. Unlike some other city parishes, there is no fear of a diminution of its numbers; and should half of them leave, it would still be large enough for the church. Three priests are required to minister to it, and they are barely sufficient; and assistance has frequently to be asked from the monastery. It is without exception the largest German Catholic congregation in Western Pennsylvania, and will number nearly, if not quite, 7000; while in point of provision for Christian training, care of the destitute, and the general spiritual welfare of its members, it is not equalled, much less surpassed, by any other.

ST. JOSEPH'S GERMAN CHURCH, MOUNT OLIVER, ALLEGHENY COUNTY.

St. Joseph's Church is not within the city limits,—although a large portion of the congregation is,—but stands like a sentinel on Mount Oliver, about one and a half miles south of St. Michael's, from which it was originally taken. The idea of erecting a church on this spot had long been entertained by the Catholics residing in the vicinity; and a committee of them purchased three fourths of an acre of ground as a site, before the breaking out of the civil war. No selection could have been better. It is a round knoll large enough for a church and the other necessary buildings, and is the highest spot of ground in the vicinity of Pittsburg. Lying to the south, it is free from the perennial cloud of smoke that hangs like a pall over the city.

But the civil war broke out before it was thought necessary to undertake the erection of a church; and Pittsburg was for a time thought to be in danger. The little church property was too commanding a spot to escape the attention of those who planned the earthworks that were thrown up at different points around the city, and a fortification known as Fort Jones was constructed upon it. The danger passed, the fort mouldered away, the temporal gave place to the spiritual, and instead of the booming of cannon, the clatter of musketry, and the glitter of polished swords are the peal of bells, the tones of the organ, and the bloodless thrusts of the sword of the spirit. It is now a citadel for the soldiers of Christ.

The time at length arrived for the division of St. Michael's congregation and the organization of a new parish. Father Luke, then assistant at St. Michael's, assembled the people on Sunday, July 12th, 1868, and discoursed to them on the necessity of erecting a church on the Mount, on which a large number of Catholic families then resided. This done, he set out at the head of a procession which advanced to the spot, that appears to have been lost sight of by its purchasers. All were pleased with the site. Work was commenced, and the corner-stone was laid by the Bishop October 4th of the same year. Father Luke, to whom the organization of the congregation was confided, and who is still its pastor, purchased additional lots adjoining those already held. The church was finished at the end of two years, and dedicated by the Bishop, under the patronage of the chaste spouse of the Blessed Virgin, November 20th, 1870. It is of brick, fronts to the north, and is 155 feet in length by 80 in width in the transept and 55 in the nave; and is built in the Roman style of architecture. It is very beautiful in the interior. The ceiling is 55 feet high, and rises somewhat higher at the point where the nave and transept intersect. No pillars rise to intercept the view; but a beautiful cornice supported by pilasters extends around the whole of the interior walls at the spring of the roof, adding greatly to the appearance. The head of the nave ends in a semicircular apse forming a sanctuary for the high altar. There are three altars, all of which are as yet temporary. The style of the pulpit, pews, confessionals, and organ is in harmony with that of the church. Contrary to the style of the present day, the windows are not filled with stained but frosted glass, which affords better light and presents the interior of the church to better advantage. The building is without a steeple, but has in its stead a simple belfry in which is a chime of bells. It would be difficult to find a church better calculated by its style and finish to please than St. Joseph's. No pastoral residence has yet been built; but the rooms over one of the sacristies serve as a lodging for the pastor, who takes his meals elsewhere.

A school was opened perhaps twenty years ago near the spot where the church now stands, and was conducted by lay teachers under the superintendence of the pastor of St. Michael's. Father Luke placed it under the care of the Sisters of St. Francis, who have a convent there. A small school was also opened by a lay teacher at Spiketown, about a mile south-west of the church. The congregation is composed principally of miners, many of whom own their humble homes, and a few farmers; but the number of persons in independent circumstances is small. It is gradually but slowly increasing and must continue to increase. A considerable part of it was taken off to form St. Wendeline's congregation in 1875; but it will still number perhaps two hundred and fifty families.

ST. MARTIN'S GERMAN CHURCH, PITTSBURG, SOUTH SIDE.

This church is situated in the extreme south-west of Pittsburg, in what was known as Temperanceville before its consolidation with the city; and is located about half a mile south of the Ohio River. The congregation cannot with strict propriety be said to have been formed from any other.

Part formerly attended St. Michael's Church, part St. Philomena's, part St. Mary's, Chartier's Creek, and the remainder heard Mass in St. James' English Church near by. When the number of families had sufficiently increased to form a congregation, the church was undertaken by the independent movement of a self-constituted committee in the summer of 1869. As the most influential of these lived on the side of the hill, they determined to consult their own convenience and build the church there. This is much to be regretted, for the hill is steep and there is neither street nor thoroughfare passing near the church. The corner-stone was, however, laid by the Bishop August 15th of that year; and the church was dedicated in his absence by Father Hickey, V.G., May 1st, 1870. It is a frame building 85 feet in length by 40 in width, and is furnished with a neat little spire over the entrance. It cannot be said to be of any particular style of architecture, but like the greater number of our smaller churches is constructed after the independent style, which leaves greater scope than any other for the display of native genius. The interior is neatly finished and frescoed. The inclination of the ground upon which the building stands secured a basement-room about half the length of the church, and here a school was immediately opened.

Rev. F. X. Paulitigi was appointed first pastor. After remaining about two years he was succeeded by Rev. Joseph Bœhm, who at the end of a year gave place to Rev. Edward Hanses. The latter built a brick pastoral residence in the summer of 1874. Father Hanses withdrew from the congregation and was succeeded by the present pastor, Rev. H. Gœbel, September, 1877. The Sisters of Divine Providence, a branch of the house at Sts. Peter and Paul's Church, Pittsburg, came to take charge of the schools at the appointment of Father Gœbel.

The congregation is composed of a variety of elements—rolling-mill hands, miners, farmers, and gardeners—and will number about one hundred and fifty families, with fair prospects for a future increase.

ST. PETER'S GERMAN CHURCH, PITTSBURG, SOUTH SIDE.

The growth of the German Catholic population of the South Side was very rapid during and after the war, and was confined principally to Brownstown, as the eastern portion of that part of the city was then called, because here the land was level and well suited for building. St. Michael's Church began, as has been said, to be crowded to excess; and although the erection of St. Joseph's afforded a relief, it was only temporary. Seconded by the pastor of the parent church, the Catholics of Brownstown purchased lots at the corner of Twenty-eighth and Sara streets, February 21st, 1871. True to the cause of Catholic education, they planned a building the first story of which should furnish school-rooms, and the second a temporary church; and when the congregation should increase so as to require a larger church, the temporary one could be converted into additional school-rooms. The building was undertaken in the latter part of 1871, and the corner-stone was laid by the Bishop on the 8th of October. The congregation was not as yet an independent organization, but was under the care of the pastor of St. Michael's. But Rev. J. B. Döffner was appointed pastor November 7th of the same year, and he still continues to preside over the congregation. Upon his arrival he found only the rising walls of a building upon which little could be done before the opening of spring. To supply a temporary place of worship he rented a hall. The new building was completed early in the spring of 1872, and was dedicated by the Bishop March 17th. It is a substantial brick structure, 55 feet in length by 27 in width.

The congregation, which daily increased in numbers and ability, soon required more ample accommodations; and in the summer of 1873 the pastor commenced the erection of what was to be their parish church. The Bishop laid the corner-stone July 13th. The church was finished in the autumn of the following year, and dedicated by the same prelate with unusual pomp November 24th. Fr. Döffner could now contemplate a finished work upon which indeed he had expended much time and toil, but in which he had been ably seconded by a generous people; and although a heavy debt was necessarily contracted, it is gradually melting away, and must after a few years entirely disappear. The church is brick, and approaches more nearly to the Gothic than to any other style of architecture. It is 170 feet in length by 70 in width, and has a steeple in the centre in front 180 feet high. There are no columns, but the ceiling is ribbed with stuccowork, and rises from the sides to the centre, which latter is 59 feet from the floor. The high altar as well as those of the Blessed Virgin and St. Joseph, to the sides of it, are wood, but of superior workmanship. The organ, which cost $4700, is an instrument of unusual power and sweetness of tone. But the frescoing of the church has not been executed in good style: it is crowded, and, the darker shades predominating, has a tendency rather to lower and contract than to expand the prospect, which latter painting should be made to do.

The school, as has just been said, was opened simultaneously with the organization of the congregation, and was under the direction of lay teachers. But in the autumn of 1876 an arrangement was made by which the girls and smaller boys are taught by the Sisters of St. Francis, who come daily from St. Joseph's Convent. A large brick pastoral residence was built to the rear of the church in the summer and fall of 1877. During the time that St. Wendeline's Church was attended from St. Peter's the pastor had an assistant, but at present he performs the onerous work of his congregation unaided.

When it is remembered that in less than four years from the organization of St. Peter's it was one of the leading German congregations of the city both in numerical strength and in the style and finish of its buildings, an idea can be formd of the rapid growth of the Catholic population. Being in the outskirts of the city, the congregation must continue to increase until such time as it becomes necessary to form others from it. It is composed principally of persons employed in the rolling-mills, glass-houses, and mines. The American Iron Works, which employs about twenty-five hundred men, and is said to be, with one exception, the largest rolling-mill in the world, is situated within the limits of this congregation. Its condition is a fair criterion by which to judge that of the congregation. If the mill is in active operation, the congregation is flourishing; if not, it is seen in the reduced circumstances of many in the parish. Fr. Döffner still presides over the parish, which will now number perhaps four hundred families.

CHAPTER XI.

GERMAN CHURCHES OF PITTSBURG AND ALLEGHENY CITY (CONCLUDED).

St. Mary's Church, Allegheny—Death and sketch of Rev. John Stiebel—St. Joseph's Church—Church of the Holy Name of Jesus—St. Winceslaus' Bohemian Church—Holy Trinity Church, Pittsburg—Death and sketch of Rev. Francis Grimmer—and of Rev. Charles Schuler—The Carmelite Fathers—Sts. Peter and Paul's Church—Death and sketch of Rev. Aloysius Hune, D.D.—St. Augustine's Church—Death and sketch of Rev. Philip Schmidt—The Capuchin Friars—St. Joseph's Church—St. Stanislaus' Polish Church—Recapitulation.

ST. MARY'S GERMAN CHURCH, ALLEGHENY CITY.

ST. MARY'S congregation was the third in point of time to be cut off from St. Philomena's. The first steps toward the organization of the parish were taken by the Redemptorist fathers from the mother-church. They selected the site upon which the church now stands; but a number of members insisted strongly upon having it built a few squares further back from the river. The Bishop, however, decided in favor of the present location — between Washington and Liberty streets, to the south of North Street. Very Rev. John E. Mosetizh, V.G., was appointed pastor, and immediately commenced to build the church. The building, which has since been torn down, was frame, 90 feet in length by 40 in width, but without attempt at architectural display, and was dedicated by the Bishop December 17th, 1848. The school-house and pastoral residence were next to engage the attention of pastor and people, and a plan was formed that should embrace both in the same building. A brick house, two stories high, was commenced in March, 1851, the first floor of which should be divided into two small school-rooms, while the second should be the pastoral residence. It was finished and occupied in July. Fr. Mosetizh was succeeded early in October by Rev. John Stiebel, in whom were united in a remarkable degree the learning, prudence, and virtue which constitute the saintly priest. Though young, he soon gave evidence of unusual energy and administrative ability, which won for him a high place in the esteem and affection of the Bishop and his brethren in the sacred ministry.

The congregation increased and a larger church was ere long demanded. Work was commenced upon it, and the corner-stone was laid by the Bishop April 17th, 1853. It was finished in the autumn of the following year, and dedicated in the absence of the Bishop by Fr. M'Mahon, V.G., December 10th. The church, which is of brick, cannot be said to be of any particular style of architecture. It is 150 feet in length by 65 in width, and has a small Byzantine dome on each corner in front; and between these is a porch supported by columns. The nave and aisles are arched with the tunnel or barrel vault, and supported by two rows of columns with cushioned capitals. A transverse arch crosses the ceiling in the middle, and at the point of intersection with the nave a small dome is erected. This dome, added to the peculiar construction of the interior, so affected the acoustic properties of the church that it was with difficulty a speaker could be heard. To obviate this difficulty the pulpit was afterwards moved to a spot near the middle of the church. There are three altars, all of which are wood. That in the centre occupies an apse at the head of the nave, and is one of the most artistically finished in the diocese. It was erected by Fr. Celestine, O.S.B., and dedicated by the Bishop April 7th, 1872. The interior of the church is finished in chaste and simple style, the object having been to erect a spacious and substantial rather than an elegant structure.

The completion of the church afforded no respite to the indefatigable pastor. Additional school accommodations were demanded; and in 1856 he erected a building with four rooms. As yet the children were under the care of lay teachers; but in 1861 he secured the services of the Sisters of Mercy from the House of Industry, near by, who taught the whole school for a number of years, and the girls for some time after giving up the boys.

The German Catholic population continued to increase, and members of the congregation were found at so great a distance and in such numbers that a new church was required on Troy Hill, to the north ; at Manchester, to the south ; and at Perrysville, to the west. All were begun about the year 1866. But no fears were entertained of the parent congregation ever becoming too small. On the contrary, the church is filled at three Masses, besides that for the children.

In the course of a few years the school accommodations again became too limited. To remedy the deficiency for all future time, Fr. Stiebel determined to erect a large building that should supply this and several other pressing wants. With this object in view he purchased lots on the side of North Street opposite the church, upon which he erected a large brick block about the year 1868, 135 feet in length by 60 in width. Exteriorly the building is one, but the interior is not. About thirty feet of the end fronting on Washington Street is arranged for a pastoral residence, and is four stories high. In this the priests, now five in number, reside. The lower story of the rest of the building is divided into four school-rooms, for the girls of the parish. The next story is a chapel, capable of seating nine hundred persons, and is for the use of the children. Over this is a hall for fairs, meetings, etc. Soon after the completion of this building the congregation and the diocese were destined to sustain an irreparable loss in the death of Fr. Stiebel. The zealous and saintly pastor, worn out by incessant toil and the voluntary mortifications which he inflicted on himself in no stinted measure, calmly yielded up his pure soul to God, after a lingering illness, early in the afternoon of January 13th, 1869, being in the 49th year of his age.

REV. JOHN STIEBEL was born of poor but pious parents, at the village of Cryon, near Trieste, at the head of the Adriatic Sea, in the Austrian Empire. Little could be learned of his parentage or his early life even by his most intimate friends, and it was only from incidental remarks, as I have been informed by a priest who was for years his assistant, that the little information we possess has been obtained. Absolutely nothing is known except that he studied in his native land, was ordained, and a year afterwards came to this country and to St. Mary's Church at the solicitation of Fr. Mosetizh, arriving, as has been said, in the autumn of 1851. From that time he is best known in his works. But his inner life, which would afford edifying details, was wholly "hidden with Christ in God." Besides his labors in St. Mary's and the congregations formed from it, he visited the German Catholics to the west as far as Beaver, and took an active interest in all that pertained to their spiritual welfare. He was also for many years diocesan secretary for the Germans. He leaves a name that will never be forgotten in the places which he illustrated by his learning and piety. His remains repose in the cemetery belonging to the church.

Fr. Stiebel was succeeded by Rev. Ignatius Reiser; and he, in April of the same year, by Rev. John A. Shell. The latter built a mortuary chapel in the cemetery on the hill to the west of the city, the corner-stone of which was laid April 24th, 1870. The dedication was performed by the Bishop November 6th of the same year. Fr. Shell was succeeded by the Benedictine fathers from St. Vincent's Abbey, who established a priory at St. Mary's in October, 1872. The church is still under the care of the fathers of that order. But before leaving, Fr. Shell secured the services of the Brothers of Mary Immaculate as teachers for the boys. They occupy the old pastoral residence as a monastery. In September, 1879, the Benedictine nuns succeeded the Sisters of Mercy as teachers of the girls' school. The priests of St. Mary's minister to the spiritual necessities of the Little Sisters of the Poor and the inmates of their Home.

St. Mary's is the second German congregation in size in the two dioceses, and will probably number about 6000 souls. It will undergo little change in the way of increase for many years to come.

ST. JOSEPH'S GERMAN CHURCH, ALLEGHENY CITY.

The rapidity with which the southern part of Allegheny was built up added many souls to St. Mary's Church and rendered the foundation of a separate parish necessary. Fr.

Stiebel took the matter in hand and purchased very eligible lots on Fulton Street, extending from Franklin to Decatur streets. Work was commenced on the church in the spring of 1866, and the corner-stone was laid by the Bishop on the 24th of June. The dedication took place about a year later, but the precise date has not been ascertained. The building, which is brick, differs in plan from all the other churches of the diocese with the exception of that on Troy Hill. It is 120 feet in length by 50 in width; but 90 feet only of the front is used as a church. The remaining 30 feet, though similar to the rest exteriorly, is two stories high, the upper being meant for a pastoral residence and the lower for a school. The object had in view was to have an opportunity of accommodating a larger congregation in after-times by removing the partitions and converting the whole into a church when it should become necessary. The front of the church is surmounted by a small spire. The interior is neatly though not expensively furnished, and contains three altars.

After its completion the church was visited every Sunday for about a year from St. Mary's; but at the end of that time Rev. Ignatius Reiser was appointed resident pastor. On the death of Fr. Stiebel he was transferred to St. Mary's, but at the end of three months returned and remained until January 15th, 1873. He was then succeeded by Rev. Peter Kaufman, the present pastor. Little change beyond a gradual increase had marked the passage of these years in the congregation. One of the first acts of Fr. Kaufman was the erection of a brick pastoral residence on Franklin Street, opposite the rear of the church. This enabled him to effect another necessary reform—that of placing the schools under the care of a religious community. He procured a sufficient number of Sisters of St. Francis from the mother-house on the South Side in September, 1873, who used as a convent the rooms formerly occupied by the pastor. But soon after the division of the diocese the Sisters returned to the mother-house, and were succeeded, in September, 1876, by Benedictine nuns, who have still charge of the schools. For the better accommodation of the children a new school-house was built about a year later, and the rooms formerly occupied by the children were given to the nuns.

St. Joseph's congregation is slowly increasing and must continue to augment, and will number at present perhaps two hundred and fifty families.

GERMAN CHURCH OF THE HOLY NAME OF JESUS, TROY HILL, ALLEGHENY CITY.

Troy Hill is a narrow strip of elevated ground extending into the northern end of Allegheny City, and lying between the Allegheny River and Spring Garden Run. On the top is a plateau which is closely built for half a mile north from the point of the hill, and forms a part of the city. As one leaves the upper part of the city he begins to ascend the hill on the eastern side, and having gone half a mile reaches the summit. Here the German Orphan Asylum, with its extensive grounds, appears close on the left, and beside it the German cemetery with its countless crosses and its neat little mortuary chapel. A square further he has the House of the Good Shepherd before him, while the church now engaging our attention lies two squares to the left of it, on the western brow of the hill. If he wishes to pass further to the north and west beyond the limits of the city, a most pleasing prospect greets his eyes. It is not the superb mansions of the wealthy, but the smiling gardens and vineyards of the laborious and frugal Germans, which speak of the contentment and independence that ever reward industry and economy. It is the paradise of the poor. To the west of Spring Garden Run green fields and extensive vineyards please the eye and enkindle the imagination. The population of Troy Hill is German, and Catholic for the most part.

As the population increased Father Stiebel took measures toward the erection of a church in the northern part of St. Mary's congregation, at the same time that he commenced St. Joseph's Church in the south of it; and having named one church in honor of the august Mother of God and another in honor of her chaste spouse, he would satisfy his devotion by completing the earthly trinity, and gave this church the holy name of Jesus. To this end he purchased lots fronting to the south on Clarke Street and extending back on Hazel to Diensberry Street. Work was begun, and the corner-stone was laid by the Bishop August 26th, 1866; but the church was not dedicated until June 7th, 1868, and as yet the interior was not completed. At the same time Rev. S. T. Mollinger, then pastor of St. Teresa's Church, Perrysville, was appointed pastor. The church is of the same dimensions and after the same plan as St. Joseph's, last noticed, but is somewhat more artistic in its interior finish. At the time the church was dedicated there were about fifty families in the congregation. A school was at once opened by a lay teacher in the lower rooms in the rear of the building, while the pastor occupied the second floor. The finishing and decorating of the interior early engaged the pastor's attention. Two superb wooden side-altars were erected in the early part of 1869, and a magnificent marble high altar after the Byzantine style was completed in August, and consecrated by the Bishop on the 15th. A statue of St. Boniface and one of St. Teresa have since been placed on brackets on either side of the altar, and one of St. John the Baptist on the right, against the pilaster that supports the arch of triumph. Against the pilaster on the left is the pulpit. A painting of St. Teresa over the altar of St. Joseph is a work of merit; but that of St. Antony of Padua over the altar of the Blessed Virgin is a work of the rarest excellence. All the altar vessels and furniture are unusually rich.

A brick school-house, 68 feet in length by 48 in width, and two stories high, was built to the rear of the church in the summer of 1874; the lower story of which is divided into two rooms, the upper being a hall. Since the completion of this building the girls have been taught by the School Sisters of Notre Dame from the German Orphan Asylum, and the boys, as before, by a layman. In the year 1877 Father Mollinger built an elegant brick pastoral residence.

The building up of this part of the city has increased the congregation to about two hundred and fifty families; but unlike other congregations, it has suffered comparatively little from the financial condition of the times, from the fact that few of its people are employed in public works.

Father Mollinger had an assistant, sometimes two, for several years who said Mass and ministered to the spiritual necessities of the communities and inmates of the German Orphan Asylum and the House of the Good Shepherd. For a time he had also charge of St. Anne's Church, Millvale: but these are now attended from other places, and he is alone.

But Father Mollinger is in possession of a treasure deserving of special mention—the large number of sacred relics which he has brought together. The collection amounts to perhaps four thousand, and is arranged in order in a room specially prepared for its reception. The greater part is placed in costly reliquaries. It would be difficult to enumerate even those deserving of special mention; but the collection may safely be said to be one of the largest and rarest in America, and few persons or institutions in the entire Christian world are permitted to congratulate themselves on the possession of such a treasure.

ST. WINCESLAUS' BOHEMIAN CHURCH, ALLEGHENY CITY.

For many years a number of Bohemian Catholics existed in St. Mary's congregation; but from the fact that Father Stiebel was familiar with their language they experienced no difficulty in complying with their religious duties, and consequently attracted no attention. At his death, however, they were in a measure deprived of the consolations of religion, there being no priest in either city capable of hearing their confessions or preaching to them. Finding a priest at length, and being anxious to organize them into a separate congregation, the Bishop encouraged them to purchase a Methodist Episcopal Church on Main Street, near St. Mary's, which was then exposed for sale. It was bought in 1871, and after undergoing the necessary alterations was dedicated by the Bishop under the invocation of St. Winceslaus. It is a brick building, perhaps 65 feet in length by 40 in width, and has been built for fifteen or twenty years. The front is surmounted by a short tower, and the interior has a front and side galleries. Rev. John Videnka, lately arrived in the diocese, was appointed pastor. A frame house on the church lot was used as a pastoral residence, and another for a time as a school-house. After remaining with the congregation for about four years, Father Videnka was succeeded by the present pastor, Rev. Siegfried Klima, O.S.B., who resides at St. Mary's.

Soon after that date the school was reopened, but this time in the basement of the church. Here the Bohemian, German, and English languages are taught the children.

The congregation should number about two hundred families, but the inroads made by secret societies, and the want of attachment to the faith in other respects, has reduced it at least one half. So unpromising was it that about the year 1873 the late Bishop seriously entertained the thought of attaching the members of the congregation to St. Mary's, and of organizing an English congregation in the upper part of the city with St. Winceslaus' as their parish church. The same thought is entertained at present, and will doubtless soon be carried into execution. There can be but little doubt that the people will eventually lose their native language and cease to exist as a Bohemian congregation ; and from the fact that no increase is received by immigration, this will be the work of comparatively few years.

HOLY TRINITY GERMAN CHURCH, PITTSBURG.

A large proportion of those who first settled on the hill, then known as Reisville, were German Catholics. To accommodate them, as well as to relieve St. Philomena's, the Redemptorist fathers determined to build a church in that part of the city ; and for this purpose purchased lots on Centre Avenue, extending from Fulton to Crawford streets. The site is about a mile from the Point and equidistant from the two rivers. A temporary chapel was opened in the spring of 1857, and at the same time work was commenced on the foundation of the church. The corner-stone was laid by Fr. M'Mahon, V.G., on the 7th of June; and the church was dedicated by the Bishop November 22d. The church was then

88 feet in length by 44 in width, and 26 feet to the ceiling, which is flat. It is furnished with three altars, and has a small wooden spire.

The church was attended by the Redemptorist fathers from St. Philomena's for some time, until at length Rev. Jos. Kauffman, a secular priest, was appointed resident pastor. About this time a brick pastoral residence was built. The church was under the care of secular priests until 1867, when it passed into the hands of the Benedictine fathers from St. Vincent's Abbey, who established a priory there. In the mean time two of the secular pastors had died. The first was Rev. Francis Grimmer, who died of apoplexy July 9th, 1859, and was buried in the cemetery at the east of the city belonging to the congregation. He was born at Taubenbischofsheim, Baden, May 12th, 1794; came to this country at the age of fourteen years, and was ordained in 1827. Little more is stated in the biographical notices of him than that he served on the mission in different parts of the country and of this diocese. The second was Rev. Charles Schuler, who died of consumption at the Mercy Hospital September 18th, 1863. He was born at Schwytz, in the canton of the same name, Switzerland, about the year 1832; came to this country and completed his studies at St. Vincent's College, where he was ordained by Bishop Domenec February 8th, 1861, being one of the first if not the first priest ordained by that prelate. His remains repose by the side of those of Fr. Grimmer.

The Benedictines withdrew from Holy Trinity at the close of 1870, and were succeeded by Rev. A. Rosswogg. From this date the pastor has always had an assistant. In the summer of 1872 the church was enlarged by the addition of twenty-four feet to its length in front—the length of the lot permitted no more; and such a steeple was erected over the entrance as had been over it before. During the following summer new and very neat wooden altars replaced the old ones; and two paintings of considerable merit, an *Immaculate Conception* and a *Crucifixion*, were placed over the side-altars. The church was also handsomely frescoed and painted, making it one of the most attractive in the city. It may be remarked, in passing, that our German friends are far in advance of the

English in the manner in which they finish and decorate the interior of their churches and brush off the dust of the city.

Fr. Rosswogg was succeeded in the autumn of 1874 by Rev. J. Tamchina, who in turn gave place to a colony of priests of the Order of Our Lady of Mount Carmel, who, banished from Prussia by the tyranny of Bismarck, found a home among us and took charge of Holy Trinity July 23d, 1875. During the summer of the following year they built a brick monastery fronting on Centre Avenue and extending 86 feet in length from Fulton Street to the church. It is 30 feet in width and three stories high, besides the basement. The chapel, rooms, and cells, though breathing the true spirit of poverty, are spacious, well ventilated, and form in all a comfortable home for the good religious. The pastor of this church had charge of the inmates of St. Paul's Orphan Asylum from 1874 until recently, when a resident chaplain was appointed.

A school was opened simultaneously with the erection of the church, and was conducted by lay teachers until the year 1878, when they were succeeded by a number of the Sisters of Divine Providence, from Sts. Peter and Paul's Church, Pittsburg, who occupy the old pastoral residence as a convent. An addition was built to the school-house about the same time that the church was enlarged. But additional accommodations are still required, and it is probable that a new school-house will soon be built.

The congregation has increased gradually since its organization, and it must continue, as it is not probable that a new one will be formed from the outskirts of it for many years.

STS. PETER AND PAUL'S GERMAN CHURCH, PITTSBURG, EAST END.

Soon after the completion of Holy Trinity Church, which accommodated part of the Catholics living in the outskirts of St. Philomena's congregation, the Redemptorist fathers turned their attention to a portion of their charge still more distant, and undertook the erection of a church for the Germans residing in East Liberty. But the

East Liberty of that day would compare very indifferently with that of the present. At that time it was a village about four miles from the city, on the line of the Pennsylvania Railroad; now it is a part of the city, an active business place and the home of many of our wealthiest and most influential citizens. Since the annexation, which took place in 1867, it is called the East End, or East Pittsburg, although its former name is frequently applied to it. The people were ably assisted in the erection of the church by the generosity of Mr. Peter Hauch, who donated half an acre of ground as a site for it. The corner-stone was laid by the Bishop on Thanksgiving Day, November 26th, 1857; but notwithstanding that the building is small, it was not finished till the end of two years, when it was dedicated by the same prelate on the same national holiday, November 24th. The church is situated on Larimer Avenue, is of brick, about 75 feet in length by 40 in width, and has a tower rising from the centre in front to the height of about 100 feet. There are three altars and a gallery which accommodates the choir and a part of the congregation. The church, though neatly finished, lacks the leading characteristics of any particular style of architecture.

The congregation was attended as a mission by the Redemptorist fathers until May, 1860, when Rev. C. Klœker was appointed resident pastor. He purchased a lot adjoining the church with a small frame house upon it, which served for many years as a pastoral residence; and he was succeeded at the end of a year by Rev. Ignatius Reiser. After improving somewhat the interior of the church, he gave place to Rev. John M. Bierl, August 15th, 1865. By this time the congregation had increased from fifty to two hundred and fifty families. But a part was English and withdrew upon the organization of the congregation of the Sacred Heart, as we have seen. Father Bierl was succeeded by Rev. F. X. Paulitigi in the summer of 1872. During his pastorate he frescoed and otherwise improved the interior of the church. But his most important work was the erection of a commodious brick pastoral residence. He gave place to Rev. Geo.

Allman in August, 1874; and he in February, 1875, to Rev. Aloysius Hune, D.D.

With the organization of the parish a school was opened by a lay teacher in a rude wooden building until such time as the congregation should be able to erect a better one. A colony of Ursuline Sisters came, most probably in the summer of 1869, who taught the school about five years. They then withdrew, and the school passed into the hands of the Sisters of St. Agnes from Fond du Lac, Wis. Their sojourn was brief, and they were succeeded by the Benedictine Nuns in the summer of 1875. A year later and they also withdrew to give place to the present teachers, a colony of Sisters of Divine Providence, expelled from Germany by the tyranny of Bismarck. Fr. Hune built a large brick school-house and convent combined, which was blessed by the Bishop September 2d, 1877, and has since been occupied. But the congregation was called upon to sustain a great loss in the sudden demise of its learned and gentle pastor, who after retiring in his usual health on the evening of December 31st, 1877, was found dead in his bed on the following morning.

REV. ALOYSIUS HUNE was born of pious German Catholic parents in Pittsburg, August 11th, 1844. In his childhood they moved to Latrobe, Westmoreland County, and at a proper age sent him to St. Vincent's College to begin his studies. He was sent to Rome in the autumn of 1869, where he continued his course until the fall of the city, when he retired to Innsbrück. Returning to the Holy City, he took his degree of Doctor of Divinity, and was ordained by Cardinal Patrizi June 7th, 1873. On his return to the Diocese of Pittsburg he was appointed pastor of the church in Cambria City, and after six months was transferred to East Liberty. Though by no means robust in health he was not feeble, and was always able to discharge the duties of his mission. His life was a constant study to follow in the footsteps of his holy patron. His remains were taken to St. Vincent's Abbey, where they repose.

After four months, during which the congregation was attended by one of the Capuchin fathers from St. Augustine's

Church, Rev. Joseph Sühr was appointed pastor, an office which he continues to fill.

Early in the year 1879 the Sisters purchased the schoolhouse from the congregation in order to use the entire building as a convent for their increasing community. They also purchased from another source a large lot of ground adjoining it. To accommodate the schools Fr. Sühr bought the First U. P. Church, a brick building two stories high and about 75 feet in length by 40 in width, with the large lot upon which it stands, for $2000. The lower story is divided into rooms sufficient for the children, while the upper, which is fitted up with pews, will serve as a hall.

The growth of the congregation, though fair some years ago, is now tardy; which is in part due to the financial depression of the times, and in part to the recklessness with which the city has been plunged into debt in the course of a few years by the construction of suburban avenues. These needless improvements have so increased the taxes that people seem rather to be renting their homes from the tax-collector than owning them. But the congregation must continue to increase, notwithstanding the difficulties against which it has to contend. It numbers at present about two hundred families.

ST. AUGUSTINE'S GERMAN CHURCH, PITTSBURG.

St. Augustine's congregation is the last of those formed from St. Philomena's. So large a number of German Catholics were found in the rapidly increasing population of this part of the city that the formation of a parish and the erection of a church were comparatively easy. The congregation was organized in the spring of 1860, and in April lots were purchased on Butler Street, between Thirty-sixth and Thirty-seventh streets. Being Germans, the first care of the people was to open a school, which they did in a rented room. The foundation of the church was begun in the spring of 1862; and the corner-stone was laid by Fr. M'Mahon, V.G., June 22d. Rev. Philip Schmidt, from St. Mary's Church, Allegheny, organized the congregation and built the church, which was finished in a year, and dedicated by the Bishop on Thanksgiving Day, November 26th, 1863. Fr. Schmidt now withdrew, and returned, it would appear, to St. Mary's. From there he retired to the Mercy Hospital, and died after a short illness in the summer of 1866, in the 48th year of his age. He was interred in the German cemetery, Allegheny. He was a native of Freiburg, Germany; and having studied and been ordained, he exercised the duties of the sacred ministry for some years in his native land. Coming to this country, he entered the Diocese of Pittsburg a few years before his death.

Rev. John N. Tamchina was now appointed resident pastor. The church, which, as will be seen, has since been enlarged, was a brick structure, and was then about 100 feet in length by 60 in width. It has a tower rising to the height of about 150 feet in the centre in front, and is approached by a flight of stone steps owing to the inclination of the ground upon which it is built. The ceiling is about 50 feet high, and approaches the tunnel vault in the manner in which it is arched. The elements of the Romanesque style of architecture predominate in the whole edifice, although it is not after that style in all its purity.

The next care of the congregation was the erection of the pastoral residence, a brick house standing a little distance to the rear of the church. The increasing congregation soon filled the church at two Masses, which was formerly too spacious for them at one; and in 1868 an assistant priest became necessary. In the same year the school-house, which had been built before the church, was enlarged. In October Fr. Tamchina withdrew, and was succeeded by Rev. Geo. Kircher; but he returned in September, 1871. The Sisters of St. Francis then took charge of the schools, which had from the commencement been taught by laymen; and came daily for that purpose, as they still do, from St. Francis' Hospital, not far distant from the church. St. Joseph's congregation, Bloomfield, had been cut off in 1870.

The congregation continued to increase rapidly and to embrace within its limits many of the leading German Catholics of the city, so that a second assistant priest became necessary in

1872. In other respects it witnessed little change until April, 1874, when Fr. Tamchina was succeeded by a colony of Capuchin friars, exiles from Prussia, under the leadership of Rev. Hyacinth Epp, the present pastor of the church and guardian of the community. The church became once more inadequate to the accommodation of the people, and plans were prepared in the fall of 1874 for its enlargement. This addition is in the form of a transept, with an extension of the nave, giving the ground-plan of the church the form of a cross. The new part is of the same style as the original building, but develops its leading characteristics to a greater extent. Although not yet finished in the interior, the church was dedicated by the Bishop July 4th, 1875.

The church at present is about 175 feet in length by about 110 feet in width in the transept and 60 in the nave, and is the same height to the ceiling as was the original building. The apse at the head of the nave forms the sanctuary of the high altar, and this one only is enclosed within the altar-railing. To the left stand two altars side by side, and one at the end of the transept; while on the right there is but one and the baptistery. All the altars are of wood, but are very artistically carved and finished. The high altar especially is a masterpiece of artistic skill, and contains three life-size statues. What is most remarkable, however, is that the altars and the pulpit were planned and built by the skill and labor of one of the lay brothers of the community. I had the pleasure on two occasions of entering the workshop of this humble son of St. Francis and witnessing the skill with which he executed his difficult work. And yet we never hear the last of "lazy monks," "drones," etc., while in our midst—did our Protestant friends but open their eyes—is presented a most irrefragible refutation of these threadbare calumnies. The Redemptorists, the Benedictines, the Passionists, the Carmelites, the Capuchins, all have united in erecting monuments that give the lie to popular prejudice; yet men "have eyes, and see not; have ears, and hear not."

A brick monastery was about the same time built against the rear of the church and connected with the existing pastoral residence which forms a part of it. This new building fronts on Thirty-seventh Street, and is spacious, comfortable, and well ventilated—the home of the community, the silent witness of their toil, their studies, their devotion, their austerities and repose.

A more spacious school building is necessary, and will soon be undertaken.

Besides ministering to the congregation, one of the fathers has charge of the community and patients of St. Francis' Hospital. They had charge of St. Joseph's Church also until the beginning of 1877, at which time a resident pastor was appointed.

The congregation will continue to increase both in numbers and wealth, although it is at present the third in population of the German congregations, and by far the wealthiest for its size. It bids fair to be ere long the leading German congregation in this part of the State.

ST. JOSEPH'S GERMAN CHURCH, PITTSBURG.

The suburb of Bloomfield, which forms a part of the northeast of the city and has not changed its name since its annexation, is about a mile distant from the Allegheny River and three miles from the Point. The first Catholics who settled here were Germans from the more central parts of the city, who in the days of our prosperity purchased lots and built humble residences, and they are principally those in moderate circumstances. In the beginning they heard Mass at St. Augustine's Church, but they were soon desirous of having a church of their own, and more especially a school. Admirable instinct of our German Catholic friends! A Catholic school —who can tell the blessings it brings with it! Fr. Tamchina, who was at that time pastor of St. Augustine's, seeing the flattering prospects of the growing suburb, favored the undertaking, and in 1867 lots were purchased by the united efforts of twenty of the heads of leading families, for school and church purposes, at a cost of $2200. A small frame building about 26 by 35 feet and two stories high was erected, and in the following year a school was opened in the lower story by a lay teacher. The pastor of St. Augustine's had now an assistant; and as the number of Catholics had considerably increased, the second story was fitted up for a church in 1870, and Mass was celebrated every Sunday. But the church was soon unable to accommodate the increasing throng. To remedy the defect an addition was built across the end of the existing church in 1872, making it about 65 feet in length by 40 in width in the transept and 26 in the nave. An humble belfry surmounts it, and the interior is neatly finished. The church was dedicated by the Bishop November 3d of the same year.

Rev. Ed. Hanses was now appointed resident pastor, who continued to exercise the duties of his ministry until succeeded by Rev. Julius Kuenzer, in the fall of 1873. But in the follow, ing July he was transferred to another parish, and St. Joseph's was again attached to St. Augustine's. The church, however, regained its independence early in 1877, when the present incumbent, Rev. John Staub, was appointed pastor. A brick residence was built in the fall of 1877, before which time the pastor had occupied a rented house.

After the school had been for some time in the hands of a lay teacher it was committed to the care of the Sisters of St. Agnes during the pastorate of Fr. Hanses. But after a short time they were succeeded by the Sisters of St. Francis, who continue to the present time, and who walk daily from St. Francis' Hospital, half a mile distant.

The congregation will number at present perhaps two hundred families, and, being in the outskirts of the city, must continue to increase. It will be but a few years before a larger church will be demanded.

ST. STANISLAUS' POLISH CHURCH, PITTSBURG.

When the good people of Pittsburg were informed, in the fall of 1875, that the Fourth Presbyterian Church, on Penn Avenue, between Fifteenth and Sixteenth streets, with the large lot upon which it stands, had been purchased for $10,000 and was converted into a Polish church, they first began to realize that there were Catholics of this nationality among us. They reside principally in the eastern section of the South

Side, and near their present church; but it would be difficult to determine the time at which they came to this city. The manner in which they were formerly ministered to is almost equally mysterious. During the lifetime of Fr. Stiebel, who died in January, 1869, they could have found a confessor in him. Soon after his death the Bohemian church was opened, the pastor of which, Fr. Videnka, was also master of the Polish language. A priest capable of conversing with them may also have sometimes been found among the Redemptorist fathers at St. Philomena's, or at the Passionist Monastery. But they felt the inconvenience of their situation, and accordingly wrote to their native land, about the year 1874, asking for a priest. They did not, however, succeed.

But in April, 1875, Rev. Anton Klowitzer, a Polish priest, entered the diocese and lodged for a time with the pastor of St. Michael's Church, South Side. He visited his fellow-countrymen in the different parts of the city, and said Mass for them in the basement of that church. Believing that the greater part resided near St. Philomena's—which is now known to have been an error—he purchased the church, as has been said, in the autumn of 1875. After undergoing the necessary alterations it was dedicated by the Bishop October 10th of the same year, and is the only Polish church in the two dioceses.

The building has stood perhaps twenty years, and shows signs of age. But it is still substantial, and is about 60 feet in length by 40 in width, and has no steeple. The interior has a gallery over the entrance and along the sides. The style of finish is chaste and simple but not expensive. But the colors are too striking to please an American taste. Here our Polish friends indulge on certain festivals in devotions and ceremonies that appear novel to us, but which have been brought from Fatherland and serve to carry the memory and affections back to it. A part of the basement, which is half beneath the surface, has been fitted up for a school, and here the good father himself taught the children till after some months, when a teacher was employed. Another small portion was made to answer the purposes of a pastoral residence, where the zealous priest, like the prophet Elizeus, rested after his labors. But a brick house was built in 1877. Toward the end of that year Fr. Klowitzer withdrew to a Polish colony in the north-west, and was succeeded by Rev. E. Bratkiewicz. But he withdrew in December, 1878, and the church was without a pastor for some months. One of the Fathers of the Holy Ghost from the Catholic College offered up the Holy Sacrifice for the people on Sundays, and one of the Passionist fathers, acquainted with their language, visited their sick. At length, in August, 1879, Rev. John Gratza came to Pittsburg and was appointed pastor of the congregation.

The congregation comprises about two hundred families, all of whom belong to the poorer class; but they are possessed of a faith and piety quite unusual in our day. There is little probability that any material change will take place for years to come in their numbers or condition. Besides these there are no other Polish Catholics in the two dioceses, with the exception of a dozen or more families at Natrona, twenty-three miles up the Allegheny River.

RECAPITULATION.

To recapitulate. We have seen that the Catholic population of Pittsburg and Allegheny was so small and insignificant in the early years of the present century that the place was visited as a station from Brownsville. In 1810—but seventy years ago—the first priest, Rev. F. X. O'Brien, had just taken up his residence here, and had undertaken to build the first church, a diminutive edifice. There were no more perhaps than a dozen Catholic families at that time. But mark the change. In the two cities there are now, instead of one priest, a Bishop and sixty-two priests. Instead of an unfinished church and one Mass perhaps once, or at most twice, in the month—for, as Very Rev. Felix de Andreis remarked in a letter, already quoted, Father O'Brien had a parish as large as ten dioceses—there are now two Cathedrals, fourteen English, eleven German, one Polish, and one Bohemian church, and nine large chapels, in which eighty-seven Masses are celebrated every Sunday. Where there was then no religious order there are now seven orders of men and nine of women. To this must be added seven charitable institutions, one college, two large and a number of smaller academies, with twenty-four parish schools taught by religious and three by laics. The Catholic population, which did not at that time exceed seventy souls, may now be fairly estimated at 70,000. "And the mustard-seed grew and became a great tree."

CHAPTER XII.

CHURCHES IN ALLEGHENY COUNTY.

St. Joseph's Church, Verona—Chapel of the Sacred Heart, Plum Creek—St. James' Church, Wilkinsburg—Braddock's Field—Chapel at Tarra Hill—St. Thomas' Church—Death and sketch of Rev. Peter Hughes—St. Joseph's German Church—M'Keesport—St. Peter's Church—Death and sketch of Rev. M. Hœrer—and of Rev. Cajetan Klœker—St. Agnes' Church, Bull's Run—St. Patrick's Church, Alpsville—St. Michael's Church, Elizabeth—Death and sketch of Rev. M. J. Brazill—Transfiguration Church, Monongahela City, Washington County.

THE congregations of Allegheny County, being in many cases offshoots of those of the two cities, are now to engage our attention. And first of those that lie east of the Allegheny and Monongahela rivers and belong to the Diocese of Pittsburg.

ST. JOSEPH'S CHURCH, VERONA.

Verona is situated on the eastern bank of the Allegheny River, ten miles above Pittsburg. At first it was known as Verner Station, Allegheny Valley Railroad, but in process of time it grew and was incorporated as Verona borough in 1871. The first Catholic settlers of the vicinity were Germans, who came to Pittsburg, and later to Sharpsburg, to hear Mass and comply with their religious duties. But as early as 1840 one of them, Adam Wirtz, bought fourteen acres of land and settled upon it, and when the number of Catholics had sufficiently increased fitted up a room in his house for a chapel. Here Mass was offered up at irregular intervals; but it is impossible to determine at what time or by whom it first began to be celebrated. At length Mr. Wirtz died, leaving his property to the German Orphan Asylum on condition that it should build a chapel upon it. Sufficient ground for the site was given, but the chapel was not built. After the completion of the railroad, in 1855, the congregation increased. A native and Irish element was also introduced; for up to this time it was exclusively German. Mass was now celebrated more frequently; but the church was not undertaken until 1866. The Redemptorist fathers from St. Philomena's, who were ministering to the people, then took it in hand, and the corner-stone was laid by the Bishop July 23d of that year. The building was finished before the winter, and dedicated under the patronage of St. Joseph by Father Stiebel, but upon what day I have not been able to learn. It occupies a most ineligible site on the side of the hill, about half a mile from the river; and is a frame building about 55 feet in length by 38 in width, with a belfry over the entrance. It is chaste in appearance and finish, but without architectural pretensions. Mass was now celebrated once a month each by the Redemptorist and Passionist fathers, until August, 1870, when Rev. Joseph Sühr was appointed pastor of Verona and Wilkinsburg, with his residence at the latter place. For three years he celebrated Mass at both places every Sunday, riding from the one to the other, a distance of six miles, between the Masses. Finding the church too small he built an addition to it consisting of a recess for the altar and a sacristy, and had the interior otherwise improved and frescoed. There were then about sixty families, some of whom resided several miles distant.

But in time the two congregations became too heavy a charge for one pastor, and in June, 1873, Rev. W. A. Burke was appointed to Wilkinsburg and Father Sühr was stationed at Verona. A pastoral residence now became necessary, and he purchased lots on the hill near the church, where a part of the town is built, and erected a neat brick house. Lots are reserved in the same place for a new church when it becomes necessary. The building of the railroad-shops here has induced a number of families to settle in the town, among whom are a few Catholics.

In the middle of May, 1878, Father Sühr was transferred to the Church of Sts. Peter and Paul, Pittsburg, and was succeeded by Rev. J. Rittiger, the present pastor.

"The congregation numbers at present about eighty families, but the German element is so far merged in the English that, although confessions are still heard in the former language, and the pastor is required to be familiar with it, there are no longer sermons preached in it.

The small number of Catholics, and the distance especially at which many of them live from the church, have prevented the opening of a parish school, and will for a few years at least. But the prospects for the future growth and importance of the congregation are flattering.

CHAPEL OF THE SACRED HEART, PLUM CREEK.

In the autumn of 1873 Father Sühr turned his attention to the spiritual welfare of a body of Catholic miners, about twenty families in number, that had settled on Plum Creek, about eight miles east from Verona. To this point the Allegheny Valley Railroad had lately laid a branch track for the purpose of shipping coal. Having visited the place a few times, he purchased a lot and determined to built a chapel. It was soon done, and in this simple little frame building Mass has since been celebrated at regular intervals. It cannot be doubted that this outpost will increase and become in time an independent congregation. But its growth and prosperity will depend on the traffic to which it owes its rise.

With this exception there are no Catholics in the northeastern part of Allegheny County east of the river, nor in the western part of Westmoreland County, except in the immediate vicinity of Freeport, about eighteen miles above Verona, and a family here and there along the railroad.

ST. JAMES' CHURCH, WILKINSBURG.

The village of Wilkinsburg is situated on the Pennsylvania Railroad, seven miles east of Pittsburg by that thoroughfare, although near the boundary of the city. It was founded some time prior to the year 1840, and was successively known as M'Nairsville, Rippeysville, and Wilkinsburg, the last of which was bestowed upon it in honor of Hon. W. Wilkins, at one time U. S. ambassador to Russia. When the city limits were extended, in 1867, it became one of the eastern wards; but after a protracted litigation it was permitted to withdraw, and so it remains.

The number of Catholics is small, and the principal part of the congregation resides at certain coal-mines about a mile to the north-east. At first the people formed a part of the congregation of Sts. Peter and Paul, East Liberty; but being English they were at a disadvantage, and under the direction of Rev. J. M. Bierl, then pastor of that church, undertook the erection of one for themselves. A very eligible lot was purchased near the railroad, consisting of about an acre of ground, and work was commenced on a church. Upon its completion it was dedicated, under the invocation of St. James, by Father Hickey, Administrator, November 29th, 1869. The church is a frame building, about 55 feet in length by 30 in width, is simple in architectural style, and is surmounted by a belfry. But no resident pastor was appointed, although Mass was celebrated in the church, until August, 1870, when Rev. Jos. Sühr was stationed there, as we have seen, with the additional charge of Verona. He lodged at Wilkinsburg, and celebrated Mass every Sunday, although as yet no residence was built. He continued to minister to the two congregations until June, 1873, when he confined his labors to Verona alone, and Rev. W. A. Burke was appointed to Wilkinsburg. The first care of the newly appointed pastor was to build a residence, and the elegant brick house which he now occupies—for he is yet pastor of the church—is the fruit of his labors. No school has yet been opened, nor will be until the congregation shall have grown larger. Like all the parishes depending upon mining or manufacture, St. James' suffered from the financial depression of 1873; but it is slowly recovering, and must continue gradually to increase in the future. At present it will not exceed eighty families, if it will reach that number.

BRADDOCK'S FIELD.

The reader will remember that Braddock's Field is on the eastern bank of the Monongahela River, about ten miles above

Pittsburg and a short distance below the mouth of Turtle Creek, and that it derives its name from General Braddock, who was there met and defeated by the French and Indians, after an engagement of three hours' duration, July 10th, 1755, as we have stated more at length in a previous chapter. But the town is of a much more recent date. The first white settler in the place was one John Frazier, an Indian trader. Washington speaks of him as having been driven from Venango by the French, and it is probable that he came to Turtle Creek in the spring of 1753. He established a trading post on the bank of the river, immediately below the mouth of the creek, where he was visited by Major Washington on his mission to the French. His name does not occur after the defeat of Gen. Braddock.*

A village began to spring up on the historic spot early in the present century, but it was not until the completion of the Pennsylvania Railroad to this point, in November, 1851, that it began to attain to any importance. The ground rises gently from the river, and the railroad passes through the back of the town; while the Baltimore and Ohio Railroad runs near the river. The Edgar Thompson Steel Works, built a few years ago and now being constantly enlarged, have added considerably to the size and importance of the place. The town was incorporated in 1867, and has at present a population of about 3500.†

CHAPEL AT TARRA HILL.

But Catholics were not among the first settlers at Braddock's Field. On the opposite side of the river, however, a few farmers and miners located themselves, and a small brick chapel was built for them on the brow of the hill by one of the priests attached to the Cathedral. The place was called Tarra Hill, or Green Springs, and was usually visited on one Sunday in the month until after the church had been built at Braddock's Field and a regular pastor appointed, about the year 1863. From that date Mass was not celebrated, and the

---

* Washington's Journal.
† Hist. Alleg. Co., pp. 24, 161.

chapel, which seems never to have been dedicated to any particular saint, but which is yet standing, is now devoted to other uses.

ST. THOMAS' CHURCH, BRADDOCK'S FIELD.

A few Catholic families at length found their way into Braddock's Field and Port Perry, on the opposite side of Turtle Creek, and Mass was occasionally celebrated, now in one place, now in the other, in a private house by one of the priests attached to the Cathedral. When this commenced or how long it continued is uncertain; but at length the Bishop determined to have a church erected. Rev. Jas. Treacy, of St. Bridget's Church, Pittsburg, visited the place and purchased a large lot; but the organization of the parish and the erection of the church were confided to Rev. Thos. O'Farrel, of the Cathedral. Work was commenced on the foundation, and the corner-stone was laid by Father O'Farrel April 22d, 1860. The church stands on the front of a gentle rise, and thus affords a basement under half its length. This basement was finished, roofed in, and first opened for divine service October 14th, 1860. But it was not until the end of two years that the church was finished and ready for dedication. The ceremony was performed by the Bishop October 28th, 1862, and the church was placed under the invocation of St. Thomas the Apostle. It is a brick building modelled after the Gothic style of architecture, and is rather substantial than elegant in its finish. The church was then about 50 feet in length by 40 in width,—it has since been enlarged,—with a tower rising from the centre in front, of which only the brickwork is built.

The congregation was visited from the Cathedral until February, 1863, when Rev. C. V. Neeson, one of the professors of St. Michael's Seminary, was appointed pastor, but with the obligation of residing and teaching at the seminary and visiting the church on Sunday. He was succeeded, at the end of 1866, by Rev. W. A. Nolan, who also resided at the seminary. At the end of October of the following year he gave place to Rev. Peter Hughes. He took up his residence with the congregation, and in the latter half of 1869 built an elegant brick dwelling.

About the year 1870 he built a cheap hall, which he soon after fitted up for school-rooms. Here school has since been held by lay teachers. The next year he enlarged the church, by the addition of about 25 feet to its length, and otherwise improved the interior.

At length, after he had ministered to the congregation for eleven years, it pleased God to call Father Hughes to a better life. Few of his brother-priests had heard of his illness, when they were pained with the news of his death from cerebro-spinal meningitis on the evening of November 26th, 1879. He was then in the 49th year of his age and the 24th of his ministry. His illness was of short duration, but conscious that death must ensue he received the last rites of the Church, and calmly awaited the final summons. His funeral took place from St. Thomas' Church, and his remains repose in St. Mary's Cemetery, Pittsburg.

REV. PETER HUGHES was a native of county Monaghan, Ireland. Having prosecuted his studies for some time in the seminary of St. M'Cartan, in the town of Monaghan, he emigrated to the United States and entered the seminary of St. Charles Borromeo, Philadelphia. Upon the completion of his course of theology he was raised to the sacred dignity of the priesthood by Bishop O'Connor, in the Cathedral of Pittsburg, August 15th, 1856. He remained at the Cathedral as an assistant until October, 1859, when he was transferred to Murrinsville. At the end of two years he was placed in charge of the Huntingdon mission; and when that was divided, in the spring of 1863, he located himself at Broad Top, in the same county. Here he built a church and residence; and having ministered to the congregation until July, 1868, he came to Wilmore. At the end of October of the same year he was transferred to Braddock's Field, which was destined to witness the closing scenes of his labors. Father Hughes was a zealous and energetic priest, a man of well-defined views and principles, and an ardent advocate of right.

Upon the death of Father Hughes, Rev. M. J. Mitchell, of the Mercy Hospital, Pittsburg, was appointed to the vacant post; but, owing to the size of the congregation, he is generally assisted on Sundays by a member of one of the religious orders in Pittsburg.

The greater part of the congregation resides in the town, but there are a few members scattered through the surrounding country to the distance of three or four miles. It is increasing at an encouraging rate in the present, and must continue to add to its members in the future.

ST. JOSEPH'S GERMAN CHURCH, BRADDOCK'S FIELD.

In the course of time a German element began to infuse itself into the English congregation at Braddock's Field, and in the summer of 1877 the people petitioned for a church of their own nationality. Having considered the matter attentively, the Bishop acceded to their request, and at the end of August sent Rev. Anthony Fisher, lately ordained, to organize the parish. He rented a hall for the use of the congregation until such time as it should be able to undertake the erection of a church; and Mass has since been celebrated there. He also rented a house for himself. A school was opened by a lay teacher in a room adjoining the church. Lots were also purchased as the site of a future church, and a temporary hall was built on them for fairs, etc. The congregation will number perhaps sixty families, and is still under the pastoral care of Father Fisher.

M'KEESPORT.

The borough of M'Keesport is situated on the east banks of the Monongahela and the Youghiogheny rivers at their confluence, about fifteen miles south-east of Pittsburg. The Pittsburg division of the Baltimore and Ohio Railroad passes through the town, and the Pittsburg, Virginia and Charleston Railroad passes up the opposite side of the Monongahela. The history of the place, both civil and religious, is interesting. Before the Indians had yielded possession to the white man they had a village there, the home of the celebrated Aliquippa, Queen of the Delawares. Her royal highness took offence at

Major Washington for not calling on her when on his way to the French posts, in the north-western part of the State, in the fall of 1753. But on his return, he says in his journal, "I made her a present of a watch-coat and a bottle of rum, which latter was thought much the better present of the two." In the year 1755 David M'Kee, a Scotch Presbyterian, settled there, and the place soon after became known as "the Forks of the Yough"—the name by which the Youghiohenny River is frequently designated. A ferry was soon after established, by which pioneers crossed the Monongahela, and from which the place was also called "M'Kee's Ferry." At length, in 1794, John M'Kee, a son of the original proprietor, had a town, which consisted of about two hundred large lots, regularly laid out. "The price of lots was twenty dollars, and the deeds were made by lottery for choice of position. Each person was to pay ten dollars when he purchased his ticket, and the remainder when his purchase was located and his deed secured. On the 26th of March, 1795, he had sold one hundred and eighty lots, but had as yet given no name to the town, and it was not till some time in November of the same year that the name M'Kee's Port was finally settled upon"—a name which in time assumed the present form. "As an incentive for parties to locate in the new town, it was told them that the place was 'twelve miles nearer to Philadelphia' than Pittsburg."* It was not until September 3d, 1842, when it contained a population of about 500, that it was incorporated as a borough. The present population is about 5000.

ST. PETER'S CHURCH.

The first Catholic families who settled in the town and its vicinity were Germans; but it would now be difficult to determine the date of their arrival. This much, however, is known with certainty, that prior to the year 1846 they were sufficiently numerous to excite the zeal of the Redemptorist fathers of Pittsburg, who had already begun to visit them at regular intervals. They were also visited at times from the

---

* History of Allegheny County, pp. 162, 163.

Cathedral. In that year they purchased a lot and commenced to build a church. Providence smiled upon their labors and sacrifices, and the church was finished the following spring, when it was dedicated under the invocation of St. Peter the Apostle by Rev. M. Müller, C.SS.R., April 5th, 1847. This church was built of brick, and was about 50 feet in length by 30 in width, with a small belfry. The congregation was visited from Pittsburg for about a year longer, after which time Rev. Nicholas Hœres was appointed resident pastor, with the additional obligation of visiting certain other missions further up the Monongahela. For several years he lodged in the sacristy of the church as best he could, but he finally built a small frame house near the church, in which he spent the closing years of his ministry.

Nothing of special interest occurred until the summer of 1862. At that time the railroad was opened through the town, and it was thought that by facilitating manufacture it would induce laborers to settle and thus increase the congregation, which up to that time had grown but little. But the congregation was destined to sustain a loss in the death of its zealous pastor, who for fourteen years had ministered to its spiritual necessities. Father Hœres came to the diocesan seminary in company with many other priests to perform the exercises of the annual retreat. But hardly had he entered upon them when he was taken sick. After suffering for three days he gave up his soul to God on the 18th of July, 1862, surrounded by his brothers in the sacred ministry. The funeral took place from M'Keesport, where his remains repose.

REV. NICHOLAS HŒRES was born at Schleida, in the Grand Duchy of Saxe Weimar, Germany, in March, 1802. After having completed his studies in his native land, he was ordained in 1831. He came to America and to the Diocese of Pittsburg in 1846, and was assistant at the church in Loretto until he was transferred to M'Keesport.

The first few years immediately succeeding his death were marked by numerous changes in the pastors of the church. Among these was Rev. Cajetan Klœker, who was pastor in the early part of 1865. But finding that consumption was undermining his health, he withdrew to the Mercy Hospital, Pittsburg, where he expired on the 18th of May of that year.

REV. CAJETAN KLŒKER was born at Hurbach, in Upper Bavaria, March 24th, 1819. Having finished his course of studies, he was ordained in 1853. Like many other generous souls to whom the Church in this county owes a deep debt of gratitude, he was moved by the wants of the infant church, and came to minister where the harvest was ready but the laborers were few. In the Diocese of Pittsburg he labored in various missions, among which were St. Mary's, Allegheny, where he was assistant for a time; then he was pastor of St. Mary's, Chartier's Creek; St. John the Baptist's, Harman Bottom; Sts. Peter and Paul's, East Liberty; St. Mary's, Pine Creek; and finally the church from which he was called to his reward.

Among his successors, Rev. John B. Smith remained the longest. Up to that date the congregation was largely composed of Germans. But during his stay he built, about the year 1868, a church at Bull's Run, about two miles from M'Keesport on the opposite side of the Monongahela, which drew away a large number of the Germans who lived on that side. The accessions to the congregation have been of English-speaking Catholics for the most part, so that the parish, although still containing a small number of Germans, is now English. At length, 1870, the present pastor, Rev. James Nolan, was appointed. The congregation had so far increased by this time as to demand more ample accommodations than were afforded by the little church. To this the pastor directed his attention. A school-house was also needed. Accordingly, in 1872, he commenced the erection of a brick school-house 65 feet in length by 32 in width and two stories high, the lower story of which was to be used as a school of two rooms, and the upper as the church till the new church should be built, which was to occupy the site of the old one. This building, which is neat and substantial, was finished early in the winter of the same year, and the room destined for a church was dedicated by Bishop Domenec January 19th, 1873. In the following summer a frame dwelling-house, with the large lot upon which it stood, was purchased, and soon after it was considerably enlarged and became the residence of the pastor. At the same time the church was undertaken. The cornerstone was laid by the Bishop September 14th, 1873. The congregation had been rapidly increasing in the past few years, thanks to the erection of extensive iron-works which brought a large number of Irish Catholics, who are acknowledged on all hands to be the nerve and sinew of religion in this county, so far at least as the English element is concerned. Two years were required to complete the church, and during that time the panic prostrated business and limited the resources of this as of many other congregations. Sunday, September 12th, 1875, was the day set apart for the solemn ceremony of dedicating the new church, and preparations were made in keeping with the magnificent temple that was to become the house of God and the place of his dwelling upon earth. The ceremony was performed by the Bishop of the diocese, and the sermon was preached by Bishop Ryan, of Buffalo. The church is one of the most substantial and beautiful in the diocese, and is in the pure Gothic style. It is built of brick, and is 130 feet in length by 65 in width, having a tower in the centre in front 175 feet high. In the interior the nave is 46 feet in height, but without a clerestory, and the aisles, which are separated from it by elegant pillars, are 30 feet in height. There are three marble altars in harmony with the style of the church, which are separated from the body of the church by a massive railing that runs across the building. The pews, pulpit, gallery, organ, and confessionals are finished in a style in keeping with that of the sacred edifice; while the windows are filled with stained glass in pleasing and appropriate designs. To the right of the entrance, in a recess prepared for it, stands the baptismal-font, enclosed by a tasteful railing. Taken as a whole, the church is entitled to a place in the first rank among our churches in point of purity in the style of architecture and completeness of finish.

When the church was finished the chapel in the schoolhouse was abandoned, and was divided into two school-rooms. The school was as yet in charge of lay teachers; but in September, 1876, a foundation was obtained of Sisters of Mercy from Pittsburg, who came to take charge of the schools. They took possession of the pastoral residence as a convent, which they still occupy, and the pastor rented a house for himself for a time. But in the fall of 1877 he built a frame house to the rear of the church, and thus completed all the buildings necessary for the congregation.

The erection of so many buildings in so short a time necessarily left a considerable debt; but this will yield in time to the prudence and energy that has been displayed in the management of the finances in the past. The congregation is in a flourishing condition, and will number perhaps three hundred and fifty families; and it has a far better prospect of increasing in the future than almost any other in the diocese.

ST. AGNES' CHURCH, BULL'S RUN.

St. Agnes' Church stands in a country place about two miles west of M'Keesport, on the opposite side of the Monongahela. The people residing in that neighborhood belonged in the beginning to the church at M'Keesport; but becoming sufficiently numerous in time to build a church for themselves, they determined to undertake it. Encouraged by their pastor, they commenced work about the year 1868. When finished the church was dedicated, under the invocation of St. Agnes, by the Bishop on the 1st of August, 1869. Rev. J. Döffner was the first resident pastor. The church is a neat frame building capable of seating about four hundred; and has a basement that has since been used for a school-room. When Father Döffner was transferred to St. Peter's, Pittsburg, Rev. Geo. Gunkle became pastor of St. Agnes', a position which he occupied until the fall of 1873. He was succeeded by Rev. John Willman. Prior to that date a house had been built for the pastor, and a school had been opened by a lay teacher in the basement of the church, which has continued with occasional interruptions to the present time. Towards the close of 1875 Father Willman withdrew, and the congregation was deprived of a resident pastor, but visited every Sunday by one of the Capuchin fathers from Pittsburg. At length, in October, 1877, the present pastor, Rev. Fred, Eberth, was transferred from Freeport to St. Agnes'.

The congregation is composed almost exclusively of Germans, and contains perhaps one hundred and twenty-five families, miners and farmers. Its future increase will be very moderate if we are to judge from present indications.

ST. PATRICK'S CHURCH, ALPSVILLE.

Alpsville is situated on the eastern bank of the Youghioghenny River, about twenty-one miles from Pittsburg, and on the line of the Baltimore and Ohio Railroad. Being one of the many mining villages on the river, its fortunes fluctuate with those of the coal trade. Prior to the erection of the church, Mass had been celebrated in a private house on one Sunday in the month by the pastor of Elizabeth. When at length the number of Catholics had considerably increased it was determined to build a church. The organization of the parish and the erection of the church were confided to Rev. P. M. Ward, one of the professors of the diocesan seminary. The corner-stone was laid by Bishop Domenec September 23d, 1866; and the church was dedicated, under the invocation of St. Patrick, by Very Rev. T. Mullen, V.G., September 1st of the following year. It is a brick building about 75 feet in length by 35 in width, and has a steeple rising from the centre in front. The style of architecture approaches the Gothic. There are three altars, and the whole interior is elegantly finished, making it one of the most beautiful of the smaller churches of the diocese. Father Ward resided a part of the time with the congregation and a part at the seminary, and continued to fill the position of pastor until permanently located in the city about the beginning of 1871, when Rev. Peter May became pastor of St. Patrick's. He built a small frame school-house soon after his appointment, to which he transferred the school from the rented room in which it had already been taught for at least three years. Having remained until June, 1873, he was transferred to Mansfield, and succeeded by Rev. John Staub. During his pastorate the panic fell upon the country, and Alpsville has not yet recovered from its prostrating effects.

He was succeeded after an interval by the present pastor, Rev. Jas. M'Tighe.

For a few years after the erection of the church, stations were held further up the river at Sutersville and Smithton, as will be seen when we come to treat of the church in Westmoreland County; and after having had a resident pastor for a short time, they again reverted to the pastor of Alpsville, and so they remain at present.

ST. MICHAEL'S CHURCH, ELIZABETH.

Elizabeth, or Elizabethtown as it was originally called, is situated on the eastern bank of the Monongahela River, twenty-two miles from Pittsburg, and is the oldest town in Allegheny County. The original owner of the place was Thomas Monroe, who obtained a patent for the land upon which the town is built in 1769. In 1784 Stephen Bayard purchased the land and laid out the town, naming it Elizabethtown in honor of his wife. In its early history it obtained a small measure of notoriety for boat-building. It was not incorporated, however, until April 5th, 1834; and its population in 1870 was about 1196.* On the opposite side of the river, which is very narrow here, is West Elizabeth, with a population of 590, through which the Pittsburg, Virginia and Charleston Railroad passes. Like the entire Monongahela Valley, Elizabeth is principally noted for its trade in coal.

Catholics settled in the river valley from Brownsville down early in the present century; but their number was so small as not to form the nucleus of a congregation until a comparatively recent date. They were occasionally visited by a priest from Brownsville or Pittsburg, from as early as 1830; and when their numbers had sufficiently increased to form a regular missionary station they were visited at fixed times by one of the priests attached to the Cathedral, and were known

---

* History of Allegheny County, p. 162.

as "the river missions." Time passed, and the Catholic population increased, especially after the coal trade began to assume its present gigantic proportions. The first notice we have of the formation of a parish at Elizabeth is in the year 1849 when, and for a year or two longer, the mission—for as yet there was no church—was visited by Rev. N. Hœres, of M'Keesport. The erection of a church was soon after commenced; and upon its completion it was dedicated under the invocation of the Archangel St. Michael, September 28th, 1851. It is an unassuming brick building, about 60 feet in length by 35 in width, is surmounted by a small spire, and has a sacristy built against the rear. It occupies a commanding position at the back of the town. The congregation was now placed under the jurisdiction of the pastor of Brownsville, who visited it generally on one Sunday in the month. The pastor of M'Keesport, it would appear, also paid the church an occasional visit. At length, in the summer of 1860, Rev. Thos. Quinn was appointed first resident pastor; but he withdrew after a short time. In the autumn of the following year Rev. Denis Kearney became pastor. One of his first acts was the purchase of a neat brick house near the church; for previous to that date the congregation possessed no residence for the pastor. He also purchased a small piece of ground about half a mile from the town for a cemetery. But his labors were not confined exclusively to Elizabeth. Monongahela City and a number of stations were also dependent on his ministrations. Then as now St. Michael's received but every alternate Sunday. It may be stated here, once for all, that there have always existed at different points along the river, from Brownsville down to M'Keesport, a number of stations at different coal-mines, which were, and still are, visited on week-days as often as the spiritual necessities of the people require or the circumstances of the pastor permit; for the Catholic population is composed of miners, with a very small number of farmers. Father Kearney remained at Elizabeth until the beginning of 1867, when he was transferred to Sharpsburg, and Rev. W. F. Hayes became pastor. Soon after his appointment he built a small wooden school-house, and opened a school with a lay teacher. But it was difficult to continue it, owing to the fact that a large number of the children lived on the opposite side of the river, which they could not cross without danger and expense. It was soon closed, and has not since been opened, nor will it be for many years from present indications. Father Hayes was succeeded in March, 1871, by Rev. M. J. Brazill, who remained until declining health forced him to withdraw in the autumn of 1872. He stopped at the episcopal residence for a short time, and then retired to the Mercy Hospital, where the disease, consumption, from which he suffered terminated his edifying life, November 9th, 1873.

REV. MARTIN J. BRAZILL was a native of Ireland, where, having pursued his studies for some time, he determined to devote himself to the American mission. He crossed the Atlantic and entered the diocesan seminary of Pittsburg. Having finished his course of theology he went to Dubuque, of which diocese his uncle, Very Rev. J. F. Brazill, was and is yet Vicar-General, where he was ordained in the beginning of 1867. Having labored there for about three years, he visited his native land. On returning to America he obtained permission to attach himself to the Diocese of Pittsburg, and in April, 1870, was appointed pastor of the church at Cameron Bottom. From there he was transferred to Elizabeth. At the time of his death he was about thirty years of age. Few young priests were more highly or more deservedly esteemed than Father Brazill.

Rev. P. M. Garvey now became pastor of Elizabeth, a position which he continued to occupy until the fall of 1877, when, after a brief interval, he was succeeded by the present incumbent, Rev. Francis M'Court.

Owing to the fluctuations of the coal trade, the intrigues of employers, and the strikes of miners, a congregation of miners is one of the most fickle of earthly things. It may count a hundred families to-day, and not more than half that number in half a month. This being kept in mind, the nearest approximation perhaps that can be made to the number of families at Elizabeth would be to place it at about seventy. The circumstances of such a congregation are as fluctuating as its numbers; for when "in" the miners generally make good wages, but when "out" they are frequently reduced to the verge of starvation. The Catholic will increase with the growth of the general population.

CHURCH OF THE TRANSFIGURATION, MONONGAHELA CITY, WASHINGTON COUNTY.

This church, although not in Allegheny County, is and always has been so intimately connected with that at Elizabeth that it is most appropriately sketched in connection with it. Monongahela City is situated on the west bank of the river of the same name, thirty-one miles from Pittsburg, and is on the line of the Pittsburg, Virginia and Charleston Railroad. It was first known as Parkinson's Ferry, and was a noted crossing for pioneers. During the Whiskey Insurrection—from 1791-'94—it was the scene of the most important meetings. The name was afterwards changed to Williamsport, which in turn gave place, about the year 1840, to the present designation.* Its moderate growth may be ascertained from the fact that while in 1840 it had a population of 752, it had increased to but 1078 in 1870.

The first Mass celebrated in the town was on Palm Sunday, 1835, by Rev. J. O'Reilly, from St. Paul's, Pittsburg, although Mass had been celebrated for several years at a place about three miles back of the town, where half a dozen families lived. Later the town was visited from Brownsville. But from the time that a resident priest was appointed for Elizabeth it was attached to that mission, and generally visited on every alternate Sunday. The Catholics increased very gradually, although even yet there are but few in the town, the greater part being distributed among the mines along the river in both directions; and it was not until 1865 that a church was thought necessary. The corner-stone was laid by the Bishop August 13th of that year, and the church when completed was dedicated by the same prelate some time in the course of the following year under the title of the Transfiguration. In its style, proportions, and material it is the

* Day's Historical Collections, pp. 669-671.

counterpart of that at Elizabeth. The congregation, too, is of precisely the same character, and is of about the same numerical strength. The increase will be very moderate, and it will be a long time before Monongahela City will require a resident pastor. The Protestant population of that part of the Monongahela valley, being well seasoned with Calvinistic leaven, is by no means liberal. The Catholic population suffers considerably from the evil effects of mixed marriages.

CHAPTER XIII.

CHURCHES OF ALLEGHENY COUNTY (CONCLUDED).

St. Philip's Church, Broadhead—St. Luke's Church, Mansfield—Death and sketch of Rev. J. O'G. Scanlon—St. Joseph's German Church, Mansfield—St. Patrick's Church, Noblestown — St. Mary's German Church, Chartier's Creek — St. James' Church, Sewickley—St. Mary's German Church, Glenfield—St. Alphonsus' Church, Wexford—St. Teresa's Church, Perrysville—St. Mary's Church, Pine Creek—Death and sketch of Rev. M. Eigner—St. Joseph's Church, Sharpsburg—St. Mary's German Church—St. Anne's Church, Millvale.

ST. PHILIP'S CHURCH, BROADHEAD.

THE spot occupied by this church—for there is neither town nor village—was so named in honor of Col. Broadhead, at one time commander at Fort Pitt. From an early day a few Catholic families settled in the vicinity. Before the erection of the church they attended the Cathedral, and occasionally Mass was celebrated for them in one of their own dwellings.

At length a Mr. Philip Smith, of Philadelphia, who owned property in the vicinity, donated a lot sufficient for a church and cemetery; and the erection of the building was soon after undertaken. Upon its completion it was dedicated by Bishop Kenrick, July 25th, 1839, under the invocation of St. Philip the Apostle, that name having been selected out of gratitude to the donor of the site. The church is a small brick building, about 40 feet in length by 25 in width, with low ceiling, one altar, and a little belfry, and is situated on the northern side of the Pittsburg, Cincinnati and St. Louis Railroad, near Crafton Station, about three miles south-west of Pittsburg. The fortunes of this church, like those of nearly all the smaller country churches, have been varied. At first a priest visited it from the Cathedral; but in the autumn of 1840 it, together with two or three others, was confided to the care of Rev. A. P. Gibbs, who resided in the city and visited it on one Sunday in the month. At the date of the formation of the diocese it was said by the Bishop to contain 150 souls. From 1844 it was visited for a few years by Rev. Thos. M'Cullagh, and after him by others, usually once in the month, until the organization of St. James' congregation, Temperanceville, 1854, when the two formed one mission for about twelve years. The church was then enlarged by the addition of perhaps 25 feet to its length. After that time it was attached to St. Luke's Church, Mansfield, or St. Mary's, Chartier's Creek, except for the time that it had a separate pastor, and was visited every Sunday. During the summer of 1874 it had a resident pastor, Rev. John Ward; but it again became dependent until the fall of 1877, since which time it has again a resident pastor.

Little change has taken place in the congregation beyond a very moderate growth; and a part of this was cut off for the benefit of surrounding churches. The construction of the railroad enhanced the importance of the place by inducing some of the wealthier families of the city to build residences in the vicinity. Although numbering no more perhaps than forty families, it is more flourishing than many that are larger. But its future growth will be necessarily slow, and it will be many years before its condition will undergo any notable change. The congregation has never been able to open a parish school or build a pastoral residence. The present pastor is Rev. Jas. Kenoy.

ST. LUKE'S CHURCH, MANSFIELD.

Mansfield is a flourishing borough, about seven miles southwest of Pittsburg, on the line of the Pittsburg, Cincinnati and St. Louis Railroad, at the point where the Chartier's Valley road branches off to Washington, Pa. It took its name from Mr. Mansfield Brown, original proprietor of the land, and was incorporated as a borough in 1872. The town owes its importance principally to the coal-mines in the vicinity and to the residences which business men of Pittsburg have erected there. A small amount of manufacturing is also carried on. The ground upon which the town is built is undulating, with the exception of the valley of the creek, which is low and damp and frequently threatened with inundation.

Catholics were among the first inhabitants. But in the beginning they heard Mass at St. Philip's, Broadhead, or came to the city on the cars. At length, in October, 1866, Rev. J. O'G. Scanlon was appointed pastor of Washington and the missions attached to it. It was at this time that Mansfield began to attain the proportions of a town, and give promise of becoming a place of future importance. Father Scanlon, who knew well the importance of securing property as soon as possible, cast about him for the site of a future church. He first purchased a lot in the northern part of the town near the creek, which had a frame house erected on it. A room was fitted up in it and became the first church in Mansfield. In June, 1868, Rev. Thos. M'Enrue was ordained and stationed at Washington, while Fr. Scanlon confined his labors exclusively to Mansfield, which was fast becoming a flourishing congregation. From that date the town has been favored with a resident pastor. Mass may have been celebrated before the arrival of Fr. Scanlon, but of this there is no authentic record. But the new purchase was low and damp, and unsuited for the erection of a large building. Seeing this he soon after purchased another lot, not far from the former, having a small brick residence and a little frame store-room on it which had before been used as a warehouse for wool. The store was converted into a chapel, and dedicated by the Bishop July 28th, 1867, under the invocation of St. Luke; although for a long time after it was better known as "the Catholic wool-house." But it was soon crowded to excess by the rapidly increasing congregation, and additional accommodations were demanded. A new part was then built to the rear. The front is now two stories high and the rear only one, but this one as high as the front two, which leaves the church unrivalled in style. The whole is 70 feet long by 25 wide, and is as neatly finished and decorated in the interior as its peculiar character will permit. But the purchase was an unfortunate step, the site being less fitted for a church than the former lot.

In the midst of its prosperity the congregation was destined to sustain a loss in the death of its zealous pastor. His health, which had of late been giving way under his untiring labors, was much more impaired than either he or his friends imagined. With a view of recruiting it he retired to the Mercy Hospital about the beginning of May, 1871. But his course was run, and he expired somewhat suddenly on the morning of the 8th of May, in the thirty-third year of his age and the ninth of his ministry. His funeral took place from the Cathedral, and was one of the largest ever witnessed in the city. His remains were interred in St. Mary's Cemetery; and a beautiful monument was erected over them soon after by the congregation for whose spiritual welfare he had so generously toiled.

REV. JOHN O'GORMAN SCANLON was born in the barony of Dushallow, county Cork, Ireland, in 1838, and, having completed his course of studies in the Missionary College of Carlow, he came to this country in the company of three other students in the summer of 1862, and entered St. Michael's Seminary. On the 7th of the following February he was ordained, and was appointed pastor of St. Mary's Church, Kittanning. Having labored in that mission until December, 1865, he was transferred to St. Patrick's Church, Sugar Creek, where he remained until his appointment to Washington. He was a man of unusual energy and perseverance, and had with these a degree of enthusiasm in the cause of religion which made him feel in his element when grappling with difficulties.

He was succeeded by Rev. W. A. Nolan, during whose pastorate the congregation continued to increase so rapidly as to render a new church indispensable. The unfitness of the site of the old church, as well as the fact that it was not thought by many to be sufficiently central, led them to prefer another location. It was soon found, yet work was commenced on the foundation of a new edifice near the old one in the spring of 1873. But it became necessary to discontinue until greater harmony should prevail. At the end of June Fr. Nolan was transferred to Freeport, and was suceeded by Rev. P. May

The panic soon after prostrated business, and the new church was left to a future time. About the same time a pastor was appointed for St. Philip's Church, and the priest at Mansfield has since been left to St. Luke's alone. After two years Fr. May was succeeded, in July, 1875, by Rev. Thos. Walsh. During this time the congregation, although as numerous as before, had deteriorated in wealth and importance, owing to the general prostration of business. The numerous strikes among the coal-miners in this and in every part of the coal regions are a misfortune generally as great for the miners themselves as for their employers and the public. They have their grievances as well as other classes, but they seek a most imprudent way of redressing them; and many, if not the greater part, being Catholics, their ill-directed course is not unfrequently laid to the charge of the religion they profess. Fr. Walsh gave place, April, 1877, to Rev. Hugh Haggerty, the present pastor. The condition of the congregation has considerably improved, and it is destined in time to become one of the most flourishing and important congregations outside the city. The new church was at length commenced in August, 1879, and is at present in course of erection. It will be in the Gothic style, 120 feet in length by 54 in width, with a tower in the centre in front.

A school was taught for several years in the room over the church; but it was discontinued in the year 1877, until the circumstances of the congregation should improve.

The pastor of this church also visits and ministers to the spiritual necessities of the few Catholic inmates of the Allegheny County Home, a State charitable institution situated about three miles from Mansfield, on the Chartier's Valley Railroad.

ST. JOSEPH'S GERMAN CHURCH, MANSFIELD.

In Mansfield, as in nearly all other towns, a German element soon began to infuse itself into the English. As their numbers increased they determined to build a church for themselves; and for this purpose a meeting was called on the 8th of June, 1879. A committee was appointed to carry out the designs of the meeting; lots were purchased, and work was commenced. The corner-stone was laid by Rev. W. Pollard September 21st, 1879; and the church when finished was dedicated by the Bishop, under the patronage of St. Joseph, on New Year's Day, 1880. The church is a brick building 30 by 65 feet, and is chaste and simple in style and finish. Rev. J. Stillerich was soon after appointed pastor. The congregation numbers about seventy-five families.

ST. PATRICK'S CHURCH, NOBLESTOWN.

Noblestown, on the line of the Pittsburg, Cincinnati and St. Louis Railroad, fifteen miles south-west of Pittsburg, takes its name from Henry Noble, who settled there about the year 1773. But it owes the little importance it has to the extensive coal-mines and stone-quarries operated in the vicinity. Soon after the opening of the railroad, about twenty-two years ago, a number of Catholic families began to be attracted to the mines; but it does not appear that Mass was celebrated in the village before the autumn of 1865. For some months subsequent to that date Rev. J. Stillerich, of St. Mary's Church, Chartier's Creek, visited the place, and a church was contemplated. It was next attended from Washington, and constituted a part of that mission until the appointment of a resident pastor. In the fall of 1866 Rev. J. P. Tahaney rented a hall for the accommodation of the little flock, and from that time Mass was celebrated on one Sunday in the month. He was succeeded by Rev. J. O'G. Scanlon, who bought a house for the priest. But the Washington mission was soon after divided, and he located himself at Mansfield, as has been said, Rev. Thos. M'Enrue being stationed at the former place. He immediately took the church in hand, and succeeded in erecting the existing edifice. I have not learned the date of its dedication; but it was probably in 1869. The church is a brick building about 70 feet in length by 35 in width, and has a tower in the centre in front.

Father M'Enrue was succeeded by Rev. Jas. Canivan in January, 1873. But it now became necessary to divide the

Washington mission once more and appoint a resident pastor to Noblestown, and Father Canivan was stationed there in June. But the panic soon after set in, and the congregation, which up to that time had enjoyed unusual prosperity and was growing apace, was reduced to the verge of want from the complete cessation of work in the mines and quarries upon which the people depended. No other congregation in the diocese was so utterly prostrated; and many families have since been on the verge of starvation. Father Canivan was succeeded by the present pastor, Rev. E. Murray, in September, 1877.

In the days of its prosperity the congregation numbered perhaps eighty families, American and Irish with a few Germans; but at present, although slowly rising from its prostration, it is much smaller. There are also a few families of French who should be Catholics, but who have fallen away from the faith. The future of the congregation will depend upon that of the coal trade; but the Catholic population must, in the nature of things, increase.

It remains to be seen what effect the opening of the new Pittsburg and Lake Erie Railroad, which traverses the southern bank of the Ohio River a distance of twenty-seven miles, will have upon the increase of the Catholic population. The rise of villages on the line will doubtless add to their number; but it is highly probable that manufactories will be erected, laborers brought together, and new congregations established in a few years.

ST. MARY'S GERMAN CHURCH, CHARTIER'S CREEK.

This little church stands on the banks of Chartier's Creek, about a mile south of the Ohio River and four miles west of Pittsburg, and was built under the direction of the Passionist fathers from St. Michael's Church, Pittsburg, to which, or to the church at Broadhead, three miles distant, the people had formerly belonged. The corner-stone was laid by Father Luke in the summer of 1855, and the church was probably dedicated some time in the following year, but the precise date has not been ascertained. In size, style, and material it is the exact counterpart of that at Broadhead. After having been attended for a year or two from St. Michael's, a resident pastor was appointed, an advantage which it has since continued to enjoy. But the changes were frequent, and the names of all have not been transmitted to us. The present pastor is Rev. J. Zwickert. Near the church stands a frame pastoral residence, one room of which is now, and has for many years been, used for a school, in which a lay teacher instructs the children of the parish. The congregation is composed of German farmers and city gardeners, a frugal, industrious, and thrifty people; and it will probably number no more than sixty families.

ST. JAMES' CHURCH.

Crossing the Ohio River we reach the borough of Sewickley, which is on the north bank sixteen miles below Pittsburg. "It is one of the most favorable situations on the Ohio, and has been settled by wealthy families, who have united in making it an elegant suburban place of residence. For this purpose they have strenuously opposed all attempts to introduce manufactories into the place, and have even refused to give their support to such necessary institutions as hotels. Consequently, although it is a place of between two and three thousand inhabitants, there is at present (1873) not a single public house within its limits. . . . The borough was incorporated in 1854." *

The first Catholics of the place were a few families, principally Germans, living in the vicinity and a few servant-girls employed in the houses of the wealthier citizens (for good Catholic girls are sought after, and generally find situations without much difficulty about Pittsburg.) Rev. Jas. Reid, of Beaver, was the first to look after the spiritual necessities of the people. He secured a lot; and built a cheap little frame church, probably about the year 1862. But the date is uncertain, as are all dates relating to this church; for notwithstanding that I have been at more pains to secure reliable information

* History of Allegheny County, p. 174.

regarding this than any other of the smaller churches, I cannot flatter myself with the success of my efforts. No one, it would appear, takes an interest in it. Fr. Reid continued to visit the place until the year 1868, when Rev. J. Zwickert was appointed resident pastor. Soon after his arrival he determined to replace the existing church by a more imposing edifice, and with the consent of the proper authority he undertook it, although as yet the congregation was quite small. The church was built; but, owing to grave defects in the plan, it fell to the ground when the workmen had finished the roof. Nothing daunted, he commenced another. It was completed and dedicated, and must always remain one of the most unaccountable instances of miscalculation ever witnessed in this country. For while the congregation will number no more than thirty families, with perhaps forty servant-girls, and has no prospect whatever of doubling itself in the next twenty-five years, the church, which to some extent is modelled after the Gothic style of architecture, is about 130 feet long by 50 feet wide, and has a tall spire in the centre in front. The interior is furnished with three altars, gallery, etc., and the ceiling rises steep from the sides to the centre, following the inclination of the roof. If it was not for the heavy walls and buttresses, the roof, which is not framed so as to be in a measure self-sustaining, would by its thrust force the walls asunder and leave the building a heap of ruins. The church could without difficulty be made to accommodate a congregation of five hundred families.

The history of the congregation has been uneventful save that its existence has been an incessant struggle with the heavy debt incurred in the erection of the two churches; and the future will be but a repetition of the past. As to increase, it is almost imperceptible. In the summer of 1877 Father Zwickert was succeeded by Rev. Jas. Rommelfanger, who remained until the latter part of May, 1879, when the congregation was visited by a priest from Pittsburg until the end of August, when Rev. J. Price became pastor. What the future of the parish is destined to be it would be hazardous to conjecture. A school has at different times been taught in the old church, which is yet standing. After an interval it was resumed about two years ago, and continues to the present time.

ST. MARY'S GERMAN CHURCH, GLENFIELD.

This church is situated in a country place two miles north of the Ohio River, at a point about twelve miles below Pittsburg. It was formerly called the Kilbuck church, the township in which it stands being so named from Kilbuck, a Delaware Indian chief. "It is said by some of the old residents that *Kilbuck* is buried in the township, and an Indian grave is still shown as his. As there are several warriors who bore that name, it is quite possible that the assertion is correct; but Captain Henry Kilbuck, from whom the run was named, died and was buried near Wheeling, West Virginia."* The place was then named Glendale, which has lately been changed to Glenfield.

The Catholics who compose the little flock settled here many years ago—it would be difficult to fix the date—but the church, like other German churches in this part of the diocese, is due to the zeal of the indefatigable Father Stiebel. As near as can be ascertained it was built in 1853, and dedicated some time in the course of the following year. It is a small, neat frame building, surmounted by a miniature belfry. For many years it was visited on one Sunday in the month by a priest from St. Mary's Church, Allegheny; but after the appointment of a resident pastor for Sewickley, it became a part of his mission and was visited every alternate Sunday. But about the year 1873 it was transferred to the pastor of Rochester. When Father Rommelfanger came from the latter place to Sewickley, the church was left under his jurisdiction, and was visited as before.

The congregation is composed exclusively of farmers, and will not exceed thirty families; and any change from its present condition will be very gradual.

* History of Allegheny County, p. 165.

ST. ALPHONSUS' CHURCH, WEXFORD.

The church at Wexford is situated in a country place on "the old Franklin road,"—running from Pittsburg to Franklin,—and is about twelve miles north of Pittsburg. After the division of the diocese it was uncertain for a time to which diocese it belonged; and indeed it was claimed by both in the *Catholic Directory* for 1877. But a more accurate survey of the dividing line proves it to be within the Diocese of Pittsburg. Wexford is an old Catholic settlement, the first families who arrived and the greater part even at the present day being Germans. Bishop O'Connor informs us that at the time of the erection of the See of Pittsburg—1843—there was a brick church and a congregation of about two hundred and fifty souls. The site upon which it stood was donated by a Mr. Shafer. But at what time or by whom the church was built cannot be known with certainty. It appears most probable that it was built under the direction of the Redemptorist fathers of Pittsburg, and a short time before the arrival of the Bishop. It was afterwards blown down, as the same prelate informs us, and was replaced by the present small brick edifice.* But all that we know of the date at which it occurred is that it was before the Bishop resigned his see; that is, before the year 1860. The congregation was attended from Pittsburg, Allegheny, or Sharpsburg (with the exception of the year 1846, when Rev. Jas. Reid, of Beaver, ministered to the people) until the appointment of a resident pastor, about the close of the year 1864. Rev. S. T. Mollinger was then appointed pastor of Wexford and the new congregation of Perrysville. From that time it has until lately enjoyed the advantages of a resident pastor. The congregation is composed of farmers, and, being far removed from railroad communication and manufactories, can hardly be said to have increased at all in the last thirty years. Its numbers at present will not exceed those given by Bishop O'Connor.

Early in 1879 Rev. J. Steger, the pastor of St. Alphonsus', was transferred to another field of labor, and the congregation

* Diocesan Register.

was united with that of Perrysville, under the jurisdiction of Rev. A. Holdapfel, of the latter, who offers up the Holy Sacrifice in both places every Sunday, riding a distance of six miles between the two Masses. This arrangement will probably continue for several years to come.

ST. TERESA'S CHURCH, PERRYSVILLE.

We now return to the Diocese of Allegheny. Perrysville is a village situated on "the old Franklin road," about seven miles north of Allegheny City, with which it is connected by a plank-road. The first person who settled at the place where the village now stands was Casper Reel, who built a log cabin there in 1794. The village, however, is of much later date. The Catholics who compose the little congregation were formerly attached to the churches of Allegheny; but in 1864 Rev. S. T. Mollinger was appointed pastor of Wexford, with the additional care of the Catholics of Perrysville. It is probable that he offered up the Holy Sacrifice for them in a private house for some time; but be that as it may, he undertook the building of a church in 1866, the corner-stone of which was laid by the Bishop on the 4th of July. The church was completed by the autumn of the following year, and was dedicated by the Bishop, under the invocation of St. Teresa, on the 6th of October. It is a very neat and substantial brick building, and, although small, will be sufficient for the accommodation of the people for many years to come. Father Mollinger was transferred to Troy Hill in June, 1868, since which time there have been several changes of pastors. The present incumbent, Rev. A. Holdapfel, has been there for the last three years. The congregation is mixed German and English, but the former predominate. As yet it is quite small and will not exceed thirty families in number, with the prospect of a very moderate future increase.

ST. MARY'S CHURCH, PINE CREEK.

St. Mary's Church is situated in the valley of the stream from which its name is taken, and about four miles north of

Sharpsburg. I have already stated, when speaking of St. Philomena's Church, Pittsburg, that this was the first congregation formed from it, and consequently the second German congregation organized in the county. After laboring zealously for the building up of the mother-church, the people turned their attention to the building of a church for themselves. It was erected about the year 1841, on a site donated by an Irish member of the congregation. But further particulars of its early history are not to be had, except that Bishop O'Connor states, in the *Diocesan Register*, that at the time of his consecration there was a log church and a congregation of four hundred souls. The church was under the jurisdiction of one of the priests attached to St. Philomena's, who visited it on one Sunday in the month until about the year 1848, when it passed into the hands of Rev. A. P. Gibbs, of Sharpsburg. He visited it generally twice in the month, and a German priest came out occasionally from Pittsburg. About the year 1855 it was attached to St. Mary's, Allegheny, from which it was visited until the appointment of a resident pastor, the date of which is uncertain.

REV. MICHAEL EIGNER, one of those who visited the congregation in this manner, was taken sick with consumption and died at the Mercy Hospital April 7th, 1862. Little is known of this good priest beyond that he was ordained for the Diocese of Pittsburg by Bishop Whelan, of Wheeling, in August, 1859. He does not appear to have been anywhere else than at St. Mary's, Allegheny.

The congregation, which is composed almost exclusively of farmers, nearly all of whom are Germans, had increased but little during these years. But the circumstances of the people had undergone a favorable change from the time they built the log church, and they determined at length to replace it by an edifice more becoming the exalted purpose for which it was destined. A new church was accordingly commenced in the spring of 1867, and the corner-stone was laid by the Bishop on the 22d of April. On the 28th of November of the same year it was dedicated by the same prelate. The church is a neat and substantial brick building about 80 feet in length by 40 in width, and has a steeple rising from the centre in front. A school-house was also built and a school opened by a lay teacher; but the date is uncertain. Rev. J. Kuenzer is the present pastor. The congregation, although not increasing much and having but little prospect of increase in the future, will yet number about one hundred families. It would have been larger had it not been that parts from the outskirts were attached to other congregations of a more recent date.

ST. JOSEPH'S CHURCH, SHARPSBURG.

The borough of Sharpsburg is situated on the west bank of the Allegheny River, about four miles north of Allegheny City. Pine Creek, which empties into the river immediately below, separates the town from Ætna borough. Sharpsburg takes its name from James Sharp, who settled there in the fall of 1827 and subsequently owned the land upon which the town is built. It was incorporated as a borough in 1841, and has at present a population of about 3500.* A considerable amount of iron manufacture is carried on in the town and its immediate vicinity, and it is to this especially the place owes its importance. The Western Pennsylvania Railroad passes through it, as the canal formerly did.

The first Catholics who settled in the borough heard Mass either in Pittsburg or at the church on Pine Creek; but a church was contemplated as early as February, 1847. Mass was celebrated in the town probably for the first time by Father Gibbs in the course of the same year, but in the room of a house until the erection of the church. The first baptism recorded is by him, and is dated November 21st, 1847. But the church was not undertaken until the following year, when the corner-stone was laid by the Bishop on the 25th of June. It was finished the following spring and dedicated by the same prelate, under the invocation of St. Joseph, April 29th. The church was a plain substantial brick building 85 feet in length by 40 in width, but without a steeple. A school appears to have been opened about the same time, but

* History of Allegheny County.

whether it was continued without interruption in the years immediately following cannot be stated with certainty.

As yet the English and Germans formed but one congregation, although the latter appear to have constituted the majority. But in January, 1853, they were organized into a separate congregation, although continuing to use the church until their own was built, as will be seen presently. Nothing beyond a moderate growth marked the flow of time, except that the pastor transferred his residence to Lawrenceville in the spring of 1854. But he continued to minister to the congregation until February, 1863, when he gave place to Rev. W. A. Nolan. He remained until May, 1866, during which time the congregation furnished no special matter for history. The same may be said of the pastorate of Rev. P. Kerr, who succeeded him, and who remained until February of the following year. Rev. Denis Kearney was now appointed pastor. The congregation began about this time to enter upon a season of greater prosperity than it had enjoyed at any previous period; and its numbers were increasing more rapidly.

About the year 1869 Father Kearney built a very neat brick residence, and about the same time erected a two-story brick school-house, 27 by 50 feet, which is one of the most elegant and substantial buildings of the kind in the diocese. The schools from this time until recently were taught by the Sisters of Mercy, who came daily by the cars from the House of Industry, Allegheny. A large lot was purchased, upon which it was proposed to build a convent for Sisters when circumstances should be favorable for the undertaking. The congregation was now at the zenith of its numerical strength and prosperity, and contained perhaps a little more than two hundred families. The old church was crowded, and it was thought best to build a more commodious edifice. Work was begun upon it, and the corner-stone was laid by the Bishop on the 4th of May, 1873. Occupying the site of the old one, the walls were built around it, and it was left standing for the use of the congregation as long as it was possible. The church, although not quite finished in the interior, was dedicated by the Bishop July 19th, 1874. The sacred edifice, which is modelled after the Gothic style of architecture, is 120 feet in length by about 55 in width, and has a tower in the centre in front finished at present to the comb of the roof. The ceiling, like that of several other churches built about the same time, rises ribbed from the sides toward the centre, and is supported without the aid of columns. There are three altars, which are as yet temporary, and are to be replaced by others more in harmony with the style of the church. Few churches of the diocese have been built with greater care or are more substantial than St. Joseph's. But the panic which set in before its completion reduced the congregation both in numbers and ability, and left them a burden of debt that it will require many years to liquidate.

After the division of the diocese Fr. Kearney came to St. Paul's Cathedral in April, 1876. After an interval he was succeeded by the present pastor, Rev. G. S. Grace, at the end of August.

Although the congregation must, in the nature of things, increase in the future, it is smaller now than it was ten years ago, and will not aggregate more perhaps than one hundred and fifty families. A brighter prospect seems now to be opening before it.

In August, 1879, Father Grace placed the schools in the hands of a number of Sisters of Charity from Altoona, who as yet occupy a rented house as a convent.

ST. MARY'S GERMAN CHURCH, SHARPSBURG.

German Catholics were among the first citizens of Sharpsburg. In the beginning, however, they heard Mass in Pittsburg, and later, when the church was built at Pine Creek, a number of those living in that part of the county attached themselves to the church there. But when the English church was opened in the town many of them went to form a part of its congregation, as has been said. At length it was deemed expedient for the Germans, who were already in the majority, to have their own church. The duty of organizing the new congregation and erecting the church was confided to the Redemptorist fathers of St. Philomena's Church, Pittsburg, and the work was undertaken January 1st, 1853. They used the English church, however, until their own was ready to receive them. A site was purchased at the back of the town, near the foot of the hill; work was commenced, and the corner-stone was laid by the Bishop early in the summer of 1853. Upon its completion the church was dedicated, under the invocation of the August Mother of God, on the 18th of June, 1854. But it had passed, in the course of its erection, into the hands of the secular clergy, Rev. C. N. Sorg having been appointed pastor in the preceding February. The new edifice was a brick building, 115 feet in length by 55 in width, and had an unpretending belfry over the entrance. But the whole building was not occupied by the congregation. Rooms in the rear were devoted to the purpose of a residence for the pastor. A basement extended back more than half the length of the building, and was partitioned off into school-rooms, in which a school was immediately opened by lay teachers. The congregation increased at a very encouraging rate, and was composed to a great extent of farmers, not a few of whom lived at a distance of six or eight miles. At length Father Sorg was called to another mission, February, 1856, and Rev. J. Tamchina became pastor. But in May of the same year he likewise withdrew, and the congregation reverted to the Redemptorist fathers, who ministered to it from St. Philomena's until August, 1865. It then returned to the secular clergy, and Rev. J. A. Shell was appointed pastor.

The church had never been a very substantial building, and it was soon found necessary to bind the walls near the roof by means of iron rods to prevent them from spreading. Wishing to add to the solemnity of divine worship, the pastor had a new organ built at a cost of $1800. When the building of the instrument was completed preparations were made for a grand opening of it. The church was crowded for the occasion, on the evening of January 4th, 1866, when to the dismay of all it was discovered that the building was on fire, and, despite all that could be done to arrest the flames, the entire structure with the pastoral residence was consumed. The fire is thought to have originated from a lighted candle having been placed too near some artificial flowers under the back of the altar.

Nothing was left for the congregation but to return with its pastor to the English church until such time as a frame story could be built on the basement walls of the burnt building, to serve the purpose of a temporary church. It was completed in May. Work was commenced on a new church with the opening of spring, and the corner-stone was laid by the Bishop May 27th, 1866. A year after the church was finished and ready for dedication, and in the absence of the Bishop the ceremony was performed by Very Rev. T. Mullen, V.G., June 16th. The sacred edifice is built of brick, and is 134 feet in length by 60 in width. In the centre in front is an unusually massive tower, which rises square to the height of perhaps 125 feet. It was the intention of the architect to finish it in a pyramidal spire, but the foundation began to show signs of giving way, and the design was abandoned after the tower had been roofed. The church is commodious and neatly finished, but lacks architectural design. In 1868 Father Shell built a brick residence. Having left these monuments of his zeal and energy, he was transferred to St. Mary's Church, Allegheny, April 26th, 1869, and Rev. A. Rosswogg succeeded him. He was in turn succeeded by Rev. J. B. Schmidt, January 4th, 1870. The congregation had so far increased that an assistant priest became necessary early in the summer of 1873. About the same time Father Schmidt had the church frescoed, and had a new high and two side altars erected. All three are after fine Gothic models, and are of polished chestnut and very beautiful. Having remained for four years, Father Schmidt was succeeded, April 20th, 1874, by a colony of the fathers of the Congregation of the Holy Ghost and the Immaculate Heart of Mary, who came from Alsace after it had passed under the sway of the German emperor. Rev. Joseph Strub, a man of great learning and administrative ability, and the leader of the little band, was the first pastor of the church; but he has since been elected provincial of his congregation in the United States, and another of the fathers is pastor of the church. Before his departure Father Schmidt had placed the schools under the care of the Sisters of St. Francis, from the mother-house in Pittsburg, who occupy part of the school building as a convent.

The congregation has increased but little since the panic, but is still in a flourishing condition and must gradually grow in the future. It will number at present about four hundred and fifty families, or perhaps more.

ST. ANNE'S CHURCH, MILLVALE.

The borough of Millvale is situated in a valley on the west bank of the Allegheny River, between Allegheny City and Sharpsburg. Previous to the incorporation of the borough, in 1868, the place was known as Bennett's Station, from the extensive iron-works of Graff, Bennett & Co., in operation there.

The Catholic families that had settled there attached themselves to the church at Sharpsburg until the Forty-third Street bridge was built across the river, which put them in direct communication with St. Mary's Church, Forty-sixth Street, Pittsburg, after which time they formed a part of that congregation. But as their number was steadily increasing, it was thought best to have them build a church for themselves. Lots were purchased and a church was undertaken under the direction of Father Gibbs. The corner-stone was laid by the Bishop September 24th, 1874, and the church when finished was dedicated by the same prelate May 2d of the following year. The church, which is a plain frame building about 70 feet in length by 30 in width, stands back a short distance from the river. It was attended from St. Mary's until the erection of the See of Allegheny, when it was for some time attached to Troy Hill. But later it was placed under the charge of Rev. Jas. Richert, of the Congregation of the Holy Ghost, attached to the German church at Sharpsburg, and so it remains. The congregation consists of about seventy-five German and thirty English families, the former of whom are anxious to separate and form a distinct congregation. This, although a misfortune to the other portion, which would in that case be left to carry a considerable burden of debt, must eventually take place. The Germans bought lots and built a brick school-house, some distance from the church, and opened a school in it in January, 1876. The congregation has a promising future before it.

CHAPTER XIV.

CATHOLICITY IN SOUTH-WESTERN PENNSYLVANIA.

General remarks—St. Anne's Church, Waynesburg—St. James' Church, West Alexander—Death and sketch of Rev. D. Hickey—Church of the Immaculate Conception, Washington—St. James' Church, Claysville—Other stations in Washington and Greene counties—Fayette and Somerset counties—Scenery, aborigines, Indian paths—First settlers—Brownsville—First Catholic settlers—Pittsburg visited as a station from Brownsville—St. Peter's Church, Brownsville—Uniontown—St. John's Church—Farrington mission—Gen. Braddock's grave—Church of the Immaculate Conception, Connellsville—St. Aloysius' Church, Dunbar—Le Mont Furnace mission—St. John the Baptist's Church, Scottdale—St. John the Baptist's Church, New Baltimore—St. Matthew's Church, Meyersdale—Death and sketch of Rev. Thos. Fitzgerald—Stations: Ursina, Sand Patch, Wellsburg.

In order not to pass too abruptly from one part of the diocese to another, we shall, after leaving Pittsburg and Allegheny counties, turn our attention to the south and thence to the east, where the church was first planted among us, and from which it extended its branches in various directions.

Under the name of South-western Pennsylvania is here understood Washington, Greene, Fayette, and Somerset counties, with that part of Beaver that lies south of the Ohio River. It embraces more than one third part of the Diocese of Pittsburg according to the last division; yet it is the most unfruitful portion of the vineyard, and cannot boast one thousand Catholic families, notwithstanding that laborers were engaged in it before the close of the last century. The part of Beaver County included in the territory contains no Catholics whatever, except perhaps two or three families on the river opposite Rochester. Washington County may have one hundred and fifty families, and Greene less than twenty-five. The barrenness of this district is to be attributed to two principal causes: its settlement by the strictest school of

Presbyterians, whose bigotry has successfully stood the test of time and reason,* and the absence of minerals, which prevented manufactories from being built and a foreign Catholic element from being introduced to plant the faith. Another cause of the tardy growth of the church is that, while the number of Catholics was too small to support sufficient resident priests to minister frequently to them, they lived too far from the city to be so attended from without. Their attachment to the faith, which is fostered by frequently witnessing the ceremonies of the Church and hearing its doctrines explained and defended, became weakened; the instinctive hatred of error grew less intense; and some fell away through negligence, while others became entangled in the meshes of mixed marriages. These causes operate more fatally on American Catholics than on those of foreign birth; and as they are still as powerful as ever, but slender hopes can be entertained of the future increase of the Catholic population in this part of the diocese.

ST. ANNE'S CHURCH, WAYNESBURG, GREENE COUNTY.

Greene County, originally a part of Washington, was organized by an act of Assembly of February 9th, 1796. It occupies the extreme south-western corner of the State, and has an area of 597 square miles. The rolling character of the surface and the nature of the soil are better adapted for grazing than for grain. Waynesburg, the county-seat, was

---

* As an evidence of what has been stated in the text the following incident may be given, which, although savoring of the fabulous, may yet be authenticated by any one who will be at the trouble of visiting the spot where it occurred. When the Jefferson Presbyterian College was built at the village of Cannonsburg, about ten miles north of Washington, Rev. Robt. J. Breckenridge, D.D., was appointed president. When superintending the building of the house that was destined to serve as his residence, he came one day and found that the doors, made after the usual pattern and already hung, had the semblance of a cross in the parts between the panels. So intense was his hatred of the least sign of "popery" that he ordered the doors to be removed forthwith, and others, made of ordinary tongued-and-grooved boards, substituted for them. The house, with its "anti-popery" doors, is yet standing for the inspection of the incredulous and the edification of the elect.

laid out when the county was established, and was incorporated as a borough in 1816. The land was purchased from Thos. Slater, and the lots were sold, in conformity with the law, for account of the county. The borough is situated in a delightful valley, one mile from the centre of the county, thirteen from the southern and seventeen from the western boundary of the State, and had in 1870 a population of 1272.*

Between the years 1795 and 1799—the precise date cannot be ascertained—Rev. Fr. Lanigan, O.S.F., came to the Catholic settlement in Westmoreland County, where St. Vincent's Abbey now stands, and took charge of the congregation. But finding himself unable to abide in peace, owing to the line of conduct pursued by the unhappy Fr. Fromm, he set out in company with a few members of the congregation in search of a place where they could found another colony. Coming to West Alexander, Washington County, they purchased several thousand acres of land, and returning brought out the colony. Not being pleased with the place after a closer inspection, they sold it, and purchased a site near Waynesburg, Greene County. Here the colony established itself permanently.† How long Fr. Lanigan remained with his little flock it is impossible to determine at this time; but his name occurs in the early history no later than 1801, although it is certain that he visited various settlements during that year. It is equally impossible to trace the religious history of these pioneers and to learn by whom they were ministered to. They generally, however, formed, as they still do, a part of the Brownsville mission, and shared its fortunes. The first authentic account begins with the year 1833—a period which, though long, would be marked by few changes in those days worthy of the historian's attention. In this year the erection of a brick church was commenced, but whether it was the first church built there or not I cannot learn. I am inclined, however, to the opinion that it was not, both because the colony would hardly exist so long without a place of worship and also because the first churches of the backwoods are seldom

---

* Day's Historical Collections, pp. 358, 361.
† St. Vincenz in Pennsylvanien, pp. 70, 71.

brick. Be that as it may, the church was dedicated by Bishop Kenrick, under the invocation of St. Anne, July 28th, 1839. The Catholics were few in number, and were scattered around the country to a considerable distance. Since the completion of the church Mass has been celebrated as a rule on one Sunday in the month. At the time of the erection of the See of Pittsburg, Bishop O'Connor sets the number of souls in the congregation at 164. The first settlers were Irish and German.

No changes worth recording took place until about the year 1852, when the church fell down. So few and poor were the people that they did not undertake the erection of a new one for almost twenty years, but assembled in a room to hear Mass. At length, about the year 1869, when Rev. H. M'Hugh was pastor of Brownsville, it was determined to rebuild the fallen temple. It was finished, and was dedicated by the Bishop October 9th, 1870. The congregation is smaller now than it was fifty years ago, and will count no more than twenty families, and it has little hope of increase in the future. The narrow-gauge railroad, now open from Pittsburg to Waynesburg, will render access less difficult. This will be the first sound of a steam-engine within twenty miles of the town.

ST. JAMES' CHURCH, WEST ALEXANDER, WASHINGTON COUNTY.

West Alexander is a village thirty-eight miles south-west of Pittsburg, and within a very short distance of the western boundary of the State. It was founded before the close of the last century, and owes its origin and early importance to the fact that it lay on the Southern Turnpike, the great thoroughfare between the east and west before the days of canals and railroads. But its glory has long since vanished, and although on the line of the Hempfield Railroad, which connects Washington with Wheeling, it is of no present nor prospective importance. It is the only place in the diocese in which a church existed for a time and was afterwards abandoned.

Catholics of Irish birth came here from the Monongahela valley as early as 1825, the pioneers being Ch. Dougherty and M. Egan. A log-church was built at an early day, but the date is uncertain; it was, however, before the erection of the See of Pittsburg, at which time Bishop O'Connor gives the Catholic population at 107 souls. After the first visit of Bishop Kenrick, in the summer of 1837, the church was visited at regular intervals from Brownsville. In the course of time the log church was replaced by a brick one, and in 1852 the first resident priest, Rev. D. Hickey, arrived. For two years he ministered to his small scattered flock, until his health failed, and after a brief illness he died, October 5th, 1854, and was laid to rest among them.

REV. DANIEL HICKEY was born in county Kilkenny, Ireland, and after completing, or almost completing, his studies came to this country and diocese, where he was ordained in 1852. At the time of his death he was but thirty years of age.

The cessation of traffic caused by the construction of canals and railroads opening other routes induced a number of Catholics to withdraw from the congregation, and it was found more conducive to the interests of religion to abandon the church and erect one at Claysville, to be noticed hereafter. The church was torn down a few years ago.

CHURCH OF THE IMMACULATE CONCEPTION, WASHINGTON.

Washington County was the first established by the legislature after the declaration of independence, having been taken from Westmoreland by the act of March 28th, 1781. Its dimensions were reduced in 1788 and 1796 by the formation of Allegheny and Greene counties, so that it comprises at present an area of but 888 square miles. The surface of the county is undulating and in some parts hilly; but there are no mountains, and the hills are seldom too steep for cultivation. The county was originally settled by Scotch-Irish from Bedford and York counties and from the Kittatinny valley, from Virginia, and directly from Ireland, and all belonged to the Presbyterian sect; and although Germans and others have since come in, the descendants of the original settlers still predominate, and their influence prevails in the manners and religious and literary institutions of the county.*

* Day's Historical Collections, pp. 658, 659.

Few towns in the State are more delightfully situated than Washington, or "Little Washington" as it is frequently called, which was founded in 1782. It is built on an undulating ground, near the head of the Chartier's Valley, about twenty-five miles south-southwest of Pittsburg, with which it is connected by the Chartier's Valley Railroad, and is surrounded by one of the most beautiful of landscapes. It has a population of about 6000, and contains many elegant private residences. But notwithstanding the natural advantages of the town, the Catholic population is very small, and, owing to the causes enumerated at the beginning of this chapter, gives little promise of increasing even moderately in the future. Presbyterianism in its darkest and most bigoted form here reigns supreme. Here, too, is situated Washington and Jefferson College, with its two or three hundred students and its staff of reverend professors of the same denomination. The former lodge about the town, and have an effect upon the religious and moral tone of the place of which different persons form different opinions. There is also a young ladies' academy. Under such circumstances it is not to be wondered at that there should be the profoundest ignorance of our holy religion, and that even enlightened minds should speak in good faith of priest's horns, etc.

It is impossible to determine the precise date of the arrival of the first Catholic settlers; but Rev. P. Rafferty, then assistant at St. Paul's, Pittsburg, is thought to have celebrated the first Mass in the town about the year 1831. Three years later Bishop Kenrick, without visiting the place, established a mission to be attended at regular, though distant, intervals from Brownsville, of which Rev. Fr. Mazzachelli was then pastor. In 1841 the building of a church was resolved upon, and a site was purchased. But to such a degree did religious prejudice prevail that persons who had purchased lots in the vicinity of the church lot gave them up, and no one could be found willing to build under the shadow of a Catholic church. Yet this took place in an enlightened and liberal (!) community and in the nineteenth century. While such a feeling prevailed it was deemed imprudent to build a church, and the lot was accordingly sold. But another lot was purchased in a different part of the town, March 5th, 1842, to be held until such time as a church could be prudently erected. In the mean time the place continued to be visited as before, and the changes in pastors were more frequent than those in the congregation. At length Rev. D. Hickey, noticed above, was appointed pastor in 1852, with his residence at West Alexander. Soon after his appointment he commenced to build the church, which, though small, was yet a heavy tax on the ability of the congregation. But the good pastor did not live to witness its completion, having died, as we saw above, October 5th, 1854. He was succeeded by Rev. John C. Farren. The church upon its completion was dedicated by Rt. Rev. R. V. Whelan, Bishop of Wheeling, under the invocation of the Immaculate Conception of the Blessed Virgin Mary, August 26th, 1855. It is a brick building, simple in style, and is 55 feet in length by 35 in width, has one altar, a gallery, and a small belfry. Strange as it may appear, it is almost adjoining the grounds of the college.

Soon after the completion of the church Washington became the residence of a priest and the centre of an extensive missionary district. But the priest has always been obliged to lodge in a hotel or with a private family. The Holy Sacrifice is celebrated every Sunday, except during a part of the winter, when it is offered up alternately here and at Claysville, as we shall see. The pastor of Washington has care of the few Catholics in the entire county, with the exception of the Monongahela valley. He celebrates Mass once a month on a week-day at Cannonsburg, on the Chartier's Valley Railroad, about twelve miles north of Washington, for a very few families, principally employed on the railroad. He also visits the Pennsylvania Reform School (House of Refuge) at Morganza Farm, a few miles further north, once a week on a week-day, gives instruction, and generally says Mass. This is a great advantage to the Catholic youth, who number about one third of the three hundred inmates. But so long as they are obliged to assist in the chapel on Sunday at the services of whatever minister chances to officiate, there is much still to be desired. The managers and officers, however, afford every negative though but little positive facility to the priest on his weekly visits. I shall treat more fully of our destitute youth when speaking of St. Paul's Orphan Asylum.

Rev. John Malady is the present pastor of Washington, and it may be questioned whether his congregation is larger now than it was thirty or forty years ago. If it be, the increase is almost imperceptible, and the past may be taken as a fair index of its prospects in the future. It will number at present about twenty families.

ST. JAMES' CHURCH, CLAYSVILLE, WASHINGTON COUNTY.

Claysville is a small village eleven miles south-west of Washington, on the Hempfield Railroad. For several years before the abandonment of the church at West Alexander it was visited as a station by the pastor of Washington. But the number of Catholic families having increased, it was thought best to erect a church for their accommodation. It was accordingly undertaken, was finished in the fall of 1875, and dedicated, by the Bishop under the invocation of St. James, September 25th. It is a brick building, is 80 feet in length by 35 in width, and has a tower in the centre in front. The interior is neatly finished, and the whole is modelled after the Gothic style. From May to November Mass is offered up every Sunday, the priest celebrating an early Mass at Washington and then driving to St. James for the late one. But in winter this is impossible, owing to the condition of the roads, except when sleighing is good. Mass is then celebrated in the two places alternately.

The future prospects of St. James' congregation are good —better than those of any other congregation in this part of the diocese; and the day is probably not far distant when the pastor will reside here instead of at Washington. It will number at present about twenty-five families, composed principally of farmers, with a few men employed on the railroad.

Besides the churches and missions already mentioned, the pastor of Washington visits a few scattered families in two or three other places; but their number is so small as not to entitle them to special mention. The church at Monongahela

City, in this county, has been noticed in connection with that at Elizabeth, Allegheny County, from which it has always been visited.

FAYETTE AND SOMERSET COUNTIES.

No part of Western Pennsylvania presents more varied and beautiful scenery than that which is at present to engage our attention. Traversed by the Allegheny Mountains and the Laurel and Chestnut ridges, it is calculated to present all that is pleasing to the eye in natural scenery, and travellers on the Baltimore and Ohio Railroad, between Connellsville on the west and Bridgeport on the east of the mountains, can bear witness to the surpassing grandeur of the mountains. We cannot pause to dwell upon this, however, as being foreign to our subject, but may occasionally refer to it in the course of our history.

The political history is no less interesting. In the early settlement of the West, Fayette County especially played an important part. A warlike though less barbarous class of inhabitants appear to have occupied the territory prior to the Indians who were found upon it by the pioneer Europeans. Ruins of their fortifications are to be met with in various places.* Numerous Indian paths traversed the country, and were of considerable importance, particularly in the mountain regions, in determining the best routes for emigrants to follow, and afterwards for the State roads or turnpikes. The principal of these was *Nemacolin's Path*, which led from the spot where the city of Cumberland stands to the forks of the Ohio, the site of Pittsburg, as we saw when speaking of the latter city. A branch of this path led to Red Stone, the present Brownsville. There were other branches of minor importance.

But from a religious point of view the history of these counties, though dating far back and promising much in the beginning, is almost as barren as that of Greene and Washington counties. It was originally settled by Dunkers, whose

---

* The Monongahela of Old, pp. 17-23.

hostility to the Church has to a great extent withstood the levelling hand of time. While this may have discouraged the settlement of Catholics to some extent, the principal reasons were the delay in developing the mineral resources and erecting manufactories; but more especially is it due to the opening of the Pennsylvania Canal, which became the great thoroughfare from the East to the West and drew the attention of emigrants to other parts of the country. But recently the mineral resources of the northern part of Fayette County have been considerably developed, manufactories have been erected to a limited extent, and in consequence a strong Catholic population is springing up, as we shall have occasion to note in the course of our remarks. To proceed, however, to the history of the separate congregations.

BROWNSVILLE, FAYETTE COUNTY.

Brownsville appears very early in the history of the western part of the State, and occupies a conspicuous place from the beginning. The advantages of its location will appear as we proceed and account for the prominent position it held during the latter half of the last and the early part of the present century—advantages which it was destined, in the nature of things, to lose with the march of civilization. Where the town of Brownsville now stands there existed at the date of the first settlement by the white man the ruins of one of those fortifications of which I have already spoken, known from the Red Stone Creek, which empties into the Monongahela at that point, as Red Stone Old Fort. Here, after the withdrawal of Ensign Ward from the fortification he was erecting at Pittsburg in the spring of 1754, Major Geo. Washington built a small fort, which was used after settlements began to be made in the surrounding country for the storage of ammunition and supplies.* It is believed that the first settlers here were Wendel Brown and his two sons, who came in 1751 or 1752.† But the great importance of Brownsville was that it stood at the head of navigation of the Monongahela, fifty-

---

* The Monongahela of Old, p. 22.   † Ibid. p. 79.

three miles by the river south of Pittsburg, and hence the spot—for the town was not yet laid out—became a place of rendezvous for emigrants "down the river" to Kentucky and other places. By this route came nearly all the early missionaries to Kentucky, beginning with Father Whalen in 1787. It was also the headquarters of spies during the Indian wars. " The protection afforded by the posts and block-houses erected along the Monongahela attracted settlers, and soon a very considerable population found its way into the valley of that river and especially around Redstone. The importance of the place was gradually increased by the emigration that set in from the regions east of the mountains, after the close of the war, along Braddock's road to Redstone. . . . It was not, however, until 1785 that the present town of Brownsville was laid out on the site of Old Fort Redstone, and in the next year its population had increased to six hundred." * Brownsville was also the scene of the first outbreak of the excise troubles known as the "Whiskey Insurrection," in 1791-4. In 1870 it had a population of 1749.

It would be difficult to fix the date of the first arrival of Catholics in the town and surrounding country; but it is certain that a few Irish Catholics found their way thither a few years before the close of the last century. Rev. Father Lanigan visited them from Waynesburg, and a Rev. J. Sayer —whose name occurs nowhere else in our history—is said to have ministered to them for a time about the close of the century. Rev. P. Heilbron, who came to Sportsman's Hall —now St. Vincent's Abbey—in November, 1799, paid them an occasional visit before the arrival of Rev. F. X. O'Brien. What consolation they were able to derive from his ministrations it is difficult to tell, for it is said that he could never learn to express the simplest ideas in English. But of these visits we know absolutely nothing but the fact of their occurrence. Fr. O'Brien came to Brownsville, as nearly as can be ascertained, early in the year 1806, and for a little more than two years remained, attending also the few scattered families in the whole south-western part of the State. Incredible as

---

* Annals of the West, p. 430.

it may appear, Pittsburg was one of these stations. But in November, 1808, he transferred the centre of his missionary labors to that city, and attended Brownsville at intervals. For the next twenty years the history of the congregation is extremely meagre in details, and all that is known with certainty is that the number of Catholics gradually increased, and that they were visited generally from Pittsburg, although the priest at Sportsman's Hall ministered to them sometimes owing to the feeble health of Fr. O'Brien. Soon after his withdrawal the government began to construct the national roads, or turnpikes, upon which a large number of laborers, principally Irish Catholics, were employed.* The "Southern Pike," from Washington City to the West, passed through Brownsville, adding materially to its importance. Naturally enough many of the laborers settled in the towns and country along the route after the completion of the work, and thus increased the Catholic population. But it must be admitted, though with regret, that, owing to the limited facilities afforded for the practice of their religion, very many of them fell away from the Church, and intermarrying with members of the sects, became members of their false religions or practical infidels. It is impossible to estimate the numbers that have been lost to the Church in this manner in every part of the diocese, but they may safely be placed at thousands.

In the year 1807 Rev. Stephen Badin, as Archbishop Spalding informs us in his "Sketches of Catholicity in Ken-

---

* As reference will frequently be made to these roads in the course of our history, it may be well to give the reader an idea of the route of the principal among them. They were:

1. One from Washington City past Cumberland, Md., through Uniontown, Brownsville, near Washington, Claysville, and West Alexander to the West. This was known in Pennsylvania as "the Southern Pike."

2. One from Philadelphia, passing through Huntingdon, Hollidaysburg, Summitville, Ebensburg, Blairsville, and Greensburg to Pittsburg. This was commonly called "the Northern Pike." From Pittsburg it divided, one branch passing to Steubenville, O., another down the northern bank of the Ohio River, and another through Wexford to Franklin.

3. One from Baltimore, passing through Bedford and Youngstown, united with the Northern Pike near Greensburg.

4. And one from Ebensburg through Indiana, Kittanning, Butler, and New Castle into Ohio.

tucky," stopped at the village of Brownsville on his way from Kentucky to Baltimore, and preached in the Methodist chapel there, after which Major Noble, who had been much impressed by the sermon, invited him to his house, which resulted in the baptism and reception into the Church of the entire family. This Major Noble appears to have held a prominent position among the Catholics of Brownsville; for upon the visit of Bishop Egan to the western part of the State in the fall of 1811 he called at Brownsville, where he celebrated Mass and administered confirmation in the house of that gentleman. Dr. Gallitzin also paid the place an occasional visit during the construction of the turnpike. It will afford an idea of the difficulties against which our forefathers had to contend when we are told they had no priest nearer than Loretto. It also illustrates the remark of Bishop Kenrick that "some of our missionaries need the gift of tongues and a health of iron."

ST. PETER'S CHURCH, BROWNSVILLE.

We must pass over the intervening time and come to about the year 1830. A Rev. Father Curtis resided at Brownsville for a short time in the fall of this year. He was succeeded by Rev. Patrick Rafferty. What harvest the latter was able to reap in the spiritual order it is difficult to determine; certain it is his temporal recompense was meagre enough. For after laboring about a year he returned to Pittsburg, having received during that time, besides his board, the sum of $3.62½. Upon his reaching the city Father M'Guire, then pastor of St. Patrick's Church, received him, and insisted upon his remaining within until he should go out and purchase a respectable suit of clothes for him. He was no doubt satisfied to leave the field of his labors to some one else. Be that as it may, the people, although giving evidence of the zeal and disinterestness—more especially the latter—with which they had been ministered to, were deprived of a resident pastor for a considerable time, as appears from a letter of Bishop Kenrick dated January 14th, 1834. He says: "On my visit to Brownsville, a little village on the Monongahela River, I was much edified at the joy with which a French widow, residing in the neighborhood, came with her children to approach the sacraments, which she had been debarred from for years, in consequence of not meeting a priest who understood her language. The faithful of this mission are to be pitied, being able only four times a year to enjoy the presence of a priest, tne pastor of Blairsville, Rev. James Ambrose Stillenger, who visits them thus till I can place a pastor here." I remember hearing Fr. Stillenger speak in his entertaining way of his travels and adventures on this mission. He visited the place for two years, till in the latter part of 1836 it was attended monthly from Pittsburg by Rev. Patrick Waters.

I have not been able to learn the date of the building of the first church, but from the words of Bishop Kenrick it must have been before his visit, as he speaks of a cnurch without making mention of its erection or dedication. The circumstances of its erection, whatever time it took place, were these: Neal Gillespie donated three acres of ground in a very desirable place in the town as a site for the building. This gentleman was grandfather of the politician James Gillespie Blaine. Two Protestant gentlemen, J. J. Workman and E. L. Blaine, father of the above-named, undertook to erect the church, travelling for the purpose of raising the necessary funds as far as Baltimore. Both became converts, and after the destruction of the church by fire were interred in the spot upon which the altar had stood.

In the summer of 1837 Rev. Michael Gallagher was appointed pastor, with the additional care of all the Catholics in Washington, Greene, and Fayette counties. In April, 1839, the congregation sustained a heavy loss in the burning of the church, and during the time that elapsed before the erection of the new one the people accommodated themselves as best they could in a private house. The congregation was at this time at the zenith of its prosperity and numerical strength. Too sanguine of the future, Fr. Gallagher commenced the building of a splendid edifice in 1842. For this purpose he collected in different parts of the country, and happily left the church at its completion free from debt.

It was solemnly consecrated by Bishop O'Connor April 7th, 1844. It is built of cut stone throughout, is 125 feet in length by 50 in width, and has a tower in the centre in front 120 feet high. The floor is paved with stone, and the altar was of the same material, but because of the dampness was soon replaced by one of wood. Had the congregation continued to increase and been able to keep the church in the order which such a building requires, it would be the most elegant as it is the most substantial church in the diocese. But the congregation began to decline soon after its completion. About the same time Fr. Gallagher withdrew, and was replaced by so long a list of successors—for the church has always had a resident pastor—that it is impossible to give the names of all. The present incumbent is Rev. H. P. Connery. The Pennsylvania Canal on the north and the Potomac Canal on the south drew the travel and traffic from Brownsville, and it immediately began to decline rapidly in importance. A pastoral residence was purchased many years ago, but the congregation has never enjoyed the inestimable advantage of a parish school.

The congregation numbers at present no more than twenty-five families, and Mass is offered up on two Sundays in the month. What the future prospects are it is difficult to conjecture; certain it is they are not flattering. Should the Pittsburg, Virginia and Charleston Railroad, now completed to Monongahela City, be extended to Brownsville, as it probably soon will be, it will doubtless increase the trade and with it the population of the town.

Of the numerous missions formerly attended from Brownsville, Waynesburg, Uniontown, and Farmington alone remain. But besides these the pastor pays an occasional visit to certain small bodies of miners living at different places along the river.

ST. JOHN'S CHURCH, UNIONTOWN.

Uniontown, the county-seat of Fayette County, is situated near the foot of the western slope of the Chestnut Ridge, about twelve miles south-east of Brownsville. The town was laid ont by Henry Beeson, a Quaker from Berkeley County, Va., about the year 1767 or '69.* It had in 1870 a population of 2503. But the history of the place and of the surrounding country begins from a period prior to the foundation of the town. The route by which General Braddock crossed from Cumberland to Fort Du Quesne in the early part of the summer of 1755 lay but a short distance north of where the town now stands. This route was, as we have seen, one of the paths by which emigrants penetrated to the West, and so favorably was it known that the Southern Pike, when laid out, followed closely the footsteps of the unfortunate Briton. Passing on its way through Uniontown, it added to the traffic and importance of the place.

Nothing is known with certainty of the early Catholic settlement of Uniontown, but it is probable that a few scattered families were found in the town and in its vicinity very early in the present century; for Dr. Gallitzin and Father Heilbron both visited the place before the arrival of Father O'Brien at Brownsville—that is, prior to the year 1806. Since that town became a missionary centre Uniontown has always, with but little exception, been attached to it. Passing over the first half of the present century, during which time the visits of a priest were more or less frequent, according to the extent of the field of his missionary labors, but never more than once in the month, we come to the year 1849. Mass was at that time celebrated once in the month on Sunday by Rev. Thos. M'Gowen, then pastor of Brownsville, and the number of Catholics, though small, was still such that it was deemed expedient to build a church for their better accommodation. Suitable lots were purchased, and in the following year the church was undertaken. It was not finished until the close of the year after, at which time Rev. John Larkin, at present

* Historical Collections, p. 340.

of Holy Innocents' Church, New York City, was pastor. It was dedicated, under the invocation of St. John the Evangelist, by Rev. Father Krutil, C.SS.R., December 7th, 1851. The church is an unassuming brick structure without a steeple, and is about 50 feet in length by 25 in width, has one altar, and is finished in a simple and inexpensive style in the interior. The affairs of the congregation remained unchanged, except that it was soon deprived of the advantages of a resident pastor until February 5th, 1863, when the church was blown down, or at least seriously damaged, by a storm. It was rebuilt without alteration, and again the little congregation pursued the even tenor of its way.

At length the condition of the congregation was improved, but hardly for its own sake, as may be inferred from what follows. About the end of September, 1877, Rev. Ed. Brennan was appointed resident pastor, with the care also of Farmington and LeMont Furnace. But after remaining until May of the following year he was transferred to another field of usefulness, and the congregation reverted to the pastor of Brownsville. It will not exceed twenty-five families in number, and may even fall below that figure, and never was it greater than at present. Being beyond the influences that ordinarily tend to increase the Catholic population, it is probable that it will undergo little if any change for many years to come.

FARMINGTON STATION.

The village of Farmington is situated on the national turnpike in a mountainous region twelve miles east of Uniontown. The scenery between the two places is grand beyond description. Soon after leaving the latter place the traveller ascends the Chestnut Ridge by a tortuous route, and having reached the summit at the distance of six miles there is presented on the west and north-west a prospect extending to a distance of more than forty miles. Little Washington, though thirty-five miles off, is seen distinctly with the aid of a glass. On the top of the ridge are Fayette Springs. It was near this spot that Major Washington built Fort Necessity immediately after the retreat of General Braddock. Passing three miles further east, one comes to the historic spot where reposes all that is mortal of the brave but imprudent General Braddock —a place which was known in the annals of Indian warfare as the Great Meadows. Here the general was laid to rest July 13th, 1755. He was first buried in the route which bore his name, to prevent the French or Indians from discovering the spot, but about the beginning of the present century his remains were removed to a spot about one hundred yards north of the road. It is surrounded by about half a dozen other graves and as many small trees, dating from the beginning of the century. The grave is marked by a flagstone without any inscription, and the wild-cherry-tree that stood at the head of it is long dead, and will soon cease to point out the spot where our hero was buried.*

The few Catholics in and around the village of Farming-

---

* The death of Gen. Braddock being the first important event of the war between the French and English, of which the territory included in this history was the scene, it may not be uninteresting to give the following account of it from Day's "Historical Collections" (p. 335), and the more so as I do not find it stated anywhere else :

"There had long existed a tradition in this region that Braddock was killed by one of his own men, and more recent developments leave little or no doubt of the fact. A recent writer in the *National Intelligencer*, whose authority is good on such points, says: 'When my father was moving with his family to the west, one of the Fausetts kept a public house to the eastward from and near where Uniontown now stands. This man's house we lodged in about the 10th of October, 1781, twenty-six years and a few months after Braddock's defeat, and there it was made anything but a secret that one of the family dealt the deathblow to the British general. Thirteen years afterwards I met Thos. Fausett in Fayette County, and then, as he told me, in his seventieth year. To him I put the plain question and received the plain reply, "*I did shoot him.*" He then went on to insist that, by doing so, he contributed to save what was left of the army. In brief, in my youth I never heard the fact either doubted or blamed that Fausett shot Braddock.'

"In spite of Braddock's silly order that the troops should not protect themselves behind the trees, Joseph Fausett had taken such a position, when Braddock rode by in a passion and struck him down with his sword. Tom Fausett, who was but a short distance from his brother, saw the whole transaction and immediately drew up his rifle and shot Braddock through the lungs, partly in revenge for the outrage upon his brother and partly, as he always alleged, to get the general out of the way and thus save the remainder of the gallant band who had been sacrificed to his obstinacy and want of experience in frontier warfare."

ton settled there most probably at the time the road was made. They are all farmers, and number no more than about fifteen families. The place has always been attached to Uniontown and attended at irregular intervals, but never more as a rule than once in the month on a week-day. No church has yet been built, nor is one likely soon to be, and there is every prospect that the future history of the place will be as monotonous as the past has been.

CHURCH OF THE IMMACULATE CONCEPTION, CONNELLSVILLE.

Connellsville is situated on the northern bank of the Yohioghenny River, fifty-eight miles south-east of Pittsburg, and took its name from Zachariah Connell, who laid out the town about the year 1790. It was incorporated as a borough in 1806, and had in 1870 a population of 1292. New Haven, on the opposite side of the river, was laid out in 1796 by Col. Isaac Meason, and had in 1870 a population of 333.* The site of Connellsville was known in frontier history as Stewart's Crossing.

Although an old town, it did not attain to any importance until the completion of the Pittsburg and Connellsville Railroad, now known as the Pittsburg branch of the Baltimore and Ohio Railroad, in 1862. The opening of this road gave an outlet to the coke trade, of which this is the centre and for which it has a world-wide reputation,† and in doing so increased the population and the importance of the town.

From an early day Catholic settlers found their way to this part of the country, and for more than a quarter of a century Mass was celebrated in the town or near it, at distant intervals, and generally on a week-day. At length the number of Catholics had sufficiently increased to render the building of a church and the appointment of a resident pastor neces-

---

* Day's Historical Collections, p. 344.

† There were in the immediate vicinity of Connellsville, according to an account drawn up in the autumn of 1879, nearly 4000 coke-ovens in full blast, yielding 250,000 bushels or 400 car-loads per day and giving steady employment to more than 2000 men, as miners, coke-drawers, and laborers, and the trade is daily increasing.

sary. In 1870 Rev. Robt. Waters, of Brownsville, began to visit it monthly on a Sunday. In the beginning of the following year he was transferred thither, and, after having offered up the Holy Sacrifice for a short time in a house, he purchased, or had purchased for him, an old Methodist Episcopal church in January, 1871. The building, which is of rough stone, is 66 feet in length by 38 in width, without a steeple, and is an interesting relic of the past. It was built, as tradition informs us, before the close of the last century, and having been used for many years by the congregation, was sold, and by a somewhat unusual transformation became a foundry. Again it was abandoned till it was purchased for a church. After the interior had undergone the necessary alteration, it was dedicated, under the title of the Immaculate Conception, by the Bishop July 9th, 1871.

Fr. Waters next purchased a large lot adjoining the church, upon which he built a frame residence in the summer of 1872. In the same year he opened a school, which was continued in a temporary frame building until June, 1878, when it was closed for the present, owing to the stringency of the times.

The congregation has not increased since the outbreak of the panic, but it still counts about one hundred families, consisting principally of Irishmen and Americans.

Besides ministering to the congregation Father Waters also visits a number of places on the line of the railroad, the principal of which are Jamestown, four miles below Connellsville, where he says Mass on one Sunday in the month; Indian Creek, seven, and Ohio Pyle Falls, sixteen miles above, each of which he visits monthly on a week-day.

The condition of the congregation and its dependencies must gradually improve in the future.

ST. ALOYSIUS' CHURCH, DUNBAR.

The village of Dunbar is on the creek of the same name, on the Fayette County branch of the Baltimore and Ohio Railroad, and on the South-western Railroad, four miles south of Connellsville. It derives its name from Col. Thos. Dunbar, who was second in command of Braddock's expedition.

About three miles east of the village, on the Chestnut Ridge, is the spot where the defeated forces first halted to rest in their retreat; and the spot is yet known as " Dunbar's Camp."

The congregation of St. Aloysius' and the village also owe their origin to the presence of a blast-furnace built there a few years ago, which naturally drew a number of laborers to the place, the greater part of whom were Irish Catholics. Mining and coke-burning have since added to their number. Mass was first celebrated by Father Waters in March, 1869, and from that time forward he visited the place once in the month on a week-day. In 1873, when the congregation had increased considerably, he began to visit it once in the month on Sunday. But the distance from Connellsville did not prevent the better disposed among the people from going there to Mass occasionally.

After the retirement of Rev. Thomas Fitzgerald from Meyersdale on account of failing health, Rev. Philip Brady was appointed pastor of that place in the beginning of 1874, with the additional obligation of visiting Dunbar on every alternate Sunday. As yet there was no church. But early in the summer of the same year, the size of the congregation, which now numbered about forty-five families with every prospect of an increase in the future, made the building of a church both necessary and feasible. A site was purchased which, although not the most eligible that could have been found, is still good, and work was commenced. The cornerstone was laid by the Bishop June 21st. The church was finished the following summer and was dedicated by the same prelate July 25th, under the invocation of St. Aloysius Gonzaga. It is a brick building 75 feet in length by 35 in width, but without a steeple, and is very neat and substantial both in its external and internal appearance and finish. The growing importance of the place induced Father Brady to transfer his residence thither in October, where he has since lived. He continued to visit Meyersdale until September, 1876, and has also had care of Le Mont Furnace from the time it became a missionary station, as we shall presently see.

A school-house was built, and a school was opened by a lay teacher in the summer of 1878.

The congregation has now increased to about one hundred and twenty families. Its future prospects are also flattering. Should additional iron manufactories be built, which is very probable, and for which there is every encouragement, the Catholic population of this part of the county must be augmented.

LE MONT FURNACE MISSION.

This mission is on the line of the railroads that connect Connellsville with Uniontown, and is four miles north of the latter. A blast-furnace was built here in 1876, which with a small trade in coke soon drew a little congregation of Catholics, Irishmen for the most part, to the place. This nationality, it would appear, is destined in the dispensations of Providence to lay the foundations of the Church nearly everywhere in the land. Father Brady, of Dunbar, began immediately to visit the place on two Sundays in the month, riding from St. Aloysius' Church between the two Masses, which he celebrated on the same day. This arrangement has since continued, with the exception of the few months from September, 1877, until May of the following year, when a priest resided at Uniontown. During that time Le Mont was, as we have seen, under the care of that missionary, but the congregation was visited in the same manner as it had been before. No church has yet been built; but the erection of one cannot long be deferred, as the congregation already numbers perhaps sixty families. The Catholic population must in the nature of things continue to increase, and it seems probable that at no distant day there will be a resident pastor, to whom will also be entrusted the Catholics of Uniontown and Farmington. The prospects of the future growth of religion in the whole northern part of Fayette are as flattering as they are in any other part of the entire diocese.

ST. JOHN THE BAPTIST'S CHURCH, SCOTTDALE.

Everson, or Fountain Mills as it was formerly called, is a little village six miles north of Connellsville, on the boundary line between Fayette and Westmoreland counties, and on the line of the South-western Railroad at the point where it is crossed by the Mount Pleasant branch of the Baltimore and Ohio Railroad. But since the incorporation of Scottdale as a borough, which lies immediately across the line in Westmoreland County, the place is better known by that name. The town owes its importance to the presence of a rolling-mill and a blast-furnace lately built there. Prior to that time a small amount of mining was carried on, in which, among others, a few Catholics were engaged. From about the year 1874 Mass was celebrated in a private house by the pastor of Connellsville, once in the month. When the iron-works at length brought a larger number of Catholics together more frequent ministrations became necessary. To supply the wants of the people Father Waters purchased a little frame Episcopal church, 20 by 40 feet, that was offered for sale, and blessed it as a church April 23d, 1876. An assistant was then assigned to him, and Mass was celebrated in the new church every Sunday. Scottdale was erected into an independent parish in the beginning of the summer of 1878, and Rev. Thos. M'Enrue, assistant at Connellsville, was appointed resident pastor. As yet there is neither school nor pastoral residence. The congregation consists of about a hundred and twenty-five families, with very flattering prospects for the future.

Father M'Enrue was succeeded by Rev. M. A. Lambing, brother of the writer, early in July, 1879.

But the church is too small for the congregation. To remedy the evil Fr. Lambing commenced, in the fall of 1879, to build a frame church, 71 by 37 feet.

The pastor of this church also says Mass on one Sunday in the month at Bridgeport, on the Bradford and Mount Pleasant Railroad, four miles east of Scottdale. There are besides this place one or two other stations where Mass is celebrated once a month on a week-day. Scottdale is perhaps the most promising place in Fayette County; and it is not improbable that the congregation will double its numbers before the end of two years.

ST. JOHN THE BAPTIST'S CHURCH, NEW BALTIMORE, SOMERSET COUNTY.

The success of Dr. Gallitzin in planting a Catholic colony at Loretto induced Rev. Thos. Heyden, of Bedford, to make a similar experiment. A Mr. Ridelmoser, a wealthy German Catholic of Baltimore, owned large tracts of land at a place known as Harman's Bottom, in Somerset County, on the eastern side of the Allegheny Mountains, about twenty-two miles west of Bedford. Here it was that Father Heyden hoped to realize his plans of an exclusively Catholic colony. In 1832 he proposed to Mr. Ridelmoser to draw Catholic settlers to his lands on condition that a church should be built and the land reserved exclusively for Catholics. That gentleman entered heartily into his plans, built a stone church, about fifty feet in length by thirty-five in width, in a simple style, and a pastoral residence, and donated 100 acres of land to the church for the support of the pastor. The church, which he furnished with vestments and plate, was dedicated, under the invocation of St. John the Baptist, January 1st, 1836. He named the place New Baltimore, but it is yet generally known by the name of Harman's Bottom. Besides this he donated 600 acres of land for the support of a Catholic school, and placed the management of it in the hands of three members of the congregation to be elected at the times and in the manner prescribed by him. It was his intention, as also that of Father Heyden, to make the new settlement a seat of learning as well as of piety. No sooner were the foundations of the settlement laid than plans were formed, as we learn from an article in the *Bedford Gazette*, for the erection of a Catholic university. The size and style of the buildings were specified, and expectations were excited that were never to be realized. Lying, as the land does, between the Northern and Southern turnpikes, the two great thoroughfares from the east to the west, it was thought to possess every advantage. But the Pennsylvania Canal lately opened drew all travel from these roads and left New Baltimore, as we shall see, with little hope of future greatness. But before condemning the projectors of the university for being too sanguine, we should note the changes that we ourselves sometimes see pass over certain localities in a single decade of years.

Upon the completion of the church there were about one hundred and fifty families, and at present there are no more. The school was not opened, and the land reserved for its support has been always rented out for the benefit of the pastor. But owing to the absence of minerals and the want of ready communication with the outer world, it is not so valuable as might be imagined. From the time of its completion until the appointment of a resident pastor, in 1854, the church was generally visited on one Sunday in the month by Father Heyden. During this time there was little change in the congregation from the fact that those who lived there owned land and cared not to leave it, while to persons from without it offered no inducements to settle.

In 1854 Rev. Richard Brown was appointed resident pastor and assigned one or two missions in connection with the congregation. Having remained until 1859, he was succeeded by Rev. J. N. Tamchina, who after a brief space gave place to Rev. Patrick Brown. After a few years he was succeeded by Rev. Robt. Byrne, who exercised the pastoral duties for about two years. At length, in 1870, the Carmelite fathers were placed in charge of the congregation, and so it remains. They enlarged the church by the addition of about thirty feet to its length, and thus improved it was dedicated by the Bishop August 3d, 1871. Two years later they built a brick pastoral residence.

A school was opened in the old residence in the spring of 1877, but after a short time it was temporarily closed. It is the intention of the pastor to have it opened permanently as soon as possible.

The congregation numbers at present about one hundred and fifty families, all of whom speak English with the exception of perhaps a dozen of the original German settlers. Its future has every prospect of being as monotonous as the past has been.

ST. MATTHEW'S CHURCH, MEYERSDALE.

Meyersdale is a village situated on the western slope of the main ridge of the Allegheny Mountains near their summit, and on the line of the Baltimore and Ohio Railroad, one hundred and twelve miles south-east of Pittsburg. The most noteworthy event in the history of the town was the difficulty it experienced in hitting upon a name. In the days of its minority it was known as Meyers' Mills; but in time it aspired to the title of Dale City. A lively discussion arose between the old and the new school which was happily adjusted by the present euphonious compromise.

A few German Catholic families located themselves in the town and surrounding country more than thirty years ago, and were visited at distant and irregular intervals either by the pastor of Bedford or by the Redemptorist fathers from Cumberland, Md. The church was undertaken about the year 1850, and when finished two years later by Rev. Joseph Gezowski, then pastor, was dedicated, most probably by Father Heyden, under the invocation of the Apostle St. Matthew, May 2d, 1852. It is a very small frame building with a little belfry. The congregation consisted at that time of eighteen families. Soon Father Gezowski was transferred to another field of labor, and the congregation was visited, generally on one Sunday in the month, from New Baltimore. This arrangement appears to have continued until about the year 1868, when Rev. Patrick Brown was transferred from New Baltimore to Meyersdale, with the care of the missions also that belong to it. During all this time the congregation had undergone no perceptible change, except that the Germans had become somewhat Anglicized and a few families had been added to the original number. At the close of the year 1872 Father Brown was succeeded by Rev. Thomas Fitzgerald, who in the course of the following summer built a frame pastoral residence at a considerable distance from the church. Failing health obliged him to withdraw from the congregation in the middle of December, and he retired to the home of his parents in Pittsburg, where he died of consumption April 21st, 1874, at the age of 26 years.

Rev. Thomas Fitzgerald was born of Irish parents in the cathedral parish, Pittsburg, and at an early age showed signs of a vocation to the sacred ministry. He entered St. Michael's Seminary March 3d, 1863, and eagerly prosecuted the course of studies necessary to fit him for the priesthood. This done, he was ordained December 20th, 1871. Shortly after he was sent to Altoona as assistant to Father Tuigg. A few months later he was appointed pastor of St. Patrick's Church, Sugar Creek. A field of labor was here opened to his zeal that was far from encouraging. The church, with all it contained, had but lately been burned to the ground, and the congregation was forced to retire to the old log church that had not been used for thirty years. He entered upon his labors with an energy that proved at times too great for the strength of his naturally feeble body, and until the close of the year 1872 toiled with unabated zeal for the spiritual and temporal welfare of perhaps the most discouraging parish in the diocese. From there he was taken to Meyersdale, as has been already stated. His remains repose in St. Mary's Cemetery, Pittsburg.

He was succeeded by Rev. Philip Brady, who divided his attention between St. Matthew's congregation and that at Dunbar. Having ministered to both until September, 1876, he took up his residence at the latter place, and Rev. R. Brown, the present pastor, was appointed to Meyersdale. The congregation does not exceed twenty-five families, and there are no hopes of increase in the immediate future.

The pastor of St. Matthew's has charge of about half a dozen stations on the line of the railroad in both directions from Meyersdale, nearly all of which are visited once in the month on a week-day. But in none of them are there more than a very few families, principally railroad men. Ursina—sometimes known as Brook's Tunnel—twenty miles west of Meyersdale, is the principal station. Here Mass is celebrated in a school-house on one Sunday in the month.

Sand Patch, five miles east of Meyersdale, at the summit of the mountain, was during the construction of the railroad an important mission, owing to the large number of hands employed in the tunnel opened through the mountain at that point. A temporary frame church 60 feet by 30 was built for their accommodation about the year 1857 and dedicated to St. Patrick. But when the tunnel was completed, a few years later, the laborers withdrew and the church, being no longer needed, was torn down. It is now an unimportant station.

WELLSBURG, across the mountain to the south-east of Meyersdale and near the State line, has had a small number of Catholics for perhaps twenty-five years. No church has ever been erected for their accommodation, and the place has never been more than a monthly station, attended sometimes from New Baltimore, but generally from Maryland. For many years it has been under the care of the pastor of Mount Savage, Md., from which place it is but a few miles distant. Its condition is destined to undergo but little change.

CHAPTER XV.

BEDFORD AND HUNTINGDON COUNTIES.

General remarks on the early Catholic settlements — Bedford, St. Thomas' Church — Death and sketch of Very Rev. Thomas Heyden — St. John's Church, Clearville—St. Mary's Church, Shade Valley—Huntingdon—Early Catholic settlement — Holy Trinity Church—Death and sketch of Rev. P. B. Halloran—Mount Union—Church of the Immaculate Conception, Broad Top.

THE tract of country that is now to claim our attention was settled at a very early date in our history, from the fact that it lay in the route west from both Philadelphia and Baltimore. For the same reason it early possessed a number of small Catholic settlements. But notwithstanding this, it has never been a fruitful field for religion, and if we except the congregation at Broad Top, which is of recent growth, the Catholic population has not more than doubled itself in seventy years. The difficulty of visiting and ministering to the pioneers, and the more rapid increase of the population of other places, which rendered it necessary to leave a very wide field here in later times for one priest to visit, the stations of which could only be visited at distant intervals, prevented religion from exercising that influence over the minds of the people, but more especially of the young, which was necessary to prevent them from being led astray by the temptations to which they were exposed. Hence there is no place in the two dioceses in which so large a number has fallen from the faith, and no place where the evil effects of mixed marriages are more plainly seen. What the future is destined to bring with it cannot be conjectured in a country like ours, where changes are so frequent and unexpected; but from present indications it offers a prospect by no means flattering.

ST. THOMAS' CHURCH, BEDFORD.

Bedford, the seat of justice of the county of the same name, is on the Philadelphia and Pittsburg turnpike, 200 miles from the former and 100 from the latter place. It is situated in a luxuriant limestone valley, and enjoys every advantage that pure mountain air and water and picturesque scenery can impart. By order of the governor of the colony the town was laid out in June, 1766, by the surveyor-general, John Lukens. The settlement had originally been called Raystown, but from the time of laying it out it was called by its present name.*

The population in 1870 was 1247. The growth of the town, it will be seen, has been very moderate, owing to the want of ready communication with other places and the absence of minerals, upon which, as is well known, the prosperity and in a great measure the increase of the Catholic population in Western Pennsylvania depend. But it has been long famous for its mineral springs, and has for many years been a summer resort. Within a few years the Huntingdon and Broad Top Railroad has been extended through Bedford to Cumberland, Md., which increased the facilities for communication, but did not materially benefit the town.

Being on the route from Maryland to the west, along which many of the pioneer Catholics passed, a small number of families settled there, making it the second Catholic settlement in the two dioceses. Doctor Gallitzin visited it soon after his arrival at Loretto, and very probably before it, inasmuch as it lay on the route from Taneytown, where he was stationed, to the colony which he established on the mountains. The Holy Sacrifice was offered up in a private house—most probably that of Mr. Heyden, a merchant of the place—until a church was built. This church was erected, as Father Bradly informs me, during the time Dr. Gallitzin continued to visit the town; that is, prior to the year 1820. But the exact date cannot be ascertained with certainty. It is needless to state that the visits of a priest were necessarily made at distant inter-

---

* Day's Historical Collections, pp. 115-122.

vals. In 1806 a Rev. Mr. Phelan was for a time at Bedford contrary to the wishes of Dr. Gallitzin, as may be learned from a letter of his to Bishop Carroll dated December 19th of that year.

Thomas Heyden, son of the merchant of Bedford, was destined to become the most prominent figure in the congregation's history. Having completed his studies at Mt. St. Mary's College, Maryland, he was ordained to the sacred ministry by a dispensation before he had attained the canonical age, May 21st, 1821. For a short time he was stationed at St. Joseph's Church, Philadelphia, after which it appears. —for the biographical notices of him differ—he was sent to minister to the congregation of Bedford. In October, 1826, he was appointed assistant at St. Mary's Church, Philadelphia, of which he soon after became pastor. The length of time he remained cannot now be determined, but it must have been short. Again we find him at his native town, but it is said that he returned to St. Mary's for a short time in 1835. His firmness, moderation, and tact admirably adapted him to the management of difficult undertakings; and the care of St. Mary's congregation in those days is admitted on all hands to have been pre-eminently such. Returning to Bedford he remained until April 1st, 1837, when he was appointed pastor of St. Paul's Church, Pittsburg, a position which he filled until the 22d of November of the same year, when the bishopric of Natchez, Miss., was offered to him. He declined the proffered dignity, which was the highest tribute that could have been paid to his zeal and administrative ability, and once more betook himself to his native town. Again he was called to Pittsburg, May, 1843, when Very Rev. M. O'Connor set out for Rome. Upon the return of that prelate as Bishop of the new See of Pittsburg, Fr. Heyden came back to Bedford, never again to leave it until called to his final rest.

He replaced the old church by another, the time of which is uncertain; but he lived in a house which he had inherited, and had no occasion to build a pastoral residence. As the Catholic population increased and priests became more numerous new missionary centres were formed, and the sphere of his labors was gradually narrowed down to Bedford and New Baltimore, which latter place he visited on one Sunday in the month till a resident pastor was appointed in 1854, as has been elsewhere stated. From this time there remained to him only Bedford and Clearville, yet to be noticed. When Bishop O'Connor visited the congregation in 1847, there were, as I learn from his Notes, 250 souls; a fact which proves the extremely moderate growth of the Catholic population. Gradual, however, as was the growth of the congregation, it was found necessary to replace the old church by a larger one, and the present edifice was undertaken. The corner-stone was laid by the Bishop October 22d, 1868, and the basement was dedicated by the same prelate July 18th of the following year. In this condition it remained for several years, until it was finished by the present pastor. It is of brick, 75 feet in length by 40 in width, neatly but not elegantly finished in the interior, and has a steeple rising from the centre in front.

But the career of Father Heyden was run, and the time had come for him to enter into the joy of his Lord. Naturally of a robust constitution, he gave little indication of his coming dissolution. He performed the usual routine duties of the Sunday, and preached with his wonted vigor and eloquence August 23d, 1870, but was almost immediately prostrated by sickness. The malady increased in an alarming manner, and, strengthened by the sacred rites which he had so often administered to others, he expired at five o'clock on Tuesday morning, August 25th, at the age of 72.

REV. THOMAS HEYDEN was born in county Carlow, Ireland, in 1798. His parents emigrated to this country in his infancy and settled at Bedford, where he spent his childhood and youth until he entered Mt. St. Mary's College. His subsequent career is before the reader. He was somewhat above the medium height, of a gentle but dignified and commanding appearance, and very measured and deliberate in his motions and in the expression of his opinions. He was a diligent student during his whole life, a profound scholar, an able administrator of the affairs of the Church, and one of the most eloquent and impressive preachers of this country. But he loved retirement and seclusion, and seldom appeared outside the limits of his parish, unless duty or the earnest request of a fellow-priest called him to assist at some of the more solemn functions of the Church. Although of a literary turn of mind, he has left but few writings after him. With the exception of a small number of printed lectures and sermons, there is nothing save a Life of his early and devoted friend, published in 1869, and entitled " A Memoir on the Life and Character of the Rev. Prince Demetrius A. de Gallitzin, Founder of Loretto and Catholicity, in Cambria County, Pa., Apostle of the Alleghenies." The work, although containing considerable information and a fair estimate of the character of the illustrious subject, did not realize the expectations of the author's numerous friends.

Father Heyden's remains repose in the cemetery at Bedford.

He was succeeded by the present pastor, Rev. Andrew J. M. Brown, A.M., formerly president of St. Francis' College, Loretto. Since his appointment he finished the church, as has been stated, and built a brick pastoral residence.

The growth of the congregation has been somewhat more encouraging in later than in former times, but it has no prospect of becoming large. It has never had the advantage of a parish school, from the fact of its being spread over a large tract of country.

ST. JOHN'S CHURCH, CLEARVILLE.

The only mission at present attached to Bedford is Clearville, about twelve miles to the south-east. Having visited the few Catholic families in the village for a time, Father Heyden built a chapel for their better accommodation, the corner-stone of which was laid by him October 10th, 1853. It was finished and dedicated at the end of about two years, and has since been visited once in the month on a week-day. Besides this there are no other missions in Bedford County, the whole Catholic population of which will not exceed three hundred souls.

ST. MARY'S CHURCH, SHADE VALLEY, HUNTINGDON COUNTY.

The congregation that I am now about to notice is, with two or three exceptions, the oldest in the diocese. Shade Valley lies between the Shade and Tuscarora mountains, two spurs of the Alleghenies, and is about twenty-five miles in a direct line south-east of Huntingdon. It lay on the route from Baltimore, Taneytown, and Conewago, to the western part of the State, which passed through the mountains at Shade Gap. The fertility of the soil, the strongest attraction for pioneers, induced a small number of emigrants to settle there between the years 1790 and 1800. The disturbances which then agitated the Westmoreland settlement, to which nearly all emigrants directed their steps at that early day, were not without influence on the minds of those who had been taught to look upon a disagreement between a pastor and his people as one of the greatest of evils. To the same lamentable cause is due in a measure the early settlements of Frankstown, Sinking Valley, and other places in Huntingdon and Blair counties. The settlement at Shade Valley was visited by Dr. Gallitzin from Taneytown in 1796. After locating himself at Loretto three years later, he was accustomed always to call at the settlement when on his way to Baltimore, and at such other times as his circumstances permitted. Besides these periodical but rare visits the people were sometimes favored with a call from the priest at Conewago. The tracing of their history prior to 1820 is attended with difficulties. Archbishop Hughes is said to have preached there when but a deacon, and the echo of his praise has not died out to the present day. When Rev. Thos. Heyden was stationed at Bedford in 1820 Shade Valley was embraced within the field of his missionary labors, and received a visit from him once in the month or once in two months. He continued to minister to the little flock until about the year 1850, although during that time it was occasionally visited by other priests. It was then for a time attended by one of the priests of the Philadelphia (now Harrisburg) diocese. But since 1853 it has formed a part of the Huntingdon mission.

A small stone church was built by Father Heyden about the year 1848. The congregation is now and has for many years been visited on one Sunday in the month, and it numbers about thirty-five families, all farmers and native born. The number was as large perhaps fifty years ago. The absence of mineral resources and of railroad communication with other places makes it very probable that it will not increase for many years.

HUNTINGDON.

Huntingdon, the seat of justice of the county of the same name, is situated on the north bank of the Juniata River, just above the mouth of Standingstone Creek. The town is built upon an elevated bank sloping gently up from the river, and behind the town rising into a hill. It was laid out a short time previous to the Revolutionary war by Rev. Dr. W. Smith, Provost of the University of Pennsylvania. When in England soliciting funds for the university he found the Countess of Huntingdon a munificent donor, and in return for her liberality he gave her name to the town. Previous to that time the place had been noted as the site of an ancient Indian village called Standing Stone. A tall slim pillar of stone, four inches thick by eight inches wide, had been erected here by the resident tribe many years before, perhaps as a sort of Ebenezer, or "Stone of Help." *

---

* Day's Historical Collections, pp. 368–370.

The same author gives the following account of the superstitious veneration with which this stone was regarded : " A tradition is said to have existed among the Indians that if the stone should be taken away the tribe would be dispersed, but that so long as it should stand they would prosper. A hostile tribe once came up from the Tuscarora Valley and carried it off during the absence of the warriors ; but the latter fell upon them, recovered the stone, and replaced it. It is said that Dr. Barton, of Philadelphia, learned in some of his researches that *Oneida* meant standing stone ; and that nation, while living in New York, is said to have had a tradition that their ancestors came originally from the south. It is generally understood about Huntingdon that the original stone had been destroyed or taken away by the Indians, but that the whites erected a similar one, a part of which remains. It is certain that the whites removed it from its original position (at the east end near the river) to the centre of the town. When Mr. M'Murtrie came here in 1776–77 it was about eight feet high, and had on it the

The scenery around Huntingdon is beautiful beyond description, being mountainous and broken and generally wooded. To one who ascends the hill or mountain to the north of the town there is presented a prospect on the north, west, and south, extending in places to the distance of more than thirty miles over a broken mountainous country until the view is intercepted by the loftier summit of the main ridge of the Alleghenies.

The growth of the town has been very moderate, and in 1870 it had a population of but 3034. The increase since that time, however, has been considerable, and it will now probably reach 5000 souls.

Catholics were among the first settlers in the town and surrounding country, and there is no part of the two dioceses in which so many have been lost to the faith by intermarriage and apostasy. Dr. Gallitzin visited the place as early as the year 1796, and from that time forward continued to do so until Father Heyden was stationed at Bedford, who then relieved him of all the missions on the eastern side of the mountains. It was a preacher of this town, a Rev. Mr. Johnson, who by his violent attacks on the Church gave occasion to Dr. Gallitzin to publish his world-renowned "Defence of Catholic Principles," etc., as we shall see more fully hereafter. The laborers who were employed on the northern turnpike, some of whom settling in and near the town after the completion of the work, increased the Catholic population. Rev. John O'Reilly, who was ordained in 1826, relieved Fr. Heyden of the northern portion of his extensive district, and resided for a time at Huntingdon. Immediately after his arrival work was commenced on the canal, and there being a large number of Irish Catholics among the laborers, he determined to build a church for his increasing flock. The dedication was performed July 4th, 1830, by Bishop Conwell, assisted by his coadjutor, Bishop Kenrick. But it

---

names of John Lukens, the surveyor-general, with the date of 1768; Charles Lukens, his assistant; and Thomas Smith, brother of the founder of the town and afterwards judge of the Supreme Court. It stood there for many years until some fool in a drunken frolic demolished it. It is evidently a stone from the bed of the creek, bearing marks of being worn by water." (p. 370.)

had then been finished for a considerable time. Speaking of the church and its dedication, a correspondent of the *United States Catholic Miscellany* says: "The church, which was commenced towards the end of September, 1828, under the care of Rev. John O'Reilly, is of brick, solid and substantial. 62 by 35 feet, including a sanctuary, which is built in the form of an offset with a small vestry-room on the left, which is also used as a confessional. It has a front gallery, supported by four columns, which together with the nave numbers 57 pews. The height of the ceiling from the floor is 25 feet. The whole is tastefully executed, for the most part, according to the Gothic style of architecture. . . . It is but just to remark that this church, as well as many others recently erected, has been raised principally by the generosity of poor Irishmen working on the canal."

Father O'Reilly remained until the autumn of 1831, and built churches in Bellefonte and Newry. He was then transferred to Pittsburg, where he became the assistant and afterwards the successor of Fr. M'Guire. Huntingdon was then visited for a short time by Rev. Jas. Bradley, then as now pastor of the church at Newry. In 1834 Rev. Patrick Leavy resided for a time in the town, attending it and the surrounding missions. After the erection of the church Mass was usually celebrated on one Sunday in the month. In 1837 Father Bradley again visited it; and in 1844 it was under the care of Rev. Patrick Pendergast, of Bellefonte. Soon after it was attached to the new mission of Hollidaysburg. When Bishop O'Connor visited the congregation in 1847, there were, according to his Notes, 130 souls. When the Pennsylvania Railroad was opened, about the year 1851, Huntingdon became, and has since remained, an independent mission, embracing the entire county. From that time Mass was celebrated twice in the month until the Broad Top congregation was detached from it in 1863, since which time Mass is offered up on all the Sundays but the one given to Shade Valley. The first resident pastor was Rev. Peter M. Doyle, who remained until the breaking out of the Rebellion, when he was succeeded by Rev. Peter Hughes. But in the beginning of the year 1863 the growing importance of Broad

Top induced the Bishop to make a further division of the mission, and the latter became an independent congregation. Father Hughes was transferred to it, and Rev. S. Wall became pastor of Huntingdon. Having ministered to the congregation until October, 1865, he was appointed president of the diocesan seminary, and Rev. O. P. Gallagher succeeded him. During his pastorate he built a brick residence by the side of the church, besides making other improvements in the church and its surroundings. In July, 1868, he was transferred to Wilmore. Among his successors changes were frequent until July, 1871, when Rev. Martin Murphy was appointed. His immediate predecessor was Rev. Patrick B. Halloran, whose feeble health forced him to retire from active duty. Soon after withdrawing from the congregation he determined to cross the ocean to his native land, in the hope of recruiting his failing health. But it was not so ordained; for no sooner had he landed than he was obliged to retire to the hospital of the Sisters of Mercy at Cork, where a few days later, October 11th, 1871, he gave up his soul to God, being then in the 26th year of his age, and not having quite completed the second in the sacred ministry. His remains were taken to Broadford, in the county Clare, where they were honored by interment in the same church in which he had been baptized.

REV. PATRICK B. HALLORAN was born at Broadford, county Clare, about the year 1845, and having almost completed his studies at Killaloo College, Waterford, he came to this country in the summer of 1868 and entered St. Michael's Seminary. Upon the completion of his course of theology he was ordained and stationed at Broad Top, but was soon after transferred to Huntingdon, from which he also visited Lewistown, in the Diocese of Harrisburg, where he commenced the erection of a church.

Father Murphy, soon after his appointment, purchased a piece of ground near the town for a cemetery. A new impetus has been given to business in the last few years, and the population has considerably increased. The congregation has also been benefited a little, but the increase is not considerable, and it will not number more than fifty families.

if so many. But its future prospects, though by no means flattering, are yet more encouraging than they were at any previous period of its history. Father Murphy was succeeded by the present pastor, Rev. Arthur Devlin, in the middle of November, 1878.

The pastor of Huntingdon has also to attend a small mission at Mount Union, ten miles east on the Pennsylvania Railroad, which he visits once in a month on a week-day. The number of families is quite small, but a Catholic gentleman, Mr. John Dougherty, has donated a few acres of ground as the site for a church which will probably be erected at no distant day.

CHURCH OF THE IMMACULATE CONCEPTION, BROAD TOP.

Broad Top City is situated on a short branch of the Huntingdon and Broad Top Railroad, about twenty-two miles south of the former town, and owes its rise to the rich coalfield in which it stands. In the beginning of its history the congregation was visited from Huntingdon, but the number of Catholics increasing, Father Doyle built a frame church, 50 feet in length and 30 in width, in the summer of 1859, which was dedicated, under the title of the Immaculate Conception, by Very Rev. James O'Connor, Adm., October 30th of the same year. The church stood in the village of Dudley, about one and a half miles west of Broad Top, and was long known as the Dudley church. Immediately before the breaking out of the Rebellion mining began to be carried on very extensively, the Catholic population increased, and it became necessary to appoint a resident pastor that the Holy Sacrifice might be offered up every Sunday. Rev. P. Hughes, who had for some time visited the congregation from Huntingdon, was transferred thither in the beginning of 1863, and became the first resident pastor. From 1861 to the close of the Rebellion was the season of the congregation's greatest numerical strength and prosperity. Fr. Hughes built an elegant frame pastoral residence, and finding the church too small he replaced it by a large frame edifice, which was dedicated by the Bishop September 18th, 1864.

Four years later Rev. W. A. Nolan succeeded to the pastorate, and Fr. Hughes was transferred to Braddock's Field. The congregation met with a serious loss in the total destruction of the church by fire, November 28th, 1869. It was replaced by another frame building, which was dedicated by Very Rev. J. Tuigg, V.F., July 21st, 1870. Father Nolan was soon after succeeded by Rev. P. B. Halloran, who in turn soon gave place to Rev. R. Brown. Owing to the partial cessation of work in the mines and the imprudent strikes of the miners the congregation had for several years been declining in numbers and importance, though still large. Fr. Brown was succeeded, in December, 1875, by Rev. Jas. P. Tahaney. Again the congregation sustained a loss in the burning of the church and pastoral residence, on Holy Saturday, April 15th, 1876. The destruction of the church is confidently believed to have been the work of an incendiary, for great dissatisfaction had long existed regarding its location. It stood at Dudley; one and a half miles east was Broad Top, and four miles further east was East Broad Top. Many wished the church to be at Broad Top, as being more central, and feeling on the matter was stronger than it was Christian.

Upon the destruction of the church the Bishop decided that a new one should be built at Dudley and another at East Broad Top. But the condition of the congregation, reduced as it was by the hard times, did not favor the undertaking, and Father Tahaney purchased a property for $1500 consisting of about an acre of ground with a large frame dwelling and several other buildings on it. The dwelling is used as a pastoral residence, and one of the other buildings has been transformed into a temporary church. Father Tahaney was succeeded by Rev. Jos. Gallagher September, 1876, and he by Rev. J. Bullion, the present pastor, February 8, 1879. For the accommodation of the people of East Broad Top, Mass is now offered up for them once or twice in the month in a school-house.

The mission, although much smaller than it was formerly, will yet number perhaps one hundred and fifty families. What it is destined to be in the future will depend upon the future of the coal-mines; but any increase is not to be expected, at least not for many years.

CHAPTER XVI.

IN BLAIR COUNTY.

General remarks—St. Patrick's Church, Newry—Rev. Jas. Bradley—St. Luke's Church, Sinking Valley—Hollidaysburg—Early Catholic settlers—St. Mary's Church—Conversion of Hayden Smith—St. Michael's German Church—St. Joseph's Church, Williamsburg—Altoona—St. John's Church—Lloydsville mission—Church of the Immaculate Conception, German—St. Matthew's Church, Tyrone.

BLAIR COUNTY, which was formed from Huntingdon and Bedford in 1846, though smaller than either, possesses a Catholic population far larger in the present than both, and affords better promise for the future. It is the only portion of the diocese east of the mountains upon which we are permitted to look with satisfaction. Favored rather by circumstances than by nature, it was at first traversed by the Pennsylvania Canal, which, terminating in its eastern division at Hollidaysburg, made that the most important town between Harrisburg and Pittsburg. In later years it reaped and is still reaping a yet greater advantage from the Pennsylvania Railroad, especially at Altoona, as we shall have occasion to remark in the following pages. It is the third county in the two dioceses in point of Catholic population, and contains perhaps nine thousand souls.

ST. PATRICK'S CHURCH, NEWRY.

The village of Newry is situated near the foot of the eastern slope of the Allegheny Mountains, about nine miles south of Altoona, with which it is connected by a branch of the Pennsylvania Railroad. Here resides Rev. Jas. Bradley, the patriarch of the secular clergy of the two dioceses, full of health and vigor and giving promise of many more years of usefulness and edification before being called to his reward. Leaving Ireland, his native country, to dedicate himself to the cause of religion in the wilds of America, he emigrated to the United States, in 1825, and entered Mount St. Mary's College, Md., to complete his studies. Having spent five years there under the spiritual direction of the venerable Simon Gabriel Bruté, afterwards Bishop of Vincennes, Mr. Bradley was ordained to the sacred ministry in the church of Conewago, Pa., September 20th, 1830. It is worthy of remark that he is the first priest ordained by the saintly Bishop Kenrick. Writing of his entering upon the mission, Father Bradley tells me: "I soon after (ordination) set out from Emmittsburg with Father Stillenger for the Pennsylvania mission. . . . I offered up my first Holy Mass in the mission at Bedford on Sunday, and drove the same day thirty miles to Newry, where I said my second Mass. I then drove to Loretto, and after spending a few days with Rev. Dr. Gallitzin, I took charge of the Ebensburg congregation." When noticing that congregation I shall have something further to remark on the labors of the venerable missionary. Having remained at Ebensburg about two years, ministering to the spiritual necessities of a very large district, Father Bradley was transferred to Newry, which from the beginning had been embraced within the range of his missionary labors.

Writing of the foundation of the town and congregation of Newry, Father Bradley says: "The first settlers of Newry were Patrick Cassidy and Henry M'Connell, who emigrated from Newry (county Down), Ireland, and laid out the town and called it Newry, after their native place, about the time that Dr. Gallitzin began his laborious mission at Loretto (1799). It was one of Dr. Gallitzin's stations for sixteen years, until the number of Catholic settlers increased and undertook to build a stone church in 1816. It was dedicated under the patronage of St. Patrick. My predecessors here were Dr. Gallitzin, Fathers M'Girr, Kearns (of Chambersburg), Heyden, Archbishop Hughes, and Father O'Reilly. The old stone church was still in use when I came to Newry, on the first Sunday of Advent, 1832. The present church was then in process of erection." Since that date, a period of forty-

eight years, there has been no change of pastors. But with
Newry the good priest had many other places to visit, as will
appear in the sequel. The new church, which is built of
brick and is still occupied, was dedicated by Bishop Kenrick
August 11th, 1833. The congregation had Mass at that time
on one Sunday in the month; then, as new missionary centres
were formed and the sphere of Father Bradley's labor was
narrowed, the Holy Sacrifice was offered up twice in the
month, and finally the good pastor's labors were confined, as
they have now been for thirty years, to Newry alone. When
Bishop O'Connor visited the congregation in 1847 it numbered, as he states in his Notes, four hundred souls. About
twenty years ago Father Bradley built a chapel for week-day
Masses adjoining his residence. The congregation has continued for many years, as it will in the future, gradually to
increase. The people are almost exclusively farmers, and are
Irish or of Irish parentage. They have grown up around
their common father, who has baptized nearly all, and has
watched over them and guided them with a father's care;
and they, in turn, as is but right, entertain for him sentiments
of filial affection. All will unite with them in wishing their
good pastor many years of life before he is called to the joy
of his Lord. In the fall of 1879 Rev. J. Ward was appointed
assistant to Father Bradley.

ST. LUKE'S CHURCH, SINKING VALLEY.

Sinking Valley extends south from Tyrone, between two
spurs of the Allegheny Mountains, the distance from that town
to the church being about six miles. The valley owes its
name to a peculiarity of the surface of the ground, which
sinks in many places as if acted upon by a subterranean current. Being near the line of emigration from the East to the
West, a small number of Catholic families settled there before
the close of the last century. When Dr. Gallitzin wrote from
Taneytown, where he was then stationed, to Bishop Carroll,
in March, 1799, requesting permission to enter the Pennsylvania mission to labor among the Catholics of the mountain
district, he named Sinking Valley as the seat of a Catholic

colony.* He was the first priest to visit the place, and he continued his visits until the arrival of Father Heyden at Bedford relieved him of the country east of the mountains. It remained under the jurisdiction of the latter until 1840; but his visits, like those of his predecessor, were necessarily made at distant intervals. In that year Father Bradley took charge of the congregation, and in the same year built the little frame church which is yet standing, and dedicated it to St. Luke. Little change took place in the congregation during that time, or indeed since, for it is as large now, and no larger, than it was seventy-five years ago. For thirteen years, as he informed me, Father Bradley continued to visit the church on one Sunday in the month, until Rev. J. Tuigg was appointed to Altoona, when Sinking Valley became tributary to that church. So it remained for perhaps eight years, until a resident pastor was appointed to Tyrone, when it passed under his care. Slender were the hopes that its condition would ever improve, owing to the small number of Catholics. But at length, in April, 1877, Rev. Ed. M'Sweeny was appointed the first and only resident pastor. Speaking of the congregation he said there were less than half a dozen families, and remarked that when he had a full attendance at Sunday-school there were two children present. He remained until September of the same year, when he was transferred to Williamsburg, and St. Luke's reverted to Tyrone. So it remains, and in all probability will remain.

Sinking Valley, like all the early settlements, was selected on account of the fertility of its soil; but when the attention of the native and foreign population was turned to other pursuits than agriculture it lost its attraction, and with it all hope of improvement. For unfortunately farming is not esteemed as it should be among us.

ST. MARY'S CHURCH, HOLLIDAYSBURG.

Hollidaysburg, the county-seat of Blair County, is situated near the foot of the eastern slope of the mountains. It lies

---

* Life of Dr. Gallitzin, by Miss Brownson, p. 111.

also on the route of the early emigrants, and for that reason it attracted the attention of the first settlers. The date of the foundation of the town is uncertain, but it was probably about the beginning of this century. The town takes its name, however, from William and Adam Holliday, who settled here in the year 1768. It was incorporated as a borough in 1836, and had in 1870 a population of 2952. Gaysport, on the opposite side of the Juniata River, had at the same time a population of 1799. Being at the western terminus of the eastern division of the canal, and lying in the midst of a fertile country, it was for many years a place of considerable activity. At present it manufactures pig and bar iron to a limited extent.

Catholics were found among the residents of Frankstown, a village three miles east of Hollidaysburg, before the close of the last century, and it was in behalf of these among others that Dr. Gallitzin asked permission, as we have seen, to enter the Pennsylvania mission. It may be that he visited the place as early as 1796. Frankstown, though but a small village, dates back to the middle of the last century and is mentioned by Col. Armstrong as a well-known place in 1756.[*] The few scattered families of the neighborhood formed a part of Dr. Gallitzin's missionary field until the arrival of Father Heyden. After Rev. H. Lemcke took up his residence at Ebensburg in 1834, he paid Hollidaysburg a few visits. At length it was transferred to the jurisdiction of Father Bradley of Newry, a place but three miles distant from it. The importance of the town, which ranked next after Pittsburg, in the western part of the State, in business, refinement, and politics, had attracted so large a number of Catholics that a church was deemed necessary. As early as the summer of 1831 Bishop Kenrick had asked the views of Dr. Gallitzin on the propriety of building a church, but we are not told what opinion was held by the venerable missionary. It was not until 1841 that the present church was commenced by Father Bradley. The dedication did not, however, take place until March 17th, 1844, when the ceremony was performed by Father Heyden. The church is a substantial brick building

---

[*] Annals of the West, p. 143.

87 feet in length by 63 in width, with a steeple in the centre in front, which was not, however, built until some years later. There are three altars, that in the centre being an elegant piece of workmanship. Over it is an altar-piece, a crucifixion, which is a painting of considerable merit.

The life and conversion of Mr. Hayden Smith, the architect of this and several other churches, offers so forcible and fitting an illustration of the feeling of the sects towards the Church in that part of the State, and in the earlier years of our history, that, without offering any apology for the digression, I shall present it to the reader. Speaking of the conversions effected by the writings of Dr. Gallitzin, Miss Brownson says:*

"One of the best known is perhaps that of Hayden Smith, the architect, son of Irish Protestants, brought up in such hatred of the Church that his father, when dying, enjoined upon him never to associate with Catholics, or touch their books or anything belonging to them, of course never to enter a Catholic church, and, if possible, to avoid living in the same town with Catholics. So solemn and earnest, we should say so horrible, was this death-bed injunction that it made the deepest impression, and the youth determined to carry it out to the very letter; he journeyed from city to city in England, Ireland, Canada, and the United States, but everywhere the cross was before him, the Catholics about him; finally he found himself in one of the bitterest towns of Pennsylvania, where the most violent animosity to the Catholics was freely displayed. In that very stronghold of ignorance and prejudice Mr. Smith met with a copy of the 'Defence of Catholic Principles.' He was about to throw it down in disgust, when it occurred to him that nothing could afford him better arguments against the despised Catholics than one of their own absurd books; he read, and he believed; he could not doubt, was received into the Church, and spent the greater portion of his long life in planning Catholic churches; he was the architect of the brick church in Loretto, of St. Mary's in Lancaster, and many others, and at the time of his death was oc-

* Life of Dr. Gallitzin, pp. 311, 312.

cupied in beautifying the famous Central Park in New York."

To return to our subject: Father Bradley celebrated Mass in the new church on two Sundays in the month for one year from its dedication, after which a resident priest was appointed. Mass was then celebrated on three Sundays until 1853, since which it is offered up every Sunday. Rev. R. A. Wilson, D.D., was the first resident pastor. At the end of a year he gave place to Rev John C. Brady, who remained until the autumn of 1848. The growth of the congregation in the years immediately following the erection of the church was more rapid than was that of any of the surrounding parishes; and from the Notes of Bishop O'Connor we learn that at the time of his first visit, in 1847, it contained seven hundred souls. Father Brady was succeeded after a short interval, December 20th, 1848, by Rev. John Walsh, whose tenure of office was destined to be more prolonged than that of his predecessors. He built a brick residence in 1851. When the Papal Nuncio, Cardinal Cajetan Bedini, visited the United States, he stopped at Hollidaysburg on his way to Pittsburg in the beginning of December, 1853, and administered confirmation in St. Mary's Church. During the construction of the New Portage Railroad, by which it was intended to connect the eastern and western division of the canal by rail, instead of drawing the freight and passengers on cars by stationary engines, as on the Old Portage, as well as during the construction of the Pennsylvania Railroad, the labors of Father Walsh were greatly increased. The distance to be travelled, the impassable nature of the roads in the mountains, the number of hands employed on the works, and the frequent occurrence of accidents rendered the duties of the priest a herculean task, and it is a matter of astonishment how one man was capable of performing so arduous a ministry. A little congregation was then springing into life, which, prior to the appointment of Father Tuigg, was, as we shall see, annexed to the mission of the pastor of Hollidaysburg.

In May, 1854, a number of Sisters of Mercy from Pittsburg took charge of the schools, which had for some time been conducted by lay teachers; and the large and elegant convent, school, and academy buildings which yet stand were elected for their reception.

But the completion of the Pennsylvania Railroad, which gave birth to Altoona, the supplanter of Hollidaysburg, diminished the importance of the latter. In 1868 Father Walsh erected another brick building, the lower story of which is used for a school and the upper is a hall. At length, after having presided over the congregation for almost thirty years, he was transferred to Altoona, upon the promotion of Father Tuigg to the See of Pittsburg, in March, 1876. He was succeeded by his brother, Rev. Thos. Walsh, who is yet pastor of the congregation. The Sisters of Mercy were also transferred to other fields of usefulness in the summer of the same year, and were succeeded in the school and academy by the Sisters of St. Joseph from Ebensburg.

The congregation of St. Mary's, like the town in which it is, has fallen from its former prosperous condition, and will not number more at present than it did thirty years ago. The future is not reassuring.

ST. MICHAEL'S GERMAN CHURCH, HOLLIDAYSBURG.

A part of the first settlers in the vicinity of Hollidaysburg were Germans, but, like their countrymen in many other parts of the diocese, they had to content themselves in the beginning with such advantages as circumstances placed within their reach, and live in the hope of better times. But while they waited in expectation the greater part of them lost their language, and their children grew up more familiar with the English than with their mother-tongue. Nearly all the present German congregations are largely—many exclusively—composed of emigrants.

The germ of the present congregation appears to have first attracted attention about the year 1856, when one of the Benedictine fathers from St. Vincent's Abbey visited the German Catholics of Blair County once in the month. This arrangement continued until the erection of the German church at Altoona, in 1860, when Hollidaysburg was attached to it. Rev. G. Kircher, who was then pastor of that parish, organized the congregation of which we are now treating and commenced the erection of a church. Upon its completion it was dedicated by the Bishop, December 20th, 1863, under the invocation of St. Michael. The church, which is comparatively small, is neat and substantial and is elegantly finished in the interior, being furnished with three altars. The whole is modelled after the Gothic style of architecture, and is furnished with a steeple in the centre in front. Soon after its completion a school-house was also built and a school opened by a lay teacher. Father Kircher was transferred thither in 1864 and became the first resident pastor. A residence was also secured, which, though small, was occupied for a few years until a larger one was erected. In 1868 Father Kircher was succeeded by Rev. J. B. Schmidt, and he, after a time, by Rev. Geo. Allman. About the year 1873 he placed the school under the care of the Sisters of St. Agnes, whom he introduced into the parish and provided with a convent, and they still continue to conduct it. Toward the close of the following year he was succeeded by Rev. J. Keuenzer. The congregation is small and its future increase will be very gradual. Fr. Keuenzer was succeeded in November, 1878, by the present pastor, Rev. J. Kaib.

ST. JOSEPH'S CHURCH, WILLIAMSBURG.

Williamsburg is situated on the Juniata River, thirteen miles east of Hollidaysburg, with which, as well as with Altoona, it is connected by a branch of the Pennsylvania Railroad. The scenery on the river in the vicinity of the town is very fine. The town was laid out in 1794 by a German named Jacob Ake, who called it Akestown; but previous to his death he changed its name to Williamsburg, in honor of his son William, who was about to leave him to penetrate further into the wilds. The plan of selling lots on lease by the payment of one Spanish milled silver dollar yearly forever was adopted by him, and to this day most all the lots pay that tax. One of the finest springs of water to be met anywhere flows through the town, furnishing water for a number of mills.*

* Day's Historical Collections and Renner's Altoona and Pennsylvania Railroad Guide, 1878, 1879.

It cannot now be ascertained with certainty when the first Catholics settled in the town and its vicinity, but until Mass was offered up for them they attended one of the surrounding churches. At length, about the year 1860, it was determined to build a church, and encouraged by Father Walsh, of Hollidaysburg, under whose jurisdiction the town was, and aided by their Protestant friends, the few Catholic families commenced. The church was finished in the autumn of 1861, and was dedicated by the Bishop on the 9th of October. It is a beautiful little edifice modelled after the Gothic style of architecture, and has a steeple in the centre in front. For a time it was visited from Hollidaysburg, and then by one of the priests attached to St. Francis' College, Loretto. The writer visited it from that institution in the autumn and early winter of 1869, and it was the first church committed to his care. When the congregation performed the exercise of the Jubilee at that time there were but twenty-eight communicants. Soon after this time it was again attached to Hollidaysburg, and so it remained until the spring of 1876, when it was visited from Altoona. At length, in the fall of 1877, Rev. Ed. M'Sweeny was transferred thither from Sinking Valley and Mass was offered up every Sunday. With the exception of his brief pastorate, Mass has always been celebrated on one Sunday only in the month. Not long, however, after his appointment Fr. M'Sweeny was rendered incapable of further exercising the office of the sacred ministry on the mission by a paralytic stroke, which forced him to retire to the hospital. Again the church was placed under the care of a priest of St. Francis' College, and so it remains. There are no more than twenty families in the town and its vicinity, and no flattering prospects can be predicted at least for the immediate future.

ST. JOHN'S CHURCH, ALTOONA.

The city of Altoona is situated at the foot of the eastern slope of the main ridge of the Allegheny Mountains, and at the head of what was known in frontier history as the Tuckahoe Valley. The ground rises north and south from the railroad, which at that point is 1164 feet above the level of the Atlantic Ocean. The name is said to have been derived from the Italian word *alto*, high. It is a creation of the Pennsylvania Railroad Company, upon which its inhabitants almost wholly depend, and it is 116 miles east of Pittsburg by that thoroughfare. Here in 1850 the company began to erect their shops, which they have since constantly been enlarging, until they are now perhaps the most extensive in the world. Here are built all the locomotives and cars for the main line and its branches, and here, too, the principal part of the repairing is done, as well as work for other roads. From being little less than a wilderness in 1849, when the site was purchased and the city laid out, the population reached 3951 in 1860, 15,329 in 1875, and it can now be little less than 20,000, about two fifths of which is Catholic. Altoona was chartered as a city in 1868.*

A large number of Catholics, it is superfluous to state, were employed in grading the railroad up the mountain side, and when Altoona was laid out and the shops erected it is probable that some of these were among the first to find employment and a home in the incipient city. Be that as it may, the number of Catholics was such that Rev. J. Walsh began to celebrate Mass there, being assisted for a time by Rev. R. Brown. He soon found it necessary to purchase lots—which lie three squares north from the railroad station—and begin the building of a church. This must have been about the close of 1851 or the beginning of the following year. The church was finished by Father Bradley, as he informs me, and was also visited by him for some months. It was dedicated in the early part of 1853, but the precise date has not been ascertained. The church was a frame building, simple in style and finish, and was 60 feet in length by 35 in width. The name of Rev. J. Neuper also occurs in 1852 and 1853 as occasionally ministering to the Catholics of Altoona.

But the rapid growth of the town and the promise it already gave of future importance made it apparent that it could not long depend on priests from other places. Accord-

---

* Compiled principally from Renner's Altoona City Directory for 1878-79, pp. 67 *et seq.*

ingly in July, 1853, Rev. J. Tuigg, till then of Pittsburg, and the present Bishop of the diocese, was appointed first resident pastor. He purchased a house by the side of the church, which he occupied as his residence. He also bought a few acres of ground in the suburbs for a cemetery. Time went on, the congregation increased, and although the Germans built a church, St. John's was no longer capable of accommodating the numbers who thronged to it on Sundays. With a view of afterwards building a large brick church Father Tuigg put an addition to the rear of the existing edifice, which, while enlarging it in the present, was destined afterwards to become a part of the new church. When finished it was dedicated by Bishop Domenec, November 16th, 1862.

In 1869 the Bishop appointed Fr. Tuigg Vicar Forane for the eastern part of the diocese. Prior to this time he accomplished another work which is one of the most noble monuments of his zeal and activity. Although a school had long been in existence, he was anxious to provide a more suitable building and also to place the school upon a more permanent basis. He accordingly erected a large and elegant brick block, four stories high, by the side of the church. The building is so arranged that the part towards the church is divided into school-rooms, while the other half is finished for a convent for the religious who teach the school. It is large, beautifully located at the corner of two streets, and presents a very pleasing appearance. Into the convent he introduced a colony of Sisters of Charity from Cincinnati in August, 1870, of which mention will be made in its proper place.

But the congregation increased more rapidly than ever, and Father Tuigg, who in the beginning had sometimes extended his missionary labors to Tyrone, Sinking Valley, and perhaps one or two other places, now found himself unable to minister to the single congregation of St. John's without the aid of an assistant. The first was appointed in 1871.

At length the period seemed to have arrived for the erection of the new church, and it was undertaken in 1872, the corner-stone being laid by the Bishop on the 22d of June. The work progressed under the pastor's vigorous administration; but before its completion the panic fell upon the country, the number of hands was reduced in the shops, and the wages of those who were retained were cut down to a low figure. Notwithstanding this the work was brought to a successful termination at the end of three years, and Father Tuigg had the satisfaction of contemplating an edifice of which he might well feel proud. Preparations were made for the dedication on a scale in keeping with the grandeur of the temple, and the ceremony was performed by the Bishop on the 30th of May, 1875. The church is of brick, is 120 feet in length by 60 in width, and is modelled after the Gothic style of architecture. At the front corners are twin towers that rise to the height of about 180 feet. There is a basement under the entire building, which is wholly above the level of the ground. The length of the lot did not permit the entrance to be made from the front, it being the object of the pastor to make the church as long as possible; and hence it was made from the two sides at the front. After entering, a flight of stairs is ascended from each side into a vestibule which opens into the church. This, although a saving of space, cannot be regarded as a happy arrangement. The means of egress are not sufficient for a building of its size, and would appear to great disadvantage in case of a panic. The distinctive characteristics of the Gothic style are not so prominent in the interior as in the exterior of the sacred edifice. It is without pillars, and the ceiling follows the inclination of the roof for some distance from the sides and is then horizontal. There is a deep gallery for the use of the people, and another above it for the organ and the choir. The pews are arranged without a middle aisle. There are three beautiful Gothic altars, and the windows are filled with stained glass in appropriate designs. The interior is also tastefully frescoed. On the whole it is one of the largest, most substantial, and elegant churches in the diocese.

About the time the church was finished the pastoral residence was also considerably enlarged and improved. Having been faithful in a few things, Father Tuigg was called by the voice of the Sovereign Pontiff to be placed over many, and was nominated to the See of Pittsburg upon the division of the diocese and the transfer of Bishop Domenec to the new

See of Allegheny in January, 1876. He was consecrated on the 19th of the following March, as was stated at length in a previous chapter.

Upon the promotion of Father Tuigg, Rev. J. Walsh, of Hollidaysburg, was appointed pastor of Altoona, and he returned to it after an absence of twenty-five years. He has since remained, but owing to the increase in the congregation he has always had two assistants. In September, 1878, he placed the boys' school in the hands of a number of Franciscan Brothers from Loretto, who opened a monastery in the city at that time.

The Catholic population of Altoona is gradually increasing, and must continue to increase with the growth of the city; and the day cannot be far distant when St. John's, now the largest English congregation outside of Pittsburg, will have to be divided and another church erected.

LLOYDSVILLE MISSION.

In 1872-3 a narrow-gauge railroad was laid from Bellwood (formerly Bell's Mills), seven miles east of Altoona, on the Pennsylvania Railroad, north-west up a grade averaging 158 feet to the mile, through delightful mountain scenery, to a spot seven miles distant where extensive coal-mines had been opened. A village soon sprung up that was at first known as Bell's Gap, but which afterwards took the name of Lloydsville; and such was the number of Catholics found among the miners that it became advisable to have the Holy Sacrifice offered up in their midst. It is now a regular monthly station, but as yet there is no evidence that it will be necessary to build a church for some years.

It is probable that a mission will also be formed soon at a point in the mountains five miles west of Altoona and three north of the railroad, to which a branch road has been laid, and in which mines have lately been opened and coke-burning commenced; and although in Cambria County, it is probable that it will be attended from Altoona. As yet the number of Catholics is small.

CHURCH OF THE IMMACULATE CONCEPTION, GERMAN, ALTOONA.

A few German Catholics were found among the first settlers in Altoona. From about the year 1855 they were committed to the care of one of the Benedictine fathers from St. Vincent's Abbey, who crossed the mountains once in the month to minister to their spiritual necessities. At length a church was contemplated, lots were purchased a few squares south of the railroad station, and work was commenced in 1860. Before the completion of the building Mass is said to have been offered up for the people for a short time in the English church. But the church was soon finished, and was dedicated on the 18th of December, 1860. It is a frame building 70 feet in length by 40 in width, simple and plain in its style and finish. Mass was not, however, offered up every Sunday until the appointment of the first resident pastor, Rev. Christian Schuler, February, 1862. He was succeeded in September of the same year by Rev. J. M. Bierl, who in the following March gave place to Rev. G. Kircher. Having remained until August, 1864, he was transferred to Hollidaysburg, and the vacancy was filled by the appointment of Rev. Anthony Rottensteiner. During his administration he built a frame pastoral residence. In August, 1866, he gave place to Rev. A. Roswogg. He opened a parochial school, for the people up to that time—strange for a German congregation—were without it. He was succeeded, April, 1869, by Rev. Jos. Deyermeyer; and he, November 26th, 1870, by the present pastor, Rev. John A. Shell. The congregation had all this time been gradually increasing and sharing in the prosperity of the city, and it now crowded the church to suffocation. A new church was imperatively demanded. But instead of erecting it at once the more prudent course of dividing the work and finishing part at a time was adopted. Plans were prepared for a church that when finished should be 120 feet in length by 50 in width; and it was resolved to erect the rear half at first against the back of the existing edifice, tear away part of the latter, and unite the remainder to the new building until such time as the whole plan could be carried out. The corner-stone was laid by the Bishop August 20th, 1871, and when finished the church was dedicated by the same prelate, June 22d, 1872. The second half of the new church would have been commenced towards the close of 1873, and arrangements were being made for it when the panic came. It was evidently no time to be making a debt that could at all be avoided, and the congregation is still awaiting such an improvement in the times as will enable it to finish the church. In 1876 Father Shell enlarged the pastoral residence, and in January of the following year he placed the schools under the care of the Sisters of St. Agnes, for whom he purchased a house to answer the purposes of a convent.

Although arrested in its growth, the congregation must continue to increase and prosper. At present it will number about one hundred and seventy-five families.

ST. MATTHEW'S CHURCH, TYRONE.

Tyrone is situated on the Pennsylvania Railroad, fifteen miles east of Altoona, and like it is an outgrowth of the opening of that line. It stands at the opening of the Bald Eagle Valley, and is the most northern point reached by the railroad between Pittsburg and Philadelphia. It was incorporated as a borough in 1856, and it has a population at present of about 3500. The growth of the town is owing to the coal and lumber trade of Centre and Clearfield counties. Two branches of the Pennsylvania Railroad connect with the main line at this point—the one from the Clearfield coal and lumber regions, the other running through Centre and Clinton counties and connecting with the Philadelphia and Erie Railway and Lock Haven. A new branch is being constructed from Lewisburg to connect with the main line at Tyrone, which when completed will add to the importance of the town.*

The construction of a railroad invariably brings a number of Catholics who settle at different points along it, and

---

* Renner's Altoona City Directory, 1878–79, p. 252.

Tyrone was no exception. Scarcely was the road completed when we find Rev. J. Bradley, of Newry, visiting the place and for a time offering up the Holy Sacrifice in a private house. Having ministered to the wants of the people from the close of 1851 till the beginning of 1853, the Bishop determined that a church should be built. Lots were purchased and work was commenced in the spring of 1853. The cornerstone was laid on the 29th of May by Rev. W. Pollard, who appears to have been pastor of the church for a short time. But it was soon after attached to Altoona, from which it was attended until about the close of the year 1858. The church was dedicated September 24th, 1854, under the invocation of St. Matthew the Apostle. It is a brick building, modelled after the Gothic style of architecture, and is 75 feet in length by 40 in width, with a steeple rising from the centre in front.

About the end of 1858 Rev. P. M. Sheehan was appointed, and remained until about the year 1862, when he was succeeded by the present pastor, Rev. John C. Farren. A residence was built, and a school was held as regularly as circumstances permitted.

But the ground upon which the church is built yielded in course of time, and the sacred edifice was in danger of falling. Part of the wall was accordingly taken down in 1876 and rebuilt. The members of the congregation are mainly employed on the railroad and in the town, although there is a small number of farmers. From what has been said of the town it will be seen that the congregation is likely to go on increasing in the future.

CHAPTER XVII.

CAMBRIA COUNTY.

General features of the county—First settlers Catholics—Captain M'Guire—First visit of a priest—First appearance of Dr. Gallitzin—His parentage and early life—He visits America—Resolves to become a priest—Is ordained—His first missions—M'Guire settlement—He takes up his abode in the future Loretto—St. Michael's Church—His estates—Loretto.

CAMBRIA COUNTY, being the scene of the labors and sacrifices of the illustrious Prince Gallitzin, as well as the most Catholic county in the western part of the State, is entitled to a larger share of our attention than any other. Its Catholic population may be roughly estimated at from 15,000 to 18,000 souls. The notice of its civil history is compiled principally from the work of Mr. Sherman Day, already frequently quoted in these pages. "The county," says this author, "occupies one of the most elevated positions in the State on the western declivity of the great Allegheny Mountain. To the traveller passing westward this mountain presents a bold, precipitous front, but on crossing the summit the declivity is very gradual, not exceeding that of ordinary hills, thus demonstrating the existence of a broad elevated table-land between the Allegheny Mountain and the subordinate range of Laurel Hill. The latter mountain skirts the western part of the county, becoming depressed and broken as it passes northward. The surface is exceedingly rugged and broken, and the soil is comparatively cold. The principal occupations of the inhabitants are agriculture, lumbering, and the labor connected with the immense transportation business on the public improvements. The latter also furnish a convenient market for the surplus produce of the country.*

* Historical Collections, pp. 178, 179.

"Near the northern line of the county there is said to be an ancient circular fortification. The embankments are four or five feet high, and overgrown with immense trees. There were very old clear fields or open prairie lands not far from these fortifications, which probably gave the name to Clearfield County. . . .

"Previous to the year 1789 the tract of country which is now included within the limits of Cambria County was a wilderness. 'Frankstown settlement,' as it was then called, was the frontier of the inhabited parts of Pennsylvania east of the Allegheny Mountain. None of the pioneers had ventured to explore the western slope of the mountain. A remnant of the savage tribes still prowled through the forests and seized every opportunity of destroying the dwellings of the settlers and butchering such of the inhabitants as were so unfortunate as to fall into their hands. The howling of the wolf and the shrill screaming of the catamount, or American panther (both of which infested the country in great numbers at the period of its first settlement), mingled in nightly concert with the war-whoop of the savages.

"It is believed that Captain Michael M'Guire was the first white man who settled within the present bounds of Cambria County. He settled in the neighborhood of where Loretto now stands in the year 1790, and commenced improving that now interesting and well-cultivated portion of Allegheny township, a large portion of which is still owned and peopled by his descendants.*

"Four or five years afterwards the captain's brother Peter, with his bride, followed him from Maryland, and before a great while six log huts, with roofs of evergreen, standing on the little patches of land cleared by the stout arms of half a dozen stalwart men, formed M'Guire's settlement. Their first, and for many years their only, near neighbors were the settlers at Blair's Mills, twelve miles away [to the south-east], with a dense forest between. Captain M'Guire lost no time in providing for the Church, for which his wonderful faith alone could have given him hopes, and took up

* Historical Collections, p. 179.

four hundred acres of land, which he made over to Bishop Carroll." *

Rev. Felix Brosius, of whom more hereafter, as well as Father Pellentz, visited M'Guire's settlement from Conewago perhaps two or three times prior to the arrival of Dr. Gallitzin. "When Mr. Brosius visited it he set apart a portion of the ground donated by Captain M'Guire, and consecrated it for a cemetery, although as yet unneeded. When Mr. Lanigan visited 'Sportsman's Hall' and 'O'Neill's Victory' he, too, stayed a few days at the settlement, said Mass in the captain's cabin, and, distressed at seeing cattle on consecrated ground, had the men and boys band together to enclose it. Too soon afterwards, November 17th, 1796, Captain M'Guire, like Father Brauers, found a final resting-place in the land he had given to the Church." †

But some time before the death of this Christian hero a figure enters upon the stage for a moment that was destined to be one of the most conspicuous in the history of the Church in America. The manner of his first coming displays so much of the Christian heroism and charity of the pioneers, illustrates so admirably the labors of our first missionaries, and affords so striking an instance of the way in which Providence sometimes brings about the most important results by means that appear to the eye of man to be merely accidental, that I cannot forego the pleasure of giving it to the reader at length, nor convey it in more fitting language than that of Miss Brownson, who collected the account of it from a traditional history which I have more than once heard recited in the homes of the mountaineers:

"In the summer following Dr. Gallitzin's ordination (1795), Mrs. John Burgoons, a Protestant woman, living beyond the limits of civilization, a week's journey from Baltimore, by unbroken forests and now and then an Indian path, far up the Allegheny Mountains, was taken very ill, and begged so hard to see a Catholic priest that Mrs. Luke M'Guire, a good Cath-

---

* Life of Demetrius Augustine Gallitzin, Prince and Priest, by Sarah M. Brownson, p. 115.
† Ibid., p. 117.

olic neighbor, in company with another person, undertook the long and dangerous journey to Conewago to find one who would be able and willing to visit her. The message came to Mr. Gallitzin, and he hastened to join the good Samaritans and carry the strengthening Sacraments of the Church to the stranger in the wilderness. Mrs. M'Guire fretted very much at the many delays necessarily incident to the journey, fearing the woman would die before they could reach her; but she was comforted and made confident by the priest's assurance that if Mrs. Burgoons so desired to see a priest as they said, God, who had given her that desire, would not permit her to die until it was fulfilled. His words were so far made good that she recovered her health, after being instructed and received into the Church, and lived a good Catholic life for many years afterwards. His coming was hailed with joy by the few families scattered in that unbroken country, to which only at long intervals a priest had ever penetrated. He said Mass in the principal log-house of the settlement, administered baptism to a number of children and even one or two grown persons, exhorted them all to faith, prayer, courage, and perseverance, and having a liberal allowance from his mother—his father, since he had chosen to be a priest, did not interest himself in furthering his temporal affairs—he considered it not a bad investment, and perhaps a kindly act, to purchase a quantity of land on the mountain for himself." * Four years later he made the summit of these mountains the field of his future missionary labors. But before proceeding with our narrative it will be necessary to cast a brief glance at the early life of this distinguished man. His subsequent career will be identified with the fortunes of his colony.

" DEMETRIUS GALLITZIN, afterwards called Augustine, was the only son and heir of one of the oldest and most famous houses of the Old World: a Russian family with a pedigree longer than that of the reigning czar, which has always influenced, often controlled, and at times all but filled the throne of Russia, numbering in its ranks men of every talent and all renown."† The name *Gallitzin* is traced back with certainty

---

* Life, etc., pp. 98, 99. † Ibid., pp. 1, 2.

to the early part of the sixteenth century. Demetrius Alexeivitch Gallitzin, the father of the subject of our remarks, was born about the year 1735, and was sent as ambassador to France in 1763. August 28th, 1768, he married the Countess Amelia von Schmettau, only daughter of the celebrated Prussian field-marshal of that name, then just twenty years of age. They soon after determined to take up their residence at the Hague, to which Demetrius had been appointed ambassador. They rested for a while on their way at Berlin, where Princess Marianna, their only daughter, was born, December 7th, 1769. The future Apostle of the Alleghenies was born at the Hague, December 22d, 1770. The position which his father held under the government prevented him from spending all his time with his family; but his wife was a woman of extraordinary mental endowments, and she bestowed the utmost attention upon the education of her children. Although residing occasionally in other places, the principal part of her time was spent at Münster, in Germany, where she became the centre of an intellectual circle in which the most celebrated literary characters of the country figured. She had been brought up a Catholic from childhood, but her son was not of the true faith. Speaking of his conversion he afterwards said: "'Raised in prejudice against revelation, I felt every disposition to ridicule those very principles and practices which I have adopted since. I soon felt convinced of the necessity of investigating the different religious systems, in order to find out the true one. Although I was born a member of the Greek Church, and although all my male relations were either Greeks or Protestants, yet did I resolve to embrace that religion only which, upon impartial inquiry, should appear to me to be the pure religion of Jesus Christ. My choice fell upon the Catholic Church.'* This occurred when he was about seventeen years old; he took the name of Augustine in confirmation to please his mother. . . . He heard Mass every day with his mother and sister—there were frequent communions of the little group—and he even went so far as to mention a desire to become a priest, an idea in-

---

* Letter to a Protestant Friend, etc., p. 19.

stantly frowned down by his indignant father and passed over by his mother as the caprice or enthusiasm of an inconstant boy whose resolves were traced in sand." *

Of his personal appearance when he obtained his majority the same authoress remarks: " Mitri was the very *beau ideal* of a stately young officer; he was rather tall, being about five feet and nine or ten inches high, with the peculiar reticent, dignified, high-bred air which has the effect of the most imposing height; he had a slender and lithe yet compact figure, a fine clear complexion, not too fair for manliness, and the handsomest dark eyes that ever glanced love or anger from the shadow of a military cap—eyes fathomless in their tenderness, flashing fire at the slightest contradiction, full of mischief and merriment the instant anything amusing crossed their outer or inner vision; masses of shining black hair clustered around a delicately formed, haughtily set head, while a long large nose, very prominent and slightly aquiline, gave that character, force, and dignity to his countenance which seldom if ever accompany features of perfect regularity." † Towards the close of his life there was remarkable resemblance between his countenance and that of Peter the Great of Russia, as may be seen by any one who is curious enough to compare the two pictures.

The education of a young man in his position could not be regarded as finished until he had seen other lands; and it was the wish of his parents to have him make a tour of the countries of Europe. But the unsettled state of nearly the whole continent at that time forced them reluctantly to turn their thoughts elsewhere. America, which was then basking in the sunshine of its newly acquired independence, and under the administration of the illustrious Washington was making such rapid strides in material progress as to excite the jealousy of old Europe, naturally arrested their attention and determined them to send Mitri—as the Prince was familiarly called—to that country. After much consultation and reflection, Rev. Felix Brosius was selected as his guardian. The princess procured letters of introduction from the Prince-Bishops of

* Life, etc., pp. 54, 55. † Ibid., p. 58.

Hildesheim and Paderborn to Bishop Carroll, of Baltimore, to whose care she wished to confide her son. To avoid the expense and inconvenience of rank, he took the name of Augustine Schmet, from his mother's family name of Schmettau, which was afterwards Americanized to Smith, the name which he bore after his ordination and of which more remains to be said hereafter. But the last days he spent in the Old World were little in harmony with the part he was destined so soon to play in the New. Says Miss Brownson:

"He had said good-by to Münster August 8th (1792), but not to his mother so soon, as she with some friends was to accompany him to Rotterdam and see him on board the ship. Every one did his utmost to make the last days pleasant, and it was said that the young prince told afterwards that the night before sailing, or else the night before leaving Münster, report is not clear which, he attended a grand ball given for him, at which he danced from dark to daylight; for Mitri was young and enjoyed the luxuries of wealth and the pleasures of life with a light heart and to the utmost. But when the hour came to say his last good-by he was completely discouraged, and had no heart for the work. . . . All at once the whole journey looked very unnecessary to him; . . . even at that moment, though his baggage and attendants were on board, though they saw as they walked along the pier that the boat sent to take him to the ship was coming near, he would gladly have turned back and given it all up; with the simplicity of his character he made no concealment of his dread and fear, eagerly begging his mother, whose grief increased as the moments passed, restrained and controlled as it was, showed her more yielding, more tender than he had ever seen her, to let him stay, and as she, who had always led him, now clung silently to him, her eyes soft with unshed tears, he looked at her and impulsively declared he could not go, he would die away from home, he was afraid of the ocean dashing up at his feet, afraid of the strange people beyond. 'Mitri, Mitri!' exclaimed his mother, shocked into sudden action, and turning instantly with flashing eyes upon him, 'Mitri! I am ashamed of you!' He was between her and the water, on the very edge of the pier, and her sudden and unexpected movement, at a time when he was absorbed in his own entreaties, caused him to lose his balance and fall over. But the boat sent out for him was close at hand and he was an excellent swimmer, so he was quickly rescued, and with one last look at his mother standing on the pier, he was swiftly rowed to the ship. He sailed from Rotterdam August 18th." *

The seemingly unaccountable reluctance with which he left the Old World may have been in part a temptation such as those with which Satan frequently assails persons whom he is permitted to foresee will be instruments in the hands of God for wresting a portion of his kingdom from him. Be that as it may, he arrived at Baltimore October 28th, in company with several priests for the American mission, and soon after waited on Bishop Carroll. In the urgent demand for missionaries it could not be expected that Father Brosius could accompany the young prince in his travels, nor that the latter would be content to follow the missionary in his. But young Gallitzin soon began to compare the tranquil state of the youthful republic with the turmoil of the Old World, and insensibly felt his heart becoming attached to it, at the same time that the religious atmosphere in which he lived for the present elevated his thoughts and desires to holier aims than those to which his noble birth would naturally have led him to aspire. He began ere long to hear within him the whisperings of a vocation to the ecclesiastical state. In this unexpected turn of affairs the Bishop thought it best to permit him to remain for a time at the Seminary of the Sulpicians in Baltimore, that he might have leisure for serious reflection on the nature of the new state of life to which he felt himself called. "While the Bishop with Mr. Nagot (Superior of the seminary) maturely considered the application he had made to enter the service of the Church, and knowing well the charges given to the young man by his father, the Bishop desired him at the same time to apply himself carefully to the study of the constitution, laws, manners, and geography of the country, and to assist him in doing so took him with him

---

* Life, etc., pp. 64, 65.

in visiting different parts of his diocese, taking him into the home circle of the most distinguished American families. In the book of the Sulpician Seminary at Baltimore it is recorded that the frank and honest manners of the young Prince Gallitzin and his excellent education gave Bishop Carroll the liveliest pleasure during his journey, but he was astonished to find that he travelled only with reluctance, and that nothing could make him forget his beloved seminary—a most precious disposition which the prelate considered a certain sign of his vocation to the ecclesiastical state, as was indeed the opinion of all who knew him. In truth it was soon apparent that Mitri had 'no other ambition than to acquire the science of the saints, and every day to die to himself and the world.'"*

The Bishop informed the princess of the course he had thought best to pursue, and at the same time paid a high tribute to the amiable qualities of her son. As to the prince, his mind was fully made up, and, with that tenacity of purpose and strength of character which marked his subsequent career, he applied himself with loving obedience to the course which Heaven had marked out for him. Upon hearing later of the choice he had made, his mother was disappointed and disposed to find fault with the Bishop, thinking that he and others had exercised an undue influence over his youthful mind; but the spirit soon triumphed over the flesh and caused her to acquiesce in the designs of Providence. His father, however, was planning for his promotion in the army and had already obtained a commission for him. His proud spirit could ill brook the thought that his only son, the heir to his titles and estates, should conceal himself in the wilds of America and devote his talents and his life to the service of the poor. He hastened to inform him that his elevation to the priesthood would of itself, according to the laws of Russia, render him incapable of inheriting the estates to which his birth had given him a claim. But I cannot dwell further upon the trials to which the young hero was exposed, nor enlarge upon the influence that was in vain brought to bear upon him. He heard the divine call, and, with St. Peter, he

---

* Life, etc., pp. 73, 74.

thought it better to obey God than man. The thorough education he had received enabled the Bishop to permit him to enter upon the study of theology after he had devoted a little time to American geography, history, and government, and so rapid was his progress that he received minor orders soon, and on November 14th, 1794, was ordained subdeacon. "At the commencement of January" (1795), says his little French note-book, "God gave me the desire to unite myself to the Society of the Sulpicians. Communicating this to Mr. Nagot, he advised me to refer it to our Lord; this desire continues as if it were already accomplished." He was admitted a member on the 13th of February of the same year, but he afterwards withdrew, although not for many years, as we shall see, a step which he could take from the fact that the members are bound by no religious vow. On the 18th of March, 1795, he was raised to the sacred dignity of the priesthood, being the second priest ordained in the United States and the first which this country can claim as wholly her own. For although Rev. Stephen Badin was the first ordained a priest, yet he was a deacon before leaving his native France. But Rev. D. A. Gallitzin, or Rev. Augustine Smith, as he was then called, passed through all the successive steps, from the clerical tonsure, on American soil. With a view of recruiting his health, impaired by his assiduous application to study, he was sent to the mission at Port Tobacco. But finding that he was not improving, the Bishop wished to send him to the extensive mission of which Conewago was the centre and at which his friend, Father Brosius, then was. But he urged such reasons against it as drew from the Bishop a letter of paternal rebuke and an order to repair without delay to Baltimore. Here he was placed in charge of the German Catholics of the city, and it was while ministering to them that he received the call to go to the theatre of his future labors, as we have already seen. Returning to Baltimore, he remained until some time in the year 1796, when he entered upon the Conewago mission. He visited a number of places in Maryland and Pennsylvania, and resided, for at least a part of the time, at Taneytown. It was at this time that the extraordinary affair of the Livingston family occurred, near Martinsburg,

Va., in which he played an important part, and for an account of which the reader is referred to Miss Brownson's Life (pp. 100-107).*

But the young priest's zeal was not always according to prudence; he saw abuses and was too hasty in attempting to correct them, and complaints of his arbitary measures were made to the Bishop. The latter, under date of October 20th, 1798, wrote him a letter admonishing him in paternal yet forcible terms not to be too anxious to correct all abuses at once, nor too desirous of imposing his views upon others. No one would for a moment venture to question his zeal and his desire of spending himself and being spent for the good of his people—his entire life is a striking evidence of both—but it is equally unquestionable that he inherited and to his dying day retained no little of that sense of superiority inherent in the nobility of the Old World; and with it he possessed a will the dictates of which no one was permitted to resist, dictates which his commanding figure, fiery eye, and thrilling voice aided him no little in carrying into execution. To the day of his death he could not brook opposition. The terms of the Bishop's letter are so applicable to his character during his whole life that one or two extracts from it are presented to the reader, and the more so as that prelate was fully capable of reading his character. Says the Bishop: "I have already often admonished you, and others in whom you have perhaps placed more confidence have urged you, to try more to win the affections of your congregations, to lead them by mildness, even here and there to overlook some things which are not precisely as they should be, that afterwards you may correct them by gentle persuasion, instead of at once making use of your authority, and carrying that authority to its utmost limits. . . . And then, what a doctrine it is that all who are under your charge should be bound also to yield to every opinion you may have, to every proposal you make, without being permitted a question." †

---

* The affair has recently been treated at length in a small work entitled "The Wizard Clip," by the late Rev. J. M. Finoti.

† Leben und Wirken des Prinzen Demetrius Augustin Gallitzin, von P. Heinrich Lemcke, p. 147.

At length the Catholics of M'Guire's settlement presented a petition to the Bishop asking him to send them a priest who should be permanently stationed among them, and stated as an inducement that the land given by the Captain to the church would, when cultivated, serve for the priest's subsistence. Dr. Gallitzin, through whom the petition was presented, united with them, and the Bishop granted it in a letter to him dated from Washington City, March 1st, 1799. Dr. Gallitzin reached his mission in the latter part of the summer following, but the precise date has not been transmitted to us. He found about a dozen families in the settlement, which, with a few persons who had come up with him, or about the same time, from Maryland and Conewago, formed his parish. But we have seen that the field of his missionary labors for many years embraced a large tract of territory with its scattered families east of the mountains. "He commenced by putting things in order, thankful enough that as yet the field was unploughed, consequently free from the tares which had so choked up the wheat and tortured him in the older and more important stations he had attended. He at once divided his own land, which had cost about four dollars an acre, into lots which he sold for a mere trifle on long credit, *credit so long that much of it still lasts*, and he held out the same inducements for all who, unable to procure the first means for subsistence, would wish to join him, providing always that they were honest, industrious, or desirous of becoming so; he wanted no wolves in sheep's clothing in his fold."* His people were all poor, and the country in which they lived was still infested with bears, wolves, and Indians. The winter, too, on the mountain is unusually long and severe, so that it required strength of both body and mind to lay the foundation of a colony there. But the priest's presence inspired new life into the settlement. The state of his farm and the erection of his church and house are thus graphically described by his enthusiastic biographer:

"When he arrived he found that Captain M'Guire had very thoughtfully given a few animals as stock for the farm to

---

* Life, etc., p. 118.

be prepared for the use of the priest who should live on the church property, and had placed a man in charge of it and them, hoping thus to have a portion cleared and made somewhat productive while awaiting its reverend occupant. Father Gallitzin gave some of these to the tenant whom he displaced to live in the houses of the settlers until his own log cabin could be built. This was put up on the slope of the hill, on the church land, which was about two miles from the chief M'Guire farm and was made of round logs. . . . With uncontrollable eagerness he watched the progress of the log church, which fast took size and shape under the strong and willing arms of his parishioners, his own inspirations and generosity. As soon as the harvest was gathered he gave employment to them all upon the church, and even had the women employed in making a great number of candles for it, and on Christmas eve of that year it was finished, placed under the protection of St. Michael, and ready for midnight Mass, the only house of God from Lancaster to St. Louis. . . . He had instructed the men to bring in branches of the beautiful evergreen trees, which grew thick upon the mountains and at their very doors; the women set their candles amongst the dark green foliage covering the rude walls; and just at midnight, when the people who had gathered from immense distances through the wilderness of snow were hushed in rapt expectation, he came out upon the altar, with all the ceremony of the grandest Cathedral, and intoned the Mass." *

Writing to the Bishop under date of February 9th, 1800, he says: " Our church, which was only begun in harvest, got finished for service the night before Christmas; it is about 44 feet long by 25, built of white pine logs, with a very good shingle roof. I kept service in it at Christmas for the first time, to the very great satisfaction of the whole congregation, who seemed very much moved at a sight which they never beheld before. There is also a house built for me, 16 feet by 14, besides a little kitchen and a stable. I have now, thanks be to God, a little home of my own, for the first time since I

---

* Life, etc., pp. 119, 120.

came to this country, and God grant that I may be able to keep it. The prospect of forming a lasting establishment for promoting the cause of religion is very great; the country is amazing fertile, almost entirely inhabited by Roman Catholics, and so advantageously situated with regard to market that there is no doubt but it will be a place of refuge for a great many Catholics; a great many have bought property there in the course of these three months past, and a great many more are expected. The congregation consists at present of about forty families, but there is no end to the Catholics in all the settlements round about me; what will become of them all, if we do not soon receive a new supply of priests, I do not know. I try as much as I can to persuade them to settle around me."

In this extract we perceive the enthusiasm with which he burned to found a Catholic colony, and the little account he made of the many and great obstacles which stood in his way. The statement of his biographer that his was the only church from Lancaster to St. Louis is true as far at least as relates to this State; for although a church was commenced at Greensburg in the spring of 1790, it was never finished,* as we shall see in its proper place. That his midnight Mass was the first celebrated west of the Allegheny Mountains, as is represented by some writers, is undoubtedly incorrect; for other priests had visited the mountains, as we have seen, before Dr. Gallitzin came; and besides, would he abstain from celebrating Mass during the time in which the church was being built? The first Mass celebrated west of the mountains, with the exception of those at Fort Duquesne, was most probably by Rev. John B. Causey, in the house of John Propst, ten miles west of Greensburg, in June, 1789, of which more hereafter.†

Dr. Gallitzin continued to invite settlers to his colony and to supply them with homes on easy terms, waiting until such time as they would be able to pay for them. Rev. J. A. Stillenger, a few years before his death, showed me a large roll of papers referring to these lands, and stated that Dr. Gallitzin

---

* St. Vincenz in Pennsylvanien, p. 54.
† Ibid., pp. 49, 50.

had bought more than twenty thousand acres of land for the settlers. This, although a high figure, is the statement of one who was next neighbor to the venerable priest for ten years, and was intimately acquainted with the history of the settlement. These mountain lands were owned by wealthy persons in the eastern cities, who had bought them low with a view of speculating, and who were willing to sell on time provided they had proper security. Although a princely estate would seem to be sufficient, the poor priest was often forced to claim the indulgence of his creditors. We shall see that in his expectation of realizing from his inherited estate he was doomed to cruel disappointment. He was naturalized and became a citizen of the United States in 1802. In May 6th, 1803, his father died suddenly at Brunswick, in Saxony, and it was thought advisable for him to cross to Europe to look after the estate. But he preferred to remain with his people. "Immediately upon the prince's death, his relatives in Russia took possession of his estates as his heirs, considering Mitri as thrown out altogether on account of his profession, as the prince had always expected; the Princess Mimi was by the laws of Russia only entitled to one fourteenth of the real estate and to one eighth of the personal property. By the advice of his mother, Father Gallitzin appointed Baron von Fuerstenberg, Count Frederic Leopold von Stolberg, and Count Clement Augustus von Merveldt, his agents, with full power of attorney to bring a suit against his relatives who claimed the estates, while the princess took every possible step to secure the property for him, or, if that could not be, for herself, through her marriage contract, which resulted in an expensive litigation, of which Father Gallitzin from time to time received some reports." *

His estates, as valued by these three noblemen, consisted, as Father Heyden tells us: "1st. Of seventy thousand rubles in money; and 2d. In real property the village of Lankoff, in the government of Wadalmir, and the villages of Fabanzin and Mikulskin, in the government of Kostrom, with all the

---

* Life, etc., pp. 157, 158.

lands, mills, and other property thereto belonging, with one thousand two hundred and sixty male subjects." *

But the settlement of these claims required time, and however sanguine the good man may have been of success, his mind became a prey to apprehensions which the impatience of some of his creditors was too well calculated to keep vividly before him. But we must not forget that he was a missionary in the wilds, and, although the temporalities of his colony claimed a great part of his time and attention, the care of the souls of his people received still more. From his mountain home there was no priest in the west nearer than Sportsman's Hall, nor in the east nearer than Conewago, while to the north and south there was none in the State, nor for a great distance beyond its boundaries. Nor was his position similar to that of the other missionaries. The whole settlement was in a measure the work of his hands; to him it owed not merely its spiritual but also its temporal existence; and he was both its prince and priest.

Some years after the erection of his humble residence, described above, he built a larger one of hewn logs adjoining it. He also put up a mill worked by two horses to grind the grain of the settlers; but as it was found to be too expensive, it was afterwards replaced by one run by water. And the visitor to Loretto, as he enters the town from the east, may see the remains of the old mill in the shape of a broken wheel or two in a field near the brook. While teaching at St. Francis' College, in the village, in the fall of 1869, I visited the old mill, then entirely fallen to ruins; but at present nothing of the building remains. A part of his own land he laid out into a village in the year 1803, and named it Loretto, out of his devotion to the august Mother of God. At the time of his death, 1840, it contained but 150 souls; and in 1870 the population had increased to only 280. It is situated about four and a half miles northwest of Cresson Station on the Pennsylvania Railroad, which is one hundred and two miles by the road from Pittsburg; but by an air line the village is but seventy-

---

* A Memoir on the Life and Character of Rev. Prince Demetrius A. de Gallitzin, etc., p. 50.

two miles east of that city. The village is built on a rising ground which falls gently to the east and south, and is longer from east to west than it is in the opposite direction. The principal street in the former direction is St. Mary's, which is but a part of the public road with board sidewalks, after the manner of mountain towns and villages. Before you have quite entered the village the ruins of the old mill will be seen on the left; a little further on the old pastoral residence appears on the right, with the chapel attached to it. Beside this is the old frame church—known in the different *Lives of Gallitzin* as the "new church"—but neither it nor the residence is now used by the congregation, the former having been replaced by the present church, and the latter by the pastoral residence lately built. A little further on, as the road winds gently to the right, on the same side, is St. Aloysius' Academy for young ladies and the girls' parish school, both in a handsome brick building under the care of the Sisters of Mercy. The road, or St. Mary's Street, as it now becomes, resumes a direct course, and you enter the village having the large brick church with the tomb of the Apostle of the Alleghanies in front of it on your right. But more of all these hereafter. Parallel with this street and on the left of it runs St. Joseph's. St. Peter's crosses these about the middle of the village, and, after descending to the west to cross a little brook, rises to the level of the village and leaves you at the gate of St. Francis' Monastery and College. When I was at the college in 1869, the village was wholly Catholic with the exception of one Jewish family and a Protestant woman whose husband was of the true faith; and the same, I believe, is true to-day.

CHAPTER XVIII.

CAMBRIA COUNTY (CONTINUED).

Dr Gallitzin as a land agent—as a pastor—Regulations for Mass, etc.—Sermons—Troubles—Death of the Princess Gallitzin—Wolves in sheep's clothing—Settlement of the litigations regarding his estate—Gradual extension of the colony—Bishop Egan visits Loretto–Dr Gallitzin as a writer—A new church—Scanty remittances from his estate—He asks aid from his friends—The crisis—Relief—The little chapel—Bishop Kenrick of Philadelphia—Rev. Henry Lemcke arrives at Loretto—Sunday at Loretto—Fr. Lemcke at Ebensburg—Other writings of Dr. Gallitzin—The end approaching—Last illness—Death of Dr. Gallitzin—Remarks on the Loretto settlement—Church property—Dr. Gallitzin's successors.

WHEN Cambria County was laid out—March 26th, 1804—Dr. Gallitzin used his influence to have Loretto made the seat of justice, but Ebensburg was finally selected as being more central. "The formation of the new county," says Miss Brownson, "threw increased business into Father Gallitzin's hands, he was agent of several firms in Philadelphia and other large cities for the sale of lands in Western Pennsylvania, and there was an endless amount of papers to be drawn up, registered, and attended to in regard to it, even of that kind known as ejectments, leading sometimes to lawsuits, for there were not lacking swindlers and impostors to take advantage of his well-known charity, obtain land from him for a trifle and on credit, and sell it again at a good profit, or occupying it to the annoyance of their peaceable and orderly neighbors, without any intention of ever paying for it. And he was not one to be imposed upon with impunity at any time, least of all when he no longer regarded himself as his own property, but as the servant of the poor, the agent of the Lord in a noble work. He was as swift and keen in justice as in charity, and the more so that he knew the full danger of establishing precedents or giving dishonesty of any kind the slightest foothold in the new county. The temporal interests of his settlement required him to attend the courts in other counties and to make long journeys to Greensburg, in Westmoreland, and even to Lancaster, frequently necessary, which, in addition to the increased missions he had to attend in the discharge of his spiritual duties, kept him constantly moving."* Of his immediate relations with his people, the same writer adds: "He had his rules for all spiritual exercises as clear, distinct, and unalterable as the famous laws of the Medes and Persians. Everything with him was exact, precise to the minute, and this not only from habit, from long training, but of very necessity for his own time as well as for their discipline and order. When it drew near the time for Mass on Sunday, he would come from his house to the church, the long train of his cassock thrown over his arm, passing with his peculiar rapid step from group to group of the men gathered on the church grounds, talking together before Mass, while the women were devoutly saying their prayers. . . In the church there were no pews nor benches; the utmost ever allowed in it consisted of two or three stools, for the use of several very aged persons who came there; the children knelt in front, by the altar rails; the women were placed on one side, the men on the other, with a narrow passage between them, which neither ever ventured to decrease. All superfluous dress had to be left behind, and at the church door every woman, young or old, was required to take off her bonnet and put a kind of handkerchief over her head. The slightest impropriety in dress—and the fashions of the day admitted plenty of it—was so well known to be hateful to him that if brought there it would be sure to be considered as a defiance of his admonitions, an insult to the house of God, and bring upon its wearer a scathing rebuke. As much as Father Gallitzin hated meanness in a man he despised coquetry in a woman—not that pleasant sparkle which comes with good health and a clear conscience, for he liked that within reasonable limits, but whatever showed

* Life, etc., p. 166.

itself in the lowering of the immortal to give precedence to that which perishes was to him a crime and a folly for which no denunciation could be too severe. He knew, also, the poverty of the generality of the people, and was careful that there should be no extravagance, no rivalry, no room for envy, by permitting even those whose circumstances would perhaps have admitted some display to make any beyond the means of the simplest and poorest, and so clearly did he make all feel that they were alike children of God, so well did he know the right word to say in confession, that to a stranger looking over the congregation they would have appeared as children of one father, dressed with different tastes, it is true, but with equal plainness. Father Gallitzin dreaded the advent of finery into the settlement as he would the small-pox or cholera, especially as there is no known remedy for the diseases it brings." To this picture of the rule of the zealous missionary is added the following account of his manner in the matter of hearing Mass, both of which are amply confirmed by tradition. "When the greetings outside the church door were all made, or whenever the moment arrived for the people to enter, he left them, and when later there was a gallery for the choir, went upstairs, other times remained at the back of the church, while they went in. When all was quiet—and that had to be very soon—he would sing the Litany, and, that ended, go twice round the outside of the church, lest any one might be lingering there instead of preparing for Mass inside. Then, in the stillness which he insisted upon, every ear would be strained to hear behind them that never-to-be-mistaken step, quick but never hurried, that marked his progress up the narrow passage, through the church to the sanctuary, while every one, however demurely kneeling with clasped hands and downcast eyes, knew well that his keen glances were piercing to the inmost heart, for then it was that the least irregularity of dress or posture was made note of. . . . He always preached two sermons at Mass, one in English and one in German, neither of which was his mother-tongue, for French was the language most natural to him; he spoke English with perfect ease, German not so well; his sermons were plain, but suited to the times, the circumstances, and needs of his people, with which he was as familiar as with his own."* In these lengthy extracts we have a fair picture of Dr. Gallitzin. He was indeed always intent on doing good, but it was in his own way—a way which no one dare question or resist. The following passage will complete the picture: " It was even true, as began to be whispered, that he was arbitrary and capable of terrible anger, with a look of fire, a voice of thunder, and a will of iron, like that grand old Sixtus Quintus who declared: ' While I live the criminal shall die,' and made the watchword of Rome, *Sixtus reigns.* There are no words fitly to describe his mastering spirit, that never was broken and could not be bent. The mere strangers to him and his religion, who strode up to see a funeral pass, baptism administered, or a sermon preached, who had never bowed at any command, at his word, ' Kneel down, sir; take off your hat,' obeyed, powerless to resist, while the rapid words were yet on his lips. At other times his voice rang out until the very rafters thrilled and trembled; the fast coming words, the cutting sarcasm, the broad, trenchant blows of his doctrinal sermons once heard could never be forgotten. Magnificent in his wrath, he seemed born to hurl the thunders of the Church at the head of sacrilegious kings, and announce the scourging of God to cowering nations, and it was felt instinctively there was a power there not well to arouse. He was careful to honor the self-respect and family reserve which he knew to be a safeguard against the petty gossip and scandal which are the bane of all small communities, but at the same time in his eyes they were all members of one family and he their father, and he would sometimes speak to all of the errors of one, not indeed personally, but too plainly intending only to use it as an illustration and a warning to others." †

But the object of his greatest solicitude was the neatness of the altar and the good order of the church; and he could truly say with the Psalmist, " The zeal of thy house hath consumed me," and " I have loved, O Lord, the beauty of thy house." However poor it might be, and it was certainly

---

* Life, etc., pp. 166-170.   † Ibid., pp. 183, 184.

never very rich, it must show at least no sign of neglect. At the door of the chapel to the rear of his residence, framed and hanging in the little vestibule, were the following printed rules, which are still there, as I have seen and read them times without number:

"*Notice.*

1. Scrape the dirt off your shoes on the iron scraper provided for that purpose.
2. Do not spit on the floor of the chapel.
3. Do not put your hats and caps on the chapel windows.
4. Do not rub against the papered walls of the chapel.
5. Do not put your heels on the washboards.
6. After coming in at the passage door, shut the door after you.

DEMETRIUS AUGUSTINE GALLITZIN,
Parish Priest of Loretto."

His rigorous enforcement of rules and regulations, as well as his credulity—which was one of his few weak points—in believing reports made to him, did not fail to make enemies, some of whom were persons who were deeply indebted to his kindness. When brought face to face with them, his indomitable will, which always triumphed, frequently embittered their feelings. The Bishop, while he sustained the good man, counselled prudence and moderation. The first serious trouble was in 1804. The Bishop sent a letter bearing date of November 30th, of that year, in which he expressed the confidence he felt in Dr. Gallitzin, and which he commanded to be affixed to the doors of the church, hoping thereby to put the disturbers at peace. But it was not sufficient to restore good feeling.

The death of the princess, his mother, April 27th, 1806, while it was a great affliction to Dr. Gallitzin, also caused him no little anxiety concerning the recovery of his portion of the estate. But his sister hastened to relieve his mind by assuring him that nothing should prevent her from forwarding him his part as promptly as it was in her power. Another source of affliction was the occasional presence in his flock of a priest unworthy of his sacred calling. We need not be either surprised or scandalized at the appearance of such men in the early days of our history. The government of the Church was not then fully organized; people were so seldom permitted to enjoy the consolations of religion that they could easily be imposed upon; the Bishop resided at so great a distance, and communication with him was so difficult and required so much time, that unworthy priests could pass from place to place and impose upon the people with impunity. And if out of the twelve whom our Saviour himself chose, "one was a devil," we need not think it unaccountable that a wolf should occasionally appear in sheep's clothing in our day. To one so thoroughly imbued with the ecclesiastical spirit as Dr. Gallitzin was, an occurrence of this kind was peculiarly trying. The divisions caused by one of these reached such a pitch that accusations were made to the Bishop against Dr. Gallitzin, and at home the zealous missionary was threatened with personal violence. Writing of it to the Bishop in a letter dated June 20th, 1807, he says among other things: "After having tried (in vain) all those means which charity and a desire of bringing my enemies to repentance could suggest, finding that they wilfully and maliciously persevered, and that even coming to church on Sunday and holy days was only a cloak to propagate their poison and trying to gain proselytes, I publicly excluded them from the benefits of the church; debarred them from polluting the floor of the church, or the holy ground on which it stands, with their presence; I refused sprinkling the holy water upon my congregation until those ringleaders of rebellion, those forgers of libels against the anointed of the Lord, would withdraw. I then commanded them by name to leave that church which under divine providence I had established with the sweat of my brow for the salvation of souls, and to which they only came for the ruin and damnation of their and their neighbors' souls, praying God to move their hearts to repentance, and to give them grace to re-enter the church at the gate of submission and humility. The next day I started for Greensburg; having received information as above, I immediately applied for two writs of scandal, and had them served as quick as possible, which produced a very happy change." From about the close of this year the trouble appears to have ceased; and the people from that time forward had a better appreciation of what their pastor had done and suffered in their behalf. His troubles for the future were to be of a financial character arising out of the tardiness with which he received remittances from Europe.

The settlement of the litigation regarding his estate was made known to him by his agents in a letter dated Münster, February 1st, 1808. The Senate of St. Petersburg decided that admission into the priesthood debarred him from inheriting. The Emperor sanctioned the decision, and gave it the force of law. The property reverted to his sister, who, however, could sell it. His agents concluded that he had nothing to fear, for his sister would pay him his portion, and in this opinion he seemed to have found consolation.

The Loretto colony appears to have had as yet but one common centre, although it was increasing in numbers and widening in extent; for the persecutions of which the pastor had been the victim served to make him better known, and attracted more settlers from the east. The log church was now filled to excess, and in 1808 he enlarged and otherwise improved it, at his own expense; for it may be stated here once for all that he never received any salary or income from the people, but paid out of his own resources the expenses of the church as well as the maintenance of his own household. In fact, it was his extreme antipathy to the pew-rent system that induced him to apply to the Bishop for permission to leave Taneytown and come to the mountain, where he could mould the affairs of the Church after his own views. The colony began to branch out and lay the foundation of other congregations that will arrest our attention after a little—Ebensburg, Carrolltown, St. Augustine, Wilmore, Summitville, etc.—but at what precise time stations began to be held in these different places, it is now impossible to determine. More will be said on the subject under the head of these respective congregations. In September, 1808, he wrote to the Bishop, asking for a priest to take a part of his territory, and leave him to labor for the Catholics of Cambria County alone, and to manage the temporalities of Loretto; but owing to the scarcity of priests, that prelate was unable to comply with the request. The temporalities gave him no little anxiety. His just expectation of receiving aid from Europe was constantly doomed to partial, often to total disappointment, so that for almost thirty years his mind had but meagre repose.

He now passed from the jurisdiction of the Archbishop of Baltimore to that of the newly appointed Bishop of Philadelphia. His real name also began to be generally known, and the confusion consequent on the promiscuous employment of the name of Smith and Gallitzin induced him to petition the State Legislature, December 5th, 1809, to authorize him to use the name Demetrius Augustine Gallitzin, since he had been naturalized as Augustine Smith. The petition was immediately granted, and the name of Smith, which had already begun to lose its hold on the public mind, was soon forgotten.

In the summer of 1811 the good pastor had the happiness of welcoming Bishop Egan, the first incumbent of the new See of Philadelphia, to his mountain home. Confirmation was then administered for the first time, if not in the entire original Diocese of Pittsburg, at least in that portion lying west of the mountains. Contrary to the ordinary custom in the administration of this sacrament, children were confirmed at a tender age. In a small memorandum of Dr. Gallitzin's which I have seen, and which contains a list of the persons confirmed at this visit, as well as other interesting matters to which reference will soon be made, I found the names of infants of but one year who were then confirmed. Nor was it an unwarranted departure from the ordinary custom, for it was nineteen years before Loretto again saw the shadow of a mitre. There were one hundred and eighty-five persons confirmed upon this visit. The same memorandum contains a list of the Easter communicants for the years 1810, 1811, and 1813. The list for 1810 comprises 219 names, of which 82 are men and 137 women; of the latter 68 were married, 5 were widows, and 64 unmarried. In 1811 there were 424 persons, of whom 171 were men and 253 women; and in 1813 there were 555 persons—203 men, 265 women, 47 boys, and 40 girls. One would be led to infer from the names that the Irish element at that time prevailed over the German. But the question arises: Over how large a tract of country were these Catholics distributed? For if it embraced all the territory under Dr. Gallitzin's jurisdiction at that time, it can afford but an imperfect idea of the population of the Loretto settlement. Be that as it may, this memorandum, as well as another to be referred to presently, contains some valuable scraps of information that have evidently escaped the notice of all his former biographers.

Not satisfied with his other duties, which were certainly arduous and numerous enough to occupy the time of the most zealous priest, Dr. Gallitzin now entered the field as a writer, and produced a couple of small works which even in our day have a high reputation. They were the instruments of numerous conversions, as well as the means of dispelling much of the ignorance and consequent bigotry in the public mind of that day regarding the religion of which he was the illustrious champion. The circumstances which called forth these precious volumes were briefly these: Late in the summer of 1814, when the British troops were advancing on Washington City, President Madison appointed a day of public fasting and prayer, in the celebration of which a certain Rev. Mr. Johnson, of Huntingdon, preached a sermon, in the course of which he indulged in a considerable amount of misrepresentation of the Church, from its august head to the humblest of its members. The sermon created quite a sensation in the mountain country, and when the echo of it reached the ears of Dr. Gallitzin he addressed the preacher through the *Huntingdon Gazette*, demanding an apology for the insults he had offered to religion. But he elicited no reply. He then published several *Letters* in the same newspaper explaining the teaching of the Church and answering such of the preacher's arguments as were deserving of attention. The *Letters* attracted great attention, and, being soon after published in pamphlet form, went through several editions. Later they were amplified and in other respects somewhat changed, and then published in their present form under the title of "A Defence of Catholic Principles in a Letter to a Protestant Clergyman. By Rev. Demetrius A. Gallitzin. 12mo, pp. 174. 1816." His fame as a controversial writer was now established, and he is believed to have been the first to enter the field of polemics in the American Church. Four years later he published another small work, a continuation of the "Defence," under the title of "A Letter to a Protestant Friend on the Holy Scriptures, etc. Ebensburg. Printed by Thos. Foley, 1820. 12mo, pp. 150." The publication of these works had a marvellous effect in promoting conversions among settlers whose hostility to the Church arose principally from a misapprehension of her true character, and it was not unusual for the pastor of Loretto to find a dozen or more converts stand together in the little chapel claiming admission into the one fold. So numerous were the applications for a more detailed exposition of the Catholic doctrine than was contained in these books that he published the following unique notice in the *Cambria County Gazette:*

"*Notice.*

"A certain number of Protestants having manifested a great desire of becoming members of the Roman Catholic Church, I hereby acquaint the said Protestants, and the public in general, that I have appointed the second Sunday after Easter (17th April) for admitting them into the Church, according to the rites and ceremonies of the Roman Ritual.

"DEMETRIUS A. GALLITZIN,
"Parish Priest.
"LORETTO, March 22, 1825."

At the end of two years Mr. Johnson published a reply to Dr. Gallitzin's works, entitled "A Vindication of the Reformation," which was admitted on all hands to be inferior to the works to which it was an answer. The pastor of Loretto contented himself with publishing "An Appeal to the Protestant Public," in which he showed up the weak points of the "Vindication," and exhorted all to seek the truth earnestly. The only practical result attained by the enemies of the

Church was the awakening of a spirit of inquiry, which, as we have seen, multiplied conversions.

In 1814 the See of Philadelphia became vacant by the death of Bishop Egan, and in the following year Dr. Gallitzin lost his most steadfast friend and prudent counsellor by the death of Archbishop Carroll. His labors were also increased about this time by the construction of the State roads, or turnpikes, one of which, known as the northern pike, passed but three miles south of Loretto. About the same time he withdrew from the Society of St. Sulpice. The feeble health of Father O'Brien of Pittsburg, and the death of Father Heilbron of Sportsman's Hall, in 1816, added for a time to his missionary duties. But his name had now become famous, and he was spoken of as a candidate for the bishopric of Bardstown, Ky.* He was afterwards, it appears, actually nominated to the See of Detroit.† Bishop Conwell, who had named him Vicar-General for the western part of the State soon after his consecration, determined later to nominate him his coadjutor, as we learn from a letter of his to Father Heyden of December 3d, 1827.‡

But he had hoped to see his beloved Loretto the home of a Bishop, as was stated above in the chapter on the erection of the See of Pittsburg. Writing to Archbishop Marechal under date of October 28th, 1823, he says:

"Several years ago I formed a plan for the good of religion, for the success of which I desire to employ all the means at my disposal when the remainder of my debts are paid. It is to form a diocese for the western part of Pennsylvania. What a consolation for me if I might before I die see this plan carried out, and Loretto made an episcopal see, where the Bishop by means of the lands attached to the bishopric, which are very fertile, would be independent, and where with very little expense could be erected college, seminary, and all that is required for an episcopal establishment! . . . It could be commenced by establishing a Bishop here who would be merely *Vicarius in Pontificalibus* to the Bishop of Philadelphia, who would give great comfort by administering confirmation in

---
* Life of Bishop Flaget, by Rt. Rev. M. J. Spalding, p. 166.
† Life, etc., pp. 332, 345. ‡ Ibid., p. 364.

all parts of Western Pennsylvania; at the death of the Biship of Philadelphia two dioceses could be formed."

About the year 1817, the log-church, which had once been enlarged, began to be no longer capable of accommodating the constantly increasing congregation. A new one was imperatively demanded, and was undertaken. It is a frame building standing near the pastoral residence, and is perhaps 40 by 65 feet. But it has not been used for many years.

At this time, when the good pastor began to feel a little security in his finances, he received intelligence from Europe that his sister was married. The result was that he afterwards received but a few small remittances from the sale of his estates, although large sums were placed in the hands of his sister and her husband to be forwarded to him. It is not for us to inquire upon whom the blame rests. There was a valuable collection of Greek and Roman antiquities, which had been left by his mother in the hands of a trusty friend to be disposed of for some charitable object, and the custodian, judging rightly that it could not be applied to a better end than the building up of religion in the New World, sold it to Dr. Gallitzin's friend and former schoolmate, the King of the Netherlands, for the priest's benefit. But the funds arising from the sale, though considerable, were far from liquidating his debts; and when he had done all in his power, he was yet forced to apply to wealthy Catholics in different places for assistance. I have examined a small memorandum-book, the companion of the one already referred to, in which are the names of a number of contributors, principally citizens of Baltimore. The book opens with a brief sketch of Dr. Gallitzin's life and the object he had in view in settling at Loretto, written in his own small but very neat hand. A part, however, is erased so as to be utterly illegible. To this is added the following valuable letter in very nervous handwriting:

"I hereby earnestly recommend to all charitable persons to subscribe such sums as their inclination and ability will permit, to second the views detailed in the opposite page by the Rev. Demetrius A. Gallitzin.

"CH. CARROLL of Carrollton.

"November 13, 1827."

The venerable signer of the Declaration of American Independence gave an example to others by subscribing one hundred dollars. The name of Cardinal Capellari, afterwards Pope Gregory XVI., also appears as the contributor of two hundred dollars. Referring to the Cardinal's letter in which his eminence addressed the missionary as *Amplitudo Tua*, the latter playfully remarked that it should have been *tenuitas tua;* for Dr. Gallitzin was of slender form. But the amount raised was not sufficient to meet the urgent demands of the moment, and he thought of crossing over to Europe to see what he might be able to raise among his numerous and wealthy friends there. But the idea was soon abandoned. At length the crisis seemed to have been reached, and in 1828 the miserable log-hut for which he had exchanged a princely title and estate was advertised at sheriff's sale. With the aid of money collected from the faithful Irish laborers on the canal between Johnstown and Blairsville, and from other sources, he was enabled to avert the impending calamity; and from that time forward his financial condition so far improved that by the time of his death he was free from pecuniary embarrassments. All told he expended about $150,000 on the Loretto settlement.*

In 1832 Dr. Gallitzin built a small chapel to the rear of his residence and adjoining it, in which he could offer up the Holy Sacrifice on week-days, and where he could be more comfortable in the severe mountain winters than in the church. But it is proper to remark that a new residence had by this time taken the place of the primeval log-house. In this chapel confessions were heard on Saturday evenings until the new residence was built, as we shall have occasion to observe, a few years ago; and I have both frequently heard in the same confessional which the illustrious missionary used, and said Mass at the same altar before which he so often stood.

The nomination of Rev. F. P. Kenrick as coadjutor to the aged and infirm Bishop Conwell of Philadelphia was not in harmony with Dr. Gallitzin's views, and he accordingly wrote the newly appointed prelate a very plain and strong though

---

* Memoir, etc., by Very Rev. Thos. Heyden, p. 92.

respectful letter on the subject. The course pursued by the Bishop in reference to certain irregularities in one or two congregations was so far out of harmony with the good missionary's ideas that he resigned the vicar-generalship in a characteristic letter. Bishop Kenrick visited Loretto early in the fall of 1830, and administered confirmation to five hundred persons, expressing himself much edified with the piety of the people and the able and skilful administration of the pastor.

In September, 1834, a priest entered upon the mountain mission who is deserving of special mention. Rev. Henry Lemcke was born in Rhema, in the territory of Mechlenburg, Prussia, July 27th, 1796. He entered the army at an early age, and was at the battle of Waterloo. Leaving the army he became a Lutheran preacher; but being soon after converted, he began a course of study for the priesthood, to which he was ordained on the 11th of April, 1825. He came to this country in 1834, and was placed in charge of a German congregation in Philadelphia. He was desirous, however, of exchanging it for some other, when he accidentally learned that Prince Gallitzin was a priest on the American mission. He came West, as we shall presently see; was the intimate friend of the prince, succeeded him at Loretto, and gained possession of all the papers left by the illustrious missionary. After remaining about six years longer in Cambria County, he was transferred to the eastern part of the State upon the arrival of the Benedictine Order at Carrolltown, in 1846. He became a member of the order in 1851, and two years later made his solemn vows.* "It was the doctor's custom," he says, in the work about to be referred to, "to preserve not merely all the letters he received, but copies of all he wrote, if of the least importance; more than this, he kept every paper in which there was any notice of events, even the most ordinary, which had any interest for him; in a large chest there were papers and letters of every description, from the memoirs of his mother to his last tailor's bill; notice from the princess to his tutors, to her children; in a word, the accumulation of half a century." †

---

* St. Vincenz in Pennsylvanien, p. 347.
† Leben und Wirken, etc., p. 11.

From these and personal recollection Fr. Lemcke composed his "Leben und Wirken des Prinzen Demetrius Augustin Gallitzin," which upon a subsequent visit to Europe he had printed at Münster in 1861. The past few years of his life, until recently, were spent at the priory of his order at Newark, N. J., but he has been for some time with the Benedictine fathers in the western part of Pennsylvania. He is hale and active, and has an inexhaustible fund of anecdotes relating to all the varied scenes through which he has passed in his eventful career, which he loves to recount in his inimitable style. He is at present engaged in preparing an autobiography, which will be a valuable addition to the history of the Diocese of Pittsburg.* Having introduced the reader to the venerable priest, we shall return to the year 1834, leaving him to tell the story of his coming to Loretto in his own picturesque style. The passage is translated, with some omissions, from his "Leben und Wirken."

"I had before this somewhere read a biography of Princess Gallitzin, and gathered from it that she had a son, a Catholic missionary in America, but no one could give any information concerning him. At last I asked the Bishop. 'He is at Loretto,' was the answer, 'in Western Pennsylvania, in this diocese.' 'Is he then still living?' 'Certainly, but he is old and delicate, greatly in need of assistance in his widespread congregation. As you desire to be removed from here, and I have now a German priest to take your place, you can go to him. But he is a singular old saint; many others have tried to live with him, but it seems as if no one could get along with him.' I consented to go, and as soon as

* In the summer of 1879 he commenced the publication of the work in the columns of the *Northern Cambria News*, a weekly newspaper published at Carrolltown, where the venerable missionary is now stopping. The work is entitled "Cambria County in the Olden Time, embracing the Life of the Prince, Priest, and Missionary, D. A. Gallitzin, and also an Autobiography of the Writer, Rev. Henry Lemcke." It was the intention to publish it afterwards in book form; but when it had continued about six months, and had brought the life of the author down to the year 1855, it was unexpectedly discontinued for the present, November 22d, 1879. It is much to be regretted that the work, although containing valuable information, should be disfigured by certain strictures on two prelates who have always been regarded throughout the country as models of learning, prudence, and piety.

I could, set out on my journey. . . . I arrived at last in safety at Munster, a little village laid out by Irish people on a table-land of the Allegheny Mountains, only four miles from Gallitzin's residence. The stage stopped at the house of a certain Peter Collins, a genuine Irishman, who kept the post-office and hotel. . . . The next morning—for it was evening when I arrived, and they would not on any account let me go on—a horse was saddled for me, and Thomas, one of the numerous Collins children, stood ready to show me the way and to bring back the horse. . . . We had gone but a mile or two in the woods when I saw a sled coming drawn by two strong horses (N. B. In September, in the most beautiful summer weather). In the sled half sat and half reclined a venerable-looking man in an old, much worn, overcoat, wearing a peasant's hat which no one, it is likely, would have cared to pick up in the street, and carrying a book in his hand. I thought, seeing him brought along in this way, that there must have been an accident, that perhaps the old gentleman had dislocated a limb in the woods; but Thomas, who had been on ahead, came running back and said, '*There comes the priest*,' pointing to the man in the sled. I rode up and asked, 'Are you really the pastor of Loretto?' 'Yes, I am he.' 'Prince Gallitzin?' 'At your service, sir. I am that very exalted personage.' Saying this he laughed heartily. 'You may perhaps wonder,' he continued, when I had presented him a letter from the Bishop of Philadelphia, 'at my singular retinue. But how can it be helped? We have not as yet, as you may see, roads fit for wagons—we should be either fast or upset every moment. I can no longer ride on horseback, having injured myself by a fall, and it is also coming hard with me to walk; besides, I have all the requirements for Mass to take with me. I am now on my way to a place where I have had for some years a station. You can now go on quietly to Loretto and make yourself comfortable there: I shall be at home this evening; or if you like better, you can come with me: perhaps it may interest you.' I chose to accompany him, and after riding some miles through the woods we reached a genuine Pennsylvania farm-house [probably at Summitville, soon to be noticed].

"Here lived Josua Parish, one of the first settlers of that country, and the ancestor of a numerous posterity. The Catholics of the neighborhood, men, women, and children, were already assembled in great numbers around the house, in which an altar was put up, its principal materials having been taken from the sled; Gallitzin then sat down in one corner of the house to hear confessions, and I, in another corner, attended to a few Germans. The whole affair appeared very strange to me, but it was extremely touching to see the simple peasant home, with all its house furniture and the great fireplace, in which there was roasting and boiling going on at the same time, changed into a church, while the people, with their prayer-books and their reverential manners, stood or knelt under the low projecting roof or under trees, going in and out just as their turn came for confession. After Mass, at which Father Gallitzin preached, and when a few children had been baptized, the altar was taken away and the dinner-table set in its place. It was, of course, too small, but it was understood to remedy this evil for one party to sit down after another party had dined, the children meanwhile standing about in the corners with their hands full, while the mother and daughters of the house went back and forth, replenishing the empty dishes from the pots in the fireplace, and pressing the food upon their guests. In a word, all was so pleasant and friendly that involuntarily the love-feasts of the first Christians came to my mind. In the afternoon we went slowly on our way, Gallitzin in his sled and I on horseback, arriving at nightfall at Loretto. . . .

"In the evening we had much to talk about. Forty-two years had already passed since Gallitzin had left Germany, and in that time how much had happened! . . . And while all this was passing, this man, destined by his birth as well as his talents to play a grand *rôle* in the world's theatre, had been announcing in the Allegheny Mountains the kingdom of the Prince of Peace. . . . While we were thus deeply engaged in conversation it grew very late, and then I saw an illustration of old-time Catholic discipline and home regularity. One of the old women, of whom there were several living in the house, put her head in the doorway, asking if there would be prayers that night. 'Certainly,' said Dr. Gallitzin, rising at once, and a signal being given, the household came together. The old nobleman knelt without any ceremony near the table by which he had been sitting, took his rosary from his pocket and began it. After the prayers were over he took his breviary, I did the same; the house was as quiet as a monastery. When I left my room the next morning I met the prince with his arms full of wood, intending to make a fire, as it had grown quite cold during the night. Afterwards when I went to the chapel to say Mass, he insisted upon serving me."

To this graphic picture of the early missionary life and customs of the pioneer priests, Father Lemcke adds the following on the Doctor's Sunday routine, which will be no less interesting:

"The next day was Sunday. The people began to come very early in the morning, from all directions, to go to confession. At ten o'clock I celebrated High Mass, at which the organ was played, and there was some pretty good singing. After the gospel the old pastor stepped quickly towards me at the altar, put me to one side, and began to preach, of course in English, of which I understood but little. As well as I could make it out it was strong against pride and vanity. Nothing in the world excited the humble man more than to perceive any luxury, love of finery, or new fashions creeping in among his children, though I must admit there was scarcely ten dollars' worth of superfluities and luxuries to be seen in the entire congregation; what special thing had just then aroused him I could not tell. Perhaps it was that at this time the first modern carriage made its appearance at the door of the Loretto church; for a man of the neighborhood who had grown rich, and now and then went to Philadelphia on business, had brought back with him a very fine carriage, in which with his family, all adorned to suit, he drove to church on Sundays, creating a great sensation. At the time the marvel was expected to make its appearance, the boys would climb the trees and fences, keeping their eyes fixed in the direction from which it would probably come; in a word, it was like the Indians on the upper Missouri when the first steamboat was seen.

"When Gallitzin had finished his English sermon, he began another in German, but to me it sounded altogether foreign ; it is true he had received a German education, although at the time when the influence of the French language was at its height, but in his forty-two years in America he had had little or no practice in speaking it. . . . He introduced me formally to the Germans, who were then pretty numerous, intimating to them that for the future I would attend to them, and that I would now preach them a German sermon, which they had not heard for a long time. He then moved aside, bowing to me with a mischievous smile, as much as to say : 'I have got through, now it is your turn.' There had been nothing of the kind intimated to me previously ; he had merely requested me to celebrate High Mass; there was no alternative but for me to preach, more decidedly extempore than ever before in my life. When I spoke to him about it later, he laughed and said that he wished to know whether I was fitted for a missionary, for he would have a treasure in one who could at any moment bring out the old and new.

"I lived in the belief that I was now at home with Gallitzin, and made my plans accordingly—how I could live with this singular old gentleman, how I would go to work to break through the crust which had formed over his noble nature in the long battle with an ungrateful and wicked world, and how I would win myself a place in his heart. But I found I had reckoned without my host.

"On Monday morning he was ready to start out again ; the horses were hitched to the wagon, for now it was to go to Ebensburg, the county-town, to which the roads were so good that the sled was only required for them in winter-time. We stopped at the house of a Mrs. Ivory, who had grown up in Gallitzin's house, while her mother and two of her sisters still remained with him, keeping house for him. The old gentleman went around all the morning from one house to another, and I could not imagine what he had on hand. After dinner the matter was explained. He handed me a paper, saying : 'Here is a list of the Catholics of the place. Each one of them has bound himself by this paper to contribute a certain sum annually for your support. There is a little church here, but for some time there has been no priest; the congregation is small and hardly able to support one. But you will stay in this house; there are some really pretty rooms upstairs; Mrs. Ivory is a good cook, and will treat you in the best manner possible. I will pay the board for you in advance, and in return you will come to me once a month to preach to the Germans and assist in the confessional; you will also have to attend to the stations and sick-calls which I can no longer reach.' 'But,' said I, 'what are you thinking of? What am I to do here among the English? for, as far as I can learn, there is not a German in the place.' 'That makes no difference; it is all the better for you; you will then learn English *nolens volens*. You have already made a good beginning, and as you by no means appear to have fallen on your head, you will soon be able to preach.' 'It may be so, but we can speak English in Loretto also, and it would in every way be better for me to live with you, and save paying for board.' 'Well, you see,' he said, rubbing his nose, as was his way when he was embarrassed, 'winter is near, and, as you have observed, there is only one room in my house, besides the kitchen, in which there is a fireplace.' I could hardly refrain from laughing at this, for the Bishop had told me he would not let another priest live with him, and had arranged his house in a way to have a good excuse for declining." Speaking of his appearance at that time, he being then in his sixty-fourth year, Father Lemcke says: "When I first saw Gallitzin, he was certainly very thin, and his general appearance fragile, but he was erect, his walk firm and rapid, his voice loud and sonorous, his look keen and decided."

Just before this time his pen had again been at work. A Presbyterian synod was held at Columbia, Pa., toward the close of the year 1833, in which the assembly, in the charitable language peculiar to that sect when discussing the subject of *Popery*, warned their ministers of the rapid strides it was making in their midst, and in six resolutions labored to enkindle their zeal in opposing its further progress. Dr. Gallitzin addressed them in "Six Letters of Advice to the Gentlemen Presbyterian Parsons who lately met at Columbia, Pa., for the purpose of Declaring War against the Catholic Church." The first of these letters appeared January 14th, 1834, and the others followed weekly in the newspaper in which they were first published. They were afterwards issued in pamphlet form by Canan & Scott, Ebensburg, 1834, pp. 28. The letters are written in an easy, almost a playful, but ironical style, and must have pierced those to whom they were addressed like an arrow. They have long since been out of print, but are given almost entire by Miss Brownson—an act for which the Catholic public should be sincerely grateful.* The following will afford an idea of the style of the letters. Having stated that he had heard of the synod, and having given the preamble and the six resolutions, he begins after this manner:

"Well done, gentlemen! Thus you have sounded the tocsin of war; you have drawn the sword, and thrown away the scabbard. Like so many heroes you stand in battle array, to fight the battles of the Lord against Pope and Popery. Fame, which hath already wafted across the Atlantic the account of your heroic deeds during the ravages of the cholera, will bring your declaration of war to Rome, and fill the Pope and his cardinals with terror and dismay.

"But now, gentlemen, let me tell you it is not sufficient to know how to declare war; you ought also to know how to carry it on; and as I am somewhat acquainted with military tactics (having formerly held a commission in the Russian army), charity impels me to assist you with my advice.

"To secure a little respect for my advice, I wish you to observe: 1st. That I am in my sixty-fourth year; 2dly. That I was educated in the Greek Protestant Church, the members of which bear a greater hatred to the Pope than ever you did; 3dly. That I am now and since the year 1795 have been a minister of that religion which you very gentlemanly designate by the nickname of *Romanism* or *Popery*, and which I call the Roman Catholic Church, *alias* the Church of Jesus Christ.

"From the premises the conclusion is rational that, knowing both sides of the question, I ought to be tolerably well qualified to advise you how to carry on a war successfully against the Pope."

---

* Life, etc., pp. 407, 409 *et seq.*

But the veteran missionary's career was fast drawing to a close. He had found a wilderness and made of it a flourishing Catholic settlement, with all that was necessary for its permanence and future development. Its ramifications had extended many miles in almost every direction, and had become either new congregations or the nucleuses of new congregations to be organized at no distant day. His financial difficulties, which were one of the heaviest crosses that he had been called upon by his Master to carry, and one peculiarly galling to a person of his refined feelings and high sense of honor, were now things of the past. Troubles from false brethren were now happily adjusted; and after a life stormy in its own way there succeeded the calm which his soul desired before its departure. But even in his old age Dr. Gallitzin did not give himself up to repose. His labors ceased only with his life. We have seen that when no longer able to ride on horseback he visited his stations on a sled, for better conveyance he had none.

It was the autumn of 1839. "In the winter following," says Miss Brownson—"a very severe one, it was noticed, with forebodings, instantly repressed as too painful for consideration, that he no longer carried himself as formerly, that the once ringing step all knew so well was at times slow and uncertain—his voice failed him in preaching, and in his exhortations tears would fall from the beautiful eyes which once flashed accompaniment to his thrilling words—tears and a look more touching than the most powerful sermon of his youth. 'Sometimes in the course of these sermons,' one who heard him relates,* 'he became truly eloquent. At such times he would lean forward a little, his face would light up, and his eyes shine with heavenly radiance; but this would last only a few minutes, being repressed as soon as he perceived it, as if it were against his calmer judgment, and after a few sentences he would resume his conversational tone; his sermons, if such they could be called, did not last quite thirty minutes.' Those who observed him closely or saw him but seldom could not doubt that he who had never cared for the world was now

---

* Father Lemcke, Leben und Wirken, p. 356.

more than ever detached from it, that he who had waited so long for heaven was looking wistfully to the promised rest. . . . The trouble resulting from a fall from his horse one night, years before, when returning from a sick-call, which had prevented his ever riding again, now assumed a very serious form always painful, and at times exceedingly so ; Dr. Rodrigue, his physician,—an excellent one,—his friends, his brother priests urged him to rest, but as long as it pleased his Master to leave him at his post he refused to consider himself incompetent to fulfil its duties, let the result be what it would; all they could say was met by a smile that tenderly acknowledged their solicitude, but put aside all hope of compliance with their wishes." * His physician urged him to remain in his room, but could not prevail on him to comply with his advice. "He went through all the services of Holy Week, heard confessions for half a day at a time, at what cost can never be told. Early Easter morning (April 19th) he was in the confessional again, but was so exhausted by ten o'clock that he could only say a low Mass, and give a short exhortation on the Resurrection, which he ended with the words spoken on the cross: '*It is consummated.*' They were the last to his congregation." †

Word was immediately sent to the neighboring priests. Father Lemcke, though suffering from an accident, had himself conveyed to Loretto on a sled, and prepared his venerable friend—for he had been his confessor for six years—for the operation which his physician deemed it necessary to perform, by offering up the Holy Sacrifice in his room immediately after midnight, and administering the last sacraments to him.

"Soon afterwards Dr. Rodrigue performed the operation, to which the Doctor submitted with heroic fortitude ; but for it the physician had no hope that he could survive the night. During the following nights Dr. Rodrigue scarcely left his side ; after riding all day to attend to his other patients, he would hasten back over the wretched roads to watch all night with the dying priest. On the 4th of May (Rev.) Mr. Heyden arrived, but the doctor was only able to welcome him with a

---

* Life, etc., pp. 434, 435.   † Ibid., p. 436.

faint smile and a few whispered, broken words. . . . So he lay there resting until the evening of (Wednesday) the 6th of May, between six and seven o'clock. When the hour came for the laborers to go home from their work, they saw that he was going too. Mr. Heyden read the prayers for the dying, the room-doors were opened, the crowds in the house and chapel prayed with tears and sobs, and in a few minutes, without any perceptible sign, all was over, the heavens were open, all their joy-bells were ringing a welcoming peal; he had gone home to his own country." *

It is impossible to describe the impression which the news of the death of the venerable man everywhere created. His own flock were inconsolable, and as they pressed around the casket containing the remains of their good pastor, their grief knew no bounds.

It was his wish to be buried between his house and the church, which stood but a few yards from it; but, in order to satisfy the devotion of the people who were anxious to take part in bearing his remains to their last resting-place, the funeral procession moved through the principal streets of the village before the interment. The solemn Mass of requiem was celebrated by Father Heyden, who also delivered the funeral oration in English, after which Father Lemcke addressed the congregation in German. But the resting-place selected was not to be permanent. He had long wished to build a large church in the village, and had set apart a number of lots for that purpose. In front of it was to be the place of his final repose. The work was left to other hands, as will soon appear, and when the church was completed, about eleven years later, a monument of "shapeless sculpture," altogether unworthy the noble founder of the colony, was erected in front of the sacred edifice. Thither the remains were transferred with great pomp, and were deposited in the vault prepared for their reception; and there the coffin, enclosed in its zinc case, reposes on a stone on the middle of the floor of the cellar-like vault under the monument, as I

---

* Life, etc., pp. 437, 438.

have seen it. On the monument is the following inscription, composed by Archbishop Kenrick of Baltimore:

> Sacrum Memoriæ
> DEM. A. E PRINCIPIBUS GALLITZIN,
> nat. XXII Decemb. A.D. MDCCLXX,
> qui Schismate ejurato ad
> Sacerdotium evectus, Sacro Ministerio
> per tot. hanc reg. perfunctus.
> Fide, Zelo, Charitate insignis, heic obiit
> die VI Mai, A.D. MDCCCXL.

> Sacred to the Memory of
> DEM. A., PRINCE OF GALLITZIN,
> born December 22, 1770,
> who having renounced Schism was raised to the Priesthood,
> exercised the Sacred Ministry through the whole of this region,
> and, distinguished for faith, zeal, charity,
> died May 6, 1840.

The question of erecting a more fitting testimonial to the memory of one who, renouncing the brilliant prospects which the world presented to him, planted the colony, gave away much of the land to its members for nothing, or for promises worth nothing, who fed its poor, and devoted his days and nights, his youth and old age, to the welfare of its people, from whom he never asked nor received any compensation whatever, has been frequently mooted, but has been permitted to fall ineffectually to the ground.

Different opinions may be formed regarding the prudence of Dr. Gallitzin's course in founding a colony on the summit of the Allegheny Mountains; but in our day there are few who would consider the choice a happy one. The summer season is much shorter and the winter longer and more severe than in the lower country; while the soil is surpassed in fertility by that of almost every other part of the dioceses, except the mountain districts. Allowance must, however, be made for the imperfect knowledge people had at that early day of the relative advantages of different localities. Nor should we lose sight of the object which Dr. Gallitzin proposed to himself, that of founding an exclusively Catholic settlement, where, under his immediate direction and control, it would grow up free from many of the evils which he was forced to witness and lament in other places. The object was a good one and much to be desired, but at the same time one which no person can hope to attain in a country so enslaved to material pursuits and empty show as ours, and hence his success was but partial. He might declaim against extravagant fashions and other novelties; he might lecture those who would presume to appear in his humble church with the latest Philadelphia styles of dress, or who rode to church in a handsome carriage instead of a farm-wagon; but the world will move on in its own way despite the efforts of any one man to stay its progress. But although he may have erred in expecting to do what no man can hope to accomplish in our day, however desirable it may be, yet the Church in this part of the country owes him a deep debt of gratitude. Through his labors and sacrifices he succeeded in making Cambria County largely Catholic, and in forming a number of congregations which will remain to all future time an evidence of his disinterestedness and zeal in the cause of the religion for which he renounced all that rank and wealth could offer, and to the promotion of which he consecrated his whole being and such remnant of his vast estates as he was able to recover. Another good work he did that must not be overlooked. In the early settlement of almost every part of this country in which Catholics were mingled with Protestants, many lost their faith by contact with heretics, and more especially by intermarriage with them; and hence it is no exaggeration to say that hundreds of thousands have been lost to the Church in this country, and families are yet multiplying, and to the end of time will continue to multiply, in whose homes, in all human probability, the light of the true faith will never shine. Through the efforts of Dr. Gallitzin the Church was spared this affliction to a great extent, and pioneers wishing to come West were not exposed to the danger of doing so at the peril of their religion. After making all due allowance for the errors of his views or his policy, he is yet entitled to the highest meed of praise; and even the errors into which he may have fallen were committed in seeking what he took to be the greater good for the souls of his people. With him the temporal was ever made subservient to the eternal; and no higher praise can be bestowed upon man than to say, what is eminently true of Dr. Gallitzin, that in all things he sought "first the kingdom of God and his justice."

At the time of his death Dr. Gallitzin left about two hundred acres of land to the church at Loretto; of which a considerable part was made over to the Franciscan brothers, sometime after their establishment there, in 1847; a few acres also passed into the hands of the Sisters of Mercy on their coming in 1848: a part has since been sold as being more to the interests of religion, and the remainder is still in the possession of the Church. For several years before his death the good priest's labors had been confined exclusively to the parent church of Loretto.

Rev. Thos. Heyden, of Bedford, was appointed his successor, but preferring to remain in his former place, he was permitted to do so. Father Lemcke was then appointed; but he did not reside at Loretto all the time that he was pastor. After presiding over the congregation for about four years, he was succeeded by Rev. Hugh P. Gallagher, who remained about the same length of time. During his pastorate the Franciscan brothers established the mother-house of their order in the diocese at Loretto, and soon after opened a college, as will be seen more at length in its proper place.

When Bishop O'Connor visited Loretto in 1847 there were 2500 souls in the congregation, as he informs us in his Notes.

Rev. Jas. Gallagher now succeeded to the pastorate. The congregation had been gradually increasing, and the church was no longer able to accommodate it. To remedy this defect the present church was begun in 1851, and when finished was dedicated by Bishop Neuman, of Philadelphia, on the 6th of January, 1854. It occupies the spot at the eastern end of the village that had been long before set apart for it by Dr. Gallitzin. The church is a brick building 130 feet in length by 80 in width, and lays little claim to architectural style. At first it had a steeple in the centre in front, but the mountain storms have long since removed it. The interior is divided into a nave and side aisles separated by two rows of columns; the ceiling of the nave being that known as the tunnel vault, while that of the aisles is flat. There are three altars. In making his tour through the diocese in the autumn of 1853, Cardinal Bedini visited Loretto and the grave of its founder. In 1848 the Sisters of Mercy came to the village, where a house was built for them, to which they have since made considerable additions, and the girls' school was placed under their charge, which they have since conducted. They soon after opened an academy for young ladies, as will be stated more at length hereafter. Some time in the course of the following year Father Gallagher was succeeded by Rev. W. Pollard, during whose stay the pastoral residence was enlarged by an additional story. He was succeeded by Rev. T. S. Reynolds in November, 1859. But for several years before this time and ever after, the pastor has required the aid of an assistant. The latter, however, has usually resided and taught at St. Francis' College, assisting at the church on Saturday afternoons and Sundays. In the summer of 1868 Father Reynolds gave place to Rev. M. J. Mitchell, who remained until February, 1870. During the latter half of the year 1869 the writer of these pages was assistant to the pastor, but resided at the college.

Upon the retirement of Father Mitchell, Rev. E. A. Bush, the present pastor, was appointed to the vacant post. Soon after his arrival he put the church through a thorough course of repairs exteriorly and interiorly, and gave it as good an appearance as a building of its singular proportions could well be made to bear. In the summer of 1874 he built a neat frame pastoral residence near the church, the old one being too far distant and out of repair. This, however, being but the smaller part of the plan he had formed, he completed it in 1879 by building a large brick house in front of it. He also restored the proper name, St. Michael's, to the church, which had been called St. Mary's, although both its predecessors had borne the former name.

St. Michael's is, with the exception of St. Augustine's, the largest country congregation in the two dioceses, and will number between three and four hundred families. Although there were originally a large number of Germans, the congregation may now be regarded as entirely English. The village and the surrounding country are almost exclusively Catholic. It is not probable that the congregation will undergo any considerable change for many years to come.

CHAPTER XIX.

CAMBRIA COUNTY (CONTINUED).—CONGREGATIONS FORMED FROM LORETTO.

St. Bartholomew's Church, Wilmore—German Church of the Immaculate Conception, New Germany—St. Aloysius' Church. Summitville—Death and sketch of Rev. Thos. M'Cullagh—and of Rev. John Hackett—St. Patrick's Church, Gallitzin—St. Augustine's Church, St. Augustine—Death and sketch of Rev. Ed. Burns—St. Monica's Church, Chest Springs.

ST. BARTHOLOMEW'S CHURCH, WILMORE.

IN tracing the history of the congregations formed from the original settlement of Loretto, we shall begin with Wilmore and form a circle around the parent church. The village of Wilmore is situated on the western slope of the mountains and on the Pennsylvania Railroad, ninety-two miles east of Pittsburg and ten miles south-west of Loretto. In the early days of its history it was known by the name of Jefferson, and it was so designated in the Catholic Directories until recently. In 1870 it had a population of 393, which showed a trifling decrease in the previous ten years. A few Catholic families had settled there before the year 1830, but at what precise time Mass was first celebrated in their midst it is impossible to determine. But from that date, and perhaps prior to it, Dr. Gallitzin visited them at intervals. Among them was a negro family from Maryland by the name of Wilmore, from which the place took its name, and in whose house—or, more correctly, barn—the priest was accustomed to offer up the Holy Sacrifice, when the threshing-floor had been swept and the barn-fowls banished out of sight, although not always out of hearing. Like the ark of the covenant on the threshing-floor of Obed Edom, the temporary altar imparted a benediction, and a flourishing congregation came at length into existence. After his appointment to Ebensburg in the latter part of 1832, Rev. Jas. Bradley ministered to the little flock until he was succeeded, about two years later, by Father Lemcke. It continued to be visited either from Loretto or Ebensburg until the year 1840, when the congregation had increased sufficiently to require a church. A small stone one was built, and was dedicated by Bishop Kenrick on the occasion of his first visit, August 22d of that year, under the invocation of St. Bartholomew the Apostle. From that time it was usually visited on one Sunday in the month; in 1844, from Loretto; in 1846, from Summitville; and after the following year from Johnstown. By this time the congregation was large, and numbered, as Bishop O'Connor states in his Notes, about 700 souls. Rev. T. Mullen was at that time pastor of the church at Johnstown, and until the close of the year 1853 he also ministered to that of Wilmore. Toward the close of this period he found it necessary to replace the small church by a larger one to accommodate the congregation, now greatly increased. But before the building was finished he was transferred to Allegheny City, and Wilmore, now separated from Johnstown, became an independent congregation, with Rev. M. J. Mitchell as its first resident pastor. The church was dedicated by Bishop O'Connor, May 20th, 1855, although not yet finished in the interior. It is a substantial brick building, 110 feet in length by 55 in width, having a tall spire in the centre in front, and is modelled after the Gothic style of architecture. Occupying an elevated position to the north of the village, it appears to good advantage. Father Mitchell was succeeded in September, 1855, by Rev. Thos. Walsh, by whom the church was finished, the balance of the debt liquidated, and a handsome frame pastoral residence built. After having ministered to the congregation for six years, he was succeeded, in September, 1861, by Rev. John Hackett. The congregation had been all this time increasing, thanks to the new life inspired into business and agriculture by the Pennsylvania Railroad. Father Hackett remained until July, 1868, when he was succeeded for a short time by Rev. Peter Hughes, upon whose transfer to another field of labor Rev. O. P. Gallagher was appointed pastor. During his administration he purchased a house in the village with a view of making it a convent for a colony of Sisters, whom he hoped to procure to take charge of a parish school to be opened. Circumstances, however, were not favorable to the undertaking, and the congregation, although as yet without a school, still owns the house. At the close of 1872, Father Gallagher was succeeded by the present pastor, Rev. Henry M'Hugh. The increase of the congregation in the last few years is but trifling, if, indeed, it has increased at all; yet it will number about two hundred families, who are all farmers with the exception of a few persons living in the village. There are also many persons living in the village, employed on the trains of the railroad, who add more to the numbers than to the moral tone of the congregation. The future of the congregation will, to all present appearances, be a very gradual increase.

GERMAN CHURCH OF THE IMMACULATE CONCEPTION, NEW GERMANY.

This church is situated in a country place, about three miles west of Wilmore, in the midst of a small German settlement, and appears to owe its existence to the fact that no priest familiar with the German language was stationed at St. Bartholomew's Church. From its organization the parish has been under the care of the Benedictine fathers, being at one time attended from Carrolltown, again from St. Vincent's Abbey, and finally from Johnstown. The first church was built in the year 1855, and was dedicated, under the title of the Immaculate Conception, by Rev. Clement Staub, O.S.B., on the 8th of December of that year. From that time the congregation has usually been visited on two Sundays in the month. There has been perhaps no increase from the beginning, but it was in time deemed advisable to replace the old church with a better one. It was undertaken, and when built was dedicated by the Bishop September 11th, 1864. Little change has marked the history of the congregation, except that of late the tide has set in against it. For, there being no parish school, the young are growing up in a measure ignorant of the parent language, and prefer the English church of Wilmore to their own. When the original founders of the congregation shall have passed away, the parish itself, which never numbered more perhaps than forty families, will be merged in that of Wilmore, and it may safely be predicted that in ten or fifteen years the congregation will be a thing of the past.

ST. ALOYSIUS' CHURCH, SUMMITVILLE.

Summitville, or "the Summit" as it is commonly called, is a village on the mountain-top about six miles south-east of Loretto, at the point where the northern turnpike crosses the mountain. In 1870 it had a population of 177, which showed the very moderate increase of one in the preceding ten years. The village owes its existence to the traffic on the turnpike, and the first settlers appear to have come soon after the thoroughfare was opened. Dr. Gallitzin held stations among the people from an early day, but the date of his first visit cannot be ascertained, although it was prior to the year 1830. After the arrival of Father Lemcke, the little flock formed a part of his extensive field of missionary labor, and until the appointment of the first resident pastor it was visited either from Ebensburg or Loretto.

The erection of the first church—an unassuming frame structure—was begun about the year 1838. In 1846 Rev. A. P. Gibbs was appointed first pastor ; but in the following year appears the name of Rev. P. Duffy, who visited it on two Sundays in the month from Ebensburg. At this time, when Bishop O'Connor visited the church and administered confirmation, the congregation, as he states in his Notes, numbered 800 souls. To supply the wants of the growing congregation, a new church was undertaken about the year 1849 ; but before its completion Father Duffy was transferred to another field, and the congregation was ministered to occasionally by a neighboring priest until the spring of 1850, when Rev. Thos. M'Cullagh became pastor. "The aspect which affairs presented, on his arrival at his new mission, was by no means encouraging. A large brick church and parsonage had been commenced by his predecessor, and left in an unfinished state. The debts, considering the available resources of the congregation, were very great. Yet many had given already all they were able to spare. The walls of the church, raw and roofless, had been exposed to all the severities of a winter peculiar to that elevated region. Under the continual action of frost and rain the brickwork in many places had crumbled away, so as to render it necessary to tear down and rebuild a great part of the structure."* But "the work on the Pennsylvania Railroad had already commenced, and the peculiar character of the route through Cambria County required for a long period a large force of laborers, who were all of that class most likely to assist Father M'Cullagh in his emergencies. Attracted by the prospect of good wages, steady employment, and the Catholic character of the neighborhood, the railroaders might be counted by hundreds as they clustered round the mountain gorges of the Alleghenies, scooping out a pathway through the rugged hills, or linking mountain to mountain by a solid causeway for the tramp of the iron horse. Under the rough exterior of railroaders they concealed honest and generous hearts; and out of their hard-won savings they were ever ready to contribute to the cause of religion with a prompt and liberal hand. Pioneers they were in more senses than one; for they were not only the scouts whose presence proclaims the onward march of modern improvement, but the vanguard also of the ancient faith whereever they appeared."†

The inspiring presence and indomitable energy of the new pastor infused fresh courage into the congregation; work was resumed on the church with the opening of spring; but it was not ready for dedication until the following year. The solemn ceremony was performed by Very Rev. E. M'Mahon, V.G., June 20th, 1851. The church is a brick building 100 feet in length by 60 in width, without a steeple, and although neat and substantial is not remarkable for architectural beauty. The house was finished and occupied prior to the completion of the church.

But Father M'Cullagh's labors were not confined to the

* Reminiscences of the Rev. Thomas M'Cullagh, of the Diocese of Pittsburg, by Rev. T. Mullen (New York, 1861), p. 44.
† Ibid., p. 45.

congregation; for in addition to his literary pursuits, of which mention will presently be made, he had ten or twelve miles of the railroad under his jurisdiction, upon which hundreds of Irish Catholics were employed. A large number was also engaged in opening the tunnel through the mountain about three miles north of the Summit; and as they were likely to remain for several years, he deemed it expedient to build a temporary church for their better accommodation. This became the nucleus of the congregation at Gallitzin, that is next to engage our attention.

In 1851 the type and press of a weekly paper were exposed for sale; and after having maturely considered the propriety of the movement, Father M'Cullagh and three or four of the priests of the mountain district purchased them, and commenced the publication of a weekly Catholic journal under the title of *The Crusader*. The editorial management was entrusted to the pastor of the Summit, who, although all contributed, was the principal writer. The first number appeared January 1st, 1852; and the paper was issued weekly until November 24th of the following year, when it was discontinued and the subscription-list transferred to the Pittsburg *Catholic*. During its brief career the *Crusader* was conducted with ability, and exercised a healthy influence in the sphere to which its circulation extended.*

In the summer of 1856 Father M'Cullagh was transferred to St. Patrick's Church, Pittsburg, and Rev. E. F. Garland, of the latter, became pastor of St. Aloysius. During this time the diocesan seminary was reopened at the Summit, but was transferred a year later to Pittsburg. Immediately after the completion and dedication of St. Patrick's Church, August 15th, 1858, Father M'Cullagh returned to his former charge, and Father Garland to his. While in the city his health had begun to become impaired, and he retired for a few weeks to St. Xavier's Academy, Westmoreland County, to recruit. But the relief afforded was only temporary; his health was permanently impaired, and on his return to the Summit it continued to grow worse, until it became evident to all that he

---

* Reminiscences, etc., pp. 49-54.

could not long continue to exercise his sacred functions. He contemplated a trip to Lake Superior, but on maturer reflection it was abandoned. He preferred to remain at his post, until, being entirely exhausted, he was forced to commit his flock to another shepherd. Coming to Pittsburg, he entered the Mercy Hospital, where he could receive the best care and medical treatment. The general debility of which he had been complaining during the last two years culminated in congestion of the brain. Several days passed without any indications of immediate danger, during which time he received the last sacraments. " On Sunday night he rested well, and on Monday morning appeared much refreshed. . . . Soon, however, another change occurred, and it was evident his last hour was approaching. He now began to sink rapidly, and at ten minutes past six, on the afternoon of the same day, the 20th of June, 1859, in the thirty-ninth year of his age and the sixteenth of his ministry, he expired without a struggle."*
His remains were conveyed by the cars to Cresson Station, Pennsylvania Railroad, one mile from the Summit, and from thence to the church, where, with all the ceremonies of religion, they were consigned to their last resting-place in the adjacent cemetery. A few years later a tasteful monument was erected by the congregation to mark the spot.

Rev. Thomas M'Cullagh was born at Cranag, parish of the Upper Badony, county Tyrone, Ireland, in the latter part of October, 1819. His parents belonged to the middle class, and were more remarkable for virtue than for wealth. After having studied in the schools of his native place, he entered Maynooth College. While engaged in the studies necessary to fit him for the sacred ministry, he pursued other branches more remotely connected with it as opportunities were offered. I have elsewhere spoken of the manner in which certain students of the college, in the fall of 1843, responded to the invitation of the newly consecrated Bishop O'Connor to labor in his diocese, where, as he told them, "he had no inducements to offer, except plenty of work and little for it." Mr. M'Cullagh sailed for America on the 9th of

---

* Reminiscences, etc., p. 60.

November, and arrived in Pittsburg just in time to assist at the first Pontifical Mass celebrated in the old church occupied by the Germans during the erection of the present St. Philomena's. "The wants of the mission, particularly in the country around Pittsburg, were at that time very great, and the physical strength of the few priests in the city taxed to the utmost. However advisable it might be, under ordinary circumstances, to allow him to prolong his studies, Mr. M'Cullagh's services as a priest could no longer be spared. He was consequently ordained on the 4th of February, 1844, in the old Cathedral, which was afterwards burnt down. His ordination was the first ceremony of the kind ever witnessed in the Diocese of Pittsburg. Immediately after his ordination he took charge of several missions around the city, thus occupying a post where his zeal was sure almost every day to find a fresh field for its exercise. Pittsburg was his head-quarters, whither he returned, from time to time, to prepare for further expeditions. . . . With little relaxation from other labors, Father M'Cullagh in 1844 assumed the editorial control of the Pittsburg *Catholic*, the organ of the diocese, and continued to discharge the duties connected with this office the greater part of the two following years. After his official connection with the paper had ceased, he was always a frequent and welcome contributor to its columns.

"During the three years immediately subsequent to Father M'Cullagh's ordination, notwithstanding the wants of the diocese, but few additions could be made to the number of priests on the mission; at last it was resolved to open a source whence a regular supply could be obtained. In 1847 St. Michael's Seminary was established in the house now (1861) occupied as a Male Orphan Asylum in Birmingham, and the interests of the institution—a most important one for the diocese—entrusted to Father M'Cullagh, who became its first president. However advisable it might be for the seminary to enjoy for a lengthened period the advantages of his scholarly attainments and beneficent rule, his health, which at the best was never robust, rendered it necessary for him to resign this position the following year. He immediately took charge of St. Vincent's congregation, Westmoreland County, where he hoped to find a region and climate better adapted to the delicacy of his constitution. St. Xavier's Academy, which was then in its infancy and in the immediate neighborhood of St. Vincent's, secured his services as chaplain. Though early convinced that his health required great care and attention, he continued to labor in his new position for the good of religion with unabated zeal. Most of the time that he could spare from duties connected with St. Vincent's and the Academy he devoted to the Catholic settlements in Westmoreland, and contrived in this way to render good service to the interests of religion in the county. When the Academy was transferred to its present beautiful site, he fixed his residence in its neighborhood and continued his vigilant supervision over its early struggles. . . . While there his constitutional delicacy had almost disappeared. The climate, the treatment, and congenial pursuits had produced a marked change in his whole appearance, and the salient points, the only drawback to his otherwise remarkably well-formed person, had subsided beneath a compact covering of flesh and muscle." *

From St. Xavier's he was transferred, as has been stated, to the Summit, where his life was identified with that of the congregation. From certain manuscripts left at his death, it appears that he had at one time entertained the project of editing a monthly periodical, when the appearance of the *Metropolitan Magazine* induced him to abandon the idea.

At the death of Father M'Cullagh, Rev. Thos. Ryan was appointed pastor of St. Aloysius and the temporary church at the tunnel. At first, like his predecessor, he was alone; but when the latter congregation, now known as St. Patrick's, Gallitzin, had increased so as to render it too laborious for one priest to minister to both, an assistant was appointed, commencing February, 1863. At length it became expedient to separate the two congregations and assign to each a resident pastor. When this division was made, November 10th, 1869, Father Ryan preferred Gallitzin, and Rev. John Hackett was transferred from Freeport to the Summit. During

---

* Reminiscences, etc., pp. 32–44.

all this time the congregation had undergone but little change; its increase, if any, had been extremely moderate, and it might be said of it more truly perhaps than of any other congregation in the diocese that it kept the even tenor of its way. At length, however, a change came, and a sorrowful one for the members of St. Aloysius' congregation. The good pastor, who had for nine years devoted his undivided attention to their spiritual welfare, after having gradually declined for a few months, although continuing to exercise his pastoral functions and to bear his infirmities with silent resignation, was taken suddenly ill on Thursday, October 31st, 1878, and died of cerebro-spinal meningitis on the afternoon of November 4th, in the 48th year of his age and in the beginning of the 24th year of his ministry. The funeral took place from the church, and the remains were laid to rest in the adjacent cemetery by the side of those of Father M'Cullagh and Rev. Peter Brown, of Johnstown.

REV. JOHN HACKETT was born in the parish and near the town of Connel, in the Diocese of Waterford, Ireland, in the year 1830. Having finished his course of theology in the missionary college of All-Hallows, he came to America and to the Diocese of Pittsburg, where he was ordained by Bishop O'Connor November 25th, 1855. At first he ministered to the congregation of Temperanceville and Brodhead, and resided at the Cathedral; but at the end of about two years he was transferred to the church at Latrobe, and thence to Cameron Bottom. From there he passed to Wilmore, September, 1861, and in July, 1868, to Freeport. While there he built the little church at Natrona. Finally he was transferred, as we have seen, to the Summit, which in the inscrutable design of Providence was to be the closing scene of his labors. Few priests of the diocese were more highly or justly esteemed than Father Hackett. Unassuming in his manner and wholly devoted to the welfare of his people, the affairs of the world made little impression upon him, while the simplicity of his character and his eminently clerical bearing endeared him to all with whom he came in contact.

Rev. Thos. Davin, the present pastor of St. Aloysius', succeeded Father Hackett. The congregation is composed principally of farmers of Irish and German descent with a small number of coal-miners, and owing to its scattered character has never been able to organize a parish school. It will number perhaps a little less than two hundred families, and its future career will in all probability be as uneventful as its past has been.

ST. PATRICK'S CHURCH, GALLITZIN.

The village of Gallitzin is situated on the summit of the Allegheny Mountains, and is 105 miles east of Pittsburg by the railroad. Here, after ascending the mountains westward from Altoona and rising about eleven hundred feet in eleven miles, in which the road passes for the most part along the northern side of a deep ravine, presenting some of the most beautiful scenery in America, a part of which is the famous Horseshoe Curve, or Kitanning Point as it is more commonly called, the railroad passes through the summit of the mountain by means of a tunnel 3670 feet in length. "One is hurried onward through dense and unbroken darkness, and just as the first ray of light, the first breath of glorious mountain air breaks in there is heard the echoing cry, GALLITZIN! the far-sounding name of him who with feet *beautiful upon the mountains* opened to the entrancing sunlight of faith the gloomy caverns of heresy and sin—a name shouted there with startling appropriateness, rendered the more striking that its deep significance was neither intended nor suspected."[*] Having passed through the village, or, more correctly, under it,—for the greater part is built over the western end of the tunnel,—the road makes the descent of the mountain, perhaps twelve hundred feet, in twenty-five miles to Conemaugh borough, near Johnstown.

Although it is probable that a few Catholic families settled in the vicinity of where the village now stands, and that Dr. Gallitzin held stations among them at intervals, the present congregation owes its existence to the railroad. Work was commenced on the tunnel in 1849, and continued for

---

[*] Life, etc., p. 405.

about four years, during which time a large number of men, principally Catholics, were constantly employed. The better to accommodate them Father M'Cullagh built a cheap temporary frame church there in which he offered up the Holy Sacrifice once or twice in the month on Sundays, riding thither from the Summit, a distance of three miles, between the two Masses. After the completion of the tunnel a village sprung up composed principally of coal-miners and men in the employ of the railroad company, and in honor of the Apostle of the Alleghenies it was named *Gallitzin*. The church remained, and was visited on one Sunday in the month by the pastor of the Summit. When at the death of Father M'Cullagh the church at the latter place passed into the hands of Father Ryan, he had charge, like his predecessor, of that also at Gallitzin. At first he visited it once in the month, but soon the congregation increased and he began to offer the Holy Sacrifice in both places every Sunday. In 1860 or a little later he replaced the temporary church, which was now ready to fall, by a more substantial frame building about 60 feet in length by 35 in width, of a plain and simple style. It stands on the highest summit of the Alleghenies, and commands a view that is at no point less than ten miles, while at some it will extend to forty miles. But the cold in winter is intense. The congregation continued to increase, so that in the beginning of 1863 it became necessary to appoint an assistant to aid the pastor in his ministrations. An enlargement of the church was also necessary, and a frame addition 60 feet in length by 40 in width was built across the end of the existing edifice in the summer of 1869, and was dedicated by the Bishop on the 12th of September.

Gallitzin was separated from the Summit, as was said above, and became an independent parish with Father Ryan as its spiritual head in November of the same year. About this time a neat frame residence was also built for his reception, but beyond that nothing more than a moderate growth of the congregation has marked the lapse of time. The pastor remains with his flock, which has not yet had the advantage of a parish school. The village and the surrounding country is almost entirely Catholic, and is either Irish or of

Irish descent. The congregation will number about two hundred and forty families, composed of miners, men in the employ of the railroad company, and farmers, and it will grow in the future as it has done in the past.

ST. AUGUSTINE'S CHURCH, CAMBRIA COUNTY.

St. Augustine's Church stands in a country place about nine miles north of Loretto; and the locality, owing to the peculiar formation of the surrounding mountains, is familiarly called "the Loop." The Catholic settlement is an offshoot of the Loretto colony, and was first visited from that place. It is uncertain at what time stations first began to be held at the Loop, for the name "St. Augustine" was unknown until after the church was dedicated; but there can be no doubt that Dr. Gallitzin was there as early as 1835. It continued to be under the jurisdiction of the pastor of Loretto until 1848. When Bishop O'Connor paid his first visit to it in the summer of the previous year, a church was in course of erection though unfinished, as he informs us in his Notes, and the incipient congregation already numbered five hundred souls. When detached from Loretto in 1848, it, together with the little flock at Cameron Bottom, was placed under the care of Rev. Jas. Gallagher, who most probably resided at the former place. The church was not dedicated until the following year, when it was placed under the invocation of St. Augustine, but the date of the ceremony has not been ascertained. A frame residence was also built for the pastor. In the summer of 1850 Rev. John Burns succeeded Father Gallagher. Time sped rapidly and the congregation increased, but beyond this its history for many years is uneventful. In 1859 a little church was built at Chest Springs, as will presently appear, for the better accommodation of a part of the people. Father Burns entered the Benedictine Order May 26th, 1866, and was succeeded by his brother, Rev. Ed. Burns. Soon after his arrival he found it necessary to enlarge the church. A new portion was accordingly built, and when finished was dedicated by Bishop Domenec, August 28th, 1868. The church is frame, is 170 feet in length by 70 in width, but so unique in construction as to defy description. An additional priest was now demanded to aid the pastor, and the congregation has since been under the care of two, with the exception of brief intervals. At length it sustained a loss in the death of Father Burns, which took place somewhat suddenly at Pittsburg, December 29th, 1872. At the time of his death he was in the 37th year of his age. His remains repose in St. Mary's Cemetery, Pittsburg.

REV. EDWARD BURNS was a native of county Tipperary, Ireland. Having there pursued his studies for some time, he came to America, and entered the diocesan seminary at Pittsburg. From there he was ordained in the autumn of 1862 and stationed at the Cathedral, where he remained until transferred to St. Augustine's.

He was succeeded by Rev. Thos. M'Enrue, who presided over the congregation until September, 1877, when he gave place to Rev. F. X. M'Carthy, who was succeeded in August, 1879, by Rev. M. Ryan. The congregation still continues to increase, and is composed exclusively of farmers. In point of nationality it is American. The distance at which the greater part of the people live from the church has prevented the opening of a parish school. Few congregations in the country impose a heavier tax on the strength of the pastor than St. Augustine's, owing to its size, its scattered character, the indifference of the roads, and the inclemency of the mountain weather in all seasons except summer. It is by far the largest country congregation in the western part of the State, and will number between five and six hundred families.

ST. MONICA'S CHURCH, CHEST SPRINGS.

The village of Chest Springs is six miles north of Loretto and about four south-west of St. Augustine's Church, and in 1870 contained a population of 269. As the congregation of St. Augustine's increased, and it was difficult for many of the people living at a distance to hear Mass during a considerable portion of the year, it was deemed advisable to accommodate a part at least by erecting this church, near which a large number resided. It is a small frame building, was erected in

1859, and was dedicated March 20th of the following year by Rev. J. Burns, then pastor of the parent church. Mass was at first celebrated on two Sundays in the month, but is now offered every Sunday; but it has always and is still regarded as an outpost of St. Augustine's, and cannot for that reason be said to have a congregation properly so called. It is probable, however, that the time will come when it will be detached and become an independent parish.

CHAPTER XX.

CAMBRIA COUNTY (CONCLUDED).

Church of the Holy Name of Jesus, Ebensburg—Carrolltown—St. Joseph's Church, Hart's Sleeping-Place—St. Benedict's Church, Carrolltown—St. Lawrence's Church, Glen Connell—St. Boniface's Church, St. Boniface—St. Nicholas' Church, St. Nicholas—Johnstown—St. John Gualbert's Church, Johnstown—Death and sketch of Rev. P. Brown—St. Joseph's German Church—German Church of the Immaculate Conception, Cambria City.

CHURCH OF THE HOLY NAME OF JESUS, EBENSBURG, CAMBRIA COUNTY.

EBENSBURG, the county-seat of Cambria County, is a flourishing town on the top of one of the spurs of the Allegheny Mountains, about ten miles west of the summit of the main ridge, and commands a grand and extensive view of the surrounding country. The turnpike from the east to Pittsburg passes through it, and another runs to Indiana. It is also connected with the Pennsylvania Railroad at Cresson by a branch road thirteen miles in length. It was the wish of the railroad company to have this branch pass through Loretto, which would have conferred a great benefit upon its Catholic educational institutions; but the people would not take the required amount of stock—a refusal of which they now fruitlessly repent—and the road passes two miles south of the village. Ebensburg was settled by the Welsh, and Rev. Rees Lloyd, who came about the year 1796 and gave the town the name it bears, was the first to arrive. But the land upon which it stands had been purchased about two years before by Rev. Morgan J. Rees from Benjamin Rush, one of the signers of the Declaration of Independence. The town was founded about the close of the last century, was made the county-seat in 1805, incorporated as a borough in 1825,* and had in 1870 a population of 1240.

Although Ebensburg was originally settled by Protestants of the most illiberal school, it was not long before a small number of Catholic families found their way into the town and its immediate environs, who, like those of all the surrounding country, were under the jurisdiction of Dr. Gallitzin. It cannot be ascertained with certainty at what time he began to say Mass among the people, but Father Bradley informs me that a small frame church was erected there about the year 1816 and dedicated to St. Patrick. It continued to form a part of Dr. Gallitzin's extensive mission until the arrival of Rev. Patrick Rafferty, who came to reside there most probably in 1829, although he does not appear to have remained more than a few months. Then came Rev. P. Duffy, whose name will occur further on, and who is known with certainty to have been pastor of the congregation in July, 1830.† Rev. Jas. Bradley, the present pastor of the church at Newry, was appointed pastor of Ebensburg in October, 1830, immediately after his ordination. Making this the centre of his mission, he visited a large number of stations in Cambria and Indiana counties, giving to the church at Ebensburg not more than one Sunday, or at most two, in the month. "In 1831," he tells me, "the Portage Railroad from Johnstown to Hollidaysburg (connecting the western and eastern divisions of the Pennsylvania Canal) was under contract, and a good number of hands were employed in grading it. Attending to them and to all Dr. Gallitzin's sick-calls kept me very busy that year. In (October) 1832 Father O'Reilly was appointed to assist Father M'Guire, of Pittsburg, and I had to take charge of his large district of Newry in addition to the Ebensburg district for two years longer. I was relieved of the Ebensburg district in the fall of 1834 by Father Lemcke." He then took up his residence at Newry and confined his labors to the country east of the mountains.

In the history of Loretto we have seen the manner in

---

* Historical Collections, pp. 180, 181.
† *U. S. Catholic Miscellany.*

which Dr. Gallitzin introduced Father Lemcke to the people of Ebensburg. But it would appear that although he succeeded Father Bradley, there was an interval between the departure of the one and the arrival of the other. For the next ten years Mass was celebrated no more frequently than it had been before, for the pastor's field of labor was still very extensive. Father Lemcke resided at Ebensburg until 1837, when he removed to his farm at Carrolltown, nine miles to the north, but he continued to visit the congregation until about 1844. During the two following years it was visited monthly from the Summit. When Bishop O'Connor made his first visitation, his Notes, so frequently referred to, inform us that it contained 300 souls. The church was now too small, and being old was out of repair, and the Bishop encouraged the congregation to undertake the erection of a new one. They complied with his request, and he laid the corner-stone on the 3d of August, 1848. The date of its completion and dedication is not known. It is a small plain brick building, and is yet standing. Rev. P. Duffy returned in 1849 and was pastor for at least two years, if not for a longer period. The congregation was then visited monthly for two years from Loretto. Finally, at the close of 1855, Rev. M. J. Mitchell was appointed pastor, and the church has since been independent. No further change was made until after the close of the Rebellion. A part of the time Father Mitchell resided at the Franciscan Monastery at Loretto, but at length a house was purchased for him and he closed his pastorate, residing among his people. He was succeeded by Rev. R. C. Christy about the close of the year 1864. The congregation had increased but little in the past twenty years, nor has it increased much since ; but the circumstances of the people had undergone a considerable change for the better, and they began to consider the propriety of replacing the old church with a better one. A lot was purchased near the existing church, work was commenced, and the corner-stone was laid by the paster June 4th, 1867. The church was not finished until the end of two years, when it was dedicated by the Bishop November 14th, and the title was changed from St. Patrick —under whose invocation the two former had been placed—

to that of the Holy Name of Jesus. It is an elegant brick building, modelled after the Gothic style of architecture, and is 100 feet in length by 50 in width. There are three altars. The tower in the centre in front is at present completed only to the comb of the roof.

Shortly before the completion of the church Father Christy introduced a number of Sisters of St. Joseph from New York, for whose reception a convent was built, and who, besides taking charge of the parish school now first called into existence, also opened Mount Gallitzin Seminary for very small boys. A little later the old pastoral residence was disposed of, and a new brick one erected at the rear of the church and adjoining it. But Father Christy's health, which had been seriously impaired by toil and exposure while he was chaplain of the Seventy-eighth Regiment in the Army of the Cumberland during the Rebellion, was since gradually declining, and he was forced to seek an easier field of labor in the beginning of 1874. He was succeeded by Rev. John Boyle, the present pastor. The congregation has undergone but little change for many years, and there is nothing to show that its future history will be more eventful than its past has been. It will number about sixty families, farmers and business men in the town.

ST. BENEDICT'S CHURCH, CARROLLTOWN, AND ST. JOSEPH'S CHURCH, HART'S SLEEPING-PLACE.*

The village of Carrolltown, which was founded about the year 1839, is situated on the summit of the Laurel Ridge, a spur of the Allegheny Mountains about twelve miles northwest of Loretto, at a point where the ridge begins to lose its distinctive character and becomes assimilated to the surrounding country. It was the wish of Dr. Gallitzin to see a Catholic colony planted at Carrolltown, as he had founded that at Loretto, and at his earnest solicitation Father Lemcke undertook to found it. A number of settlers had already located themselves a short distance north of where the village stands,

---

* Compiled principally from "St. Vincenz in Pennsylvanien," pp. 199 *et seq.*

and in 1836 Father Lemcke purchased four hundred acres of land there, upon which he soon after took up his residence. But the idea of founding a colony on the top of the ridge was as ill-advised as that of Dr. Gallitzin in founding one upon the summit of the Alleghenies. It was the intention of Father Lemcke to name the rising village *Gallitzin*, in honor of his friend ; but the latter would not consent to it, and suggested that of the first American Prelate, Archbishop Carroll, which was adopted. In 1870 the village had a population of 416.

But the Catholic history of this section of the country dates from a period long anterior to the arrival of Father Lemcke. A colony of Trappist monks sought to establish a house of their order at a spot about half a mile from Carrolltown about the beginning of the present century, although, strange as it may appear, there is no mention of it in any of the extant letters of Dr. Gallitzin. Driven from France by the revolution in 1791, a number of the monks found a temporary home in Switzerland, where they remained until the influence of the French Government began to be felt in that country in 1798, when they were again forced to fly. They now passed into Russia and soon after into Prussia, and finally set sail for the New World under the guidance of Father Urban Guillet, May 29th, 1803. They landed at Baltimore on the 4th of September, and came to the vicinity of the future Carrolltown; but failing to make a foundation there, they next proceeded to Pigeon Hill, Adams County, Pa., and abandoning that also, they went further west.

The first settler near Carrolltown was John Weakland, one of the most courageous and powerful of men, and one of the most famous Catholic pioneers of Western Pennsylvania. Leaving Loretto in 1819, he purchased a large tract of land for himself and his numerous family about three miles north of the site of Carrolltown, at a spot called Hart's Sleeping-Place, in memory of a celebrated fur trader by the name of John Hart, who had frequently rested there. Among the settlers, the greater part of whom were Germans, was a man by the name of Luther, said to have been a descendant of the Father of the Reformation. About the year 1830, or perhaps earlier, John Weakland donated four acres of ground as the site of a church, and, in company with the other settlers and under the direction of Dr. Gallitzin, he built a log-church, which was dedicated to St. Joseph and is yet standing. Dr. Gallitzin visited the church until the arrival of Father Bradley at Ebensburg in the fall of 1830, who then took charge of it until he was succeeded by Fr. Lemcke. Bishop Kenrick visited the church and administered confirmation October 16th, 1832. When Father Lemcke purchased a farm at Carrolltown four years later, he built a small house for himself over a spring of water which is the source of the West Branch of the Susquehanna River. Some time later he built a frame chapel near it, in which Mass was celebrated on week-days, although St. Joseph's was the parish church until the summer of 1850, as will appear further on. Father Lemcke continued to preside over the congregation until about 1844, when he crossed the Atlantic to Germany to try to collect money to aid him in erecting a large church and to secure German priests for the new diocese.* During his absence St. Joseph's was visited for a time from Loretto, and later was under the pastoral care of Rev. M. Stauber.

When the Benedictine fathers entered the diocese in the fall of 1846, they at first thought of establishing themselves at Carrolltown, but were dissuaded from doing so by the Bishop, who, better informed than they, recommended the site of the present Abbey of St. Vincent's in Westmoreland County. The father prior, however, soon contemplated the erection of a second house, and on visiting, Father Lemcke, in the summer of 1848, made an arrangement with him for the purchase of his farm and for taking charge of the congregation. The Bishop gave the necessary permission for founding a priory, and also committed the care of the congregation to the Benedictine Order by an instrument dated October 16th of that year. The foundation was made December 16th, and Rev. Peter Lechner, one of the most learned and energetic members of the order, became the first prior and pastor. Father Lemcke soon after went to Kansas and thence to Reading, Pa., where he took charge of a congregation and wrote his "Leben und Wirken des Prinzen Demetrius Gallitzin."

* St. Vincenz in Pennsylvanien, p. 26.

St. Joseph's Church had by this time become too small to accommodate the ever-increasing congregation, and it was, besides, some distance north of the centre of the parish, which was principally in the vicinity of the village. The new church contemplated by Father Lemcke was undertaken in the spring of 1849, and the corner-stone was laid by the Bishop on the 10th of June. It was finished at the end of the following year, and was dedicated, under the invocation of St. Benedict —to whom the priory is also dedicated—by the prior, Rev. Father Cœlestine, on Christmas Day. The church is a substantial brick building, modelled after the Romanesque style of architecture, and is 110 feet in length by 55 in width. St. Joseph's was now abandoned as a parish church, although Mass is occasionally celebrated in it, and St. Benedict's became the future place of worship for the congregation.

A large brick priory was built during the administration of Father Agedius Christoph—from 1862 to 1868—but the precise date of its completion has not been ascertained. A parish school was still wanting, and the people of that portion of the county, who for the most part are Catholics, did all in their power to supply the deficiency—and the same may be said of other congregations in the northern section of the county— by having Catholic teachers employed in the public schools. But although this measure may have been productive of some good, the public-school system is so radically wrong and opposed to the true Christian instinct that the people of St. Benedict's were not satisfied until they had a parish school. The date of its opening is not known, but it was some time after the year 1856. The children—or rather such of them as did not live at too great a distance to attend—were under the care of lay teachers until the early part of 1870. In the previous year a large brick convent had been built near the church and placed under the patronage of St. Scholastica, and a colony of Benedictine nuns was introduced into it and has since had charge of the schools. This convent was the motherhouse of the nuns of this order in the two dioceses until recently. But the march of improvement did not stop here. The congregation continued to increase, and the church, though large, could no longer accommodate it. It was accordingly enlarged in 1867, and when completed was dedicated by the Bishop November 13th. Nor was this all. A massive tower was erected, terminating in a spire at the height of 165 feet, and was supplied with a chime of four bells, which were blessed by the Bishop September 22d, 1872. Here the people rested, being now supplied with all the buildings and accommodations necessary for many years. The congregation numbers 2000,* all farmers with the exception of those living in the village, and although originally German, it is fast becoming American both in language and customs. The future of the congregation will be as its past has been, a gradual increase in numbers and prosperity.

ST. LAWRENCE'S CHURCH, GLEN CONNELL.

St. Lawrence's Church is in a country place in the midst of a small German settlement commonly known as Glen Connell, about ten miles north-east of Carrolltown. For some time it was a missionary station visited from St. Joseph's and later from Carrolltown. A church was undertaken as early as 1853, although Mass had been celebrated at intervals long before that time, but it was not finished and dedicated till about two years later, when it was placed under the invocation of St. Lawrence, which name is fast superseding that of Glen Connell as the name of the locality. It has always been and is yet attached to Carrolltown. At first it was visited on one Sunday in the month, but more recently it was visited on two Sundays. The congregation numbers at present 180 souls, all farmers; and while it is slowly increasing, its future prospects are not very flattering, being so far removed from ready communication with other places.

ST. BONIFACE'S CHURCH, ST. BONIFACE.

St. Boniface's Church stands in a country place about six miles north of Carrolltown, and is the northern, as the latter is the southern, extremity of the Hart's Sleeping-Place settlement.

---

* These figures, as well as those of the following congregation, are taken from the *Catalogus Exhibens Nomina Monachorum*, etc., 1879, p. 55.

The congregation is German or of German descent, and consists exclusively of farmers. For a time it was a station visited occasionally from Carrolltown, to which it is yet attached; but in process of time the number of Catholics so far increased as to render it expedient to build a church for their accommodation. It was finished and dedicated under the invocation of St. Boniface a short time before the year 1869, but the precise date has not been ascertained. Mass is celebrated on two Sundays in the month. In 1873 it numbered 300 souls, and it has since been steadily increasing, as it will continue to do in the future. The proximity of the church to Carrolltown makes it probable that it will continue for many years to be visited from the Benedictine priory.

ST. NICKOLAS' CHURCH, ST. NICKOLAS.

The village of St. Nickolas, or Nicktown—as the post-office is named—is about eight miles west of Carrolltown. It was laid out, probably about the year 1865, by Nickolas Lambourn, who owned the land and who donated a lot as the site of a church. The Catholic inhabitants of the village and surrounding country are principally Germans. From the beginning the mission was, as it still is, under the spiritual direction of the Benedictine fathers of Carrolltown, under whose inspiration a church was undertaken in the spring of 1866. The corner-stone was laid by the Bishop on the 21st of June, and when finished the church was dedicated to St. Nickolas by the same prelate. It is a neat frame building containing elements of the Romanesque style of architecture, and is about 70 feet in length by 35 in width and surmounted by a belfry. From the date of its completion it was visited on two Sundays in the month, but more recently Mass is celebrated every Sunday. But the pastor does not live in the congregation, nor will he in all probability for many years. A school was opened in a rustic building by a lay teacher soon after the completion of the church, and has since continued to contribute its share to the cause of religion. The congregation is composed of farmers and numbers 650 souls. Its growth will be very moderate, owing to its comparative seclusion.

JOHNSTOWN.

Johnstown is situated on a broad flat at the foot of the western slope of the Alleghenies, and is completely surrounded by mountains. What is generally called "Johnstown" is not, however, a city, but consists of a number of separately incorporated boroughs immediately adjoining each other, and all within a radius of two miles from the centre of Johnstown borough. They have an aggregate population of 18,000, more than one third of which is Catholic. It occupies the site of an Indian village by the name of Kickanapawlin's Town, and is on the Conemaugh River, the Pennsylvania Canal, and the Pennsylvania Railroad, by the last of which it is 78 miles east of Pittsburg. About the year 1791 or 1792 Mr. Joseph Yahn, or Jahn, an enterprising German, came and settled there, and the original title-deeds of many of the town lots are in his name. As this was the head of navigation to those seeking the western waters—although the Conemaugh River was navigable only at certain seasons and for small craft, and even then dangerous—it became a place of shipment for the iron of Huntingdon County, and for the lumber and produce of the vicinity, as well as for the emigration destined for the west. Arks and flat-boats were then the only mode of conveyance. The pigs and blooms of Juniata iron were hauled over the old Frankstown road by the gap of that name. The place was then called Conemaugh.*

Being at a later date the eastern terminus of the western division of the canal, it was necessary to connect with the eastern division at Hollidaysburg; which was accomplished by means of the Allegheny Portage Railroad, commonly known as "the old Portage."† It was to the construction of the canal, and the business which it called into life, that Johnstown owed its rise; but its present importance is due to its

---

* Day's Historical Collections, pp. 182, 183.

† Being mainly the work of Irish Catholics, the subjoined notice of it will no doubt be interesting: "The Allegheny Portage Railroad is $39\frac{48}{65}$ miles in length from Hollidaysburg to Johnstown, overcoming in ascent and descent an aggregate of 2570 feet, 1398 of which are on the eastern and 1172 on the western side of the mountain. It crosses the mountains at Blair's Gap summit, and descends along the mountain branch of the Conemaugh; the top of the mountain, which is some 200

extensive iron and steel manufactories. As early as 1820 a forge or bloomery was built, and about twenty years later the first blast-furnace was constructed. In 1853 a large rolling-mill was completed, and since that time the manufacture of iron and steel has been steadily increasing till it has reached an extent that is almost incredible for the size of the town; and notwithstanding the financial depression of the times, the works are being constantly enlarged. The completion of the Pennsylvania Railroad in 1853 struck a death-blow at the canal; although it survived a few years, just at the time when, with great expense to the State, the grading of the "new Portage" Railroad, by which it was intended to cross the mountains by means of locomotives instead of stationary engines and planes, had been completed. But the railroad infused new life into Johnstown.

ST. JOHN GUALBERT'S CHURCH, JOHNSTOWN.

The introduction of Catholicity dates from before the construction of the canal. Dr. Gallitzin is thought to have visited the town and ministered to the few Catholic families before the year 1830. After the appointment of Rev. Jas. Bradley to Ebensburg, in the fall of that year, Johnstown became a part of his mission; and he visited it, as he informs me, at regular intervals. Having celebrated Mass for a time in a private house, he began the erection of a church, in 1832, on a lot in Conemaugh borough, donated for that object by a Mr. Livergood. The Catholic population at this time consisted of no more than three or four families, besides a number of transient laborers. Father Bradley was soon after transferred to Newry, and Father Lemcke visited Johnstown on one Sunday in the month from the date of his appointment to Ebensburg. The church, an unpretending brick building about 50 feet in length

---

feet higher than the culminating point of the railroad, is 2700 feet above the Delaware River at Philadelphia. The ascent and descent have been overcome by ten inclined planes, lifting from 130 to 307 feet and varying in inclination between 4½ and 5¼ degrees. The shortest plane is 1585 feet, and 130 feet high; the longest is 3100 feet, and 307 feet high. . . . The cars are elevated by stationary steam-engines at the head of each plane, and on the intervening levels locomotives and horses are used. The total cost of the road, including stationary engines, etc., exceeded $1,500,000."—*Ibid.*, p. 183.

by 30 in width, was finished, and was dedicated by Bishop Kenrick July 15th, 1835.

When the Portage Railroad was finished in 1834 the hands withdrew, reducing the congregation to thirteen families, while much of the debt contracted in building the church remained unpaid, and it was sold by the contractor in 1836. Two years later, when the congregation had increased, the church was repurchased. It was visited, generally once in the month, at one time from Ebensburg, again from Loretto, and finally from the Summit, until 1844, when Rev. Patrick Ratigan was appointed first resident pastor. He had, however, other missions in connection with it. But his health failing, he withdrew, and the church was again visited by Father Lemcke until about the close of 1846, when Rev. T. Mullen was appointed pastor with the additional mission of Wilmore. Previously to this a number of German families had settled in the town, and the prospects were that it would in time contain a considerable German Catholic population. In July, 1850, the Bishop sent Rev. Teresius Gezowski, a Carmelite, to Johnstown to minister to the Germans of the mountain district.* Soon after, however, they became a distinct congregation. The Catholic population increased rapidly owing to the commencement of the iron manufacture. To accommodate the people, as well as to secure a more central locality, Father Mullen purchased lots on Jackson Street, in the eastern part of the town, as the site of a new church, and began preparations for its erection. He also opened a parochial school conducted by lay teachers.

In the autumn of 1854 he was transferred to Allegheny City, and was succeeded by Rev. James Kearney. During his pastorate the idea of erecting a church was entertained, but work was not actually commenced. Early in 1859 he was succeeded by Rev. Peter M. Garvey, who soon after his appointment began work on the new church. Upon its completion it was dedicated by the Bishop September 25th, 1864. It is a brick building 131 feet in length by 64 in width, with a tower in the centre in front built up to the comb of the roof,

---

* St. Vincenz in Pennsylvanien, p. 231.

and surmounted by a nondescript temporary wooden belfry. The style, if style it may be called, of the church is peculiar. The nave is separated from the aisles by four columns on each side, surmounted by composite capitals. The ceiling of the nave is the tunnel vault, while that of the aisles is flat. The windows are small and square-topped and very high in the walls, and the interior is painted and pointed in imitation of stone. The altar-railing crosses the entire building, enclosing the high and two side altars. A large brick pastoral residence was also built by the side of the church. About the year 1869 the congregation purchased a large brick building near the church, which was converted into a convent under the title of St. Mary's for the Benedictine nuns, who soon after took charge of the schools. Some time later a brick school-house 45 by 80 feet was built, to which the children of the parish were transferred.

The congregation had so much increased that a second priest was required about the year 1866, and since that time, with but little exception, two priests have ministered in St. John's Church.

Rev. Peter Brown, the first to fill that office, after having labored in the sacred ministry for almost thirty years, died at Johnstown, August 8th, 1872, in the 56th year of his age. His remains were interred at Summitsville by the side of those of Rev. Thos. M'Cullagh. A tasteful monument was erected some time later to mark the spot by the members of the congregation in whose behalf he had so efficiently labored.

REV. PETER BROWN was born in Gleneely, parish of Donoughmore, county Galway, Ireland. Having almost completed his course of theology at Maynooth College, he came to America and to the Diocese of Pittsburg at the invitation of the newly consecrated Bishop O'Connor, being one of the first to accept it. He was ordained to the sacred ministry in company with two of his companions, Rev. T. Mullen and Rev. P. Duffy, September 3d, 1844. He was sent almost immediately after to Erie City, where he labored for a number of years, when he returned, after having been at several other places, to the Diocese of Pittsburg and was stationed at

Johnstown. As a pleasing, persuasive, and eloquent preacher he had few superiors in the country.

At the close of the year 1872 Father Garvey was succeeded by the present incumbent, Rev. O. P. Gallagher. Notwithstanding the panic that fell upon the country soon after his appointment, Father Gallagher has been able to make many important and necessary improvements both in the church and the pastoral residence, besides paying off a heavy debt in an incredibly short space of time. Further improvements are contemplated in the church which will add to its appearance and comfort, but which will not be undertaken for some time. The erection of new steel manufactories is now adding to the congregation. In September, 1878, when the Benedictine nuns took charge of the large school at St. Mary's Church, Allegheny City, they found it necessary to withdraw from Johnstown, and they accordingly gave place to a number of Sisters of Charity from Altoona, for whose reception a house was leased, the old convent being now very much out of repair. It is the intention of the pastor to build a new convent as soon as the circumstances of the congregation will justify the undertaking.

The congregation is at present the most flourishing outside of the cities, and with the exception of that at Altoona, and perhaps without excepting it, is the largest, and will number in all probability 5000 souls. It must continue to increase in the future until a division becomes necessary. In no part of the diocese perhaps are the prospects of the Church more flattering than in Johnstown.

ST. JOSEPH'S GERMAN CHURCH, JOHNSTOWN.*

German Catholics began to settle in Johnstown at an early day, but their number was not considerable until about the year 1850. Bishop O'Connor then sent a Carmelite father, Rev. Teresius Gezowski, to minister to the Germans there and in other parts of the mountain district. When he was transferred to Butler, about a year later, the Bishop requested the abbot of St. Vincent's to take charge of the place, and a

* St. Vincenz in Pennsylvanien, pp. 231, 232.

priest was accordingly sent, at first once in the month, then twice, from the abbey. But while a mission was being held in the English church during the same year, the Germans were encouraged to build a church for themselves. This they immediately determined to do, and what they were unable to accomplish by means of subscriptions they did by the labor of their own hands; and although the incipient congregation consisted of but twenty-eight families, the church was soon finished. It is a plain frame building, 30 by 48 feet, and was dedicated, under the invocation of St. Joseph, by Rev. T. Mullen, pastor of the English church, January 4th, 1852. A school in charge of a lay teacher was soon after opened in the basement. Since its organization the church has been in charge of the Benedictine fathers. For some years it was visited from the abbey, but in 1859 a brick pastoral residence was built near the church and a priory was established there. About this time the Germans residing in Cambria City, the western part of what is called Johnstown—St. Joseph's Church being in the eastern part—determined to build a church for their own accommodation, a determination which resulted in the present Church of the Immaculate Conception.

The congregation increased rapidly, and in time the little church was crowded to excess. A more spacious and imposing edifice was now contemplated, and the Cambria Iron Company donated a large and eligible lot as the site of it a few squares from the spot occupied by the existing church. Work was commenced, and the corner-stone was laid by the Bishop November 15th, 1868. The church was finished with the exception of the steeple, which was built only to the comb of the roof, at the end of two years, and was dedicated by the same prelate October 30th, 1870. It is a brick structure modelled after the Gothic style of architecture, but is without columns, and has the ceiling rising from the sides ribbed towards the centre. It is 120 feet in length by 66 in width, and has three altars. But the plan of the building is seriously defective. The span is too great for the strength of the roof-timbers, and there is danger of the walls eventually spreading, and in fact the rear wall is already beginning to part. Owing to this defect it is to be feared the church will probably have to be torn down to prevent accident. The spire was completed in an elegant proportion to the height of 179 feet, in the summer of 1876.

A frame school-house was built in addition to the old church, which has been used as a school since the completion of the new edifice. The lay teachers were in time superseded by the Benedictine nuns from St. Mary's Convent attached to the English church, and these gave place to the Sisters of Charity from the same church in the autumn of 1878.

The congregation is not increasing so rapidly now as formerly, but numbers 900 souls, a small part of which live outside the town. The future prospects of the congregation are very flattering.

GERMAN CHURCH OF THE IMMACULATE CONCEPTION, CAMBRIA CITY.

Cambria City is the most western of the aggregation of boroughs commonly called Johnstown. The Germans of this place, being, as was stated above, at a considerable distance from St. Joseph's Church, determined to have one for themselves. Having had the Holy Sacrifice celebrated for some time in a room in their midst by one of the Benedictine fathers, the church was built about the year 1859—the precise date has not been ascertained—and was dedicated under the title of the Immaculate Conception. A school, the inseparable companion of the church, was opened, and has since been conducted by a lay teacher. Having been under the care of the Benedictine fathers from its erection, the church passed in 1872 into that of the secular clergy, with whom it has since remained. A pastoral residence was about this time built. The present pastor is Rev. Jos. Lingel. The congregation has increased gradually since its formation, and at present will probably number about one hundred and fifty families; and it must continue to increase in the future.

CHAPTER XXI.

WESTMORELAND COUNTY.

The place it occupies in our history—General features—First Catholic settlement in Western Pennsylvania—The first Mass—The first priest—The first church—Death of Rev. Theodore Browers—Troubles—Rev. P. Heilbron—New settlements—Death of Father Heilbron—Rev. Ch. B M'Guire—Trustees—Rev. Terence M'Girr—Arrival of Rev. J. A. Stillinger—The Bishop and the trustees—The new church.

No part of Western Pennsylvania figures more prominently in the history of Catholicity than Westmoreland County. It was the scene of the first permanent Catholic settlement in the State west of the Allegheny Mountains, and east of them also as far as relates to the territory embraced within the present history. It was also for many years a kind of resting-place for Catholic emigrants to parts of the State lying farther west, being on Gen. Forbes' route from Cumberland to Pittsburg, and also on the road, or path, from Philadelphia to the same city. Westmoreland County was formed from Bedford by an act of February 26th, 1773, and included the entire southwestern corner of the State. To this was annexed, in 1785, the tract of country which constituted the last purchase from the Indians, and which came into possession of the State in the previous year, so that the county before it was subdivided embraced the entire western part of the State. At present it has an area of 1004 square miles, and is separated from Somerset and Cambria on the east by the lofty and well-defined range of Laurel Hill. Parallel to this is the lower range of the Chestnut ridge, and between them the long and elevated Ligonier Valley, about ten miles wide. The soil, except in the mountain regions, is very fertile. The county was originally settled by Irish and German emigrants.

It is said that in Wheatfield * Township there is a remarkable mound, from which in the early part of the present century several articles were dug, consisting of a sort of stone serpent about five inches in diameter; part of the entablature of a column, rudely carved in the form of diamonds and leaves; an earthen urn with ashes; and many others of which no account is now extant. It is thought to have been the ruins of an ancient Indian temple. Previous to 1758 Westmoreland was a wilderness, trodden only by the wild beast, the savage, and an occasional white trader or frontierman; but in that year a road was cut by Gen. Forbes' army on their way to attack Fort Duquesne. This road opened the way for numerous pioneers into this region; but as yet it was only safe for them to live under the protection of the forts.†

Hannahstown, which stood about three miles north-east of Greensburg, but was destroyed by the Indians, was the first place west of the mountains where justice was administered according to legal forms by the white man. There was a wooden court-house and a jail of the like material. The first prothonotary and clerk of the courts was Arthur St. Clair, afterwards a general in the war of the Revolution. Robert Hanna was the first presiding judge; and the first Court of Common Pleas was held in April, 1773.‡

The history of the first Catholic settlement is very interesting, both from the fact that it is the first in the diocese and also on account of the vicissitudes through which the colonists had to pass in matters of religion. In the years 1787 and 1788 six Catholic families left the settlement of Goshenhoppen, in Berks County, and crossing the Alleghenies, established a colony in Unity Township, Westmoreland County, not far from Greensburg.§ In March, 1789, they purchased an acre and twenty perches of land in Greensburg, as the site of a church and burying-ground, for which they paid five shillings. This was the first property owned by the Church in the western part of the State. The deed is made out in the name

---

* The name has since been changed.
† Day's Historical Collections, pp. 680, 681.
‡ Ibid., p. 683.
§ St. Vincenz in Pennsylvanien, p. 43 *et seq.*

of the following six persons, who were the original settlers: John Propst, John Young, Patrick Archbald, and the three brothers Christian, George, and Simon Ruffner.*

Before setting out from the east they had obtained a promise from the priests stationed both at Goshenhoppen and Philadelphia that one of them would pay the new settlement an occasional visit, or secure the good offices of some other missionary in their behalf. In compliance with this promise Rev. John B. Causey, a missionary at Conewago, penetrated the wilds, and arrived at the settlement in June, 1789. There being as yet no church, he offered up the Holy Sacrifice in the house of John Propst, who lived a short distance west of Greensburg. This was the first Mass celebrated in a permanent Catholic settlement west of the Allegheny Mountains, and in the entire dioceses of Pittsburg and Allegheny. After remaining but a short time, Father Causey returned to the east. Few families ventured at that early day to join the colony, but it was not entirely without accessions.

The second priest who visited the colony was Rev. Theodore Browers, of whom little more is known than that he was a native of Holland, a member of the Minorite Order, and that he had been on the mission for some time in the West Indies. He was also possessed of some wealth. He came to Philadelphia, but at what time is uncertain, and took up his residence with Rev. Peter Heilbron, whose name will occur farther on in these pages. Although urged to remain in Philadelphia, he determined to labor among the pioneers, and hearing of the Westmoreland colony concluded to make that his home and the centre of his missionary district. Before leaving the city he purchased a farm of 165 acres in Westmoreland County, at the foot of the Chestnut ridge, a short distance east of the Catholic settlement, and known as "O'Neil's Victory," the property of one Arthur O'Neil, for which he paid 106 pounds and 17 shillings. The deed is dated August 7th, 1789, and the money was paid on the 27th of September.† He set out without delay, and after the vicis-

---

* The Ruffners were natives of Tyrol, in Austria; and Simon was the great-grandfather of the writer.

† See "St. Vincenz," etc., pp. 357-60, where a diagram of the farm is traced and the deed given in full.

situdes through which the traveller of those days was necessitated to pass he reached the settlement, and was welcomed with a feeling of joy that can readily be imagined. Finding no house upon his arrival, he passed the winter with Simon Ruffner. It was his intention to build a house and church on his farm; but upon visiting it he found that it was not so fertile as he had been led to expect, and besides it was at too great a distance from the principal part of the settlement, being not less than twelve or fourteen miles east of Greensburg. There was another farm offered for sale nine miles east of Greensburg, and known as "Sportsman's Hall," which, being more central and more fertile, the settlers urged him to purchase. It was the property of one Joseph Hunter, and consisted of about 315 acres. He accordingly purchased it for 475 pounds, April 16th, 1790. It is the cradle of Catholicity in Western Pennsylvania, and the site of St. Vincent's Church, abbey, and college.* The name Sportsman's Hall was retained until the dedication of the church, July 19th, 1835, since which time it has been known by the familiar name of St. Vincent's. In the spring of 1790 a church was commenced at Greensburg, although, as we shall see, it was never finished. It was the first church undertaken in Western Pennsylvania; the second was Dr. Gallitzin's, finished at Loretto on Christmas, 1799; the third, St. Patrick's, Sugar Creek, Armstrong County, yet standing; and the fourth, "old St. Patrick's," Pittsburg.

At the time Father Browers purchased Sportsman's Hall it could not boast so much as a log-hut to shelter its new proprietor; but he employed a workman, such as the backwoods afforded, who ere long built a log-house, one and one half stories high and 17 feet square. The farm was entrusted to a man who should clear a part of the ground and till it; and there being no church, Father Browers was accustomed to ride six miles every Sunday to the home of Simon Ruffner to offer up the Holy Sacrifice under his roof. But his health had been failing for some time, and ill-suited him for a backwoods mission, although there were no other Catholics as yet

* See diagram and deed in full, "St. Vincenz," etc., pp. 360-63.

save those of this one settlement. His zeal forbade him to seek repose, and he was taken suddenly ill at the altar while celebrating Mass on a Sunday in June, 1790, and was unable to finish it. As his little remaining strength gradually ebbed away and he felt that his end was approaching, he sent to Conewago for a priest who should administer to him the last rites of the Church. Father Causey responded to the summons; but being unworthy of his sacred calling, his arrival was an ill-omen to the settlement. He was dissatisfied with Father Browers' will, and refused to administer the sacraments to him until he had altered it so as to make it harmonize with Father Causey's views. Worn out by the labors of a long and edifying career, Father Browers died October 29th, 1790, the first to close his career in the western part of the State. By his will, dated but four days prior to his death, he says: * "First, I recommend my soul to God who gave it, my Body to the Earth to be buried in a decent Christian like manner on the Place I now live Called Sportsmanns Hall, and a small neat stonewall to be built around my grave. . . . I Give and Bequeath all my Books clothing and Furniture and all the residue of my personal estate that shall not be otherwise disposed of, to Jams Pennane, in Trust and for the use of the Poor Roman Catholic Irish, that does or shall live at the Chappel, on Conewagga, . . . I give and bequeath all my Real Estate viz. my place on which I now live called Sportsmanns Hall, and one other Tract of Land on Loyelhanna Creek Called O'Neals Victory, with their appurtenances to a Roman Catholic Priest that shall succeed me in this same place, to be Entailed to him and to his Successors in trust and so left by him who shall succeed me to his successors and so in trust and for the use herein mentioned in succession for ever, And that the said Priest for the time being shall strictly and faithfully say Four Masses Each and every year for ever viz. One for the soul of the Reverend Theodoras Browers, on the day of his death in each and every year for ever and three others the following days in each year as

---

* See "St. Vincenz," etc., pp. 363-5, where the document is given in full. The extracts here given conform to the original in every particular.

aforesaid at the request of the Reverend Theodoras Browers And further it is my Will that the Priest for the time being shall Transmitt the Land so left him in Trust as aforesaid to his successor clear of all incumbrance." Christian Ruffner and Henry Coons (Kuhn) were named executors. Besides the property he had $1146, a large sum in those early days, in the bank at Philadelphia.

No sooner was the good man laid to rest than Father Causey removed to Conewago the effects bequeathed to the Catholics of that settlement, and immediately set about gaining possession of the money in the bank. He succeeded, and with the aid of it led a life not only at variance with his sacred calling, but with all sound Christian principles, until he was finally arrested and cast into prison at York, Pa., by order of Very Rev. Jas. Pellenz, V.G. He gave bail, however, and was released, and history has forgotten to record his further aberrations.

Next came Rev. Francis Fromm, a man of unfortunately the same stamp as his predecessor. Having been ordained in Germany, his native land, in 1773, and having exercised the duties of the sacred ministry in various places, he came to America in February, 1789, with a letter of introduction from the Vicar-General of the Archbishop of Mentz. Arriving soon after at Conewago, and hearing from Father Causey of the settlement and farm in Westmoreland, he set out for the spot and took possession of the farm, according to the bequest of Father Browers, as he alleged, although he was not then nor afterwards received by Bishop Carroll, nor empowered to exercise the duties of the sacred ministry in the United States. He remained, however, in spite of the remonstrances of the trustees and the Bishop, when he had heard of the usurpation, until the trustees entered a suit against him to recover possession of the property. After a delay of several years, during which the settlement was in a deplorable condition, it was finally decided against him at Greensburg in December, 1798.* Nothing daunted, he immediately appealed to the Supreme Court at Philadelphia, whither he went the follow-

---

* St. Vincenz, etc., pp. 365–376.

ing spring. He there met Rev. P. Heilbron, who in vain urged him to submit to the Bishop. He soon after fell a victim to the yellow-fever, then raging in that city.

During Father Fromm's stay at Sportsman's Hall, the Bishop sent an Irish priest by the name of Rev. Mr. Whelan, or Phelan, to take charge of the mission. After remaining for a time and finding that nothing could be done in the unhappy state of affairs then existing, he withdrew, and was some years later at Sugar Creek—if that were indeed the same person. A priest of the same name, it will be remembered, was at Bedford in 1806. Bishop O'Connor was of opinion that this Father Whelan was the same as that mentioned by Bishop Spalding as the first missionary to penetrate the wilds of Kentucky. But if the details given by the latter prelate are correct—as we must suppose they are—that opinion cannot be regarded as having sufficient foundation.* After Father Whelan came Rev. Mr. Lanigan, who also remained but a short time, when taking with him a number of the pioneers finally settled, as we have stated elsewhere, at Waynesburg, Greene County. Father Pellenz, from Conewago, also visited the colony once at least.

The settlement had increased but little during this time, owing to the state of affairs just described; and many of those who had set out from the east with a view of making it their home settled, on hearing of the disturbances, at Shade Valley, Frankstown, Sinking Valley, and other places east of the mountains, on and near the route. The Westmoreland settlement was composed of Germans and Irish, the former of whom predominated. It was as yet small, and was further reduced by the departure of those whom Father Lanigan had led to Waynesburg, so that according to the statement of Rev. J. A. Stillenger—with whom the reader will presently become acquainted—there were but seventy-five communicants when Rev. Peter Heilbron arrived from Philadelphia, November 17th, 1799. It was a happy day for the people when he first appeared among them; yet so little

---

* Sketches of the Life, Times, and Character of Bishop Flaget, by M. J. Spalding, D.D., Bishop of Louisville, pp. 73, 74.

talent had he for languages that until his death he could not learn sufficient English to carry on a conversation. The most he could acquire was a few words absolutely necessary for administering the sacraments. The person left in charge of the farm by Father Fromm would not yield possession to Father Heilbron until compelled to do it by the civil courts.

As yet there was no church, and for a time he offered up the Holy Sacrifice in a room in his own log-house. But his labors were not confined to this settlement alone. Others had now begun to spring up in different parts of the country, and the whole of these, now constituting the dioceses of Pittsburg, Allegheny, and Erie, were for several years ministered to by him and Dr. Gallitzin. The principal of these were Shade Valley, Sinking Valley, Frankstown, Bedford, Loretto, Sportman's Hall, Jacob's Creek, Waynesburg, Brownsville, Pittsburg, Donegal, and Oil Creek. Soon after his arrival he built another log-house, 26 by 28 feet, which afforded better accommodations both to himself and the congregation. The happy settlement of the troubles of the colony induced other Catholics from the east to make it their home, and it began to increase rapidly. To accommodate the congregation thus augmented, an addition was made to the house, which served for a chapel for a few years. About the year 1810 a hewed-log church 26 by 40 feet was built, and was the first church, properly speaking, in the settlement. It does not appear, however, that it was dedicated to any saint. As Father Heilbron undertook to manage the farm according to his own ideas of agriculture, it afforded him but a meagre support and left him at all times in straitened circumstances. Prior to this date Father O'Brien had been stationed at Pittsburg, but his feeble health rendered him unable to minister to the whole of his extensive district, and the greater part of it was left as before to Father Heilbron and Dr. Gallitzin. The opening of the State roads or turnpikes about the same time added to their labors, as the greater part of the hands employed were Irish Catholics who longed for nothing more ardently than the consolations of religion. Father Heilbron appears to have been of a robust constitution, but about the year 1815 a tumor appeared on his neck, and having for a long time submitted himself in vain to the treatment of such physicians as the country afforded, he set out for Philadelphia to have the benefit of physicians of greater skill. It was to no purpose, however, and he resolved to return to his mission and labor among his people as long as it might please Providence to spare his life. But he was taken suddenly ill at Carlisle on his way home, and died there at the close of 1816 or the beginning of the following year. His age at the time of his death, or any other particulars of his life beyond what are contained in this brief account of his labors, are not known.

The congregation was without a pastor until the arrival of Rev. Charles B. M'Guire in the fall of 1817, although in the mean time Father O'Brien had paid it an occasional visit and had encouraged the people to put the house in a more fitting condition for the reception of their next pastor. Father M'Guire remained two years, during which time the congregation increased more rapidly than ever before, which was in a great measure due to the increased facilities for travel afforded by the turnpikes. Like his predecessor, he did not confine his labors to one congregation, but visited many other settlements. Among these were Pittsburg, to which he sometimes came to relieve Father O'Brien, whose health was failing. When the latter was at length forced to retire from active missionary labor and seek repose, Father M'Guire came to Pittsburg in March, 1820, much to the dissatisfaction of the people of Westmoreland, whose property he is said to have left considerably in debt for improvements. The manner in which he had managed the farm also met with their disapprobation, and so strong was it that they determined to have an act of the legislature passed constituting a body of lay trustees to manage the temporalities in future. Against this Father M'Guire got up a counter-petition, but the congregation gained the victory; the act was passed and approved by the governor, Joseph Heister, March 7th, 1821. This act is the first and, so far as I know, the only one of its kind ever passed for the management of the church property in the dioceses. It vests the two tracts of Sportsman's Hall and

O'Neil's Victory in five trustees "and their successors, who shall be duly and regularly appointed, according to the rules of the said congregation, in trust for the uses mentioned and declared in the last will and testament of Reverend Theodore Browers, deceased."* Having served for a year, during which time Rev. Terence M'Girr became pastor of the congregation, "At a meeting of the Trustees and Wardens or Vestrymen of the Roman Catholic Congregation in Unity Township, Westmoreland County, on the first day of May, A.D. 1822, It was unanimously adopted and admitted by and with the consent and approbation of the Rev. J. M'Girr, their clergyman, and also by the consent of the said congregation, That trustees or wardens be appointed by ballot on Monday, the twenty-seventh inst. . . . That the said trustees be duly and regularly elected by ballot on the last Monday in May, henceforth and forever in every year."† So it continued, although the trustees never exercise full control. The arrival of Father M'Girr dates from the beginning of Lent, 1821. As the farm was still in the hands of Father M'Guire, whose brother occupied the house, Father M'Girr lived for some months at Youngstown, a village a short distance east of it. When the house was at length vacated, he took possession of it and assumed control of the farm without much regard for trustees or anybody else, his brother being the farmer. For some time he was accustomed to pay an occasional visit to the Armstrong and Butler county missions, which usually occupied him about six weeks. Though zealous in the discharge of his duties, he was possessed of strange idiosyncrasies, which made his relation with the congregation during his pastorate anything but harmonious. In 1822 he built a log-church about six miles north-east of Sportsman's Hall, which was blessed under the title of Our Lady of Mount Carmel, and is yet standing. A petition was sent to the Bishop asking to have him transferred to another mission, but it did not so much as elicit a reply. Affairs became daily more complicated, and recourse was had to the civil tribunal by the

---

* The act is given in full in "St. Vincenz," etc., pp. 376, 377.
† St. Vincenz, etc., pp. 377, 378.

trustees, September, 1826, to dispossess a man to whom Father M'Girr had leased the farm. The verdict was given in their favor on September 3d, 1829, but Father M'Girr immediately appealed to the Supreme Court, which, however, affirmed the sentence. While at Sportsman's Hall Father M'Girr ministered to the laborers on that part of the canal that traversed Westmoreland County, which added considerably to his duties. After having encountered many difficulties—which, it must be admitted, he in a great measure brought upon himself, but in which Dr. Gallitzin both as his friend and as Vicar-General stood by him—he retired to the mountain country about the close of the year 1829 and joined his illustrious supporter. When Bishop Kenrick was appointed administrator of the diocese, Dr. Gallitzin interposed in Father M'Girr's behalf, but only with partial success, and in 1837 the latter retired to the vicinity of Cameron Bottom church, where he died in 1856. His remains were interred in the cemetery at Ebensburg.

Some time after the withdrawal of Father M'Girr, Rev. Jas. A. Stillenger was appointed pastor, a man who figured more conspicuously than any other in the history of the church in Westmoreland and Indiana counties. His arrival does not, however, date from the winter of 1829, as the author of "St Vincenz in Pennsylvanien" (p. 83) states, for he was not ordained until February 28th, 1830, and Bishop Kenrick, by whom he was sent, was not consecrated until June 6th of the same year. He arrived on the 28th of November, 1830, as I have frequently heard him say, and as is stated in a manuscript of his now before me. The anomalous state of affairs at Sportsman's Hall for some years previous offered a plea, if not a justification, for the act of incorporation constituting the trustees. But the system is radically opposed to the spirit of the Church and is well calculated to produce mischief. Nor could two persons be more unlike than Father M'Girr and Father Stillenger; for while the former was impulsive by nature and singular in his manner, the latter was prudent and gentle, but possessing withal a degree of firmness that enabled him to maintain his position with dignity and to pass safely through trying circumstances. A more suitable person could not have been found. At the time of his arrival the trustees had all in their own hands, and evinced a disposition not only to manage the temporalities with a degree of self-will that too often characterizes that class of persons; they wished also to control the pastor to an extent that would deprive him of the freedom of action necessary for one in his exalted position. They made a mistake too common among even well-informed Catholics—that of imagining that church property belongs to the congregation. It belongs not to the people, but to the Church. It is given to Christ in his mystic body for the use of that body, and, like the Church herself, is to be administered by those whom the Holy Ghost, in the words of St. Paul, has appointed to rule. Hearing of the erroneous views of the trustees, Bishop Kenrick wrote to them on the 24th of August, 1831, to point out their error and remind them that the property did not belong to the congregation and had not been purchased by the money of the people, but was the free gift of Rev. Theodore Browers for the support of the priest who should for the time be the lawfully appointed pastor. While admitting that the act of incorporation served to preserve the property from loss at a time when there was no pastor, he declared that the will of the testator must be carried out to the letter, and that if Father Stillenger were not permitted to manage the property he could not allow him to remain. A meeting of the congregation was called May 28th, 1832, the day of the annual election of trustees, when it was "decided by vote that there should not be any more election of trustees, but that it should go by appointment, and that it should rest with the Rt. Rev. Bishop and the pastor to make the appointments."* This agreement was signed by sixty-six persons. May not this be taken as the number of heads of families in the congregation at that time, as it is probable that for the transaction of business so important all who could do so would attend? The skill with which Father Stillenger managed the affairs of the congregation had much to do with the happy settlement of these difficulties. No further change took place until the arrival of the Benedictine fathers.

* Minutes of the Meeting, "St. Vincenz," etc., pp. 84, 85, 380.

The Bishop had in the mean time paid a visit to Western Pennsylvania and stopped among other places at Blairsville and Sportsman's Hall, both of which were under the care of Father Stillenger. A correspondent of the *U. S. Cath. Miscellany* of September 24th, 1831, says: "On the 23d of August the Bishop took his departure from Blairsville to Sportsman's Hall. On his arrival there, there were about 100 children already collected for instruction and prepared for confession. The whole afternoon was occupied with the children, as well as the forenoon of the next day until half past ten. One hundred and five were confirmed and between sixty and seventy received Holy Communion." A fuller notice of the life and labors of Father Stillenger will be found in the history of the Church at Blairsville, where he closed his long and edifying career. There it will be seen that he celebrated the Holy Sacrifice alternately at Sportsman's Hall and Blairsville after the church had been built in the latter place, except at such times as he was obliged to give a wider range to his missionary labors.

The harmony resulting from the adjustment of the difficulties of the trustees enabled Father Stillenger to undertake necessary improvements. In the summer of 1833 he proposed to the congregation to build a brick church and a pastoral residence, a proposition to which they readily acceded. A subscription was immediately opened, upon which nearly $4000 was soon paid and the contract for the work was let, the cost of the church being fixed at $6600 and the house at $2600. The former was completed in the summer of 1835, and was dedicated by Bishop Kenrick on the 19th of July. It was the custom of the Bishop to name the churches which he dedicated after the saint whose feast was that day celebrated, and hence this church was placed under the invocation of St. Vincent of Paul. The place lost from that date its name of "Sportsman's Hall" and has since been known as "St. Vincent's," although in the neighborhood it was for a long time called "the Hill Church," from the gentle eminence on the side of which it stands. The sum of $4373.23 was still due on the building at the time of the dedication, for the payment of which the trustees gave security. The church was about 87 feet in length by 51 in width, simple in point of style, and was surmounted by a belfry. Changes have been made since its erection which will be noticed as we proceed. But it was soon found that the contractor had not done his work properly; both the foundation and the building were defective, and a balance of about $1400 still due was withheld for damages. A lawsuit was the result; but it was finally decided in favor of the congregation in August, 1843.

In September, 1844, Father Stillenger transferred his residence to Blairsville, but continued to divide his attention between the two churches until about the close of the following year, when Rev. Michael Gallagher was appointed resident pastor of St. Vincent's. But an event of greater importance was about to transpire than had as yet marked the history of the congregation—the foundation of the first house of the venerable Benedictine Order in the New World north of Mexico.

CHAPTER XXII.

WESTMORELAND COUNTY (CONTINUED)—THE BENEDICTINE ORDER AT ST. VINCENT'S.

Departure of the Benedictines from Germany and their arrival at St. Vincent's—Condition of the place—Taking possession—The first ordination—Spread of the Order—St. Vincent's an independent priory—Improvements—A seminary and college opened—St. Vincent's an exempt abbey—Further improvements—The congregation—Present state of the Order—Church of the Most Holy Sacrament, Greensburg—St. Boniface's Chapel, Chestnut Ridge—St. Vincent's Chapel, Youngstown—Ligonier—Church of the Holy Family—Bolivar Station—St. Mary's Church, New Florence.

I SHALL not enter upon the disputed question of the discovery of America and the occupation of certain parts of the New England States, the establishment of an episcopal see, and the foundation of a house of the Benedictine Order three or four centuries prior to the landing of Columbus; but coming to a time the events of which are beyond the reach of cavil or dispute, I shall briefly sketch the introduction of the Benedictines into North America, and their subsequent growth and extension; for although the history of the congregation of St. Vincent's is distinct theoretically from the establishment of the Order there, yet the two are so intimately connected that practically it is difficult to separate the one from the other.

The reader will remember that we stated, in the history of the Church at Carrolltown, that in the year 1844 Rev. H. Lemcke visited his native land with a view of enlisting German priests for the newly erected Diocese of Pittsburg. While there he met at Munich Rev. Boniface Wimmer, a monk of the Benedictine monastery of Melten, in Bavaria, who for some time had been contemplating the establishment of his Order in the United States.* Father Lemcke offered

---

* St. Vincenz, etc., pp. 26 *et seq.*

him his farm of 400 acres of land at Carrolltown for that purpose, and Father Wimmer, thinking he could not do better than accept it, immediately opened a correspondence with the Bishop of Pittsburg and offered himself to the new diocese. A proposition so favorable to the interests of religion was readily accepted, whereupon Father Wimmer made preparations to set out for America. The good father was highly esteemed, and the people of Munich manifested the liveliest interest in the contemplated foundation, supplying him with the vestments and altar furniture necessary. The Louis Mission Union donated the handsome sum of 6000 gulden, to which the venerable Charles Augustus Reisach, Prince-Bishop of Munich, added 500 more, besides promising still further pecuniary assistance.

The little band was soon chosen, fitted out, and ready to embark on its new mission for the glory of God and the extension of his kingdom on earth. There was the leader, Rev. Sebastian (in religion Boniface) Wimmer, born at Thalmassing, in Bavaria, January 14th, 1809, ordained to the priesthood July 31st, 1831, received into the Benedictine Order September 14th, 1832, and admitted to his solemn vows December 29th, 1833. He was a man in every respect admirably fitted for the arduous mission he was about to undertake, and which he has for more than thirty years so successfully conducted. With him were four students and fourteen lay brothers. At five o'clock in the morning of July 25th, 1846, all assembled in the church of St. Michael, in Munich, to assist at Mass celebrated by the venerable Prince-Bishop, and to receive from his hands the Bread of Angels to strengthen them against the trials and privations that awaited them. From Munich they took cars for Rotterdam, where they embarked on board the ship Iowa for New York. They landed on the 16th of September, and after remaining in New York three days set out for Carrolltown. They did not, however, reach the term of their journey until the 30th, for it must not be forgotten that as yet no railway traversed the States of New Jersey and Pennsylvania to facilitate travel. Having notified the Bishop of their arrival, Father Wimmer was invited to Pittsburg for an interview. The Bishop rejoiced to see the great Order of St. Benedict about to take root in his diocese, but he recommended St. Vincent's as the seat of the foundation instead of Carrolltown, and the two set out together to examine the spot. Pleased with it, Father Wimmer returned to his little band, and on the 15th of October set out from Carrolltown to the scene of his future labors.

The better to understand the condition of St. Vincent's at that time and the improvements since effected, it will be necessary to cast a glance at the place as it then appeared. There was the church, erected, as we have seen, twelve years before, and near it a two-story brick house built about the same time. But this was occupied, and had been for about a year, by the Sisters of Mercy as a convent and the cradle of St. Xavier's Young Ladies' Academy, and must continue to be so occupied until the permanent buildings of that institution, situated about a mile and a half distant, should be completed. Besides these there was a small one-story brick school-house, which had been divided into two rooms by a partition. Then there was a log-house occupied by the farmer and his family, and a miserable log-barn. The farm consisted of 315 acres of splendid farming ground, and the other tract of land, known in the beginning as "O'Neil's Victory," but now familiarly called the "Seven-Mile Farm," from it lying that distance east of the church, comprising 165 acres and far inferior to the other for tillage. Over all hung a debt of $3000. The Bishop called a meeting of the congregation, and in the address which he delivered on the occasion expressed his desire of having Father Boniface—as we shall now call him—establish a priory there. The people were delighted with the idea, and promised to do all in their power to second the undertaking. It was agreed that the Sisters should withdraw to their new home as soon as it could be made ready to receive them, which, however, would not be for some months; that the pastor, Father Gallagher, should remain to minister to the English portion of the congregation until a priest of the Order should have learned that language, and that arrangements should be made with regard to the transfer of the property. Having maturely weighed the respective claims of the two places, Carrolltown and St. Vincent's, Father Boniface determined to establish himself at the latter. Returning to Carrolltown, he departed for his new home much to the regret of the good villagers, who had hoped that he would remain with them. But if the good father and his companions had by vow embraced a life of poverty, they soon found that for a time at least that virtue must become a necessity with them. The school-house already mentioned must serve for the present for the entire community and afford, besides, a suit of rooms for the pastor. But as if nothing should be wanting in their sacrifices, the house being new was not yet plastered nor was the roof finished. Mattresses laid on the floor of the low attic or garret constituted the dormitory of the brothers and students. One of the rooms of the main story served the multifarious purposes of kitchen, refectory, community or chapter room, and infirmary for a member of the community then sick. The other room was divided into two apartments, the one of which served as a sleeping-chamber for the pastor and superior, the other was the study-hall of the students. Possession was taken on the 19th of October. But it was not until the 24th of the same month that Father Boniface, the Superior and only priest in the little band, gave the religious habit to the members of the community, who until then had been only candidates. The observance of the rule in all its details was from that time enforced, and the day is celebrated as that of the establishment of the Benedictine Order in North America.

But so indifferently were the members of the community protected from the inclemency of the weather that I have heard one of them state that when it rained at meal-time one would be deputed to hold an umbrella over the table to protect it from the drops that penetrated the roof. Such were the beginnings of an abbey, seminary, and college that are now capable of accommodating five hundred monks and students, and whose ramifications have penetrated into eighteen States of the Union.

On the 5th of November of the same year the Bishop appointed the Father Superior pastor of the congregation for the time being, and thus confirmed him for the present in possession of the property. He at the same time expressed his willingness to make the Superior of the Order the perpetual pastor of the congregation as soon as the latter was prepared to accept it and was in a condition to assume in perpetuity the discharge of the duties connected with it. He also empowered him to establish priories in the diocese, and to open a seminary and college as soon as circumstances permitted. Thus was the wish of Rev. Theodore Browers, the generous donor of the property, more than realized, who had frequently been heard to say, " My object is to make Sportsman's Hall another Conewago." Father Gallagher withdrew at the end of six months, but for several years, probably six, the chaplain of St. Xavier's convent and academy or the pastor of Greensburg was accustomed to visit the congregation twice in the month for the benefit of the English portion. On the 7th of March, 1847, Mr. Martin Geyerstanger (Father Charles) was ordained, being the first priest of the Benedictine Order to be raised to that sacred dignity in North America. May 14th of the same year the Sisters took possession of their new convent and academy buildings of St. Xavier's, and gave the house which they had occupied till that time to the Superior. The greater part of the community was immediately transferred to it.

But it was not long before the Father Superior began to show that enterprising spirit which so admirably fitted him for the field upon which he had entered. Soon he extended his ministrations to the little congregations of Saltzburg and Indiana, in the latter of which he established a priory, and to St. Mary's, Elk County, now in the Diocese of Erie. But at home he was beset with innumerable and apparently insurmountable difficulties arising from the poverty of the community and the necessity of making improvements in the property. The members of the Order increased, both by accessions at home and arrivals from Europe; and the Louis Mission Union, that had so generously aided him in the beginning, still made him remittances until he had attained a degree of independence. But before commencing to build, the Order must be confirmed in its possession of the property. The appointment of the Superior perpetual pastor of the congregation, and the consequent transfer of the property to the Benedictine Order in perpetuity, was made by the Bishop in an instrument dated February 15th, 1848. Soon after this the Superior laid the condition of the foundation before the Holy Father, and asked that it might be declared an independent priory. The request was granted, and the Superior, or Prior as he now became, was empowered to erect other priories in different parts of the country, after he should obtain permission from the respective Bishops of the places. But it was not until July 15th, 1852, that St. Vincent's was formally recognized as a non-exempt priory by Bishop O'Connor.* An addition to the building was commenced by the brothers September 29th, 1848. On the 20th of April of the following year three of the students who had accompanied the Superior from Germany were ordained priests. At the same time a seminary was commenced on a small scale. At the close of this year the community consisted of eight priests, seven clerics, and twenty-six lay brothers. A farm of 293 acres, lying on the Chestnut ridge, about eight miles south-east of the priory, was purchased principally on account of the timber with which it was covered. In 1851 the Prior visited Germany, where he received very considerable pecuniary assistance to further his good works in the cause of religion. St. Vincent's College was opened in 1849. By the year 1854 it had ninety students; additional buildings were required for their accommodation, and were erected. To secure to the Order the possession of the property and give the former a proper standing in the face of the law, a charter was obtained from the State Legislature May 10th, 1853. In December of the same year, the Papal Nuncio, Cardinal Bedini, visited the monastery, and on his arrival at Pittsburg raised three members of the Order to the sacred dignity of the priesthood. The better to secure the independence of the community, a saw-mill and a flour-mill were built in 1854, and at the same time a farm of 205 acres of land lying ten miles from the monastery was purchased. But it would require too much space to trace the gradual growth of so large and complete a "little world" as St. Vincent's. A few only of the leading features must suffice.

* St. Vincenz, etc., pp. 128, 129.

In 1855 the Prior visited Rome once more to lay the affairs of the Order before the Holy Father. But the most important result of his visit was that he succeeded in having St. Vincent's raised to the dignity of an exempt abbey with himself as mitred Abbot, having been appointed by the Pope to that dignity for a term of three years, after which the Abbot should be elected according to the provisions of the rule. The brief of the Holy Father raising St. Vincent's to the dignity of an abbey was dated August 24th, and that appointing the father Abbot September 17th. Father Wimmer was the second mitered Abbot in the United States, Rt. Rev. Father Maria Eutropius, of the Abbey of Our Lady of La Trappe, Ky., having been raised to that dignity some time before. The following statistics will show the rapid growth and spread of the Benedictine Order in the first nine years of its existence among us: There were twenty priests, of whom two were at Butler, three at Carrolltown, one at Indiana, two at St. Mary's, Elk County, two at St. Severin's, Clarion County (the last two in the Diocese of Erie), and ten at St. Vincent's. There were fifteen clerics, twenty-two novices, seven scholastics, and one hundred and twelve lay brothers—in all 176 souls.

The adjuncts of the abbey and college gradually appeared and the whole developed itself into a perfect organization. In 1858 a brewery was built to supply the community with its favorite German beverage, which soon found its way also into the market, and made a name for itself. In 1864 a printing-press was set up, and soon a photographing apparatus found a place among the improvements. A tannery was also built. Additions were made from time to time to the buildings of the abbey and college. In 1878 an immense brick barn was put up, the largest in the county.

The Abbot again visited Rome in 1865, when the Holy Father was so well pleased with the progress made by the Order under his wise and energetic management that he appointed him General, or President, of all the houses of the Order in the United States for life. But after his death the election of Abbot will be according to the provisions of the rule. While in Rome the abbot also made arrangements for the opening of a house in the Holy City, where students should be prepared to fill the position of professors afterwards in the college. It was, however, discontinued after the occupation of Rome in 1870. By an apostolic brief of August 3d, 1866, the priory at St. Cloud's, Minn., was made an abbey, and Rev. Rupert Seidenbush, the present Vicar Apostolic of Northern Minnesota, was named Abbot. He was consecrated on the 12th of the following December. In 1869 the Abbot again crossed the Atlantic to visit his native land and to be present at the Vatican Council.

During this time the congregation had been in the fullest enjoyment of all the advantages which the presence of a large number of the reverend clergy in their midst naturally afforded. It had undergone, however, but little change beyond a moderate increase. Other congregations were formed from its outskirts which drew away a part of its numbers, so that at present it counts but 750 souls. There is a parochial school attached to the abbey, and one also at St. Xavier's Academy.

From the humble beginnings which we have seen, when the pioneer members of the Order found it difficult to procure the most miserable lodgings, the abbey has grown to be one of the most important religious foundations in America. The main building, including the seminary, college, and monastery, forms a quadrangle about four hundred feet in length by two hundred in width, with the church running across the centre the shorter way. A part of one end of the quadrangle is unfinished as yet, but will be completed in a few months. The church has been enlarged at the ends so as to join the other buildings; and a number of chapels have also been formed in an addition to the side. A tall tower has also been constructed, and the interior has undergone renovation. Although struggling from the first and until lately with formidable difficulties, the career of the institution in all its departments has been one of constant success. The following will give an idea of the growth of the Order. There are now three abbeys: St. Vincent's, raised to the dignity of an abbey August 24th, 1855; St. Louis of the Lake, Stearns County, Minn., August 3d, 1866; St. Benedict's, Atchison City, Kansas, September 29th, 1876; and St. Malachy's Priory, Union County, Iowa, 1871. To sum up, we have the following: two

Bishops, three Abbots, one hundred and thirty-four priests, seven deacons, fourteen subdeacons, twenty-nine clerics, eighteen novices, one hundred and sixty-seven brothers, one hundred and fifty-seven other alumni of the Order; and about four hundred students, besides, attending their colleges. The Order is distributed into four monasteries, eleven priories, thirty-three *expositura*, or houses where priests reside having charge of congregations, forty-two stations, and six colleges and high-schools. They are, in fine, located in ninety-five places, these being in eighteen different States of the Union, in fifteen dioceses and three vicariates apostolic, and they have charge of well-nigh 40,000 souls.

The career of the seminary and college of St. Vincent's has been equally prosperous with that of the Order. Notwithstanding that additions have been made to the college buildings from time to time, the reputation which it has acquired for itself and the pains that are constantly taken to provide a numerous and efficient staff of professors have drawn as large a number of students as the buildings are capable of accommodating. After meeting with considerable opposition, the faculty succeeded in obtaining from the Legislature the right of conferring degrees, by an act dated April 29th, 1871.

Truly the mustard-seed has grown and has become a large tree.* The good work has not, however, ceased, but, on the contrary, is being pushed forward with increased activity, and the venerable Abbot, although in his 71st year, yet displays all the energy of youth. A most estimable man, he has the best wishes of all for the success of his noble undertakings.

Turn we now to the congregations formed from the parent stem; and first to Greensburg.

CHURCH OF THE MOST HOLY SACRAMENT, GREENSBURG.†

Greensburg, the county-seat of Westmoreland County, is situated in a country place on the line of the Pennsylvania Railroad, thirty-one miles east of Pittsburg, at the junction of

---

* Compiled from *Catalogus Exhibens Nomina Monachorum Ord. S. P. Benedicti*, etc., 1879.

† St. Vincenz, etc.; *Catalogus*, etc.; and Day's Historical Collections.

the South-western Railroad. It is also on the line of the Philadelphia and Pittsburg turnpike. It was laid out in 1782, incorporated in February, 1799, and had in 1870 a population of 1642. Here in the Presbyterian Cemetery repose the remains of General Arthur St. Clair of Revolutionary fame.

As regards the Catholic history of the place, it is unusually interesting. Here the first property was owned by the Church in Western Pennsylvania, and the first church was undertaken, although it was not destined to be finished. In March, 1789, the Catholic pioneers purchased one acre and twenty perches of land for a church and cemetery at a cost of five shillings, as we have seen. In the spring of the following year the erection of a log-church was commenced. Carpenters were scarce, and those to be had were not adepts in the trade. But architectural taste had not as yet attained a high degree of refinement, and people were easily satisfied. Four walls, a floor, and a roof were quite sufficient. The church was so far completed as to provide these, with the exception of part of the roof, when Father Browers died and disturbances began to mar the harmony of the little flock. Nothing further was done until after the arrival of Father Heilbron, who, in 1800, resolved to finish the long-standing edifice. But upon examination the logs of which it was built were found to be rotting, and a beginning must be made, if made at all, from the ground. The unfinished building, without the lot upon which it stood, was sold, and so matters remained for forty-five years. In the summer of 1846, however, the Catholic population of the town and environs had so far increased as to make it desirable to have a church. One was accordingly undertaken, but by whom has not been ascertained. The corner-stone was laid by the Bishop June 9th of that year, but the building was not ready for dedication before the middle of December, 1847. It was then dedicated under the title of the Most Blessed Sacrament. The church is a brick building of simple style and finish, and has a steeple rising from the centre in front. It stands on the lot purchased by the original settlers, on a gentle hill to the north of the tunnel by which the railroad passes under a portion of the town. It was at first attended from the abbey, nine miles distant, Mass being celebrated at first on one Sunday in the month, but soon after on every Sunday. About the year 1851, when the railroad was in course of construction, Rev. W. Pollard, a secular priest, was appointed pastor; and he appears to have been the only secular priest who exercised the functions of the sacred ministry regularly for the people, although from the beginning the chaplain of St. Xavier's Convent had at times visited the church to minister to the English-speaking portion of the flock. But in 1853 it reverted to the Benedictine fathers, with whom it has since remained. In 1854 Rev. Aug. Wirth, O.S.B., who was then pastor, built a residence near the church, and about the same time put up a frame school-house in which a school was opened and has since been conducted by a lay teacher. Little change marked the flight of time, and the growth of the congregation was almost imperceptible. But many of the descendants of the original settlers have unhappily lost the faith, and have gone to swell the ranks of heresy or infidelity. Additional lots were at some time purchased adjoining the original tract. At length Father Wirth returned in 1876, after an absence of nearly twenty years, during which he had labored in different parts of the West. His first care was to enlarge the church by an addition to the rear, making it 92 feet in length by 30 in width. The interior was also submitted to a course of renovation which added no little to its appearance. In the summer of 1878 he replaced the school-house by a brick building. No further improvements will be required for many years.

The congregation is and has always been mixed, German and English; but the former element has constantly predominated. Its future growth will be extremely slow. At present it numbers only two hundred and fifty souls, with thirty children in the school.

ST. BONIFACE'S CHAPEL, CHESTNUT RIDGE.

In the fall of 1850 the prior of St. Vincent's purchased, as we have already seen, a farm of 293 acres on the Chestnut ridge, about seven miles east of the abbey. Additional purchases were made at different times afterwards, until the Order owns at present about 735 acres there. Buildings were soon after put up for the accommodation of the brothers who work on the farm, and for the professors of the college, who are accustomed to spend part of the summer vacation in this quiet retreat. Mass was celebrated in a private chapel from time to time, and at length—the precise date has not been ascertained—a little stone public chapel was built. Here Mass is celebrated on two Sundays in the month for the few Catholics living in the vicinity, whose number is now estimated at sixty souls. The future prospects of the little flock are not flattering.

ST. VINCENT'S CHAPEL, YOUNGSTOWN.

Youngstown is situated on the Pittsburg and Bedford turnpike, eleven miles east of Greensburg and about two miles from the abbey. It dates from the commencement of the present century, and is one of the many villages that owe their origin to these public thoroughfares. Like the others it flourished while these roads were the medium of communication between distant cities, but sank into comparative insignificance when travel and traffic were diverted into other channels. As an evidence of this Youngstown had a population of 415 in 1840, while in 1870 it had but 301.

A little brick chapel was built here by the Benedictine fathers about ten years ago—the date is uncertain—and like the parent church was placed under the patronage of St. Vincent of Paul. It cannot be said with propriety to have a congregation, but must rather be regarded as an outpost of the abbey church, built for the better accommodation of a portion of the parish.

CHURCH OF THE MOST HOLY TRINITY, LIGONIER.

Ligonier Valley lies between the Laurel ridge on the east and the Chestnut ridge on the west, and is eight or ten miles wide. The village of Ligonier is in the valley about seventeen miles south-east of Greensburg, and is rich in historical reminiscences. While the army led by General Forbes against Fort Duquesne in 1758 was detained at Bedford, Colonel Bouquet pushed forward with 2500 men in July toward the Loyalhanna River, cutting his way through the forests as he advanced. While in the Ligonier Valley, which he did not reach until October, awaiting intelligence from Major Grant, whom he had despatched with 800 men to make a forced march to Fort Duquesne to surprise it, but who was himself surprised and defeated, Col. Bouquet was attacked by a considerable force of French and Indians. Having with great difficulty repelled the attack, he threw up an entrenchment to protect the large amount of stores collected there, and this entrenchment afterwards took the name of Fort Ligonier.* The place is named in honor of Viscount Ligonier of Enniskillen, son of a French Huguenot, Commander-in-Chief of the land forces of Great Britain. The early settlers were often compelled to seek refuge within the fort from the frequent incursions of the Indians. The old fort offered the only secure resting-place of any importance in all the country east of the fortifications at Pittsburg. Two miles north of the village of Ligonier, at a point called Hermitage, stands a portion of the house built by General St. Clair. All that now remains of the old mansion is one room, which was used as a parlor by the general and his family one hundred years ago. In time a village sprung up around the ruins of the old fort, but it was not regularly laid out until 1825. It was incorporated as a borough April 10th, 1834, and had in 1840 a population of 294. This had risen to no more than 317 in 1870. Soon after that date a narrow-gauge railroad was built, connecting the village with the Pennsylvania Railroad at Latrobe, thus affording a ready market for the timber in which the valley and the ridges abound. For a few years the population increased rapidly, but the depression of the times arrested its growth and brought it back to something of its former monotony.

A few Catholics were found among the first settlers in the valley, but as they lived only ten or twelve miles from St. Vincent's, they were able, with a little exertion—such as people were not afraid to make in those early days—to assist occasionally at Mass. At length it was deemed advisable to build a church in the village, and it was accordingly under-

---

* Day's Historical Collections, p. 681.

taken under the direction of one of the Benedictine fathers from St. Vincent's, in 1854. When finished it was dedicated, under the invocation of the Most Holy Trinity, by one of the same fathers November 25th, 1855. The church is small and simple in style, as the wants and means of the people required it to be. It was then visited from the abbey once or twice in the month, as it still continues to be visited. The congregation, if such it can be called, is still very small and numbers at present but forty-seven souls, having diminished a little in the last few years. Its future prospects are not flattering.

BOLIVAR STATION.

The village of Bolivar is situated on the southern bank of the Conemaugh River and on the line of the Pennsylvania Railroad, fifty-five miles east of Pittsburg. It owes its rise to the railroad, is noted for the manufacture of fire-brick, and it had in 1870 a population of 298. About three years ago one of the Benedictine fathers began to visit the place once a month and say Mass in a private room for the few Catholics then found in the village, and the same arrangement continues and will probably continue for many years. The number of Catholics at present is but thirty-four.

ST. MARY'S CHURCH, NEW FLORENCE.

Nine miles east of Bolivar and similarly situated is New Florence, which had in 1870 a population of 333. Catholics were among the first to make their appearance in the village; and in 1854 Rev. James Kearney, then pastor of the English church at Johnstown, commenced the erection of a church. It was finished at the end of that year, and was dedicated by Very Rev. E. M'Mahon, V.G., January 14th, 1855. The church is a brick building of simple style and finish, and is quite small. Until recently it was visited twice in the month from Johnstown; but about three years ago it passed under the jurisdiction of the Benedictine fathers of St. Vincent's, and so it remains. At present the congregation numbers but 82 souls, and its future increase will in all probability be as gradual as its past has been.

CHAPTER XXIII.

WESTMORELAND COUNTY (CONCLUDED)—INDIANA COUNTY.

Church of Our Lady of Mount Carmel—St. Martin's Church, New Derry—Church of the Holy Family, Latrobe—St. Boniface's Church, Penn—Church of St. Mary of the Assumption, Irwin—Suterville Mission—Smithton Mission. INDIANA COUNTY—St. Patrick's Church, Cameron Bottom—Church of the Seven Dolors, Strongstown—St. Bernard's Church, Indiana—Blairsville—Sts. Simon and Jude's Church—Death and sketch of Very Rev. J. A. Stillenger—St. Matthew's Church, Saltzburg.

CHURCH OF OUR LADY OF MT. CARMEL.

THIS church is situated in a country place about five miles north-east of Latrobe. It is built of hewn logs, and was erected by Rev. Terence M'Girr in 1821 for the accommodation of the few Catholic farmers residing in the vicinity. The building is quite small, being no more perhaps than 20 by 30 feet, with a little recess for the altar. The spot is lonely, and the burying-ground around the church, where "the rude forefathers of the hamlet sleep," seems a fit resting-place for the departed. Father M'Girr visited the place occasionally during his residence at Sportsman's Hall, and after his departure his successor, Rev. Jas. A. Stillenger, did the same for many years. But these visits were seldom more frequent than once in two months. There are a few acres of land attached to the church, but owing to some flaw in the title Bishop Kenrick, who visited it soon after his consecration, would not dedicate the building. It is only a few years since the deed was executed in proper form. Since the erection of the church at New Derry, four miles distant, in 1856, Mt. Carmel has not been visited more than three or four times in the year; but it has always since that time been under the jurisdiction of the pastor of the latter place. The church can hardly be said to have a congregation, for the Masses that are offered up are principally for the benefit of the aged of that portion of the parish who would find it difficult at some seasons of the year to go to Derry to receive the sacraments. The pastor of Derry had the church repaired in 1878, but notwithstanding the improvements it is but a relic of the past, and its bare walls and rafters, the absence of pews, and the box-like altar carry the mind back to the early days of Catholicity, when wealth and taste were both wanting. Its lot in the future will doubtless be what it has been in the past.

ST. MARTIN'S CHURCH, NEW DERRY.

New Derry, or Derry as it is more commonly called, is situated on one of the old State turnpikes, about four miles north-east of Latrobe, and is about the size of an ordinary country village in an advanced state of decadence. Soon after the opening of the Pennsylvania Railroad a small number of Catholics families began to settle at Derry, an important station on the line at the summit of the Chestnut ridge, and one and a half miles south of the village of New Derry. As the old Mount Carmel Church stood north of the centre of the congregation and the railroad station south of it, a compromise was effected by building a church at New Derry. It was erected in 1856, and was dedicated, under the invocation of St. Martin, by Bishop O'Connor on the 17th of September of that year. It was a small brick building without a steeple, but was large enough to accommodate the congregation, which was said at that time to consist of about sixty families, nearly all of whom were farmers. It was built under the direction of the Benedictine fathers of St. Vincent's, under whose jurisdiction it remained until transferred to Rev. Jerome Kearney, of Latrobe, in June, 1861. He continued to offer up the Holy Sacrifice in both the church at Latrobe and that at Derry every Sunday, giving to each an alternate early and late Mass, until the fall of 1873, when the congregations had so far increased as to require separate pastors. Father Kearney then confined his attention exclusively to Latrobe, and Rev. John A. Martin was appointed first resident pastor of New Derry.

But the congregation had been gradually increasing prior to that time, especially by Catholics in the employ of the railroad company and others engaged in business settling at Derry station, so that in 1869 Father Kearney had found it necessary to enlarge the church. This he did by adding considerably to its length. It was otherwise improved in the interior, and when completed was dedicated by the Bishop on the 3d of August of the same year. Soon after his arrival, Father Martin built a neat frame residence. The congregation has gone on gradually increasing and will number at present about one hundred and ten families. But this increase has been for the most part at Derry station, and the people there are anxious to have a church for themselves. No effective movement has yet been made in that direction, but it is probable that it will not long be deferred, for that place is destined, in the nature of things, to grow more or less rapidly, while the rest of the congregation will remain as it is. There can be no doubt that in a few years there will be a church, residence, and school—for as yet there is no school—at Derry station, from which the present church will be visited as a station. About the middle of March, 1879, Father Martin was transferred to another congregation, and was succeeded by Rev. Jeremiah O'Callaghan. The congregation consists of farmers, persons employed by the railroad company, and a few coal-miners at a point a short distance east of Derry.

CHURCH OF THE HOLY FAMILY, LATROBE.

The borough of Latrobe is situated on the Pennsylvania Railroad, forty-one miles east of Pittsburg, and owes its rise and whatever trade it enjoys to that road. The population in 1870 was 1127, and it has since been steadily increasing. Soon after the construction of the railroad, a number of Catholic families began to settle in the incipient town, but for the present they complied with their religious duties at St. Vincent's, two miles distant. At this time a certain Catholic gentleman, whose name is withheld at his own request, donated a large and very eligible lot of ground for a church and cemetery. Seeing the future prospects of the town, Bishop O'Connor, by a letter dated June 13th, 1855, authorized the building of a church to be for the present under the jurisdiction of the chaplain of St. Xavier's. Work was not, however, commenced until the following summer, when Rev. James O'Connor, brother of the Bishop, took it in hand. He was succeeded in November of the same year by Rev. James Keogh, D.D. The church when finished was dedicated to the Holy Family by Very Rev. E. M'Mahon, V.G., on the 18th of January, 1857. It was a brick building 60 feet in length by 40 in width. When Dr. Keogh was transferred to the diocesan seminary in October of the same year, Rev. John Hackett became chaplain of St. Xavier's and pastor of Latrobe. But failing health soon obliged him to retire for a time to an easier mission, and he was succeeded May 5th, 1858, by Rev. Jerome Kearney, whose tenure of office was destined to be more lasting. He was the first to reside at Latrobe, although he retained the chaplaincy of St. Xavier's. At that time the congregation consisted of thirty-five families. In June, 1861, the church at New Derry was placed under the jurisdiction of the pastor of Latrobe, who in September was relieved of the chaplaincy of the convent and academy. In the same year a frame school-house 23 by 34 feet was built, and a school opened by a lay teacher. The congregation sustained a heavy loss February 4th, 1863, in having the church blown down by a storm. A meeting was immediately called to take measures for rebuilding it, and in the mean time the Holy Sacrifice was offered up in the school-house. But the growth and the future prospects of the congregation showed the propriety of making the new church larger than the old had been. The old walls yet standing were used as far as they were considered safe, and an addition of 22 feet was put to the length of the church, making it 82 feet in length by 40 in width. It was dedicated by the Bishop September 6th, 1863. It is modelled after the Gothic style of architecture, with the ceiling rising gently from the side walls towards the centre. There are three altars. A neat brick residence was finished in March, 1864.

Three years later it became necessary to enlarge the school-house. In April, 1868, the schools passed into the hands of the Sisters of Mercy, two of whom come daily from St. Xavier's. In the same year a steeple was built to the front centre of the church. The size to which the congregations of New Derry and Latrobe had grown made it expedient to separate them and appoint a distinct pastor to each, and while Father Kearney remained at the latter Rev. John A. Martin was appointed to the former in the fall of 1873. A splendid brick school-house, consisting of two rooms for the children on the first floor and a spacious hall on the second, replaced the old one some time in the same year. In December a few acres of ground were purchased adjoining that upon which the church stands.

At length, after having ministered to the congregation for more than twenty years, Father Kearney was transferred to St. Bridget's Church, Pittsburg, December 6th, 1877, and was succeeded by Rev. Jas. Holland. But on the 20th of the following June he gave place to Rev. S. Wall. Nor was his pastorate destined to be much longer than that of his immediate predecessor; for, being appointed pastor of St. Patrick's Church, Pittsburg, in the middle of May, 1879, the congregation was confided to Rev. Jas. Canivan, the present incumbent.

Since the financial panic of 1873 the congregation has increased but little, if at all; and it will number at present about one hundred families, with the prospect of a very gradual increase in the future.

ST. BONIFACE'S CHURCH, PENN.

Penn borough, or Penn Station as it is commonly called, is on the line of the Pennsylvania Railroad, twenty-six miles east of Pittsburg, and it had, in 1870 a population of 820. It owes its existence to the railroad and to the very extensive coal-mines operated there. German Catholics settled in the vicinity long before the erection of a church, this being to some extent a part of the original Westmoreland County settlement. Before the erection of a church they heard Mass at Greensburg, which is only five miles distant. At length the mines were opened and the number of Catholics so far increased as to make it expedient to build a church for them. From the beginning this congregation as well as that at Irwin, next to claim our attention, was under the jurisdiction of the pastor of Greensburg, who was assisted on Sundays by a priest from the abbey. A site was secured, the church was undertaken, and the corner-stone was laid by the Bishop October 11th, 1863. It was finished in the course of the following summer, and was dedicated by the same prelate under the invocation of St. Boniface. The church is a frame building about 30 by 50 feet, and is surmounted by a belfry ; but it lays no claim to any special architectural style. A cheap frame school-house was soon after built, in which a school was opened by a lay teacher. Mass was now celebrated every Sunday. Upon the appointment of Rev. Michael Murphy pastor of Irwin, in October, 1871, this church was also confided to him, and he continued as his predecessors had done to offer up the Holy Sacrifice in both every Sunday, giving each an alternate early and late Mass. But in the summer of 1873 the congregations were separated, and Rev. John Stillerich was appointed pastor of St. Boniface. A frame residence was built near the church for his reception. But the support of a school and a resident pastor was found to be too heavy a tax on the means of the small congregation, and the school was closed and has not since been opened. Father Stillerich was at length succeeded by Rev. Ed. Troutwine, early in the summer of 1878, under whose jurisdiction the congregation yet remains. It is composed of German and Irish mixed, the former predominating, and in the days of its greatest prosperity never exceeded eighty families. Like all similar communities it is subject to frequent and sudden vicissitudes, and it is not unusual to find the condition of the people change from labor to idleness and from abundance to want in a single month.

Penn has at present greatly fallen from its former prosperity, and numbers, although it is doubtless but temporary, not more than thirty families. But notwithstanding this it is destined, in the nature of things, to go on gradually increasing.

CHURCH OF ST. MARY OF THE ASSUMPTION, IRWIN.

Irwin borough, or Irwin Station, is on the Pennsylvania Railroad, twenty-one miles east of Pittsburg. The place was so named from Mr. John Irwin, lately deceased, who owned extensive tracts of lands there. Here are located the Westmoreland Coal Company's mines, the most extensive in Western Pennsylvania. The borough had in 1870 a population of 833 souls, and it has since increased very considerably. Although a small number of Catholics lived on farms in the vicinity for many years, the congregation and the town owe their rise to the mines. But the place was settled by Scotch-Irish Presbyterians, a class after Knox's own heart, and it is one of the most bigoted spots in the western part of the State. As an illustration of their hostility to Popery, it will suffice to say that when Mass was celebrated for some time in a house of one of the miners, beginning about the year 1862, before the church was built, it was not unusual for some of the young gentlemen of the place to assemble on the side of the hill above the house and annoy the assembly by throwing stones at it. So high did feeling run, that when one of the Benedictine fathers by whom the place was at first attended came on the cars on a certain Sunday to offer up the Holy Sacrifice, and did not find a man to meet him at the station, he would not venture alone to the house where the people were assembled, but stepped on the cars again and came to Pittsburg.

But the number of Catholics increased, and they determined to have a church. A site was purchased and work commenced under the supervision of the pastor of Greensburg, who, aided by one of the priests at St. Vincent's, ministered to the congregation until the appointment of a resident pastor. The corner-stone of the church was laid by Very Rev. T. Mullen, V.G., August 15th, 1867, and the church was dedicated by the Bishop on the following Ascension Day, under the title of St. Mary of the Assumption. The church is a brick structure 62 feet in length by 32 in width, and is furnished with a belfry. The style and finish are chaste and simple. Mass was celebrated from that time forward every Sunday, and of late years it has been celebrated twice. At length, in October, 1871, Rev. Michael Murphy was appointed first resident pastor, a position which he continues to fill. Not having ground upon which to build a house, he purchased a large frame residence on a spacious lot adjoining the church in April, 1875. From the time of his appointment until the summer of 1873 he ministered to the congregation at Penn in connection with his own; but since that time, as was stated above, he has devoted himself exclusively to the church at Irwin. In December, 1876, he built a frame hall for fairs, entertainments, etc., and it is his intention to open a school in it as soon as circumstances permit. The principal obstacle that stands in his way is the fact that his congregation is distributed along the railroad for perhaps two miles in both directions from Irwin, and owing to the number of trains running parents fear to send their children.

The members of the congregation are engaged almost to a man in mining, which is known, here at least, as a very uncertain kind of employment, depending in part on the season of the year, in part on the iron trade, to some extent on the caprice of the operators of the mines, and no little on the strikes of the miners themselves; and hence it is almost impossible to estimate the numerical strength of such a congregation. A single week may effect as great a change as a year would accomplish in other places. But the congregation is the largest in Westmoreland County, and as near as can be estimated may be put at one hundred and seventy-five families, who are almost without exception natives of the Emerald Isle. The church is far too small to accommodate them, and if circumstances permitted would have been enlarged before this. The congregation must increase in the future as it has done in the past, and it is not improbable that another church will at some future day be erected between Irwin and Braddock's Field.

SUTERVILLE MISSION.

Suterville is a village on the Youghiogheny River and the Baltimore and Ohio Railroad, twenty-nine miles south-east of Pittsburg. The mission is composed, like the others last noticed, almost exclusively of coal-miners. After the erection of the church at Alpsville, about eight miles further down the river, it was visited from there generally once in the month. Prior to that date it had perhaps been visited occasionally from Elizabeth, on the Monongahela River. No church has yet been built, but Mass is usually offered up in the village school-house. In April, 1877, Rev. H. P. Connery was appointed resident pastor, and in October of the same year he rented a hall which was from that time used as a church. But the mission was unable to afford any kind of support to a pastor, owing to the fact that the small number of Catholic miners in the place did not work more perhaps than one third of their time, and in November, 1878, it was again attached to Alpsville and Father Connery was transferred to another congregation. No steps have as yet been taken towards the building of a church, nor is it probable that any will be taken until there is a permanent revival of business, for the prosperity of the place depends entirely on the mines. At present there are perhaps fifty families; and the number will increase, as the mines are rich and have been opened at a comparatively recent date.

SMITHTON MISSION.

Ten miles farther up the river, in the same county, is Smithton with ten Catholic families, miners. This place was also visited at first from Alpsville, but after the appointment of a pastor for Suterville it became a part of his mission. On his withdrawal, however, it reverted to Alpsville, and so it remains. Mass is celebrated in the school-house of the village. Both these missions are composed principally of Irish Catholics.

Although Westmoreland County is the oldest settlement

in the diocese, and possesses a fair number of congregations, yet they are generally small, so that the Catholic population is not large. In the south-eastern and north-western sections there are no Catholics, if we except a very few scattered families.

INDIANA COUNTY.

It was the misfortune of this county to lie outside the line of canals and railroads, and hence, although all the congregations were founded at an early day, religion has not flourished except at Blairsville. Nature, too, denied it the advantages of mineral wealth and left its population almost exclusively to the pursuit of agriculture, except in the eastern and north-eastern portions, which were covered with extensive pine forests. For these reasons the increase of the population has been very gradual, and that of the Catholic population still more gradual, as will be seen.

ST. PATRICK'S CHURCH, CAMERON BOTTOM.

This congregation is located in the eastern part of the county, about three miles north of the State road running from Ebensburg to Indiana, and about equidistant from both places. It is an offshoot of the Loretto colony, and dates as far back at least as the year 1820. Two years later Rev. Terence M'Girr began to pay it an occasional visit from Sportsman's Hall, and it is said to have been visited prior to that time by Father M'Guire, of the same place. A farm of about 360 acres was donated for the site of a church and the support of its pastor by a Mr. Wilcott, of Wilmington, Del.; and a stone church was commenced in 1827. It was dedicated by Bishop Kenrick on his first visit, October 21st, 1832. But it would be impossible to give the names of the numerous visiting priests and resident pastors, for it has had more than any other three congregations in the dioceses. The bare list of them is enough to convince a person of ordinary intelligence that life is but a pilgrimage.

It was generally attended from Loretto or Ebensburg at distant intervals, until 1850, when the farm was transferred to the Franciscan Brothers of the former place by the Bishop upon certain conditions, the most important of which was that they should establish a monastery and lodge and board the pastor of the church. When Bishop O'Connor visited the place in 1847 there were, as he states, 300 souls in the congregation, a larger number than at present, owing to the fact that a few families withdrew and attached themselves to the church at St. Nickolas, seven miles distant.

Upon the transfer of the property to the Brothers, a colony was sent from Loretto who built a frame house to serve as a temporary monastery until a more substantial one could be provided. From that time forward the congregation has been blessed with the presence of a resident pastor, and Mass is celebrated every Sunday. The first pastor was Rev. W. Lambert, but the changes were as frequent from that time as they had been before.

The little stone church began at length to show signs of age, and the people felt able to replace it by one more becoming the sacramental presence of our Divine Redeemer. Work was commenced, and the church was finished in the fall of 1853. The ceremony of the dedication was performed by Rev. Michael Corbett, of Loretto, on the 13th of November. The church is a small frame building capable of accommodating about three hundred, and makes no pretensions to architectural style. No steeple was built until 1868, when Rev. P. M. Sheehen was pastor.

About the same time the Brothers began the erection of the present stone monastery, which was finished in 1854. It is a large substantial building with small windows, and reminded me of a fort the first time I saw it from a distance. But it is very comfortable, and has a chapel where the priest offers up the week-day Masses. The remaining portion of the congregation's history is uneventful. In February, 1861, a number of the larger male orphans was sent to the Brothers from Pittsburg to work on the farm till they should be larger, and then to find homes with Catholic families in the surrounding county. There were generally from twenty to thirty at the farm until about 1868. But this disposition of the orphans was not successful, as will be seen more fully hereafter.

It was my lot to be pastor of the congregation during the early part of 1870, and at that time there were forty-five families, all farmers, and with a few exceptions Irish or of Irish descent. The present pastor is Rev. Philip J. Colwell. The future of the congregation is likely to be extremely monotonous.

CHURCH OF THE SEVEN DOLORS, STRONGSTOWN.

For several years two or three of the wealthier members of the southern part of the Cameron Bottom congregation complained of the distance they had to travel to hear Mass, and requested permission from the Bishop to build a church at Strongstown, four miles south of the present church. Permission was granted, and a miniature frame building was erected in the summer and fall of 1871. It was dedicated by Rev. James Canivan, pastor of the Cameron Bottom church, January 24th, 1872. Mass is celebrated in it once or twice in the month, the priest riding from one church to the other between the Masses. But on the whole it may be regarded as a supernumerary.

ST. BERNARD'S CHURCH, INDIANA.

Indiana, the county-seat of Indiana County, was laid out in 1805 upon a tract of 250 acres of land granted for that purpose by George Clymer. The turnpike from Ebensburg to Kittanning passes through it; but the principal outlet is the Indiana branch of the Pennsylvania Railroad, which connects with the main line near Blairsville. There are said to have been some traces of an ancient fortification about three miles south-west of the town.* The population in 1870 was 1605 souls. Father Bradley informs me that he visited the place occasionally during the two years he resided at Ebensburg, from 1830 to 1832, at which time there were but one English and two German families there. From the latter date until a resident pastor was appointed it was under the jurisdiction

---

* Day's Historical Collections, p. 378.

of the pastor of Blairsville. Little is known of its subsequent history until 1846, except that the Catholic population increased gradually by settlement and conversions. In that year the building of the first church was commenced, the corner-stone of which was laid by Rev. J. A. Stillenger, of Blairsville, on the 6th of June. When Bishop O'Connor visited the congregation the following year, it numbered, as he states, two hundred and fifty souls. At the same time he dedicated the church under the invocation of St. Bernard. The building was quite small and simple in style. It is but proper to state, in passing, that the greater part of what follows is taken in substance from the German history of St. Vincent's Abbey already referred to.

The congregation at Blairsville had by this time so far increased as to demand the undivided attention of Father Stillenger, and the church at Indiana was confided to the care of the fathers of the Benedictine Order at St. Vincent's Abbey. The church was at first visited on one Sunday in the month, as it had formerly been, but as it lay on the route to St. Mary's, Elk County, where the Benedictines had recently established a priory, the Father Superior wished to found one there also, both for the better management of the congregation and also as a station on the journey to St. Mary's. The requisite permission was granted by the Bishop July 15th, 1852. Hereupon the Superior purchased a property near the church with a building on it which had been used as a tavern, for $3700, and also a farm of 310 acres, four miles from the town, for $2400. Two priests were at first stationed at the priory, who ministered to the spiritual necessities of the congregation and also visited a few families at Perrysville, twenty-three miles north of Indiana; Plum Creek, twelve miles, and Crooked Creek, eight miles west; and Mechanicsburg, eight miles south-east. But regular visits to these places were not long continued, and in the autumn of 1855 one of the priests was withdrawn. In 1861 a school-house was built and a school opened by a lay teacher. In the following year a stone priory was erected.

The church at length became too small to accommodate the congregation, whose means as well as number justified them in undertaking a new one. The lot upon which it was to stand was donated by Paul Vogel & Brothers; work was commenced, and the corner-stone was laid by the Bishop August 17th, 1869. Two years later the church was completed, and was dedicated by the same prelate September 26th. The sacred edifice, which is of brick, is built after the Roman style of architecture, and is 95 feet in length by 64 in width in the transept and 54 in the nave. It is surmounted by a steeple 135 feet high. The interior is well finished, and altogether the church will compare favorably with almost any in the diocese. The entire cost was $18,000. This quite naturally left a considerable debt on the congregation, which at that time numbered 450 souls, with fifty children in the school.

In 1876 the Benedictine Order withdrew, and the congregation passed into the hands of the secular clergy. The present pastor, Rev. Geo. Allman, was appointed to the vacant office. The following year he built a convent and schoolhouse combined, and introduced the Sisters of St. Agnes to take charge of the schools, a duty which they continue to fulfil. But this improvement and change, considering the debt and the circumstances of the congregation, though desirable, are thought to have been premature.

The congregation was from the beginning almost entirely German, and that nationality still predominates, but the younger portion is rather American, and the parish may be termed a mixed one. It has, if anything, declined in the last few years, but it must increase—although it will be very slowly—as it is composed principally of farmers.

BLAIRSVILLE.

Blairsville is situated on the north bank of the Conemaugh River and on the northern turnpike, 40 miles east of Pittsburg. It was laid out about the year 1819, and was named in honor of John Blair, of Blair's Gap, Allegheny Mountain, then president of the Hollidaysburg and Pittsburg Turnpike Company. The land upon which the town is built originally belonged to a Mr. Campbell. The construction of the turnpike fostered the growth of the town, and in March, 1825, it was incorporated as a borough. From 1827 to 1834 were the palmy days of Blairsville. In 1828 the western division of the canal was completed to the town, and the eastern was gradually advancing toward the mountains. In 1834 communication was made between the eastern and western divisions of the canal, traffic and travel by the turnpike almost ceased, and Blairsville lost its former importance, for the canal did not pass through the town, but on the opposite side of the river.*

The Pennsylvania Railroad runs within three miles of the town, with which it is connected by the Indiana branch. The West Pennsylvania Railroad, which was built on the line of the canal from Allegheny City to Blairsville, about the year 1864, has its shops in the town. But the place no longer enjoys its former prosperity, as will be seen from the fact that in 1840 it had a population of 990, which had risen in 1870 to but 1054.

Catholics were among the first settlers in the vicinity of Blairsville. Prior to the construction of the canal, the Westmoreland colony, the centre of which was but ten miles distant, had extended across the Conemaugh into Indiana County. Upon the completion of the canal a number of the laborers employed upon it took up their residence in the town and its environs. The first Mass celebrated where the town now stands was by Dr. Gallitzin; the date is uncertain, but the circumstances will show that it was most probably before the town was laid out. I have the account from a man who was present. The Holy Sacrifice was offered up in the open air, under a tree in a grove back of the present church. When the grove was cut down to convert the place into a cemetery, the stump of the tree was religiously guarded by Father Stillenger, until time itself removed it. Mass was afterwards celebrated in the house of a Mr. Devinny, but for how long a time is uncertain. During the construction of the canal Mass was celebrated by Rev. Terence M'Girr, of Sportsman's Hall, but Dr. Gallitzin also paid the line an occasional visit.

* Day's Historical Collections, pp. 378, 379.

STS. SIMON AND JUDE'S CHURCH, BLAIRSVILLE.

The building of the church appears, however, to have been the spontaneous work of the people themselves. Be that as it may, the congregation cannot be said to have been organized until the arrival of Rev. James A. Stillenger, who was the first, and the only pastor for forty-three years.

The people, anxious to enjoy the advantages of a resident priest, sent a delegation to Pittsburg in the latter part of June, 1830, to meet the newly consecrated Bishop Kenrick on his way from Kentucky to his see, and lay their petition before him. But he preferred to stop at Blairsville on his way, as he did July 1st, when he administered confirmation and learned the condition of the congregation. He promised to send them a pastor, and on November 28th Father Stillenger took up his residence in the town. He finished the little church, which had not yet been completed, had it dedicated, and continued to offer up the Holy Sacrifice twice in the month; at the same time he attended the scattered families over a large tract of the surrounding country. In 1832 he was directed by the Bishop to visit the few Catholics residing east of the Allegheny River as far north as the New York State line, a distance of 110 miles, and two years later Fayette and other counties in the south of the State were placed under his jurisdiction, and received the benefit of his ministrations four times in the year. His parish during this time —which was not more than three years—embraced the entire breadth of the State, a distance of about 160 miles. About the same time, as we have seen, he built a new church and a house at St. Vincent's, and transferred his residence thither. There he resided until September, 1844, and visited Blairsville as usual on two Sundays in the month.

In the mean time, however, the congregation had so far increased as no longer to find accommodations in the church. A new one was called for, and was commenced in 1841. When finished it was dedicated by Very Rev. M. O'Connor, V.G., October 2d of the following year. It is a brick building 90 feet in length by 48 in width, having a steeple in the centre in front, and is modelled after the Gothic style of architecture. The main altar occupies a recess with a sacristy on each side, in front of which are the side-altars. Upon the return of Father Stillenger to Blairsville, his labors were confined exclusively to that congregation, with the exception of a monthly visit to Indiana until 1852. He built or bought a brick residence, and some years later—the date is uncertain—built a brick school-house and opened a school with a lay teacher. About the year 1858 he added greatly to the decoration of the interior of the church by placing nine large oil-paintings on the walls. On the right hand, uniform in size and about 6 by 9 feet, are the Agony in the Garden, the Descent from the Cross, and the Resurrection. On the left hand, and of the same size, are the Nativity, the Transfiguration, and the Ascension. Over the side-altar on the right, the titular saints, Simon and Jude, stand side by side in full-length portraits in a painting about 8 by 10 feet. Over the other side-altar is the Annunciation, of the same size. The altar-piece of the main altar is a Crucifixion, about 10 by 12 feet. These paintings are all mounted on rich gilt frames, and although of different relative merit are all works of rare excellence. They have been visited and admired by thousands, many of whom came from a distance to see them. Their history as far as it is known is briefly this, as told me by Father Stillenger a short time before his death. "When I used to kneel before the altar of the old church," said he, "and look up at the little picture of the Blessed Virgin and Child over the altar, I would wish and pray that I might be able to decorate my new church, when it should be built, with beautiful oil-paintings. The Blessed Virgin heard my prayer. There was a young man here at that time, a particular friend of mine, whose godfather was a celebrated painter in Germany, and it was through his influence that I got these pictures. I paid something for them, but of course not as much as they are worth."

During all this time the congregation had been increasing slowly both in the town and country, until it had become large. But the good pastor had one wish of which he fondly hoped to witness the accomplishment—that of placing a religious community over the schools. With this object in view, he built a brick convent near the church in the summer of 1872, which, although not so conveniently arranged in the interior as might be desired, is yet spacious and comfortable, and presents an imposing appearance in the antiquated town with its diminutive houses. Into this convent he introduced a number of Sisters of Charity from Altoona in January, 1873, and gave them charge of the schools, which they still continue to teach. This was the last improvement effected by the good pastor; but so much did he delight in it that he was frequently seen to shed tears of joy at the thought that now at length the children of the congregation had the amplest opportunity of receiving a thoroughly Catholic training.

But his course was run; the end was at hand, and he was about to be called to his final rest. For a few months he had been observed to decline more rapidly than could have proceeded from old age alone, but no apprehensions were entertained that his dissolution was at hand. Daily he offered up the adorable Sacrifice and administered the affairs of the congregation. But on the morning of September 18th, 1873, his congregation and friends were appalled with the intelligence of his sudden death. He had entered the church as usual to celebrate Mass, and at its conclusion retired to the sacristy, where he unvested, put the vestments away, and seated himself, according to his custom, to make his thanksgiving. His housekeeper, finding that he did not return at the usual time to take his breakfast, went to the church to ascertain the cause of the delay, and there found him dead upon the chair. So life-like was his appearance that she spoke to him before she perceived that his spirit had taken its flight.

VERY REV. JAMES AMBROSE STILLENGER was born in Baltimore, April 19th, 1801. His great-grandfather had emigrated from Cologne, Prussia, but his father was born in York County, Pa. His mother was a native of Baltimore, but of French descent. From his third year he lived with his grandfather near Chambersburg, Pa., and here in his sixteenth year he was employed in a German printing-office. A year after he went to Gettysburg, where he followed the same occupation, till at length, after much persuasion, Rev.

John Dubois, president of Mount St. Mary's College, induced him to enter that institution and pursue a course of studies. He entered in November, 1820, and remained until he was raised to the sacred dignity of the priesthood, February 28th, 1830. Having remained at the college ministering to the congregation attached to it until November, he came to Blairsville.* The rest of his laborious and edifying career has been traced in the history of this and St. Vincent's congregration. When Rt. Rev. M. O'Connor was promoted to the new See of Pittsburg, Father Stillenger was named the first Vicar-General, and when the Bishop visited Rome and other parts of Europe, July 23d, 1845, he was appointed administrator of the diocese. He continued to fill the position of Vicar-General for about four years, until it became advisable for that dignitary to reside in the episcopal city, when another was appointed; for as Father Stillenger frequently remarked, "he should regret nothing more than to be obliged through sickness or any other cause to be separated from his beloved congregation of Blairsville."

The closing scenes of his life have already been laid before the reader. It is worthy of remark. however, that he had always expressed a wish to die on a Friday after having offered up the Holy Sacrifice of the Mass. In itself this might be regarded merely as the expression of a pious desire, but when it pleased our Lord to grant it, we begin to understand how deeply it must have been fixed in his mind and how earnestly sought in prayer. Did the good old man have a presentiment, as he walked with faltering steps from his house to the church, that he was making that passage for the last time? Did he feel, as he passed under the loaded vines which years before his hand had planted, that never after that morning would Heaven, obedient to his word, change the fruit of those vines into the most precious Blood of Christ? And when arrayed in the sacred vestments, was it revealed to him that what he had long sought by prayer was to-day to be granted? Were those eyes bathed in tears of grateful devotion when, administering to himself his own

---

* Compiled from MS. left by him at his death.

Viaticum, he said: "May the Body and Blood of Jesus Christ preserve my soul unto life everlasting"? We know not. All we know with certainty is that his soul took its flight on a Friday after he had celebrated Mass.

His remains repose a short distance to the rear of the church, the spot where the old church had stood and the one selected by himself. Over it has since been erected a very tasteful monument.

Father Stillenger was, as it were, the connecting link between the past and the present. His recollection extended far back into the days of Dr. Gallitzin and his contemporaries. With them he had labored, from them received much of the historical reminiscences which made a conversation with him more than equal to the perusal of a history of the Church and of civilization in the western part of the State. He rendered invaluable assistance to Miss Brownson in the preparation of her "Life of Dr. Gallitzin," on which subject his interest amounted almost to enthusiasm. Besides the incidents with which his mind was well stored, he had in his possession valuable manuscripts relating to the early settlement of Loretto. The early history of Catholicity was a favorite topic with him, and he possessed an admirable faculty of interesting his hearers. He never wished for a large company, but spoke more freely in the presence of a few. He would entertain the little circle for hours, interspersing the more serious narrative with amusing incidents, "which," as he remarked, "God was pleased to scatter on our path to recreate and cheer us on; for we needed something." "At first," he would say with a smile, "my parish embraced five counties."

Father Stillenger was a little above the medium height, erect, but with the head falling gently forward, of a powerful frame, and weighing at one time only a little less than three hundred pounds. His countenance was of the German mould, although his accent betrayed nothing of his Teutonic extraction. His voice was soft and low, apparently devoid of the metallic ring and fulness that distinguish the orator, yet possessing that gentle fervor which no one finds it in his heart to resist. His eye was playful and sparkled even in his old age with a fire that might be called mischievous, but which indicated the possession of that inestimable faculty which attracts the young and fills them with confidence while it inspires them with respect.

Upon the death of Father Stillenger, Rev. Ed. M'Keever, the present pastor, was appointed to the vacant post. In the year 1875 he made some necessary repairs both of the interior and exterior of the church, had the windows filled with stained glass, and the church handsomely frescoed. At the same time he enlarged the school-house by adding a story to the old building, which was but one story high, and erecting a transverse building to the rear of it. Three rooms and a library were thus provided on the first floor, while the second is a hall for meetings, exhibitions, etc.

The congregation is composed principally of farmers, with a number of small traders, laborers, and miners, and will aggregate about one hundred and seventy-five families. It cannot be said to be increasing, and whatever augmentation there may be in the future will be extremely slow.

ST. MATTHEW'S CHURCH, SALTZBURG.

Saltzburg is situated on the north bank of the Kiskiminitis —or Kiskiminetas—River at the point where the Conemaugh and Loyalhanna unite, and from which to its confluence with the Allegheny River, nineteen miles below at Freeport, the stream takes the above name. The village owes its name to the discovery of veins of salt water, which are quite abundant along the river, and which appear to have been first discovered by a William Johnston about the year 1813.* The town owes the little importance it has to the construction and traffic of the canal, and afterwards to that of the West Pennsylvania Railroad, which, following the line of the canal, also passes through it. The most noted feature of the place is the number of preachers who make it the rendezvous from which they attend their little flocks in the surrounding country. The village had a population of 659 in 1870.

A few miles above is a tunnel on the canal 1000 feet long,

---

* Day's Historical Collections, pp. 375, 379.

and an aqueduct over the river near it. This was the scene of the first Mass offered in this part of the county. About the year 1828, when a large number of Catholic laborers were employed at this point, Dr. Gallitzin visited them and offered up the Holy Sacrifice in the tunnel. Standing under the arch, on the bed of the canal, with hundreds of feet of rock over his head, and using the towpath for an altar, he offered up the Adorable Victim in perhaps the most unique temple on earth. I have the account from a man who was present. About this time a small number of Catholic farmers, principally Germans, settled in the neighborhood; but it was not until 1847 that a church was built for their accommodation. It is probable, however, that they were occasionally visited by Father Stillenger before that time. One of the Benedictine fathers from St. Vincent's then collected and organized the little flock, and built a brick church 40 by 35 feet on a lot of ground donated for that purpose by a Mr. Rombach. It was dedicated by Bishop O'Connor September 21st, 1847, under the invocation of St. Matthew. The congregation then numbered, according to the Notes of the Bishop, 50 souls. The church has always been under the care of the Benedictine fathers, who visit it on one or two Sundays in the month.

Although originally German, the congregation can now with propriety be called American. Its prospects in the future are not flattering, and may be judged from its past history.* It numbers at present 145 souls.

* St. Vincenz in Pennsylvanien.

CHAPTER XXIV.

THE DONEGAL SETTLEMENT, ARMSTRONG COUNTY.

Character and nationality of the colonists—Crossing the ocean—Coming west—Settlement — The first visit of a priest — Armstrong 'County— St. Patrick's Church, Sugar Creek—A resident priest—The farm and church—Death and sketch of Rev. P. O'Neil—and of Rev. P. Rafferty—and of Rev. Jos. Cody—and of Rev. P. M. Doyle—Church of St. Mary of the Nativity, Freeport—St. Joseph's Church, Natrona, Allegheny County—St. Patrick's Church, Brady's Bend—St. Mary's German Church—Kittanning—St. Mary's Church—Holy Guardian Angels' Church, Easly's Settlement—Parker City, an oil-country town—Church of the Immaculate Conception.

THE DONEGAL SETTLEMENT.

THIS settlement, as I stated in a previous chapter, is partly in Armstrong and partly in Butler County. Unlike the other original colonies, it was composed exclusively of one nationality; and not only so, but from one locality—the county Donegal, Ireland. It possessed, besides, the advantage of a bard by whom the account of the embarkation, voyage, and landing was commemorated in a song that may still be heard in many a Butler County home. I have frequently listened to it in childhood. It is not, it is true, after Tom Moore's best style; but truth is not dependent upon graceful and classic diction. The bard, as he informs us in the first stanza of his song, was Jerry Monaghan, who "spent many a frolicksome day on the banks of Lough Erne," in the south-eastern part of county Donegal. The embarkation is thus narrated:

> "On the fourth of June, in the afternoon,
> We sailed from Londonderry;
> Early next day we put to sea
> To cross the tedious ferry ;
> We hoisted sail with a pleasant gale
> As Phœbus was arising,
> Bound for New York, in America,
> In the grand brig Eliza."

The only incident worthy of note that occurred during the voyage furnished material for the following stanza. Knight was the captain of the brig Eliza :

> "A British fleet we chanced to meet
> On the twenty-fourth of August ;
> A man-of-war came bearing down
> With crowded sails upon us.
> Brave Knight, being true to all his crew,
> Advanced unto the captain,
> And when he made a bow to him,
> Showed America's protection."

But instead of landing at New York the brig entered Delaware Bay, and proceeded to New Castle, "next port to Philadelphia," where the emigrants disembarked, being "both blithe and hearty"—an event which the bard, faithful to his trust, has handed down to posterity in these lines :

> "September ninth we took our leave
> Of captain, mate, and sailors,
> Likewise of the Eliza brave,
> For no less can we name her ;
> We gave three cheers for old Ireland,
> It being our former quarter,
> And then, like wandering sheep, we strayed,
> And parted from each other."

This was in the year 1792. But the bard did not accompany that part of the colony which came to the west. He preferred to remain in New Jersey, where he died many years after.* But his mantle fell, as will be seen hereafter, upon the shoulders of a worthy successor.

It was not the intention of the entire colony to make their home in the West; but such as were resolved upon doing so came without much delay, by Braddock's route,

---

* At the conclusion of a lecture on the Introduction of Catholicity into Western Pennsylvania, which I delivered in Pittsburg in the spring of 1878, and in which I had occasion to refer to the song given in the text, as I was leaving the hall an elderly lady stopped me to inform me that Jerry Monaghan, then an old man, had been a frequent visitor at her father's house in New Jersey when she was a little girl. Thereupon she began to repeat the song.

to Indian Creek in Fayette County. But the presence of hostile Indians deterred them from going further, and they settled there to bide their time. By the terms of the treaty signed at Fort M'Intosh—on the site of the present town of Beaver—January 21st, 1785, the Indians relinquished their claim to the soil of Pennsylvania. But notwithstanding this they continued to commit depredations on the pioneers, until, in the battle of Maumee, Ohio, fought in August, 1794, General Wayne broke their power forever. They were then only too glad to come to terms with a man whom they had learned from experience to recognize in fact as well as in name as "Mad Anthony Wayne." The news of their defeat coming to the ears of the colony at Indian Creek, they set out to take possession of the territory which they had long had in their mind's eye. A few families remained two years longer; but the greater part, leaving Braddock's route, came by the settlement at Sportsman's Hall, and crossed the Allegheny River at the spot where Freeport now stands. Passing up Buffalo Creek, which empties into the river at that point, they soon reached the end of their journey in 1796, and settled down in the wilderness. The settlement extended north-west eight or ten miles from the spot where Sugar Creek church now stands. But as new accessions were constantly arriving, it gradually spread in every direction except to the east. These pioneers were very primitive in their manners, as countless anecdotes related of them incontestably prove. They delighted in polemics, and if the priest found it necessary to refute some arguments of a minister of the sects, he need not be surprised to hear some elderly member of his flock enthusiastically exclaim, "Well said, your reverence," or "Let him have it; he deserves it, your reverence," or some such token of approval. If he denounced intemperance or some other disorder in his flock, a patriarchal figure might be seen rising to point a significant finger at some one, with, "That's for you; you were drunk last week. Listen to what his reverence is saying;" or more briefly, "Take that, —— ——; that's for you." Others contented themselves with a nod of approval or a glance at the offender. Another stalwart man would report to the priest at his periodical visits how many persons he had beaten for mocking at the doctrines and practices of the Church.

But the colony was possessed of a bard, as has been said, who had the happy faculty of celebrating every memorable event in verse. If the schoolmaster vanquished some unfledged preacher—for the schoolmasters of that day were like those of whom Goldsmith has written—it was soon heard sung on every side. If the neighbors met at a "frolic" or "raising," and some, after having indulged too freely in ardent spirits, broke the peace and perhaps some one's head along with it, a song commemorating the event immediately sprung from the bard's fertile brain. But with simplicity of manners they had a purity of morals and firmness of faith which are the glory of the Irish people in whatever part of the world they are found; and an insult offered to religion by a sectarian, or a scandal brought upon it by one of their own communion, was the only unpardonable sin in their decalogue.

Turning to the facilities which these early settlers possessed of hearing Mass and receiving the sacraments and consolations of religion, we can readily understand how very limited they must necessarily have been. The first priest to cross the Allegheny River and visit the settlement was Father Lanigan, in 1801. But he paid it only one visit. The next visit was that of Rev. P. Heilbron, which is thus noted by Father Stillenger: "In 1803 Father Heilbron made his first visit beyond the Allegheny River. At Slippery Rock he baptized thirteen in one day, and at Buffalo Creek thirty-eight." It may be remarked that what is now called the Sugar Creek church was long known as "the Buffalo Creek mission;" and in fact it is much nearer to the latter than it is to the former stream. With the next visit a new era dawned for the settlement; the germ of separate congregations began to spring up, and the Church commenced to show the first elements of organization.

ARMSTRONG COUNTY.

Armstrong County derived its name from Gen. John Armstrong, who commanded the expedition against the Indians at Kittanning in the summer of 1756. It was formed by an act of Assembly of March 12th, 1800, and it contains at present—for Clarion County was taken from it—an area of 639 square miles. A large portion of the population is of German descent, having emigrated from the eastern part of the State.

Nearly all the Catholics of this county reside west of the Allegheny River, and are very generally distributed over it, with the exception of that portion lying immediately northwest of Kittanning, in which there are none. On the eastern side of the river there are none of any account, except in the vicinity of Kittanning and a few German families in the northern part of the county.

ST. PATRICK'S CHURCH, SUGAR CREEK.

This congregation, which is the parent of all those west of the Allegheny River, dates, as we have seen, from the close of the last century, and its history will for that reason be unusually interesting. The church stands about twelve miles north-west of Kittanning, in a country place, and is about half a mile east of the Butler County line.

In the year 1805, or according to another tradition 1806, or as a third will have it 1807, although the first is supported by the strongest arguments, Rev. Laurence Sylvester Phelan (sometimes also called Whelen or Whalen) took up his residence at what became the site of the church. He had been for a short time at Sportsman's Hall, as was remarked in the history of that congregation; but owing to the unfortunate disturbances arising out of the irregularities of the misguided Father Fromm, he could not enjoy the tranquillity necessary for laboring successfully in the cause of religion, and accordingly withdrew. A number of the Catholic settlers followed him. Soon after his arrival at Sugar Creek the heads of families, overjoyed at the thought of having a priest among them, met to consider the best means of securing him a home and a church. Land was to be had in abundance and at a very moderate price at that time, as will appear from the fact that a man sold his settler's right to two hundred acres of ground for a set of old-fashioned plough-irons, that could have been bought at most for five dollars. Another man exchanged his right to four hundred acres for a silk dress for his wife. But money was as scarce as land was plenty, and five dollars was a small fortune. Still the people recognized the truth of the adage that "there is strength in unity," and it was resolved to make an appeal to every one. The district, at least fifteen miles square, was quartered out to four collectors, whose duty it should be to solicit donations. Casper W. Easly took the southern district, near Slate Lick; Jas. Sheridan the south-western, or Clearfield Township; Neil Sweeny, Butler and its surroundings; and Connell Rodgers the north and north-western, or Donegal Township. Soon money sufficient to buy a farm and commence the building of a house and church was collected, the highest subscription being, as we are told, two dollars. The present farm, consisting of almost two hundred acres, was bought and a little log-cabin was built for the priest. The church was then undertaken in the following novel way: Each of the four men above named was required to come on a certain day, and to bring with him as many men as would be required to fell trees and hew logs enough for one side or end of the proposed building. The more important work of making the shingles for the roofs and procuring and driving the nails was entrusted to Patrick M'Elroy. The building was ready for the roof in the fall of 1805 or '6, or '7, according to the dates given above for the arrival of Father Phelan, for this was in the autumn after his coming; but owing to the difficulty experienced in procuring the nails, it was not roofed until the following spring. It was then placed under the invocation of the Apostle of Ireland. The building, which is yet standing, is of hewn logs and is about 22 by 35 feet, with a gallery, and the altar standing against the end wall. There are three little square windows in each side, and one in each end of the gallery.

The interior is without ceiling, open to the roof, and without pews. A little porch was afterwards built in front. It is the oldest church now standing in the two dioceses and in the entire western part of the State. Hither came people from ten miles around, and frequently from a greater distance; and the father of the writer often crossed the river from his home below Kittanning, in years gone by, and walked fasting to the church of a Sunday morning, a distance of not less than twelve miles, and many others did the same. The devotion and piety of the people was truly edifying, and showed how much they appreciated the ministrations of religion. The stations of the cross, which I have frequently seen, consisted of so many crosses marked on the walls with a piece of charred wood taken from the fire. Before these the good people would commemorate the Passion of our Redeemer in a manner that showed how deeply the sense of their indebtedness was engraven on their minds. Each one as he reached the church on a Good Friday would remove the shoes from his feet, and, leaving them in the little vestibule, enter the church and perform the stations barefoot.

But so numerous were the stations which the priest was obliged to visit, and so far distant from each other and from the church, that Mass was not offered up in it more frequently than once in a month or once in two months; for at that time, and for many years after it, there was but one priest in the entire district west of the Allegheny River from Erie to Beaver. After remaining with the congregation until 1810, Father Phelan withdrew, and his name is no longer met with in the history of this part of the country. The congregation was then visited at distant intervals until 1820 by Fathers O'Brien and M'Guire, from Pittsburg, and by Father M'Girr, from Sportsman's Hall. The following year Rev. Charles Ferry took up his residence at the church, and visited and ministered to the surrounding district, which included a scope of perhaps thirty miles square and was estimated to contain at that time about one hundred and forty families. A few scattered families resided at a still greater distance. Father Ferry remained until 1826, when he was succeeded by Rev. Patrick O'Neil, who resided at Freeport and built the first church there, as will be stated further on. In 1831 he published a pamphlet of 50 pages, entitled "A Sermon on the Mystery of the Real Presence, Preached in the Court House in the Borough of Butler, by Rev. P. O'Neil, Roman Catholic Missionary in Armstrong, Butler, and the Adjacent Counties, etc. With an Analysis of a Sermon said to be Preached against Transubstantiation in the Associate Reformed Church, in the Borough of Butler, by the Rev. Isaac Niblock, A.M." The sermon is a lucid and powerful exposition of the Catholic doctrine of this adorable mystery; the Analysis is an overwhelming refutation of the sophisms, misrepresentations, and calumnies of a man whose conscience was as callous as his language was illogical and ungentlemanly. So caustic were some parts of the Analysis that, at the request of Bishop Kenrick, the author suppressed more than one fourth of the original manuscript. Father O'Neil withdrew from the congregation very early in the year 1834, and for many years after served on the mission in the west. He paid a visit to the field of his early labors in the summer of 1878, and was for a little time the guest of the writer, to whom he communicated valuable information regarding this portion of our history. He had made an arrangement with an eastern publishing house for the issuing of a new edition of his pamphlet, and the writer furnished him with the only complete copy of the work that is known to be extant. On returning to the west Father O'Neil went to the Mercy Hospital in Chicago, in which he had for some time been chaplain. He continued to exercise the duties of that office until, worn out with toil and full of days, he expired there on the 15th of June, 1879, in the 84th year of his age and the 58th of his ministry.

REV. PATRICK O'NEIL was born in the northern part of Ireland, most probably in the county Armagh, in 1797. Having pursued his studies for a time in his native land, he was sent to the foreign-mission college of the Society of Picpus, at Paris, by Very Rev. Henry Conwell, then Vicar-General of the Archdiocese of Armagh, in 1817. Upon the appointment of Dr. Conwell Bishop of Philadelphia, in 1820, Mr. O'Neil offered his services to him, which were accepted, and he was ordained at Paris in 1821, and soon after set out for the New

World. He came to Western Pennsylvania, as we have seen, in 1826. His subsequent career has already been briefly referred to.

Upon Father O'Neil's retiring, the mission was for a few months without a pastor, as will appear from the following account of an episcopal visitation, which, from the picture it affords of those early days, is given entire, so far as relates to this church:

"The church of St. Patrick, *Buffalo Creek*, Armstrong County, was next visited. This congregation is also destitute of a pastor. The church is of unwrought wood, and might vie with the apostolic times for unadorned plainness and simplicity. During five days, from Thursday until the following Tuesday (May 15th–20th, 1834), from 5 or 6 o'clock in the morning until 6 or 7 in the evening, the confessional was crowded with penitents. Many of them had come great distances and remained fasting until a late hour in the day. Among those was an old lady who, although in her eightieth year, had walked a mile and a half to be present at the Holy Sacrifice and eat of that Flesh 'which was given for the life of the world.' About 300 received communion, and confirmation was given to 90 persons, some of whom had travelled 50 miles to receive this gift of the Holy Ghost. The scenes exhibited during these five days were similar to those which excited the Saviour's compassion over the neglected people, who were as sheep wandering without a shepherd, and necessarily brought to mind his command to the Apostles, 'to pray to the Lord of the harvest, that he would send laborers into the harvest.'"*

Some time in the summer of the same year, 1834, Rev. Patrick Rafferty was placed in charge of the mission, and, like his predecessor, resided at Freeport. Little of interest marked the passage of time beyond the gradual settlement of the country and increase of the Catholic population. St. Patrick's was visited, as heretofore, on one Sunday in the month. After remaining for about two years Father Rafferty withdrew to the eastern part of the diocese, in 1836, and was

---

* *Philadelphia Catholic Herald.*

for many years pastor of St. Francis' Church, Fairmount, Philadelphia, in which position he died after a short illness, March 16th, 1863, at a very advanced age. He had labored on the mission in different parts of Western Pennsylvania from about the year 1828. During that time he wrote a number of small works, among others "A Short History of the Protestant Reformation; chiefly Selected from Protestant Authors," Pittsburg, 1831, which is a well-written work, and presents the subject as fairly as could be expected in a 16mo work of 240 pages. Another, "The Sling of David," etc., printed in 1832, is a spirited controversial work square 16mo, 128 pages, in answer to a challenge of a Rev. W. C. Brownlee, of "the Middle Dutch Reformed Church of the City of New-York," published in the *Truth-Teller*, February 2d—the year is uncertain, as the copy I have has lost the title-page—couched in the following terms: "I beg leave here, publicly and formally, to challenge Bishop Dubois, Dr. Power, or Dr. Varella, or Dr. Levins, to enter the list in a series of letters, and I shall attack or defend as duty may call me; the controversy to begin as soon as convenient. I offer to take them individually or as a body; hoping that this challenge may be accepted in the same prompt and frank manner in which it is given, and feeling anxious to hear from you or the reverend priests as soon as convenient." "My argument," as Father Rafferty informs the reader in his preface, "is this: either we are to be guided by the Catholic Church that has already lasted eighteen hundred years, or by Dr. Brownlee, a preacher without any mission, ordinary or extraordinary, and without ordination." And he proceeds to develop his argument from the Scripture, the Fathers, and reason in a most convincing though somewhat verbose manner. He also published a work of explanation of the Christian doctrine, and perhaps one or two others.

The life of FATHER RAFFERTY was very eventful. In 1798 he was an active agent of the rebellion in his native land, and for a time acted as a messenger between Emmet and Fitzgerald. He afterwards completed his studies and came to this country, was ordained—at what time is uncertain—and spent the remainder of his life on the Pennsylvania mission. He was a man of great learning and singular prudence, as will appear from the fact that he was counsellor to the Papal Nuncio in the discussion of the Bonaparte-Paterson marriage case at Trenton, N. J.*

After the transfer of Father Rafferty, St. Patrick's was without a pastor until the summer of 1837, but it was visited at distant intervals by a priest from Pittsburg. In August of that year Rev. Joseph Cody was appointed pastor, and took up his residence at the church. From this time forward Mass was celebrated on two Sundays in the month, the third being given to Freeport and the fourth to Butler. But the congregation was becoming too large for the church. A new one was accordingly undertaken in 1840, and, although not entirely finished, was dedicated by Very Rev. M. O'Connor, V.G., July 29th, 1842. This church was brick, and was about 80 feet in length by 45 in width, without a tower, with a gallery and one altar. The interior was simple in style and finish, and the altar stood against the end wall, having a semicircular railing. The sacristy was a separate building against the rear of the church. In 1844 the sphere of Father Cody's labors was narrowed by the appointment of Rev. M. J. Mitchell to Butler, with the additional care of Murrinsville and Mercer (the latter now in the Diocese of Erie). Soon, however, Brady's Bend required an occasional visit from him, and a little later a church was built at Donegal, or North Oakland as it is now called.

In 1847 the field of his labors was still further narrowed by the appointment of Father Mitchell pastor of Freeport and Brady's Bend. From that time Mass was celebrated at St. Patrick's on three Sundays in the month, the other being given to Donegal. The congregation was as large at this time, perhaps, as it was at any time in its history. In the summer of 1854 the dilapidated old log residence was replaced by a brick one, in the building of which the writer of these pages labored. After about the year 1861 Father Cody's sole attention was confined to the parent church, a circumstance rendered necessary by his age and declining health. At

---

* *Philadelphia Catholic Herald.*

length, after having borne the heat and burden of the day for almost thirty years, and having been occasionally assisted by the neighboring priests during the last two or three years, he felt no longer able to minister to his congregation, and Rev. J. O'G. Scanlon was transferred from Kittanning to St. Patrick's at the end of the year 1865. Soon after Father Cody retired to the Mercy Hospital, Pittsburg, where he was affectionately cared for by the Sisters and by his nephew, Very Rev. J. Hickey, V.G., and where he calmly rested from his labors in the sleep of death, August 7th, 1871, in the 70th year of his age.

REV. JOSEPH CODY was a native of county Tipperary, Ireland. Having pursued his studies for some time in his native land, he came to this country and entered the seminary at Philadelphia. He was ordained to the sacred ministry on the feast of Corpus Christi, May 25th, 1837, and immediately came to Pittsburg. From August of the same year, as has been said, he had charge of the Armstrong and Butler county mission; and at the time of his death there were at least ten congregations in the field which he alone had for many years cultivated. His funeral took place from St. Patrick's, and his remains repose in front of the church, the spot which he had selected, reminding those who enter of the debt of gratitude they owe him.

Father Scanlon immediately set about the improvement of the interior of the church. Plans were procured, but before he could carry them into execution he was transferred to another congregation and was succeeded by Rev. James P. Tahany in October, 1866. He collected means and made the improvements contemplated by his predecessor. Side sacristies were erected, thus making a recess for the main altar; side-altars and a new high altar were provided, the interior was frescoed, the windows filled with stained glass, and altogether the church assumed the appearance of a new building, and one of the most beautiful in the diocese.

Father Tahany was succeeded November, 1871, by Rev. S. P. Herman. But soon after his appointment the congregation sustained a heavy loss in the total destruction of the church by fire on the night of January 1st, 1872, leaving a small debt and no insurance. The burning of the church was the work of an incendiary—an act of revenge. The congregation now retired to the old church, which from the erection of the other had been unoccupied, or had served the purpose of a school for one or two summers, a granary, etc. Rev. Thomas Fitzgerald now became pastor of the congregation. But it had fallen somewhat from its former numerical strength and prosperity. He fitted up the old church as well as he could, and occupied it while he remained. Having ministered to the congregation for about a year, he was transferred to Somerset County, and was succeeded by Rev. P. M. Doyle. During this time the people continued to occupy the old church, not thinking themselves equal to the task of erecting a new one, and the more so as many of the young men had withdrawn to the oil country, thus weakening the congregation. But the health of Father Doyle, which had been seriously impaired within the past few years, became so feeble that he was no longer able to continue in charge of the congregation, and he retired to a hospital in Washington City in the fall of 1875, where he remained for a time. With his health somewhat improved he set out for the home of one of his brothers residing in Illinois, with a view of further recruiting before resuming his sacred functions. But while on his way he was suddenly taken sick at the town of Vandalia, Ill., and died almost immediately after, July 21st, 1876, in the 47th year of his age and the 22d of his ministry.

REV. PETER M. DOYLE was born in the State of Vermont, but his father moved to Armstrong County in this State during the childhood of his son. He entered St. Michael's Seminary at a proper age and pursued his studies to their completion, when he was raised to the sacred dignity of the priesthood. He served on the mission at Huntingdon till the year 1861, when he came to Clearfield, Butler County, where he remained until transferred to St. Patrick's, seven years later. His remains were brought to Freeport, the home of his father, where they were laid to rest.

Father Doyle was succeeded by Rev. Patrick Quilter, the present pastor. His first care was to replace the church that had been destroyed by fire, and so successful was he that the foundation was ready for the laying of the corner-stone in the summer of 1876. The ceremony was performed by the Bishop on the 5th of August. The church was finished the following summer, and was dedicated by Very Rev. R. Phelan, Administrator of Allegheny, July 3d. Like the former, it is brick, and is modelled after the Gothic style of architecture. It is 90 feet in length by 45 in width, and has a steeple in the centre in front. Unlike the old, however, it has a basement, one half of which is beneath the surface. The interior is furnished with three altars, and is finished in a chaste and beautiful manner.

The discovery of oil in the vicinity improved the condition of the congregation for a time. But the congregation is not large, perhaps not so large as it was twenty years ago, and will not number more than one hundred families. A portion was cut off in the formation of the new parish at Millerstown, a church which is under the jurisdiction of the pastor of St. Patrick's. Although efforts were made at different times to open a Catholic school, they have never been crowned with permanent success, nor is it at all probable that a school will be permanently established in the future, owing to the distance at which many of the people live from the church. The farm is still attached to the church, and is cultivated or leased under the direction of the pastor. No marked change is likely to take place in the parish for many years to come.

CHURCH OF ST. MARY OF THE NATIVITY, FREEPORT.

Freeport is situated on the west bank of the Allegheny River, twenty-eight miles above Pittsburg and in the extreme southern corner of Armstrong County. It was laid out by David Todd about the year 1800, although a few settlers had occupied the ground previous to that time. But it owes whatever of importance it has to the Pennsylvania Canal, which, following the Kiskiminetas River to its mouth a mile above the town, crossed the Allegheny and passed through it. In 1870 the population was 1640, a fraction less than it had been ten years before. Here it was that the famous Donegal colony crossed the river in 1796, and, while the greater part continued their journey, a few stragglers settled in the country along Buffalo Creek, which empties into the river immediately below the town. It is not known whether Father Lanigan, in his visit to Donegal in 1801, or Father Heilbron, in his of two years later, came to Freeport. It is probable, however, that they did, for the missionaries of those days usually visited all the localities in which they knew that even three or four families resided. Certain it is that Mass was celebrated in different places in the southern part of the county by the pastor of Sugar Creek, from the arrival of Rev. Charles Ferry, in 1821. The Holy Sacrifice was not offered up in the town before the year 1826. At that time Rev. Terence M'Girr celebrated Mass in the lower part of the town, in the house of a Catholic family by the name of Boland, which furnishes an illustration of the trials of those days. No sooner had the priest arrived than messengers were sent to all the Catholics of the surrounding country. The house in which Mass was to be offered up was in course of erection and was unfinished. A number of men laid a temporary floor and threw some boards over the joists of the second story, under which the altar was to stand, while the priest heard confession under a tree at a short distance. When all were heard, Mass was commenced—but not till then, for many had come fasting, perhaps eight or ten miles, and could ill afford to return disappointed.

Rev. Patrick O'Neil, who arrived in 1826, was the first resident pastor. The next year the building of the canal was begun, and, the number of Catholics increasing, he determined to build a church. He collected means from the farmers and laborers, and purchased a lot from Con. Rogers for $200. The contract for the church was let to a Protestant builder in 1827, who agreed to erect it for $600. While engaged on the work he was frequently reminded that he was using brick of an inferior quality, but his invariable reply was, "They are good enough for the Catholics." But when the work was finished they refused to pay him, and upon arbitrators being appointed by mutual consent, the work was condemned, and he was required to remove the building and leave the lot as he had found it. Father O'Neil left him the alternative of taking $200 for the building such as it was, a proposition which he reluctantly accepted; and this was the actual cost of the church. But it was soon necessary to put iron rods through it at the spring of the roof to keep it from falling apart. After the completion of the church Mass was usually celebrated on one Sunday in the month by the pastor of St. Patrick's, Sugar Creek, until 1847. It is not known at what precise time the church was finished, but it was not dedicated until the visit of Bishop Kenrick—which was the first visit of a Bishop—September 8th, 1831, when he dedicated it under the invocation of St. Mary of the Nativity. The church was plain and simple in style and finish, was 34 feet in length by 28 in width, and had a gallery. Pews were not put into it until a few years later. It was in this church that the writer was baptized. Bishop Kenrick again visited Freeport May 11th, 1834, between the date of the departure of Father O'Neil and that of the arrival of Rev. Patrick Rafferty. From a report of this event in the *Catholic Herald* the following is taken: "As there has been no pastor here for some months, the visitation occupied three days, during which time more than one hundred persons approached the sacraments of Penance and the Eucharist, and fourteen were confirmed. The lively faith and tender piety of this congregation is calculated to give partial consolation for their spiritual destitution." Soon after that time Father Rafferty took charge of the mission which embraced Freeport, and, like his predecessor, resided in that town. The congregation gradually increased with the growth of the town and the settlement of the surrounding country. After about three years— August, 1837—Father Rafferty gave place to Rev. Joseph Cody, who took up his residence at St. Patrick's, Sugar Creek.

At length we reach the year 1847. In the early part of this summer Freeport and Brady's Bend were detached from the parent church and formed into a separate mission in charge of Rev. M. J. Mitchell, who lived part of the time in each place, and gave Mass to each every alternate Sunday. In the latter part of the same summer Bishop O'Connor paid his first visit to St. Mary's, and states in his Notes that the congregation then numbered four hundred souls.

Soon after his arrival Father Mitchell undertook the erection of a new church to replace the old one that was now becoming too small. Lots were purchased beside it, and work was commenced without the ceremony of a corner-stone laying, a circumstance not unusual in those early days. About the time of the completion of the new edifice, Father Mitchell was succeeded by Rev. John Larkin. The dedication ceremony was performed by the Bishop December 28th, 1851. The church is brick, is 85 feet in length by 45 feet in width, and has a steeple in the centre in front. The interior is furnished with two altars, one of which was erected some years later. The building is modelled after the Gothic style of architecture, and is superior to almost all the churches erected at that time.

The congregation was considerably increased at this time by the building of the Soda Works (now called Natrona), five miles below; and a few years later it was still further augmented by the building of two or three cannel-coal oil-works on the opposite side of the river from the town. But the farming portion has undergone little change for many years. From the completion of the church until 1858 the changes of pastors were frequent. But in that year Rev. R. Phelan was appointed, and remained ten years. He improved the interior of the church, purchased a few acres of ground for a cemetery, and also bought a pastoral residence. It was during this time that the congregation was at the zenith of its prosperity and numerical strength. But upon the promotion of Very Rev. T. Mullen, of St. Peter's Church, Allegheny, to the See of Erie (July, 1868), Father Phelan was appointed his successor, and Rev. J. Hackett filled the vacancy at Freeport. Prior to this the congregation had declined considerably, owing to the suspension of the oil-works. During Father Hackett's pastorate a church was built at Natrona for the Catholics of that place, as we shall presently see. On November 10th, 1869, he gave place to Rev. Jas. Holland. A school was now opened in a rented room. Unsuccessful attempts had been made to found one many years before, but this one promised to be more permanent. The pastor added considerably to the embellishment of the church both in the interior and exterior, and left it upon his transfer to Pittsburg, January 16th, 1873, one of the most beautiful of the diocese. He was succeeded by the writer, who remained but six months, during which he took measures towards the erection of a school-house. Rev. W. A. Nolan now filled the vacancy, and while pastor built a substantial brick schoolhouse, two stories high and about 25 by 50 feet, on the lot beside the church. To it he transferred the school a year after his arrival. But the depression of the times consequent on the panic of 1873 soon rendered it necessary to discontinue it, and it has not since been resumed. Father Nolan was succeeded June 1st, 1876, by Rev. G. S. Grace, and he at the end of August by Rev. Fred. Eberth and C. M'Dermot; for the difficulty of going from Natrona to Freeport on the days on which Mass was celebrated in both places—the Western Pennsylvania Railroad refusing the use of the hand-car from that time—rendered it no longer possible for one priest to minister to both congregations. Since that time there have been two priests, but it is probable that ere long Natrona will be an independent congregation with a resident pastor. Father Eberth was succeeded by Rev. Jas. Canivan, September, 1877, and he by the present pastor, Rev. P. M. Garvey, at the end of April, 1879. The congregation of St. Mary's has, if anything, been declining in numbers and importance in the last few years, and will not at present exceed eighty families. The future prospects are not encouraging for its growth and prosperity, although it is probable that it will maintain its present position.

Mass is occasionally celebrated at Leechburg, five miles up the Kiskiminetas River, for a few families residing there.

ST. JOSEPH'S CHURCH, NATRONA, ALLEGHENY COUNTY.

The number of Catholics in the north-eastern part of Allegheny County is small. After leaving Sharpsburg few are to be met except a small number of farmers who hear Mass in that town, a dozen families at Hoboken, five miles further up the river, and the congregation we are now about to notice.

There were none of the older Catholic settlements between Pittsburg and Freeport.

About the year 1852 the Pennsylvania Salt Manufacturing Company built extensive works for the manufacture of salt and other alkalies at a point on the west bank of the river twenty-three miles above Pittsburg and five below Freeport. Soon a flourishing village sprung up around the works, which was at first called East Tarentum, and later Natrona, but which is generally known as "The Soda Works." The greater part of the population is Catholic, of whom there are at present perhaps seventy-five families, twenty of whom are German and almost the same number Poles. They have always been, and are yet, attended from Freeport. Mass had never been offered for them in the village until after the appointment of Father Phelan pastor of Freeport, in the autumn of 1858. Seeing that it was difficult for some of them, and impossible for others, to hear Mass regularly, he soon began to visit them on a Sunday and offer an early Mass either in one of their houses or in one of the school-rooms. These visits, at first irregular, soon became of monthly occurrence, and later still more frequent. At length the congregation had so far increased that it became expedient to build a church for their better accommodation, and early in 1868 Father Phelan obtained the donation of a lot from the proprietors of the works for that purpose. But before undertaking the church he was transferred to St. Peter's, Allegheny, and was succeeded, in July of that year by Rev. J. Hackett. In the early part of the following summer he built the church, which was dedicated by the Bishop August 22d, under the invocation of St. Joseph. It is a neat frame structure, built with little expense, and without pretensions to architectural style, and is 50 feet in length by 30 in width, and has one altar.

From that time the Holy Sacrifice was offered up on two Sundays in the month by the pastor of Freeport, who went from one church to the other between the Masses. The congregation was gradually increasing. To increase the accommodations Father Nolan built a gallery in the summer of 1874, and in the following summer made an addition to the rear of the church for the altar and sacristy. But the congregation keeps pace, and the church is a third time inadequate to its accommodation. A Catholic school was at one time attempted, but it did not succeed. Since the appointment of an assistant to the pastor of Freeport, in the summer of 1876, Mass is celebrated every Sunday, and the congregation is now in a more flourishing condition than that of which it is a dependency.

ST. PATRICK'S CHURCH, BRADY'S BEND.

The village of Brady's Bend is situated on the west bank of the Allegheny River, at the mouth of Sugar Creek, sixty-eight miles above Pittsburg, and it owes its name to a celebrated Indian scout, Captain Samuel Brady, after whom the bend in the river was called. Its more recent notoriety is due to the blast-furnaces and rolling-mill till recently in operation there. The furnaces, one mile up the creek from its mouth, were built in 1840, and the rolling-mill, at the mouth of the stream, a year later. For many years it was known as the Great Western Iron Works. Catholics, both English and German, began to settle at the works from the date of their erection; and in 1843 Father Cody, of St. Patrick's, Sugar Creek, offered up the first Mass for them. From that date they were occasionally visited by him and by the German priest from Butler.

In 1846 a small frame church was built. But so opposed were the proprietors of the works to Catholicity that they would not permit it to be erected near their premises; and not only so, but when they learned that the Catholics contemplated the purchase of a lot at a considerable distance, they bought it the better to prevent such a desecration of their sacred precincts. It thus happened that the church was built at Queenstown, a village on the hill a mile north of the furnaces. But the proprietors will yet learn, as many others have learned, that the influence of a priest over the class of people usually employed in public works, even in temporal matters, is valuable enough to be purchased at a considerable cost.

Early in the following year Rev. M. J. Mitchell was transferred from Butler, and became pastor of Freeport and Brady's Bend, to each of which he gave alternate Sundays. The presence of a pastor inspired new life into the little flock, and the church was soon inadequate to its accommodation. The pastor built a transverse addition to the rear of the church, making it 74 feet in length by 45 in the transept, and dedicated it, under the invocation of the Apostle of Ireland, November 18th, 1849. At that time the German element was strong in the congregation, and before the erection of the German church a priest was accustomed to visit the place occasionally from Butler. In 1851 Father Mitchell was succeeded by Rev. Eugene Gray, who remained until 1856. As time passed the capacity of the works was increased, and the congregation became gradually larger. After the departure of Father Gray the changes of pastors were frequent until September, 1861, when Rev. Thos. Walsh was appointed. The old church was by this time too small for the congregation, and although the Germans were formed into a separate congregation, a new church was necessary. But a greater change had come over the proprietors of the works than over the congregation. So well had they taken to heart the lessons of experience that they donated a lot of ground near the furnaces as the site of the new building, besides aiding in other ways towards its erection. The corner-stone was laid by the Bishop June 19th, 1864, and the church was dedicated by the same prelate July 29th, 1866. The building, which is modelled after the Gothic style of architecture, is frame, 90 feet in length by 45 in width, and has three altars. The finish is chaste and simple.

Not long after the completion of the church the proprietors of the works also built a commodious frame house, which with a large lot they have since given rent free to the pastor for a residence. The congregation continued to increase until the time of the panic, when it was the largest and most flourishing in the county. In the summer of 1871 the church was neatly frescoed, and a steeple was built in the centre in front, which greatly improved its appearance. But the prostration of business consequent on the panic, which caused the works to cease operation, forced many of the people to seek employment elsewhere. The works have not yet resumed and it is probable they never will, as the machinery, etc., is old and of the old style, and putting it in working order would be equivalent to erecting new works. But the discovery of oil in the immediate vicinity gave a transient stimulus to business. Father Walsh was succeeded by Rev. Peter May, the present pastor, in April, 1876. The congregation has never had a parish school.

ST. MARY'S GERMAN CHURCH, BRADY'S BEND.

German Catholics were, as we have seen, among the first settlers attracted by the new iron-works. But they were not organized into a separate congregation until 1865. In the summer of that year they were occasionally visited by Father Chilian, one of the Benedictines from Butler, who purchased for their use a small Protestant church then offered for sale. It was soon after dedicated by the Bishop under the invocation of the Mother of God. The building is frame and small, and is surmounted by a belfry, and, standing as it does on the side of the hill, has a basement under half its length, which has been used from the beginning for a school. On the 15th of October of the same year it was relinquished by the Benedictines, and passed into the hands of the secular clergy. Rev. J. Zwickert was the first pastor, and after him came Rev. L. Spitzelberger; and in the spring of 1868 Rev. Jos. Deyermeyer. At the end of about two years he was succeeded by Rev. Jos. Buss. In the mean time a frame pastoral residence had been built. The cessation of the works on account of the panic forced many of the laborers to go elsewhere; while the erection of a church on the opposite side of the river at East Brady's Bend, in the Diocese of Erie, drew away another portion. The decimated congregation being no longer able to exist as an independent organization, the pastor was transferred to another mission in the autumn of 1875, and for a time the pastor of the English church offered up the Holy Sacrifice once on Sunday at the German church and once at his own.

But the strength of the congregation returned with the

extension of the oil territory in that direction, and in the fall of 1877 Rev. J. Rittiger was appointed pastor. He was succeeded in the following May by Rev. J. Stillerich, and he in the beginning of 1879 by Rev. Jos. Steger. St. Mary's is not so numerous now as it was before the panic, and, although it may be able to exist as a separate parish, its prospects are not flattering.

KITTANNING.

Kittanning, the county-seat of Armstrong County, is situated on the east bank of the Allegheny River, 45 miles above Pittsburg. It was laid out in 1804, incorporated as a borough in 1821, and had in 1870 a population of 1889. But many years before the town was built it was a place of note. The name is of Indian origin, being properly Kittanyan, which, it is said, signifies "tall corn." When in the middle of last century the French and Indians were at war with the English, a line of fortifications was built along the Susquehanna to protect the frontier. But the Delaware Indians from their village of Kittanyan, where the famous chief Captain Jacobs, and occasionally also the chief Shingis, lived, made numerous and troublesome raids on the frontier settlers, until in the fall of 1756 Lieutenant-Colonel John Armstrong, from whom the county takes its name, who commanded the Susquehanna forts, planned an expedition for the destruction of the village and the liberation of the prisoners held by the Indians. He reached the place on the 8th of September, attacked and burnt the village, which consisted of about thirty houses and a large store of ammunition which the Indians had collected, and killed the dreaded Captain Jacobs. A fortification known by the name of Appleby's Fort was built on the site of the village for the protection of the frontier in 1776.*

"After the destruction of the Indian town, the location remained unimproved by white men until near the close of the last century. The land was in possession of the Armstrong

---

* Annals of the West, and Pennsylvania Archives.

family; and when the establishment of the county was proposed, Dr. Armstrong, of Carlisle, a son of the general, made a donation of the site of the town to the county, on condition of receiving one half the proceeds of the sale of lots.* A plan of the town was soon after prepared, known as "the Armstrong plot."

ST. MARY'S CHURCH.

The first members of what is now the congregation of St. Mary's settled about seven miles south-west of Kittanning, near Slate Lick, at the beginning of this century. The pioneers were Andrew and Casper Easly and William Shields, from the Westmoreland County settlement. The first member on the eastern side of the river was Matthew Lambing, grandfather of the writer, who came from Adams County, Pa., in the fall of 1823 and settled soon after at Manorville, two miles below Kittanning. But the scattered few were obliged to travel to St. Patrick's, Sugar Creek, or later to Freeport, to hear Mass and comply with their other religious duties, or await the stations that were held at very distant intervals in the different settlements. I have heard my father say that he walked fasting to Freeport, a distance of more than fourteen miles, on three successive Sundays before he had an opportunity of confessing and receiving holy communion. At length a few families settled in Kittanning and in its immediate vicinity, and it was deemed expedient to have the Holy Sacrifice offered up in the town. The first time this took place was most probably in the summer of 1848, and the officiating priest was either Father Cody, of St. Patrick's, or Father Mitchell, of Freeport. Both came at times, the former, however, but seldom. In those early days Col. W. Sirwell, though not a Catholic, was, as he still is, the steadfast friend of the priest; and it was generally in a room of his house that Mass was celebrated. About the year 1850 a small rolling-mill was built in the town, which attracted a number of Catholic laborers. Mass was then celebrated at

---

* Day's Historical Collections, p. 97.

shorter intervals in the court-house or academy by the pastor of Freeport.

At length, in the summer of 1853, the little congregation had increased so much that a church became necessary for its accommodation. Lot No. 1 of "the Armstrong plot," situated on the bank of the river at the northern end of the town, was purchased by Rev. E. Gray, and a church was built upon it. About the same time the grading of the Allegheny Valley Railroad from Pittsburg to Kittanning increased the congregation considerably for the time being. But the church, although occupied, remained unfinished for about ten years, without being plastered and with only temporary pews and altar. The visits of a priest were very irregular, and seldom oftener than once in two months, with frequent disappointments. It was visited in this manner by the priest from Freeport, Sugar Creek, Butler, Brady's Bend, or even by a priest of the Diocese of Erie from Clarion County. It was indeed "nobody's child." But from the appointment of Father Phelan to Freeport in the fall of 1858, Mass was celebrated regularly on one Sunday in the month.

Finally, in February, 1863, Rev. J. O'G. Scanlon was appointed the first resident pastor. But the church was yet unfinished, and the steeple with which it had been provided had been blown off to the roof in the spring of 1858. Soon after his arrival Father Scanlon set about the completion of the interior, a work in which Catholics and Protestants vied with each other in the assistance they rendered him. The work was completed and the church reopened, although not then dedicated, February 7th, 1864. Not satisfied with this, he had it neatly frescoed in the summer of the same year, and dedicated by the Bishop on the 23d of October. While the improvements of the church were going on Mass was offered up in the court-house.

In December, 1865, Father Scanlon was succeeded by Rev. J. A. O'Rourke. But the rolling-mill was burnt down a little later, and many families moved away. The railroad was now extended up the river, and as the parish with its missions embraced twenty miles of the line, it proved to be a very timely assistance to the congregation in its reduced circumstances. In the spring of 1870 Mr. John Gilpin, a Protestant gentlemen of the town, presented the church with a bell weighing twelve hundred pounds, and Father O'Rourke immediately erected the tower for its reception. It was blessed by Very Rev. J. Hickey, V.G., in the absence of the Bishop, April 3d. The church was now finished. It is a brick edifice 65 feet in length by 43 in width, having the tower in the centre in front. There is a high and one side altar, the space on the other side being occupied by the confessional. Father O'Rourke gave place to the writer of these pages on the 22d of the same April. Up to this date the pastor had lodged in a hotel or with a private family, but now a house was rented and he was more independent. Having remained until January 17th, 1873, and having made considerable improvement in the church and around it, he was succeeded by Rev. E. J. Dignam. A few acres of ground were now purchased near the town for a cemetery.

The difficulty experienced by one priest in attending the numerous missions, especially after the building of the Holy Guardian Angels' Church, next to be noticed, induced the Bishop to appoint an assistant to the pastor in the summer of 1876. But at the end of a year and a half the parish was again left to the care of one priest. The congregation has declined in the past few years, and will not exceed sixty families in number, which are, as they always have been, English and German mixed. But new and larger iron-works are now being built, and the prospects of future increase are flattering. The pastor has been obliged to give up his house and return to boarding with a private family.

A number of missions were always attached to Kittanning, and were attended monthly on week-days. One of these, eight miles above the town at the site of the old Ore Hill Furnace, consisted of about half a dozen families of railroad men. Another, two miles farther up at the mouth of Mahoning Creek, was of the same kind. Ten miles east from the latter place, at Colwell's Furnace, was another, consisting of about twenty-five families; but in the summer of 1878 the furnace blew out with the intention of never again being put into blast, and all the families went elsewhere. Finally, fifteen miles above Kittanning and two miles east from the river is a settlement, principally German, consisting of about twenty families, where—in the house of John Harman—Mass has been celebrated for thirty years. This mission has lately been attached to the German church at Brady's Bend. The Catholics have left all the other missions. There are few Catholics in the county east of the river, and west of it to the north-west of Kittanning there are but two or three families in a circuit of seven miles. Father Dignam was succeeded by the present pastor, Rev. Thos. Howley, December, 1878.

HOLY GUARDIAN ANGELS' CHURCH, EASLY'S SETTLEMENT.

For sixty years the Holy Sacrifice had been offered up at distant and irregular intervals, now in the house of one farmer, now in that of another in the Easly settlement, about eight miles south-west of Kittanning; and a lot of ground consisting of about an acre had also been set apart for half a century as the site of a church to be built when times and circumstances should favor its erection. The Catholics of the vicinity belonged at first to the congregation of St. Patrick's Church, Sugar Creek, then to Freeport, and after the erection of the church at Kittanning they attached themselves with few exceptions to it. At length the time seemed to have arrived for the building of the church; and the writer, who was at that time pastor of the Kittanning congregation, undertook it in the summer of 1872. The corner-stone was laid by the Bishop June 16th, and in the summer and autumn the building was put up, but not finished. In this condition it remained, and Mass was offered in it upon a temporary altar once or twice in the month on Sunday by the pastor of Kittanning, who drove from one church to the other between the Masses until the summer of 1878, when it was finished. It was dedicated by the Bishop, under the invocation of the Holy Guardian Angels, on their feast, October 2d of the same year. The church is brick, and is 57 feet in length by 32 in width, is modelled after the Gothic style of architecture, and is without a steeple. The interior is furnished with three altars. The site upon which it is built was donated by Mr. Casper

Easly. Mass continues to be celebrated as before. The congregation consists of about twenty families, and it will not undergo any perceptible change for many years to come.

PARKER CITY.

The last church that we have to notice in this county is situated in the extreme northern part of it. Parker City is on the west bank of the Allegheny River, 82 miles above Pittsburg. It was formerly a place of no importance, and was known only to boatmen as Parker's Landing. The little village on the hill at the southern part, where the church now stands, was called Laurenceburg. Oil was first discovered here in 1865, but it was not until July, 1869, that it was found in such quantities as to create an excitement, and no one who has not seen it can form an idea of what an oil excitement is. Hundreds of oil dealers and producers from the more northern fields hastened thither, while large numbers of others in search of work or speculation, or something worse, crowded the throng, and in a few weeks it presented a scene that beggars description. Inasmuch as it has since been the representative town of the lower oil region, a few remarks on it may be interesting to the reader. On the eastern side of the river, which is traversed by the Allegheny Valley Railroad, there is no bottom-land on which to build; but a station-house was erected and ferries started, and later a bridge spanned the river and a mushroom town sprung up on the narrow bottom and on the hill on the west. Soon it contained a population of from 2000 to 3000, and was chartered as Parker City in the fall of 1873. It contained hotels, stores, banks, machine-shops, theatres—all but churches. Here lumber, engines, pipe, tools, and all the paraphernalia of the oil business were unloaded from the cars in incredible quantities and of every conceivable variety, and hauled to the surrounding country. Derricks, or "rigs" as they are commonly called, were put up by the hundred, and pipe-lines traversed the country in every direction. From 30,000 to 40,000 barrels of oil, and frequently a great deal more, changed hands daily; property was bought, leased, and sold, and all was done peculiar to the oil business. But such a population is seldom brought together. Many were without the controlling influence of religion or public opinion, or any other restraint. Business men, crazed with speculation, forgot the principles of honesty, and not unfrequently those also of prudence; the common crowd forgot those of virtue, and hundreds plunged into the deepest ocean of immorality. To say all in one word, there was presented the bustle and excitement of Wall Street, the hurry and confusion of Broadway, and the morality of Pentapolis. Catholics who were exemplary at home found it difficult to withstand the current that set in against them; those who were remiss at home were little short of infidels here; and many of the girls who were attracted to the hotels and other places by ready employment and high wages were soon swallowed up in a vortex of hopeless depravity. So fetid was the immorality of the atmosphere that it might be felt like the Egyptian darkness of old. Such was Parker as I have seen it in the early days of its history as an oil town, and such in a greater or less degree are all the towns in the oil country while the oil excitement remains at its height among them. But after a few years business became more settled, and the unbridled throng began to disperse and go to other places. In the early part of 1874 the Parker and Karns City Railroad began to carry much of the freight directly to the "front," and the excitement and activity of Parker City was diminished.

CHURCH OF THE IMMACULATE CONCEPTION.

The ramifications of the Donegal colony appear to have extended as far as Laurenceburg, for we read in the *United States Catholic Miscellany* of Bishop Kenrick visiting the place September 6th, 1831, and confirming eighty-three persons. But these were doubtless collected from the surrounding country for a considerable distance. Be that as it may, we hear nothing more of the place until the discovery of oil infused a new life into it. Soon after that time it was visited by Rev. Joseph Haney, of Murrinsville, who offered up the Holy Sacrifice in a private house in 1869. He continued to do so until July of the following year, when lots were purchased on the hill at the southern part of the city and a church was commenced. It was occupied in October, although not finished until the middle of the next summer, and even then much remained to be done, but it was left for the present. It was then a frame building about 45 feet in length by 30 in width, but without pretension to architectural style. In March, 1871, Rev. J. Stillerich was appointed first resident pastor, and he remained until November of the same year, when he was succeeded by Rev. Jas. P. Tahany. To his energy and zeal the Church in Parker as well as elsewhere owes much of its temporal development. He built a neat frame pastoral residence beside the church, and later, when the congregation had increased, he enlarged the church by the addition of 18 feet to the front, with a belfry and certain decorations, and 24 feet to the rear in the form of a transept. The interior was also finished and the church was dedicated by the Bishop, under the title of the Immaculate Conception, November 24th, 1874. On the same day, as we shall see, the church at Petrolia, erected by the same laborious priest, was dedicated. He also opened a school, but the scattered character of the congregation prevented it from enjoying the patronage upon which its existence depended, and it was discontinued after a few months.

Father Tahany was succeeded in December, 1875, by Rev. Jas. Donnelly. The difficulty of attending the church at Parker and that at Petrolia, which has always been attached to it, rendered it necessary to appoint an assistant to the pastor, and two priests attended the churches until August, 1879. Father Donnelly gave place in October, 1877, to Rev. P. M. Garvey, and he in August, 1879, to the present pastor, Rev. F. X. M'Carthy. The congregation is now in a prosperous condition and will number perhaps a hundred families, and although oil towns have no stability as a rule, it is probable this will to some extent form an exception at least for a few years. But no considerable growth of the congregation is to be expected.

CHAPTER XXV.

BUTLER COUNTY.

The Indians and Moravians—Location of the Catholic inhabitants—St. Peter's German Church, Butler—St. Paul's Church—St. Bridget's Chapel, M'Neil's Settlement—St. Wendelin's Chapel—St. Mary's German Church, Summit—St. Joseph's Church, North Oakland—St. Joseph's German Church—St. John's Church, Clearfield—Church of the Mother of Sorrows, Millerstown—St. Alphonsus' Church, Murrinsville—Death and sketch of Rev. Joseph Haney—Chapel at Fairview—St. James' Church, Petrolia.

FROM the following extract, which is given for what it is worth, it would appear that after the withdrawal of the French soldiers and their chaplains from the western part of the State, a few Indians who had been converted to Catholicity roamed through the forests, many, if not all of them, to lose their faith, as not a few of the pioneer whites afterwards did. "From a map attached to Loskiel's history of the Moravian missions, we learn that there existed about the year 1770 an Indian village called Kaskaskunk, some eight or ten miles north-west of Butler. It appears from Loskiel that a chief of the Delawares, Pakanke, dwelt here, and a warrior and speaker of some distinction called Glikkikan. The latter had heard of the arrival of the Moravian missionary Zeisberger and his brethren among the Senecas, at Lauanakanuck, on the Allegheny above Venango, and as he had formerly been initiated in the Catholic doctrines by the priests in Canada, and had been a teacher among his own people, he determined to go and refute and resist the newly ingrafted heresy of the Moravians."* The account goes on to say that he embraced the doctrines of the sect he had come to oppose.

The English-speaking portion of the Catholics of this

---

* Day's Historical Collections, p. 172.

county are for the most part descendants of the original Donegal colony, and are principally confined to the eastern and north-eastern sections, where they named Donegal township in honor of the home they had forsaken in their native isle. The remaining portions of the county contain but a few scattered families, if we except Butler town and its immediate vicinity, in which the German element greatly predominates.

ST. PETER'S GERMAN CHURCH, BUTLER.

Butler, the seat of justice of the county of the same name, was laid out in the year 1800, was incorporated as a borough February 26th, 1817, and had in 1870 a population of 1935. It is connected with Freeport by the Butler branch of the Western Pennsylvania Railroad, and with Parker's Landing by a narrow-gauge road. The first Catholic settlers of the town and vicinity were the gradual extension of the Donegal colony. They usually heard Mass and complied with their religious duties at St. Patrick's Church, Sugar Creek, from which they were distant about twelve miles; or the pastor of that church held stations among them at distant intervals. Weary at length with travelling so great a distance for the consolations of religion, they determined to build a church for themselves. Mrs. Collins, a Catholic widow lady, donated an acre of ground immediately south-east of the town as the site of the church, and the building was begun most probably about the year 1829. There were at that time no more than six or eight families. Immediately after this German immigrants began to arrive in considerable numbers, and settle in the town and around it. Bishop Kenrick visited the place in 1831; but tradition has transmitted no further particulars than that he administered confirmation but did not dedicate the church, which was not yet finished. Soon after Mr. Evan Evans, son-in-law of Mrs. Collins, donated another acre of ground for a cemetery. After the completion of the church it was usually visited on one Sunday of the month by the pastor of Sugar Creek. The Bishop came a second time, on Wednesday, May 21st, 1834, in company with Rev. F. Masquelet and Rev. A. F. Van de Wejer, from Pittsburg, and on the following Sunday dedicated the church under the invocation of the Prince of the Apostles. Sixty were confirmed and one hundred and fifty received Holy Communion. The congregation is said to have trebled its numbers in a short time, owing to the arrival of Germans. Father Masquelet visited the town once in the month for some time; for during a few months there was no pastor at Sugar Creek, and until 1840 a German priest came regularly from Pittsburg to minister to his countrymen. In June of that year came the first resident pastor, Rev. F. Kühr, who remained until the autumn of the year following. He was then succeeded by Rev. H. P. Gallagher, who exercised the pastoral duties until the early part of 1844, when he gave place to Rev. M. J. Mitchell, who also visited Mercer and Murrinsville. A Redemptorist father came monthly from Pittsburg to minister to the Germans. Father Mitchell was succeeded in May, 1847, by Rev. M. Creedon. During this time the congregation had been increasing, and the little church could no longer accommodate the crowds that gathered to it from every side. A new church must be built. But a difficulty arose; for the Germans, who were the majority, wanted a church of their own, while the English, although greatly in the minority, claimed the same privilege. Bishop O'Connor effected a compromise by promising a priest who should be master of both languages. The Germans lived in the town and its immediate neighborhood, while the English lived for the most part at a distance. Lots, by no means the best that could be desired, were purchased in the town, and the corner-stone of the new church was laid by the Bishop August 6th, 1848. Prior to this St. Joseph's Church, Donegal (now North Oakland), had been built, which drew away a considerable number of the English families. The new church was dedicated by the Bishop October 14th, 1849. It is a brick edifice, 116 feet in length by 58 in width, and though of no particular style of architecture contains elements of Byzantine rather than of the Gothic. The massive tower was not built until about 1870, when the Benedictine fathers had charge of the congregation. The church contains three altars, and the whole is finished in a chaste rather than a decorative style. But now a new difficulty arose. In addition to what had been drawn away by the church at Donegal, a new loss of the English element was sustained by the erection of St. John's Church near Coylesville, which was built about the year 1854. The congregation of St. Peter's was now almost exclusively German, and the church has always been regarded as of that nationality.

Soon after the completion of the church a large brick pastoral residence was built by Father Creedon, the last English pastor of the congregation. He was succeeded in 1851 by Rev. J. N. Tamchina, and for some years the pastor of Sugar Creek paid an occasional visit to the English. Father Tamchina gave place to Rev. Jos. Gezowski in September, 1852, and he in 1854 to the Benedictine fathers, who established a priory. A school-house was built about the year 1864, and a school opened by a lay teacher. The congregation was still gradually increasing. The Benedictines withdrew in the autumn of 1872, and the congregation passed once more into the hands of the secular clergy. But after it had been presided over for about a year by Rev. J. M. Bierl, it was confided to the fathers of the Carmelite Order, who still have charge of it. Wishing to improve the school, they built a brick pastoral residence in 1875 and gave the old one, which is large, to a number of Sisters of St. Francis from St. Joseph's Convent, Pittsburg, as a convent. They took charge of the schools in January, 1876. They also conduct an academy for a few boarders from the vicinity.

The congregation is gradually improving, and is the largest and most flourishing in the county, containing more than one hundred and fifty families.

ST. PAUL'S CHURCH, BUTLER.

I have already traced the history of the English Catholics of Butler to the arrival of the Benedictine fathers in 1854. From that time, as before, they continued to frequent the German church, yet never felt at home in it, but looked forward to the time when their numbers should justify them in undertaking a church of their own—a period which from the tardy growth of the town seemed as yet far distant. But patience has a certain reward, and at length it came. It was not, however, their numbers, but rather the wealth of a few, that was to surmount all difficulties. Mr. Peter Duffy, then as now the leading member of the congregation, donated a very eligible lot in the town as the site of the new church. The corner-stone was laid by the Bishop June 7th, 1866, and the church was dedicated by the same prelate February 17th of the following year. It is a brick building 73 feet in length by 38 in width, with a steeple in the centre in front, and two altars. The ceiling rises from the sides toward the centre, and the interior is finished in a chaste rather than expensive manner. The wealth that erected the church also took the place of numbers in supporting the pastors. Of these there were before the year 1871 Revs. S. Barrett, James Nolan, F. O'Shea, and F. X. M'Carthy. In that year came Rev. Edward M'Sweeny, who remained until the fall of 1876, when he was succeeded by the present pastor, Rev. W. A. Nolan. A very neat brick pastoral residence was built by the side of the church in 1874. The proximity of the oil-field and the traffic which it brings to Butler have improved the town in the last few years and increased the congregation. But the latter will number no more than about forty families.

ST. BRIDGET'S CHAPEL, M'NEIL'S SETTLEMENT.

M'Neil's Settlement is about nine miles south-west of Butler, and contains about half a dozen families of farmers. When Father Nolan was pastor of St. Joseph's Church, Sharpsburg, in 1865, he visited the place, which is about seventeen miles to the north, and ministered to the little flock. On a subsequent visit he purchased the Methodist Episcopal church, a diminutive frame building, then offered for sale, at a cost of $200, and blessed it under the title of St. Bridget's Church. It is visited a few times in the year on week-days by the pastor of the English church at Butler. The congregation, if such it may be called, has little present importance or future prospect.

ST. WENDELIN'S CHAPEL.

This chapel, which stands in a country place about ten miles north-east of Butler, has a somewhat unique history. The date of its erection is uncertain, but as near as can be ascertained at present, it was about the year 1845, or before that time. Although there are different accounts, the circumstances appear to have been these: A small number of German families settled there, and among them was an eccentric school-teacher by the name of Müller, who aspired to the dignity of a teacher of divine as well as of human sciences. He possessed great influence over the simple-minded people, and induced them to purchase a few acres of land and build a chapel in honor of St. Wendelin, which should in time, as he promised them, become a place of pilgrimage like the celebrated shrine of the saint at Treves, in Prussia. The chapel was built and with it a house for the school-teacher, and here he taught school. But as the people lived far from a church and could hear Mass but seldom, he was accustomed to assemble them in the chapel on Sunday for prayers. He also discoursed to them occasionally. But proceeding further with his usurpations than they were willing to follow him, he was forced to leave the place, and he became afterwards a veritable preacher of one of the sects.

It is not known with certainty at what time the Holy Sacrifice was first offered up in the chapel, but it was the German priest of Butler who paid these occasional visits on week-days. The old chapel was at length replaced by a new one, when it began to be regularly used as a parish church. The ceremony of the dedication was performed by Very Rev. J. Hickey, Vicar-General and Administrator, January 16th, 1876. The church is a frame building 72 feet in length by 37 in width, is neatly finished, and has three altars. It is visited every Sunday by one of the Carmelite fathers from Butler, and notwithstanding that there are but eighteen families they yet have a Catholic school. Who can withhold his admiration of their devotion to the cause of Catholic education, when he sees a handful of families so courageously surmount every obstacle and make every sacrifice necessary to secure for their children the advantages of a Christian training! It is not at all probable that the little congregation is destined to undergo any considerable change for many years.

ST. MARY'S GERMAN CHURCH, SUMMIT.

This church is situated in the midst of one of the most delightful agricultural districts in Western Pennsylvania, about five miles south of Butler and near the line of the Butler branch of the Western Pennsylvania Railroad. At an early day a small number of German Catholic families settled in the vicinity of the spot now occupied by the church, and after Mass had been celebrated for them for some time in a private house by the priest residing at Butler, or by one of the Redemptorist fathers from Pittsburg, a few of the leading men sent a petition to Bishop Kenrick, of Philadelphia, early in the summer of 1842, asking permission to build a church. It was granted, and four men whose farms centred at the same spot each donated an acre of ground for church purposes, to which, some years later, each added another acre. The church was soon after undertaken, and when finished was dedicated to the August Mother of God by Rev. Joseph Müller, C.SS.R., July 6th, 1845. It was an unassuming brick building, 50 feet in length by 36 in width. Although an humble residence was built for the priest in 1847, and was replaced by a better one in 1853, the congregation continued for a little time to be visited from Butler and Pittsburg before a resident pastor was appointed. Soon after the Benedictine fathers took charge of the congregation at Butler, St. Mary's was also given into their hands. In 1855 it is said to have numbered eighty families. To enlarge the church an addition was made to the rear of it, consisting of a sanctuary and sacristies, in 1862; but notwithstanding this it was still too small. It was then enlarged to its present dimensions in 1866, but this was done by using as much of the existing building as possible. When finished it was dedicated by the Bishop, February 19th, 1867. The church is now 100 feet in length by 45 in width, has a steeple in the centre in front, and is modelled after the Gothic style of architecture. There are three altars, dedicated respectively to Our Lady of the Assumption, to the Mother of Sorrows, and to St. Wendelin. After the withdrawal of the Benedictine fathers from Butler, St. Mary's reverted to the secular clergy, with whom it remained until 1876, when it was given into the hands of the Capuchin fathers from St. Augustine's Church, Pittsburg, who immediately built a brick monastery adjoining the church, 92 feet in length by 32 in width, and established the mother-house of their order for the diocese there.

A school was opened at an early day—the date has not been ascertained—in a frame building erected for that purpose, and has since been conducted by a lay teacher. The congregation will number at present about one hundred and twenty families, about one fourth of which are English, and its prospects for the future are a gradual increase.

ST. JOSEPH'S CHURCH, NORTH OAKLAND.

The church now under consideration is about eight miles north-east of Butler, is a short distance south of the narrow-gauge railroad extending from Parker's Landing to Butler, and is near the centre of the original Donegal colony. Until recently it was known as St. Joseph's, Donegal. Although originally an Irish settlement, there were at the date of the erection of the church a large proportion of German families. This date, however, is uncertain, but according to the best information I could obtain—which, in the case of this congregation, is very limited—it was about the year 1846, or perhaps a little later. The church, a small frame building, was put up by a somewhat independent movement on the part of the people, and the independence with which it began has suffered no abatement in the lapse of time. From the beginning Mass was usually celebrated twice in the month, once each by the German priest of Butler and the English priest of Sugar Creek, and later, from about 1861, by that of Brady's Bend. But in course of time, perhaps in 1867, the church was favored with a resident pastor familiar with both the German and English languages. The first was Rev. D. Devlin, after whom came Rev. Joseph Steger. In the mean time a pastoral residence was built. Soon after the discovery of oil at Parker's Landing the field began also to extend toward North Oakland; the congregation increased, the old church became too small, and Rev. Jos. Deyermeyer, who succeeded Father Steger in the summer of 1872, undertook the erection of a new and larger one. The corner-stone was laid by Bishop Domenec September 5th, 1872, and the church was dedicated by the same prelate January 28th, 1874. It is modelled after the Gothic style of architecture, is about 90 feet in length by 45 in width, and has a steeple in the centre in front. The interior is very neatly finished, and contains three altars. Father Deyermeyer was now succeeded by Rev. John Ritter, who remained until the beginning of 1876, when he gave place to Rev. Thos. Davin. Prior to this date oil was discovered within the limits of the parish, a circumstance which greatly increased its wealth and numbers; and for the size of it, it is now by far the wealthiest congregation in Western Pennsylvania.

Father Davin built an elegant frame pastoral residence in the latter part of 1877. The congregation since the division consists of about eighty families, all of whom are farmers; but it is not probable that it will undergo any great change in the immediate future. Father Davin was succeeded by Rev. E. J. Dignam in December, 1878.

ST. JOSEPH'S GERMAN CHURCH, NORTH OAKLAND.

When the Germans of St. Joseph's congregation were deprived of a pastor who was familiar with their language, they sought to remove the disadvantage under which they labored. Having obtained permission to separate and organize a distinct congregation, they fitted up the old church, then out of repair, and had it rededicated by Very Rev. R. Phelan, Adm., July 18th, 1877, and they are now visited every Sunday by one of the Capuchin fathers from the Summit. A school-house has also been provided and a school opened, although the number of families is but thirty.

ST. JOHN'S CHURCH, CLEARFIELD.

The congregation of St. John's was formed in part each from those of Sugar Creek, Freeport, and Butler. Before the erection of the church stations had been occasionally held at Coylesville, but in time the people resolved to build a church. After considerable debating on the most central locality, the present site was adopted, and work was commenced in the summer of 1853. The church is situated in a country place about a mile south of Coylesville and of the State road from Kittanning to Butler, and is equidistant from each town. The corner-stone was laid by Rev. John Larkin, of Freeport, August 15th of the above year, and the church was finished and dedicated in the course of the following summer. It is a brick building, modelled after the Gothic style, is 85 feet in length by 45 in width, and has a steeple in the centre in front. The finish of the interior is rather chaste than expensive. Before the appointment of a resident priest the congregation was under the care of the pastor of Freeport, and it was visited on one Sunday in the month until the summer of 1855. Rev. R. C. Christy was then appointed resident pastor. He built a pastoral residence, and later a school-house, in which school was taught during a few summers, but not regularly.

Upon the breaking out of the Rebellion Father Christy was appointed chaplain of the Seventy-eighth Regiment Pennsylvania Volunteers, and was succeeded at St. John's by Rev. P. M. Doyle, in the latter part of the summer of 1862. During the time that had elapsed from the organization of the parish, its growth had been very moderate. Father Doyle remained until the close of the year 1873, when he was succeeded by the present pastor, Rev. Patrick Brown. The proximity of the oil-fields on the north and west has improved the congregation in the last two years; but the benefit it derives from this source will be transitory. It will number about one hundred and fifty families, almost all of whom are Irish or of Irish descent, whose ancestors formed a part of the original Donegal colony. Being exclusively farmers, no change is to be expected in the congregation for many years.

CHURCH OF THE MOTHER OF SORROWS, MILLERSTOWN.

Millerstown lies on the eastern boundary of Butler County, about eleven miles north-east of Butler, and it had in 1870 a population of 207 souls. It was a quiet village until the oil excitement reached it about the year 1874, when, like all places in the oil regions, it assumed a degree of activity and corruption which those only can appreciate who have the misfortune of being acquainted with the ordinary effects of the discovery of oil upon the morals of those who throng to the spot. The narrow-gauge railroad which was about that time built from Parker to Butler passes through the village.

Previous to this time the few Catholic families who lived in the village and its vicinity heard Mass either at North Oakland or Sugar Creek. But now that the floating population increased their numbers, it was deemed expedient to build a church in the village. A lot was accordingly secured and a building commenced in the summer of 1875 by the pastor of Sugar Creek, Rev. P. M. Doyle, to whose jurisdiction it pertained. When finished it was dedicated to the Mother of Sorrows, November 7th, by Father Hickey, Vicar-General, in the absence of the Bishop in Rome. The church is a neat, plain frame building, capable of accommodating about three hundred persons, and is without belfry or steeple. It has always been visited every Sunday from Sugar Creek, from which it is about six miles distant, although the labor of ministering to the two churches is very considerable, especially in inclement weather. From the time the church was finished the congregation continued to increase, and it was feared that an addition would have to be built. But in the beginning of 1878, when the production of oil began to decrease, and when new fields were developed in the northern part of the State, much of the floating population was drawn away, and the congregation was reduced by half. It is probable that the production of oil will ere long entirely cease, an event which will reduce the congregation to a small number of original residents. Should that day arrive, and it is only a question of time, the church will not be visited more than once, or at most twice, in the month. As to hopes of increase in the future by the gradual settlement of a permanent population, they are so slender as to merit no consideration.

ST. ALPHONSUS' CHURCH, MURRINSVILLE.

The village of Murrinsville is situated in the extreme northern part of Butler County and of the diocese, and is about twenty miles north from Butler and eleven west from Parker's Landing. The congregation is properly the eastern portion of the Slippery Rock settlement, which was an extension of the Donegal colony, made two years after the first settlement in 1796. Slippery Rock station—for no church was ever built there—is a few miles west of Murrinsville, and was from the beginning occasionally visited by missionaries. It is impossible to determine at present how frequent these visits were, but it is certain they were never oftener than once in two months. The first visit was that of Father Lanigan, in 1801, and the second that of Father Heilbron, in 1803. Later it depended on Sugar Creek, then on Butler, and lastly on Murrinsville, and stations are occasionally held at present, although, on account of the backwardness of the place, religion has not flourished. Murrinsville also became a regular missionary station early in the century; but prior to the year 1844 it was not visited more frequently than once in two months; but being on the line of the turnpike from Pittsburg, by way of Butler to Franklin, it enjoyed a certain amount of notoriety that would be more esteemed in those early days than at present. Bishop Kenrick's first visit took place May 27th, 1834, and the following is taken from an account of it published in the *Catholic Herald*. The description of the village, it may be remarked, will apply as well to our day as it did to his:

"The number of Catholics found here, and in the other stations of this direction, far exceeded the Bishop's anticipation and the general impression. Although Murrinsville has only four houses, thirty-five persons received communion and thirty were confirmed. The number of communions would have been doubled had a second day been given to the Catholics of this neighborhood."

At length a church was determined upon, the contract for which was drawn up August 23d, 1841, although work was not commenced until the following April. The date of its completion and dedication is uncertain. The church is an unassuming stone building, 60 feet in length by 40 in width. From the summer of 1844 to that of 1850 Mass was usually celebrated on one Sunday in the month by the priest residing at Butler. But at the end of that time Rev. M. J. Mitchell was appointed first resident pastor. He was succeeded in April, 1854, by Rev. P. M. Doyle, who remained about a year. The church was then visited once a month from New Castle till October, 1859, when Rev. P. Hughes was appointed pastor. Having remained until December of the following year, he gave place to Rev. Thos. Walsh, who lived a short time at Murrinsville before taking up his residence at Brady's Bend, from which he visited it until March, 1863. From that date until the present the congregation has enjoyed the advantages of a resident pastor. Rev. J. C. Bigham was the first, then came Rev. C. V. Neeson, next Rev. Jos. Haney, who remained until about the beginning of 1871, when his health began to fail, and he was transferred to a less arduous mission. But it was to no purpose, and he died at Carrolltown on the 6th of February, 1872, being in the 33d year of his age. His remains repose in the cemetery attached to the church there.

REV. JOSEPH HANEY was a native of Watertown, county Londonderry, Ireland. Having almost completed his studies in his native land, he came to America and attached himself to the Diocese of Pittsburg in the summer of 1862, where he was ordained on the 8th of the following February. He was at first appointed assistant to the pastor of the church at Johnstown, but before the end of a year he was transferred to the church of Brownsville, where he remained until sent to Murrinsville.

He was succeeded at Murrinsville by Father Neeson, who was pastor for the second time; and he in September, 1876, by the present pastor, Rev. Jas. F. Tobin.

A farm of 160 acres lying about a mile from the church

was bequeathed to it by Mr. John Murrin. Father Neeson built a pastoral residence.

In the summer of 1855 there are said to have been seventy families, and the congregation has increased a little since that time in numbers and wealth. But owing to the absence of traffic and travel from the locality, the increase will be very moderate in the future. The people are farmers, and are for the most part descendants of the early Irish emigrants.

CHAPEL AT FAIRVIEW.

The little frame chapel at the village of Fairview, about seven miles south-west from Parker's Landing, has never been dedicated nor honored with the name of a saint. It was built by a Mr. Charles Collins about the year 1863, from a bequest of his father for the benefit of the few Catholic families living in that neighborhood. But the bequest sufficed merely for the erection of the shell of the building, and it remained unfinished, although Mass was celebrated in it on one Sunday of the month by the pastor of Murrinsville until a resident pastor was appointed for Parker's Landing, when it passed to his jurisdiction. Soon after the arrival of Rev. J. P. Tahany at the latter place at the close of the year 1871, he took measures for its completion. He then offered up the Holy Sacrifice in it occasionally until the erection of the church at Petrolia, next to engage our attention, which, standing but a short distance off, drew away the little flock. Since that time Mass is seldom offered within its walls, and it may be said to be without a congregation.

ST. JAMES' CHURCH, PETROLIA.

Petrolia, about eight miles south-west of Parker's Landing, though of recent growth is the most flourishing town in the interior of the Butler County oil territory. The completion of the Parker and Karns City narrow-gauge railroad through it, which took place in February, 1874, added considerably to its business and importance. Catholics were early found among its inhabitants, and Father Tahany, of

Parker's Landing—to which the congregation has always been attached—rented a hall in the autumn of 1873, where he offered up the adorable Sacrifice every Sunday, riding from the one town to the other between his two Masses. Measures were at the same time taken to purchase a lot and commence the building of a church with the opening of spring. It was done; the church was built, and, as we have seen, was dedicated by the Bishop, under the invocation of St. James, November 22d, 1874. It is a neat frame building of no special style of architecture, 75 feet in length by 35 in width, without a tower, but with a basement under the rear half that would serve for a school. Mass is celebrated every Sunday by the priest of Parker's Landing. The congregation was at one time as large and flourishing as the one of that place, but it will not be so permanent. It has already commenced to decline, and will soon be reduced to perhaps one fourth of what it once numbered.

CHAPTER XXVI.

BEAVER AND LAWRENCE COUNTIES.

Visit of a French missionary—Sts. Peter and Paul's Church, Beaver—Death and sketch of Rev. James Reid—St. Cecilia's Church, Rochester—St. John the Baptist's Church, Baden—St. Joseph's Church, New Brighton—St. Rose's Church, Cannelton—St. Mary's German Church, Beaver Falls—St. James' Church, New Bedford—St. Mary's Church, New Castle—St. Francis Xavier's Church, Stonerstown—St. Teresa's Church, Clinton.

CATHOLICITY, although never in a very flourishing condition in this part of the diocese, yet dates its history from a remote period. It is related that as the French retired from Fort Duquesne when the English obtained possession of it, in November, 1758, their chaplain passed up the Beaver valley on his way to the French posts in the north-western part of the State. While doing so, he stopped at Mount Jackson in the present Lawrence County, about forty miles north-west of Pittsburg and four from the State line, to visit an Irish Catholic family of the name of O'Brien. Having remained a short time and baptized three members of the family, he passed further north-east into the present Butler County, where he visited a French family of the name of Crafiere. Soon after the commencement of the present century—to pass over the intervening time—Catholic families principally Irish, and, in the northern part, an extension of the Donegal colony, settled at different places in the valley, but principally at New Castle and Beaver, as will be seen more in detail as we proceed. The first to attract the attention of missionaries was the latter town.

STS. PETER AND PAUL'S CHURCH, BEAVER.

The town of Beaver, the seat of justice of the county of the same name, is situated on the west bank of the Beaver River, at its confluence with the Ohio, and occupies a plateau about 100 feet above the level of the rivers. It is twenty-seven miles north-west of Pittsburg, and at the most northern point reached by the Ohio River in its course. It was laid out by David Leet in 1791, and occupies the spot formerly the site of Fort M'Intosh, a fort established for the defence of the frontier, and the scene of the last treaty with the Indians, whereby their claim to the soil of Pennsylvania was forever extinguished. It was incorporated March 29th, 1802.

A few Catholic settlers found their way into the town and surrounding country in the early part of this century; and in 1830 the place became one of the regular missionary stations of Rev. Patrick O'Neil, of Sugar Creek. As the population gradually increased, a church became desirable. To second the efforts of the Catholics, whose resources were very limited, Mr. Jas. W. Hemphill, a Protestant gentleman of the town, donated a large lot of ground as the site of a new church. With this encouragement the Catholics commenced the building of the church in 1834. It was not finished until 1837, when it was dedicated by Bishop Kenrick, under the invocation of Sts. Peter and Paul. The building is frame, about 24 by 40 feet, and simple in style and finish. Rev. J. O'Reilly, of Pittsburg, visited it at distant intervals; and afterwards it became a regular monthly station, attended successively from the same place by Rev. E. F. Garland, A. P. Gibbs, J. Powers, and Thos. M'Cullagh. In 1847 Rev. Jas. Reid was appointed first resident pastor, with the additional charge of the entire Beaver valley. His first care was to give the church and its surroundings a thorough repairing, and make it a more fitting place for the offering up of the adorable Sacrifice. The increase of the congregation was almost imperceptible, and the church, though so small, has never been unable to accommodate the people. About the year 1854 Lawrence County was detached from Fr. Reid's mission, and received a pastor of its own at New Castle. In his narrower sphere the good priest kept the even tenor of his way, till old age stole upon him and he was forced to seek repose. This took place in 1866, from which time one of the Passionist fathers from Pittsburg visited the congregation on two Sundays in the month. Fr. Reid continued to reside at Beaver, where, full of years and merit, he expired February 14th, 1868, in the 75th year of his age.

REV. JAS. REID was born at Carrickmacross, county Monaghan, Ireland, in the year 1793. Coming to this country in 1817, he taught school in Westmoreland County and in the academy at Butler, and in 1822 entered the seminary at Bardstown, Ky. Having finished his studies, he was ordained by Bishop Fenwick at Cincinnati on Easter Monday, 1832. After serving on the mission in various parts of Ohio, Virginia, and Maryland, he entered the Diocese of Pittsburg in 1846. Here he attended Pine Creek and Wexford, in the latter place finishing a church, and was in about a year transferred to the scene of the closing years of his life. His remains repose in the cemetery of the church he so long and faithfully served.

After the death of Father Reid, the church at Beaver was attached to Rochester and has continued so with the exception of about a year. It is probable that the two congregations will eventually be merged into one with a new church midway between the present two. Mass is now celebrated every Sunday, except the fifth of the month, in each church, but the congregation of Sts. Peter and Paul is decreasing and will not number one hundred souls. For obvious reasons no parish school has been opened.

ST. CECILIA'S CHURCH, ROCHESTER.

The town of Rochester, which was formerly known by the name of East Bridgewater, lies on the opposite side of the Beaver River from the town last noticed, and like it is built on a table-land. In 1870 it had a population of 2091. A small number of German Catholic families settled in the town and surroundings more than twenty years ago, and not finding it convenient to attend the English church at Beaver, a separate one was built for their accommodation by Rev. J. Stiebel, of Allegheny City, about the year 1857, but I have not been able to learn the date of its dedication. It is a frame building 46 feet in length by 25 in width, and has a small belfry. The interior is neatly finished and has one altar. Upon the completion of the church, Rev. Michael Mühlberger was appointed pastor in 1858, but was succeeded the following year by Rev. J. Reiser. But the congregation was too small to support a resident pastor, and before the end of the year it was attached to St. Mary's, Allegheny City, from which it was visited generally twice in the month for nine years. The death of Father Reid at this time left a vacancy, and the churches of Beaver and Rochester were united under one pastor, in which state they have, with little exception, since remained. Rev. Adam Gunkle now became pastor, but the following year the Passionist fathers attended Beaver, and Rev. J. Zwickert was pastor of St. Cecilia's. Next came Rev. Julius Kuenzer, after whose departure it was reunited to St. Mary's, Allegheny, till, in 1873, Rev. Joseph Boehm was appointed pastor. He was succeeded November, 1875, by Rev. James Rommelfänger, and he in October, 1877, by Rev. J. Kaib, who gave place to the present pastor, Rev. Fred. Stefen, in November, 1878.

The congregation has increased but little and its growth in the future will be no less tardy, unless the Pittsburg and Lake Erie Railroad, now opened, and which crosses the Ohio River at this place, induces manufacturers to locate there. St. Cecilia's was originally a German congregation, and at present that element predominates, but there is a sufficient number of English to make it now a mixed congregation requiring a pastor conversant with both languages.

The church at Glenfield, as we have seen, was for a time ministered to by the pastor of St. Cecilia's, but is not at present. But he attends that at Baden, next to be noticed, and besides this has since 1868 visited Industry, eight miles down the Ohio, and Smith's Ferry, four miles farther, both of which are villages with half a dozen or more families, for whom Mass is celebrated monthly on a week-day. There are no Catholics whatever in that portion of Beaver County lying south of the Ohio River, except perhaps two or three families opposite Rochester. St. Cecilia's congregation will not count more than perhaps thirty families; it has never had a parish school, nor does it own a pastoral residence.

ST. JOHN THE BAPTIST'S CHURCH, BADEN.

This little church is situated six miles east of Rochester and two north of the Ohio River. It was built in 1871 by about a dozen farmers, who had formerly heard Mass at Rochester, and is a neat frame structure about 50 feet in length by 25 in width. The pastor of the church at Rochester has always had charge of the little congregation, for whom he offers up the Holy Sacrifice once a month on week-days and on every fifth Sunday of the month. The people are all farmers. It is not probable that the status of the congregation will undergo any considerable change for many years to come.

ST. JOSEPH'S CHURCH, NEW BRIGHTON.

The town of New Brighton is situated on the eastern bank of the Beaver River, three miles from its mouth, and is twenty-nine miles north-west of Pittsburg. The Pittsburg, Fort Wayne and Chicago Railroad passes through it, and on the same tracks the Erie and Pittsburg Railroad. It has a limited manufacture of wool and iron, and had in 1870 a population of 4037. The first Catholics of the town and vicinity heard Mass at Beaver, but in the fall of 1863 an old United Presbyterian church was offered for sale and was purchased by the Catholics at a trifling cost. It was a brick building, about 50 feet in length by 40 in width, situated on a large lot in the northern part of the town, and had been erected about thirty-five years before. The style of the building was rigidly simple: Presbyterian in appearance as well as in the object of its erection. Having been interiorly renewed, it was dedicated by the Bishop, December 6th of the same year, under the invocation of St. Joseph. Rev. M. J. Mitchell was appointed first pastor to reside here and celebrate Mass alternately at

St. Joseph's and at St. Rose's, Cannelton. Having remained sixteen months, he was transferred to another field of usefulness, and the church was visited once in the month by Rev. J. A. Shell, assistant at St. Mary's Allegheny, and afterwards by one of the Passionist fathers from Pittsburg. At length the present pastor, Rev. John C. Bigham was appointed, February 1st, 1866. Soon after his arrival he purchased a neat brick residence a short distance from the church, which he has since occupied; for prior to that time the pastor lodged in a hotel. He also bought five acres of ground on the hill at the back of the town for a cemetery. The interior of the church was decorated, and a frame hall was built near it for fairs, etc.

But the old church was now too small to accommodate the increasing congregation, and was, besides, ready to fall from age and other causes. It became necessary to purchase property and erect a more commodious edifice notwithstanding the limited means at the pastor's disposal. A very eligible lot, 180 feet square, was purchased adjoining his residence, plans were procured, and the foundation of the church commenced. The corner-stone was laid by the Bishop November 12th, 1871. Work proceeded but slowly on account of the limited resources and the depression of the times, and it was not until the fall of 1875 that the basement was finished. It was dedicated by the Bishop on the 17th of October. The church, when finished, will be 106 feet in length by 53 in width, after a modified Gothic style, with a tower in the centre in front. The basement, which is finished at present, and will for a number of years be used as a church, is 11 feet high in the clear, has three altars, and is otherwise finished in a suitable manner. More than half is beneath the surface of the lot, the ground being removed for a few feet on both sides and the embankments supported by walls.

The old church and hall, together with a valuable circulating library, were burnt by an incendiary while a fair was being held, June 25th, 1876.

The congregation, although not in so flourishing a condition as it was a few years ago, is yet as numerous, and consists of about one hundred families, some of whom are farmers residing in the vicinity of the town, while others, and perhaps the greater part, are employed in the public works, especially the cutlery manufactories at Beaver Falls, on the opposite side of the river, one mile above. A large number of Chinese were also employed in these works for several years, but the time for which they had contracted expired early in the summer of 1877, and they all returned to California.

The distance at which the greater part of the congregation lives from the church and other causes have prevented the opening of a parish school. The future prospects of St. Joseph's are good, although its growth will not be rapid.

Besides ministering to this congregation and to St. Rose's, Cannelton, Fr. Bigham also attended other stations at different places in the county, the principal of which were Industry and Smith's Ferry before they were attached, as we have seen, to Rochester. St. Rose's had always been, with little exception, attached to New Brighton from the time the latter became the residence of a priest until February, 1877, and the labors of Fr. Bigham in behalf of that church will next engage our attention.

ST. ROSE'S CHURCH, CANNELTON.

This church is situated in a country place about eleven miles north-west of New Brighton, six south of the Pittsburg, Fort Wayne and Chicago Railroad, and three east of the State line. Nearly all the land in that part of the county belongs to the Economites, a religious sect, founded by General Rapp, having all things in common. They are tolerant, however, of the religious views of others, as will appear from the fact of their having donated an acre of ground to the Catholics as the site of a church. They own extensive coal-mines in the vicinity of the church, and have constructed the Darlington and Cannelton Railroad from the mines to the Pittsburg, Fort Wayne and Chicago Railroad. The time of the first settlement of Catholics in this part of the county is uncertain, nor is it known whether Mass was celebrated for them prior to the time at which the building of the church was undertaken. Their number was thought sufficient to justify the building of a church in 1861, and Fr. Reid, who then visited them, erected a miniature edifice no more than about 20 by 30 feet in the cheapest and simplest style, which he placed under the invocation of the Rose of America. He continued to visit it until the beginning of 1863. It was then attended once in the month for a year from New Castle. From that time it was attached to New Brighton, and visited on every alternate Sunday. In time the congregation increased and became too large for the church, so that in May, 1871, Fr. Bigham commenced the erection of a new building. It was finished in the fall of the same year, and dedicated by the Bishop on the 21st of October. The church is 57 feet in length by 25 in width, but without a steeple. The ceiling of the interior follows the inclination of the roof, and the whole is neatly finished with one altar, frescoed walls, and stained-glass windows. A school was opened in the old church in September, 1873, but the panic set in, and it was soon after discontinued. In the same year a frame pastoral residence was built. Immediately before the panic the congregation was in the zenith of its prosperity, and numbered about one hundred families. But the panic reduced the demand for coal, so that work in the mines was almost suspended and many of the miners were obliged to go elsewhere. Work has been but partially resumed. In February, 1877, St. Rose's Church was cut off from New Brighton, and with St. Teresa's, taken from New Castle, now form a separate mission, with the pastor residing at the former. Rev. Peter M'Mahon was appointed pastor, but was succeeded in May by Rev. S. P. Herman, and he in the early part of the winter by the present pastor, Rev. Thos. Devlin. The congregation at present contains about sixty families, a part of whom are farmers scattered about the county to a considerable distance from the church, and it is not probable it will further decrease, nor will it increase except slowly.

The pastor also attends two stations on the Pittsburg, Fort Wayne and Chicago Railroad once a month on a week-day, New Galilee and Palestine, the latter of which is in the State of Ohio and Diocese of Cleveland. But the number of families is very small in both places, and neither has a church.

ST. MARY'S GERMAN CHURCH, BEAVER FALLS.

The few German families who located themselves at Beaver Falls a few years ago, and who were obliged to content themselves with the English services at St. Joseph's Church, New Brighton, or travel to Rochester, determined to build a church for themselves. By an independent movement they purchased a site, and erected a frame church 60 feet in length by 36 in width, which they furnished very neatly in the interior, and which the Bishop dedicated, under the invocation of the Blessed Virgin, July 4th, 1872. But their labors were in a measure in vain, for the church was without a pastor for about two years. The Bishop then gave it in charge of the Capuchin fathers, Pittsburg, by whom it is visited on one Sunday in the month. There are about twenty-five families in the congregation, and as the cutlery works of the town —in which they for the most part find employment—are doing but little, it is not probable that the congregation will increase in the future, except imperceptibly. There are also about half a dozen French families at Beaver Falls who attend St. Joseph's Church, New Brighton, and who are perhaps the largest body of that nationality to be found anywhere in the dioceses. Measures are now being taken to build extensive iron-works, which will no doubt have the effect of increasing the Catholic population.

ST. JAMES' CHURCH, NEW BEDFORD.

The village of New Bedford is situated in the extreme north-western part of Lawrence County and of the Diocese of Pittsburg, and within half a mile of the State line. A few families settled in that part of the county at an early day, and one of them, Mr. William Murrin, donated a farm of 247 acres of ground to Bishop O'Connor for the use of the orphans, as we shall have occasion to show when treating of St. Paul's Orphan Asylum. The people were visited from the year 1838, but it is uncertain whether a priest offered the Holy Sacrifice for them prior to that date or not. These visits were at first made at irregular intervals, but afterwards regularly once in the month. Among those who shared in this missionary work were Revs. E. F. Garland, A. P. Gibbs, and Thos. M'Cullagh. The last-named, seeing the number of families slowly increase and become more thoroughly organized into a congregation, thought it expedient to build a church upon the farm, for as yet the people had heard Mass in a private house. With this object in view he opened a subscription, but before he had collected sufficient funds with which to commence work the mission passed, in 1847, into the hands of Fr. Reid, of Beaver. He carried the plan of his predecessor into execution, and built, a short distance from the village, a frame church about 40 feet in length by about 25 in width in the simplest style, which he placed under the invocation of St. James the Apostle. He continued to visit the congregation once in the month, and to minister to the rest of the Catholics in the whole Beaver valley till the year 1854, when Lawrence County was formed, as we have said, into a separate mission with the pastor residing at New Castle. From this time forward St. James' continued to be visited generally once—though sometimes twice—in the month until it was finally relinquished, as we shall presently see.

In 1849 or 1850 an attempt was made by the Franciscan Brothers from Loretto to open a male orphan asylum on the farm in accordance with the stipulations of the donor. An additional building was erected and the larger orphan boys transferred thither, but the distance from the city, the difficulty of access, and other causes induced the Bishop to regard the work as impracticable, and the farm with its buildings was sold to the Bishop of Cleveland in 1851 for $3000. But the use of the church was permitted the people for some time ; nor does it seem that the chaplain of the community that took possession of the farm ministered to the people until recently. The Sisters of Charity from Cleveland first occupied the farm and opened an orphan asylum, having for their chaplain Rev. Fr. O'Callaghan, and after him Rev. Fr. Pugh. But they were succeeded in 1854 by the present community, the Sisters of the Humility of Mary, with their founder, Rev. J. J. Begel, as chaplain. The community numbers at present thirty-two Sisters and thirty novices, and they have an asylum with about fifty orphans. The object of the institute is the care of orphans and the sick, and the instruction of the children of the poor. They teach school at different places in the dioceses of Cleveland and Erie.

The erection of churches at New Castle and at Youngstown, Ohio, drew away many of the families that originally belonged to St. James', and the few that remain live at a considerable distance from the church. The difficulty of access to the place and the absence of minerals and manufactories make it improbable that it will ever have a considerable Catholic population. Mass has not been celebrated in the church since about the year 1873; for when the Sister senlarged their house they built a chapel in which the few families—perhaps not a dozen in all—hear Mass. The church was moved to a spot nearer the house about a year or two later, and is now used as a school for the orphans.

ST. MARY'S CHURCH, NEW CASTLE.

New Castle, the county-seat of Lawrence County, is situated on the Shenango River,* at its junction with Neshannock Creek, and is on the line of the Erie and Pittsburg Railroad, 50 miles north-west of the latter city. The town was laid out about the year 1800, but owes its importance to the construction of the Beaver Canal, which traverses the valley, and which was opened in 1832. The town was at first confined to the delta between the two streams, but is now spread far over the gently rising hills on both sides of the Shenango. The present population is estimated at 11,000. For the size of the place it has very extensive manufactories of iron and glass, and to these is due its recent rapid growth. A creature of the iron trade, its fortune changes with it, and the same may be said of the Catholic population.

A small number of Catholics settled on farms in the vicin-

---

* The principal stream of the Beaver valley bears this name till its junction with Little Beaver Creek, when it takes the name of Beaver River till it flows into the Ohio, 16 miles below.

ity of New Castle at an early date in its history; but although Mass was undoubtedly offered up for them in a private room as often as their necessities, or rather the time at the disposal of the missionary priests of the district, made it practicable, we have no reliable record of it. This much, however, is known, that priests from Pittsburg ministered to the few scattered families along the canal at such points as was necessary. When Fr. Reid first said Mass at New Castle, August, 1851, there are said to have been no more than ten or fifteen families of farmers and a small number of others. In 1852 he built a frame church, about 40 feet in length by 20 in width, on the side of the river to the west of the town in the most unlikely spot imaginable, and dedicated it to the Blessed Virgin. He was then succeeded by Rev. Peter M. Garvey, who became the first resident pastor, offering up the Holy Sacrifice alternately at that place and New Bedford. The constant residence of a pastor from that time would seem to argue a considerable increase in the Catholic population. But there was a strong Presbyterian element of a very illiberal school in the town and county, and the Catholics were, and still are, looked upon as a generation that fears the light. In June, 1855, Fr. Garvey was succeeded by Rev. Thos. O'Farrell, who ministered to the congregation and missions until August, 1859, when he gave place to Rev. John C. Farren. Upon his withdrawing in May, 1862, the congregation was visited monthly for a year by Rev. Thos. Walsh, of Brady's Bend, Armstrong County. Rev. Jas. Canivan then became pastor; and during his residence the iron trade of the town began to assume its present proportions, and to draw thither a large number of Catholics, principally Irish, who sought employment. The church was now no longer capable of accommodating them, nor could it be sufficiently enlarged. Desiring a more suitable locality, Fr. Canivan purchased a large lot in the older part of the town, corner of Beaver and North streets, and soon after commenced to build the church. The corner-stone was laid by the Bishop July 4th, 1866, but the church was not finished for five years. March 10th, 1871, Fr. Canivan was succeeded by Rev. W. F. Hayes. The congregation was now large and increasing rapidly. In April, after his arrival, Fr. Hayes opened a school in a rented room, under the direction of a lay teacher, and in May purchased a large frame dwelling across the street from the church for a pastoral residence; for previous to that time the pastor had occupied a rented house. The church was finished the same year, and dedicated by the Bishop September 17th. It is built of brick, is 110 feet in length by 45 in width, has a well-proportioned tower in the centre in front, and follows the Gothic style of architecture with some modifications in the plan of its construction. There are no columns in the interior, but the ceiling is groined over the windows and rises moderately from the side walls toward the centre, at which point it reaches the height of 33 feet from the floor. There are three altars, a large gallery, and stained-glass windows. But the lot is low and the church is damp.

Soon after the completion of the church the congregation was in the zenith of its prosperity, and contained perhaps four hundred families, besides many single men employed in the manufactories. There was also at this time a considerable number of Germans. An assistant to the pastor became necessary, and one was first appointed in February, 1873. But the panic of the same year bore heavily on New Castle, and the iron-works, after struggling against it for a time, either entirely suspended or greatly reduced the number of the hands employed. This was especially trying for the congregation, which had purchased sixty acres of land about a mile from the town in May of that year, part of which was to be used as a cemetery, and the balance to be disposed of in lots to members of the congregation according to an agreement the conditions of which they were now unable to fulfil. A new and larger school-house was also needed, and after some necessary delay it was built in 1876. It is one of the most substantial and best arranged school-houses in the diocese, and is 60 feet in length by 35 in width, and three stories high. The first and second floors are each divided into two rooms, while the third is a hall with stage for exhibitions, fairs, etc. The schools were placed under the care of the Sisters of St. Joseph, from Ebensburg, in September, 1875. As yet a convent has not been built for their accommodation.

In February, 1877, St. Teresa's Church, Clinton, which had to that time been under the care of the pastor of New Castle, was detached to form part of a new parish, and with it the assistant withdrew from St. Mary's.

The congregation is now greatly reduced in numbers, and will not count more perhaps than one hundred and fifty families, with many single persons. But this is only temporary. With the revival of the iron trade New Castle will be itself again, and St. Mary's will enjoy its wonted prosperity. Fr. Hayes was succeeded February 8th, 1879, by the present pastor, Rev. Jos. Gallagher.

ST. FRANCIS XAVIER'S CHURCH, STONERSTOWN.

The little village of Stonerstown is situated on Slippery Rock Creek, about twelve miles east of New Castle. The scenery along the creek, especially at the mouth of Muddy Creek immediately above, is very romantic and beautiful. Tradition also points to this as the spot where the Indian tribes for a great distance round were accustomed to hold their annual council. A blast-furnace was built here many years ago, which was replaced by another more recently, and since the latter date a few Catholic families settled in the village and around it. But Mass is not known to have been celebrated there until after the appointment of Fr. Hayes to New Castle. For a few years he offered up the Holy Sacrifice monthly on a week-day in a private room, but in the summer of 1875 he built a frame church 47 feet in length by 22 in width, with a steeple. It is dedicated to the Apostle of the Indies, and is one of the most chaste and beautiful little churches in the diocese. A priest from New Castle visited it on one Sunday in the month until the furnace blew out about a year later, when all the Catholics, with the exception of half a dozen families, moved elsewhere. It is now visited once in the month on a week-day. Little change is likely to take place in the miniature congregation for many years to come.

ST. TERESA'S CHURCH, CLINTON.

Homewood Furnace, about thirteen miles down the river from New Castle, employed in its day a number of Catholic laborers, and was for many years while it was in blast attended at regular intervals; but these visits ceased after the erection of the church at Clinton. This church is situated at Clinton station, on the Erie and Pittsburg Railroad, twelve miles below New Castle.

There is neither town nor village, and the congregation is composed principally of miners, although there are a few farmers and railroad men. From the beginning it was attached to the New Castle mission, from which it was visited monthly for four or five years prior to the erection of the church. When the congregation had so far increased as no longer to find accommodations in a room, the church was undertaken in May, 1871, and the excavations were dug and foundations laid by the people under the guidance of Fr. Hayes, then pastor of New Castle. The building was completed the same year, and was dedicated by the Bishop October 15th, under the invocation of St. Teresa. It is an elegant frame building, 66 feet in length by 33 in width, and surmounted by a chaste steeple. After its completion it was attended twice in the month on Sundays. But the congregation was increasing rapidly, and the church immediately after its completion was no longer able to accommodate it. An addition was then built to the rear, consisting of an apse for the altar with a sacristy on each side; the interior was frescoed, and it was reopened by the Bishop November 16th, 1873. The congregation consisted at this time of about sixty families, besides a large number of unmarried men employed in the mines. But with the well-known financial crisis came an almost total suspension of work, and the congregation declined rapidly. At present it will not exceed thirty families, who are for the most part farmers residing in the vicinity.

In February, 1877, the church was detached from the New Castle mission and with St. Rose's formed into a separate pastorate, as has already been remarked. The fortunes of St. Teresa's are bound up with the coal-mines which called it into existence, and these depend in a great measure on the iron trade. This last is reviving slowly from its recent prostration, but it does not appear at all probable that this congregation will attain its former prosperity for many years to come. It is still visited on two Sundays in the month, but for obvious reasons it has never enjoyed the advantages of a parochial school.

CHAPTER XXVII.

RELIGIOUS ORDERS OF MEN—COLLEGES.

Remarks—St. Michael's Seminary—The Brothers of the Presentation—St. Vincent's Abbey and College—The Franciscan Brothers—St. Francis' College—The Congregation of the Holy Ghost and the Immaculate Heart of Mary—The Pittsburg Catholic College—Other religious orders—The Passionists—The Oblates of St. Charles Borromeo—Death and sketch of Rev. P. M'C. Morgan.

From the fact that the members of several of the religious orders now established in the diocese are engaged in teaching, and from the impossibility of treating of their colleges without at the same time entering more or less into the history of the orders themselves, it has been thought best to give in the present chapter a combined sketch of both. The first place has for obvious reasons been given to the diocesan seminary.

ST. MICHAEL'S THEOLOGICAL AND PREPARATORY SEMINARY.

Conscious of the advantages of having the candidates for the sacred ministry trained under his immediate supervision, one of the first objects that attracted the attention of the newly consecrated Bishop O'Connor was the opening of an ecclesiastical seminary. Humble in its beginning, it was yet destined to be productive of incalculable benefit to the diocese. Early in the year 1844 he assembled a small number of students at his residence on Smithfield Street, not far from the Cathedral, under the presidency of Rev. R. A. Wilson, D.D. As this was only meant to be temporary, he resolved to build a seminary on the Cathedral lot. But this idea was abandoned, and the students remained with him; and when his new residence was built by the side of the Cathedral they followed him to it. Here they remained for a short time.

Soon after his arrival in Pittsburg, Bishop O'Connor purchased a farm of about one hundred acres from the Economites for $16,000. It lies on the side and top of the hill to the south of the Monongahela River in what was then Birmingham borough, but which is now a part of Pittsburg. The investment was a profitable one; for after building lots, to the amount of about $100,000, had been sold, and after other large lots had been donated to the orphan asylum, the Passionist monastery, and St. Michael's Church, the remainder was valued by the city at $162,000 before the panic. Parts of it were sold for as much as $6000 an acre. A frame dwelling stood on it at the foot of the hill, near St. Michael's Church, and this the Bishop transformed into a seminary at the close of 1846 or early in the following year. Rev. Thomas M'Cullagh was appointed president. But failing health soon obliged him to relinquish the arduous duties connected with it and the missions, which, owing to the scarcity of priests, he was also obliged to visit, and to seek repose for a time. He accordingly withdrew to St. Xavier's Academy, and the seminary was placed in the hands of the fathers of the Congregation of the Oblates of Mary Immaculate, in November, 1848. But they did not succeed in laying a permanent foundation in the diocese. On the event of their withdrawal, in the course of the following year, Rev. James O'Connor was appointed president. Little change took place beyond a gradual increase in the number of students, until the summer of 1851, when the cholera broke out with great violence in the city, and it was deemed advisable to close the seminary. The students were transferred to other institutions, and the seminary became soon after a boys' orphan asylum.

The Cathedral had been burnt down in the previous May, and the present imposing structure undertaken, which, owing to the limited resources of the diocese, made it expedient to curtail expenses as much as possible, and not open the seminary for a few years. In the mean time the diocese was divided and the new See of Erie erected.

At length, after no little speculation as to the most suitable place for reopening it, the seminary was located at Summitville, Cambria County, in September, 1856, under the presidency of Rev. C. M. Sheehan. Here it remained for a year.

But the site was not a happy selection. The buildings were very indifferent; the place, being on the summit of the mountains, was extremely cold in winter; and the distance from Pittsburg, 102 miles, added to its other inconveniences. To secure a more fitting place a lot of ground consisting of about eight acres, with a large frame summer hotel standing on it, and lying at Glenwood, on the east bank of the Monongahela River five miles from its mouth, but at present within the city limits, was purchased April 8th, 1857, for $6600. Here the seminary was opened in the beginning of September of the same year, and Rev. James O'Connor was soon after appointed president. Besides the preparatory and theological departments, there was also a separate department for lay students until the summer of 1863, when it was discontinued. The building soon became inadequate to the accommodation of the number of students required to meet the demands of the diocese, and an additional wing was built in the summer of 1862.

At the end of October, 1863, Father O'Connor was succeeded in the presidency by Rev. James Keogh, D.D., who had long been vice-president; and Father O'Connor soon after withdrew to the Diocese of Philadelphia. Ill-health prevented Dr. Keogh from discharging the duties of his office during a considerable part of his administration, and he resigned at the close of June, 1865, and made his home also for several years in Philadelphia. Rev. S. Wall was appointed to the vacant post October 23d of the same year, a position which he occupied until the seminary was finally closed.

A public chapel, as we have stated when speaking of St. Stephen's Church, was opened in the seminary when it was located at Glenwood, for the benefit of the Catholics living in the vicinity. It was not closed until after the erection of St. Stephen's Church. The largest number of students in the seminary at any time was about seventy-five, but that was more than the building was capable of accommodating properly.

After the division of the diocese and the erection of the See of Allegheny, the Bishop of the latter withdrew his students and placed them in other institutions. The parent diocese, burdened as it was with debt and deprived of a large portion of its former revenue, was no longer able to maintain the seminary, and it was closed at the end of the year 1876. The pastor of St. Stephen's Church is now the sole occupant of the deserted building. Such of the students as were necessary to supply the wants of the diocese were transferred to other institutions and the remainder were dismissed. It is not probable that the seminary will be again opened for many years, owing to the financial straits of the diocese, and when it is opened it will not be in the old building, for it is now almost ready to fall with age.

THE BROTHERS OF THE PRESENTATION.

Having provided teachers for the girls of the city by the foundation of a house of the Sisters of Mercy, Bishop O'Connor sought out an order to take charge of the boys. When on his visit to Europe in 1845, he called at the city of Cork, Ireland, and applied to the mother-house of the Brothers of the Presentation for a foundation. His request was granted, and a small number accompanied him on his return to America. They took charge of the boys' school attached to the Cathedral, and lived in Birmingham, not far from St. Michael's Church. But the time did not appear to have arrived for the Brothers to locate themselves in this part of the country. One of them died, another returned to Ireland, and a third joined the Augustinian Order at Philadelphia and became a priest. At length, as if to show that Providence did not wish the foundation to be permanent, two of the three remaining Brothers, Paul Cary and Francis Ryan, were struck by lightning, on the street, July 2d, 1848, as they were returning to their residence after teaching Sunday-school in the school-house attached to the Cathedral. Their death was most extraordinary. They had almost reached their home, when, as they hastened along, one on each side of Mr. H. S. Bowen, who carried an umbrella, it was struck by the lightning and both were instantly killed, while Mr. Bowen remained unhurt. Many years after he was ordained a priest, and he is now a professor at St. Francis' College, Loretto. But one professed Brother and two novices now remained, and they were not

ST. VINCENT'S BENEDICTINE ABBEY AND COLLEGE, WESTMORELAND COUNTY.

I have already treated at length of these institutions when sketching the church of the same name, to which the reader is referred.

THE FRANCISCAN BROTHERS—ST. FRANCIS' COLLEGE, LORETTO.

Catholic education was ever dear to the heart of Bishop O'Connor, and he spared no pains to place it within the reach of the children and youth of his diocese. The Sisters of Mercy, whom he had introduced in the beginning of his episcopate, were meeting with the most encouraging success in training the girls, but the boys were not as yet so well provided for. The Presentation Brothers, who were destined to flourish but for a brief period, had charge of a small portion only of the children, and although the Benedictine fathers were preparing to open a college, the Bishop felt that still more could be done. He accordingly resolved to introduce the Brothers of the Third Order of St. Francis. Application was made to the Archbishop of Tuam, Ireland, upon whose solicitation the communities of Clifton and Roundstone gave six members to the new diocese. They arrived at Pittsburg in 1847, and located themselves at Loretto, the spot made famous by the labors and sacrifices of Dr. Gallitzin. Part of the land left by the illustrious missionary was transferred to them upon certain conditions, and they took possession of some old buildings standing upon it until such time as more suitable ones could be erected. A monastery was commenced in the following summer, the corner-stone of which was laid by the Bishop on the Feast of St. Joseph Calasanctius, August 27th. The Order flourished; numerous candidates sought admission, and the Brothers soon found themselves enabled to extend the sphere of their usefulness. A house was established at Pittsburg in the fall of 1848, and on the 4th of October the Brothers took charge of the boys' school attached to the Cathedral after the withdrawal of the Presentation Brothers from the diocese. Later they also, for several years, taught the boys of St. Peter's, Allegheny.

When the new buildings were completed at Loretto in 1850, an academy for boys was opened, which, four years later, was chartered by the Legislature and empowered to confer collegiate honors and degrees. The college has since continued to hold an honorable place among our institutions of learning. The average number of students in attendance is a little less than one hundred.

In 1849 or the following year a number of Brothers took possession of a farm at New Bedford, Lawrence County, and opened a male orphan asylum, as was elsewhere stated; but it was abandoned at the end of about a year. In 1852 they opened a house at Cameron Bottom, an account of which was given in connection with the church at that place.

But the great work of the Order, the erection of the new college buildings, was not undertaken until the year 1863. At that time the energetic Brother Lawrence commenced the work, and it occupied his attention for about eight years. They consist of a central building 75 feet front by 50 feet deep and four stories high, which is flanked by two wings each 50 feet front by 30 deep and three stories high. Against the north wing is the exhibition-hall, 40 feet front by 80 deep and four stories high; while to the south wing is the chapel building, 40 feet front by 100 deep and four stories high. This gives a front of 255 feet, which, with the study-hall built some years before, and standing north of the college, with which it is connected, presents an imposing appearance. All the buildings are brick and have finished attics. Although the entire college is finished in good style, the chapel is deserving of special mention. It is modelled after the Gothic style of architecture, and is finished in the interior in immaculate white, which, far from smoke and dust, will long retain its original lustre. The windows are filled with stained glass, and the little marble altar is one of the most beautiful in the diocese.

Here it is that the priests of the diocese perform the exercises of the annual retreat. Previous to the year 1870 the retreats were held every second year, and continued for nine days, all the clergy being required to perform the exercises. But at that time a system in many respects preferable was adopted, and is still followed. It is that of two annual retreats of five days each, one half the clergy attending the first and the other half the second. By this arrangement all the clergy are enabled to reap the fruit of the exercises without depriving their congregations of Mass on a Sunday.

Additional lands were purchased at different times, until the Brothers now own about six hundred acres at Loretto. The Order has not flourished recently as it did in former years, although new members are being received from time to time. Nor has the college met with the full measure of patronage expected. With accommodations for perhaps one hundred Brothers and two hundred students, the latter have never exceeded one hundred, and have generally fallen far below that number. It has suffered doubtless from being situated at a distance from the railroad. But if an institution of learning is to flourish in the competition found at the present time, pains must be taken to maintain a competent staff of professors. While the members who founded the college were ripe scholars, their successors, it is to be feared, fall somewhat below them. The future prospects of the college, though fair perhaps, are not flattering.

In September, 1878, the Brothers established a house in Altoona, and have since taught the larger boys of St. John's congregation. The house at Pittsburg was discontinued in the summer of 1866. The Order numbers at present three houses, with about thirty-five professed Brothers and a few candidates.

THE CONGREGATION OF THE HOLY GHOST AND THE IMMACULATE HEART OF MARY.

This religious congregation was founded by the venerable Paul Marie Lieberman at Amiens, in France, in 1844, and although of but recent date is fast spreading throughout the world, the members being engaged principally in teaching and in the work of foreign missions. When Alsace passed under the rule of the German Emperor, a number of the fathers of the congregation came to this country under the guidance of Very Rev. Joseph Strub, as we stated in the history of St. Mary's Church, Sharpsburg, and after some time entered the Diocese of Pittsburg, and established the first house of the Order in the United States at Sharpsburg, April 23d, 1874. In October, 1876, St. Anne's Church, Millvale, was also confided to the pastoral care of one of the fathers. In the following year Father Strub secured a very large tract of land from one of the railroad companies in Franklin County, Arkansas, with a view of establishing a Catholic colony; and taking with him five priests and twenty Brothers, he founded a house of his congregation there. But the most important work of the Order for this diocese was the establishment of the Pittsburg Catholic College.

THE PITTSBURG CATHOLIC COLLEGE.

In the organization of his diocese Bishop O'Connor was not satisfied with merely placing within the reach of the children of both sexes the means of acquiring an elementary training; he would also afford them facilities for securing a higher education. For this purpose he established a highschool for boys in Pittsburg in 1844, and named Rev. T. Mullen principal. The school continued under his administration until the arrival of the Brothers of the Presentation, when it passed into their hands. It was discontinued for want of patronage about the year 1849. No attempt appears to have been made to revive it until about 1864, when a similar school was opened. But neither was it destined to be permanent, and at the end of two or three years it was numbered with the things of the past.

But although there were other colleges in the diocese, it seemed to be, and it was, a reproach that Pittsburg and Allegheny, with a Catholic population at that time numbering sixty thousand, should not possess a Catholic school for the higher education of boys. In 1873 a third attempt was made to found one. It took the name of the Catholic Institute, and entered upon its career with fair promise of success. But the times were not favorable, and it was impossible for a priest to superintend the school and at the same time discharge the duties of pastor of a congregation. At the end of about three years it went the way of its predecessors. It had long been apparent to every one capable of forming an opinion in the matter that, while there was no lack of youth desiring an education, a college could only be successful in the hands of a religious community whose sole business it should be to promote the interests of the institution.

At length, in the summer of 1878, the fathers of the Congregation of the Holy Ghost determined to open a day-college. It was an undertaking that would doubtless be attended with difficulties, not the least of which would come from a want of confidence in its ultimate success on the part of the public, owing to previous failures. Still the announcement was hailed with pleasure. Five fathers, three natives of Ireland and two of Germany—but all experienced professors—opened the Catholic College, as it was named, in rooms near the Cathedral, on the 1st of October, Rev. W. Powers being president. Two more fathers have since been added to the staff of professors. The system of training was soon found to be such as far to surpass expectation, and the number of students increased until it exceeded a hundred before the end of the first year. The course embraces all the departments that a young man could wish either to fit him for business, for the learned professions, or for the study of theology; while the many advantages arising from the lessening of expense to parents, the good effect of having the children always at home, and others, are such as to commend the college still more to public favor. It is probable that ere long permanent college buildings will be erected, as the success of the college is now placed beyond question.

OTHER RELIGIOUS ORDERS.

The Congregation of Our Most Holy Redeemer has already been spoken of in the history of St. Philomena's Church,

Pittsburg; and the Capuchin and Carmelite orders have been noticed in the sketches respectively of St. Augustine's and Most Holy Trinity, Pittsburg; while the Brothers of Mary Immaculate were referred to in the history of St. Mary's Church, Allegheny. It remains to speak of the Passionists and the Oblates of St. Charles Borromeo.

THE PASSIONIST FATHERS.

The Discalced Clerks of the Most Holy Cross and Passion of Jesus Christ, or Passionists as they are more commonly called, were founded by Paul Danei, now St. Paul of the Cross, at Mount Argentaro, not far from Rome, in 1737. His object was to unite in one the spirit of the ascetic and the missionary orders, the contemplative and the active life, and form a congregation of missionary priests somewhat differing from any then existing in the Church.

The first colony of the Passionist fathers to enter the New World came at the request of Bishop O'Connor, sailing November 14th, 1852, and landing at Philadelphia on the 6th of December. There were three priests—Fathers Anthony, Stanislaus, and Domenec—and two lay brothers. They celebrated the feast of the Immaculate Conception at the Seminary of St. Charles Borromeo, Philadelphia, and immediately after set out for Pittsburg, the term of their journey. They stopped for some time at the episcopal residence, where they devoted their leisure hours to the study of English. The Bishop donated certain lots, upon which the monastery now stands, and to which the fathers have since added by purchase; and they commenced the erection of the first monastery, or *retreat* as their houses are usually called, in the New World. The monastery stands on the brow of Mount Oliver, south of the Monongahela River, and is of brick. The main building extends east and west, and is 120 feet long and three stories high. A wing 100 feet long and two stories high runs south from the western end of the main building. From the southern extremity of this wing runs the church or public chapel still farther to the west. But all were not built at the same time. The first section was undertaken in the summer of 1853, and the corner-stone was laid by Father M'Mahon, V.G., on the 7th of August. It was dedicated by Bishop O'Connor on the 4th of June in the following year. The building included a public chapel, but not the present one.

Although the rule is one of the most austere in the Church, the good work the fathers were accomplishing soon made a favorable impression, and they began to receive applications for admission. Sunday, June 25th, 1854, witnessed the first accession to their number, and to Mr. Theodore Lobomiller —in religion Brother Bernard—belongs the honor and privilege of being the first to be invested with the habit of the Passionists in the New World. Members of the congregation also arrived at different times from Europe. So large had the community become that as early as 1855 the buildings were enlarged to their present proportions.

Soon the present large public chapel was undertaken, the corner-stone of which was laid by Father M'Mahon July 25th, 1858. It was dedicated by Bishop Young, of Erie, November 13th in the following year. But it did not at that time present the appearance it does to-day. Many of its most attractive features remained to be added before it should become one of the most beautiful chapels in the country. It is 75 feet in length by 45 in width, and is a fine specimen of Corinthian architecture, the only one in the diocese. The ceiling is supported by elegant fluted pillars. The building is lighted by small windows placed high in the walls, leaving space below for altars and confessionals. Of the former there are five—a high and two side altars, besides two others in chapels in the side-walls some distance back. All are finished in a high style of art and are in harmony with the rest of the interior, and all have been planned and built by the skill and labor of the industrious members of the community. The high altar particularly is one of the most splendid pieces of workmanship to be found anywhere in the country. A few years ago a beautiful altar-piece, representing St. Paul of the Cross ascending to heaven borne by angels, was executed in Rome at a cost of $400 in gold.

The community, as has been remarked, has purchased additional lots occupying the front of the hill below the monastery. The industry of the Brothers has converted this into a garden and vineyard, which add to the attractions of the place and make it more agreeable for the community and for those who, touched by divine grace, retire to this sacred retreat to devote a few days to the important affairs of salvation.

But though the congregation laid its first foundation at Pittsburg, and though this monastery is still the motherhouse and novitiate in the United States, it was not to be circumscribed within the limits of a single diocese. At the urgent request of Bishop Timon, of Buffalo, the Monastery of the Seven Dolors of Mary was established at Dunkirk, N. Y., May 26th, 1861. Two years later, August 9th, 1863, that of St. Michael the Archangel was founded at West Hoboken, N. J. The provincial usually resides there. On the 28th of April, 1867, St. Joseph's Monastery was established at Loudon Park, near Baltimore. The Monastery of Holy Cross, Mount Adams, Cincinnati, dates from May 28th, 1871, and that at Louisville, Ky., from November 14th, 1878. Thus we perceive that the mustard-seed has become a great tree, and in every place to which its branches have extended it has bórne most abundant fruit.

THE OBLATES OF ST. CHARLES BORROMEO.

Early in the year 1870 Rev. H. Denny and Rev. P. M'C. Morgan, with one or more lay brothers from England, sought to found a house of the Oblates of St. Charles Borromeo, which they had both recently joined in London. They selected East Liberty as the site of the foundation, and named the house Our Lady of Victories. But after it had been opened for about a year circumstances were found to be so unfavorable that it was reluctantly discontinued. The lay brothers returned to England; Father Denny entered the Society of Jesus, of which he is now a distinguished member; and Father Morgan, whose health was seriously impaired by the ravages of consumption, soon after retired to the home of his parents in Pittsburg, where he terminated his life by an edifying death on the morning of April 14th, 1872, in the 38th year of his age.

REV. POLLARD M'CORMICK MORGAN was a native of Pittsburg, and the son of a prominent Presbyterian gentleman who is yet living. At a proper age he entered the Western Theological Seminary (Presbyterian), in Allegheny City, where he completed the course of studies that was to fit him for entering the ranks of the ministers of that sect. But Providence had different designs upon him. He crossed over to England, where he joined his friend Mr. Harmer Denny, like himself a student and member of the same sect. Both were converted. Returning to America, he determined to consecrate himself to the preaching of the true gospel, to the knowledge of which he had been brought by the mercy of God. He entered the diocesan seminary at Pittsburg, and having finished his course of theology, was ordained on the 7th of February, 1863. He was now appointed pastor of Brownsville, and at the end of about a year was transferred to Loretto, to assist at the church founded by Dr. Gallitzin. We next find him at the seminary filling a professor's chair. At length he crossed over to England and entered the Congregation of the Oblates of St. Charles Borromeo. Returning to Pittsburg in the early part of 1868, he was appointed pastor of St. Andrew's Church, Allegheny, on the 1st of April, to remain until such time as circumstances should favor the opening of a house of the congregation of which he was a member. It was at length opened, as we have seen, but discontinued.

His funeral took place from the Cathedral; his parents and relations, still attached to the errors of their sect, occupied the front pews, and his devoted friend Father Denny pronounced the funeral discourse. These circumstances, in connection with the solemn chants of the Office and Mass, made the ceremony extremely touching and impressive.

Father Morgan was considerably below the medium size, and of slender form. In manner he possessed the candor and simplicity so strongly enjoined upon His followers by our Divine Redeemer. But his zeal in the cause of religion was far beyond his strength, and in death he could truly say, "The zeal of thy house hath consumed me."

CHAPTER XXVIII.

RELIGIOUS ORDERS OF WOMEN—ACADEMIES.

The nuns of St. Clare—St. Clare's Academy—The Sisters of Charity—The Sisters of Mercy—St. Xavier's Academy—St. Aloysius' Academy—The Sisters of St. Francis—The Sisters of St. Joseph—Mount Gallitzin Seminary—The Benedictine nuns—The Ursuline nuns—Other religious communities.

THE NUNS OF ST. CLARE—ST. CLARE'S YOUNG LADIES' ACADEMY, ALLEGHENY CITY.

IN the year 1828 Sister Frances Van de Vogel, a nun of the Order of St. Clare, belonging to a wealthy Flemish family, arrived from Belgium accompanied by another nun of the same Order, and established a convent in Pittsburg. For a short time they occupied a house on the cliff overlooking the Allegheny River, but at length purchased sixty acres of land on the hill west of Allegheny Town, where they erected a large frame convent and academy. Rev. Charles B. M'Guire, pastor of St. Patrick's Church and their ecclesiastical superior, took a lively interest in the foundation and encouraged it by his influence and counsel. The spot where the convent, which is yet standing, was built was named Mount Alvernio, but has since been known as "Nunnery Hill." Rev. Vincent Raymacher, O.S.D., was the first chaplain, but he was soon succeeded by Rev. A. F. Van de Wejer, O.S.D., a Belgian, who remained until the convent was abandoned. When Bishop Kenrick visited it in company with Bishop Conwell, June 27th, 1830, the community had increased to fourteen members, and the academy, although not enjoying the degree of patronage expected, was still in a flourishing condition.

This was the only house of the order in the United States at that time; for although a foundation was made many years before at Georgetown, D. C., it had long since been abandoned. Another house was established at Green Bay, Wisconsin, in 1830. The nuns continued in their quiet and unobtrusive way to work out the ends of their institute, and little further is known of their history until the storm arose which resulted in their expulsion and the sale of their property. This untoward event, which was painted at the time in the darkest colors by sectarian bigotry, is simple in itself and easily explained, although even yet it is looked upon by some as a dark spot in our history. And since I am of necessity constrained to give a sketch of the community, I deem it best to enter into a circumstantial account of the whole affair and thereby set the matter at rest. I have been at great pains to collect and sift the accounts of the very few who remember it, and the statement will be found to coincide with the card which Bishop Kenrick found it necessary to publish. The circumstances are briefly these: A young lady, remarkable for the eccentricities of her piety, lived in Allegheny and by visiting the convent became known to the nuns. It is also probable that she asked to be admitted into the community, and was not accepted. She went at length to Wisconsin and taught school for some time near the convent of the Order in that State, and was finally admitted into the community. In time she was sent to the convent at Allegheny, but not having the requisite letters was not admitted. She stopped with a friend until she could write for letters and receive them. But these did not secure her reception, for Madam Van de Vogel was not aware that she had an ecclesiastical superior in this country after the death of Father M'Guire. The consequence was that Bishop Résé, of Detroit, who held that office, interposed, and, after inflicting certain censures on two members of the community, ejected all the nuns from the convent, May 17th, 1835, and sold the property. Madam Van de Vogel went to Rome, and the other members of the community, after remaining in a house in Allegheny for about two years, supporting themselves by needlework or living on the charity of their friends, either returned to Europe or attached themselves to other religious communities.

All manner of slanderous stories were circulated by the sectarian press and certain ministers of the sects, and so damaging were some of these to the character of Rev. J. O'Reilly, pastor of St. Paul's Church, that his friends had recourse to the civil courts for redress. They forced a certain minister to publish a card retracting his statements; but this not proving satisfactory, he was obliged to publish another more explicit. Bishop Kenrick also published a card dated August 1st, 1835, in which he states the cause of the closing of the convent substantially as given above, and vindicates the character of Father O'Reilly from the aspersions thrown upon it.*

Father O'Reilly himself published a denial of ten false statements contained in an article that appeared in *The Conference Journal*, a sectarian publication of August 27th, dated the following day.† To these the physician of the institution, H. D. Sellers, M.D., a Protestant gentleman, added his statement in a card of August 1st, in which he vindicates the characters of all persons concerned, and denies the calumnies circulated against them.‡

Thus ended the only attempt ever made to establish the Nuns of St. Clare in Western Pennsylvania.

THE SISTERS OF CHARITY.

We have seen that the Nuns of St. Clare closed their academy and retired from their convent in the middle of May, 1835. In the summer of the same year Father O'Reilly, then pastor of St. Paul's Church, applied to the Sisters of Charity at Emmittsburg, Md., for a colony of their institute to take charge of the day-schools attached to the church. Such was his success that a small number of Sisters were immediately sent. He procured a house for them on Second Street (now Second Avenue), near Wood Street, where they remained for several years. They took charge of the schools, and also opened an academy for the more advanced pupils. When the orphan asylum was opened, in 1838, the care of the children was also confided to them. At the end of a few years—the date has not been ascertained—they procured a

---

* *Catholic Telegraph*, August 28th, 1835.
† Ibid., October 2d.
‡ Ibid., September 18th.

house on Webster Street, said by some to have been donated to them, where they took up their residence during the remainder of their sojourn in the city.

At length Pittsburg was raised to the dignity of an episcopal see, and Bishop O'Connor, on his return from Europe after his consecration in December, 1843, brought with him a foundation of the Sisters of Mercy, as we shall have occasion to remark hereafter, who immediately gained the ascendency. About the close of the year 1845 their superiors recalled the Sisters of Charity, and they withdrew from the diocese. During the ten years of their sojourn they had effected great good, and had lived in the greatest poverty and privations. Such was the first appearance of these devoted ladies among us; their second was destined to be under more favorable circumstances.

Seeing the present growth and the future prospects of his congregation, and wishing to place within the reach of all the many blessings afforded by our holy religion, but especially that of a thoroughly Catholic education, Very Rev. J. Tuigg, of Altoona, erected a large and elegant brick convent and school building, as we have elsewhere stated more fully, into which it was his intention to introduce a religious community to take charge of the schools. After mature deliberation he applied to the superioress of the convent of the Sisters of Charity at Cedar Grove, near Cincinnati, for a foundation. His petition was favorably received, and on the 11th of August, 1870, six Sisters left to found a house at Altoona. It may be remarked, in passing, that these Sisters belong to that branch of the community established by Mother Seton that did not affiliate with the Sisters of Charity in France, but preferred to retain the rule and habit inherited from their illustrious foundress. They immediately took charge of the girls and the smaller boys of the parish, and also opened an academy for the more advanced girls.

From the date of their arrival the Sisters, both as a community and as teachers, have met with complete success. Many have sought and obtained admittance into their ranks, and their numbers have increased from six to sixty. Nor has the sphere of their usefulness been confined to one parish only. In January, 1873, they founded a house at Blairsville, and took charge of the school. Two years later another band of seven opened a convent at the Church of the Sacred Heart, Pittsburg, and took charge of the school. For the same purpose a colony of nine came to St. John's Church, Pittsburg, South Side, and added a fourth convent to those already established. Another house was opened at Johnstown in September, 1878, by ten Sisters, who teach the schools attached to St. John Gualbert's English and St. Joseph's German church. Still another was opened at St. Joseph's Church, Sharpsburg, in September, 1879. In addition to these a number of Sisters go daily by cars from the convent at the Sacred Heart Church to teach the schools attached to St. John the Baptist's Church, of which they took charge in the fall of 1879. The extent of its ramifications and the entire satisfaction it has everywhere given show the wisdom and foresight of Father Tuigg in introducing the Order, no less than the zeal and efficiency of the Sisters themselves. There is no other community in the diocese that has so flattering a prospect as the Sisters of Charity.

THE SISTERS OF MERCY.

Whatever may be said of the other religious orders of women in the diocese, and they all have a noble record, the Sisters of Mercy must ever occupy the foremost place, as well by their number, which is now almost two hundred, as by the numerous schools, academies, and charitable institutions entrusted to their care. For thirty-six years, in imitation of their divine Master, they have gone round doing good, instructing the ignorant, protecting those exposed to danger, reclaiming many from vice, caring for the sick and the orphan; everywhere and by all proper means promoting the cause of religion. Nor have their labors been confined to one single diocese. From the foundation made at Chicago at the solicitation of Bishop Quarter, in September, 1846, to that at Wilkesbarre, thirty years later, the branches of the Order have been extending and have everywhere been bearing fruit for the honor and glory of God. Not content with the opportunities which ordinary circumstances placed within their reach, they have sought others. When the Rebellion desolated so large a portion of the country and filled the hospitals with sick and wounded, a band of Sisters from Pittsburg had charge of a hospital in Washington for some months, where, like members of other orders, they did much to alleviate pain, to reconcile the suffering to their lot and make it a means of spiritual profit, to prepare the poor victims for death, and to remove no little of the prejudice which ignorance and bigotry had caused and fostered against the Church and her religious orders. An interesting chapter of American Church history would be that recounting the benefits which the Sisters of the various orders conferred thus indirectly upon religion during the late Rebellion. But to resume.

At the date of the erection of the Diocese of Pittsburg there was but one religious order of women—the Sisters of Charity—in Western Pennsylvania, and these Sisters, notwithstanding their labors and sacrifices, were not meeting with the success to which they were entitled. On his return from Rome, where he had lately been consecrated Bishop of the new See, Dr. O'Connor passed through Ireland with a view of enlisting priests and religious for his Diocese. Among other places he visited the mother-house of the Sisters of Mercy in Dublin, from which, at his earnest request, seven Sisters accompanied him to America. They sailed on the 12th of November, 1843, and arrived at Pittsburg on the 3d of December—the first Sisters of Mercy to cross the Atlantic Ocean. On their arrival they took possession of a house on Penn Street, near Sixth, where they remained until 1848. On the 14th of April, 1844, they took charge of the girls' department of the Cathedral school in the new building then finished, and in September they opened St. Mary's Academy for young ladies. The other schools and academies which they conduct and the hospital and asylum of which they have charge, have been or will be treated under the heads of these congregations and institutions. The ranks of the community soon began to increase both by accessions for a short time from Ireland and by native aspirants to religious perfection. "In 1848 several of the Sisters having fallen victims to the ship-fever, then so prevalent in the city, and serious fears being entertained for the safety of the rest of the community, Bishop O'Connor, regardless of his own comfort, gave up his own residence to the Sisters, whither they removed and remained until the present convent on Webster Avenue was finished, a period of over two years. The same house served for convent, orphan asylum, academy, and here, too, some classes of the parochial schools for girls were taught. In 1850 the Sisters went to Webster Avenue." * This convent is at the corner of Chatham Street and not far from the Cathedral. It has been considerably enlarged, however, since that time. In 1866 the Sisters took charge of the boys' department of the Cathedral schools, which is taught in the building attached to the Cathedral. A year later, upon the completion of the new orphan asylum and the transfer of the orphan girls to it, the Sisters took possession of the old asylum which stood at the back of the convent, and soon after, having torn down the building, replaced it by one much larger for the accommodation of a part of the community. An elegant brick academy, fronting 58 feet on Chatham Street by 30 feet deep and three stories high, was finished in the spring of 1875. Thus were founded and finished all the buildings—and they are both neat and substantial—necessary for the community. The Order is in a flourishing condition and is constantly increasing in numbers. We shall now turn to the educational institutions conducted by the Sisters; their charitable institutions will find a place in the next chapter.

ST. XAVIER'S ACADEMY, WESTMORELAND COUNTY.

No sooner had the Sisters of Mercy established themselves in Pittsburg than they sought to extend the sphere of their usefulness. Encouraged and directed by Bishop O'Connor, who was always their steadfast friend, they resolved to establish a house and open an academy for young ladies near St. Vincent's Church, Westmoreland County. Father Stillenger

---

*Annual Report of the Treasurer and Rector of St. Paul's Cathedral, from July 1st, 1873, to June 30th, 1874.

had transferred his residence to Blairsville a short time before, and the Benedictine fathers had not yet arrived, and the large brick residence which the former had built in 1835 being unoccupied, would serve as the temporary home for the community and the cradle of their institution. Soon, however, they secured a farm of one hundred acres of land lying about one and one half miles south of St. Vincent's and on the Philadelphia and Pittsburg turnpike. They have since purchased an additional hundred acres adjoining it. Here they prepared to establish their convent and academy. Few places could have been better chosen, as every one who has visited it in the last thirty years attests. The spot selected for the buildings rises gently above the adjacent grounds and affords a fine view of the surrounding country and of the well-defined Chestnut ridge that extends north and south about six miles east of the academy. Many a giant oak of the primeval forest is yet standing in the recreation grounds to carry the mind alike of light-hearted girl and thoughtful Sister back to the days, but a century distant, when the forests resounded with the howl of the wolf and the panther and the war-whoop of the savage. It is a paradise, if there be such on earth. To this inviting spot the Sisters transferred their convent and school when the buildings were ready, May 14th, 1847, and named it in honor of the Apostle of the Indies. The increased accommodations and facilities soon began to have their effect in establishing for the institution that reputation for imparting a thorough education which it has since so successfully maintained and enhanced. The building of the Pennsylvania Railroad, which passes two miles north of the academy, placed it in direct communication with both the east and the west. As time went on the Sisters were enabled to improve the buildings and grounds and render them still more attractive. But in the midst of their prosperity and apparent security a calamity befell them which enlisted the sympathy not only of those who had been benefited by the academy, but of all who had heard of it. The building accidentally took fire on the 1st of February, 1868, and was burned to the ground.

Nothing remained but to replace it by a new building; and

in the mean time the school was continued, with such pupils as chose to remain, in the spacious brick guest-house that had been lately built. Work was immediately commenced on a new convent and academy that should occupy the site of the former. The friends of the Sisters hastened to their aid, and contributed liberally to the new building. It was ready for occupation at the commencement of the September term in 1869. The chapel, however, was not finished until the spring of 1870, when it was dedicated by Father Hickey, V.G., on the 21st of April. The new academy is considerably larger than the old one was, is finished in better style, and, being built in one block, is more symmetrical. Since its completion it yearly graduates young ladies from all parts of the country, who will carry with them through life the solid and healthful education they have received, and everywhere bear witness to the advantages offered by the institution.

Although the Sisters, in common with others, feel the effects of the present financial depression of the country, in a falling off in the number of pupils received, it is but temporary, and the academy still enjoys a liberal share of public patronage.

ST. ALOYSIUS' ACADEMY, LORETTO.

It had long been the wish of Dr. Gallitzin, as we have already remarked, to place the children of his Loretto settlement under the care of religious teachers; but, although he made an attempt to establish a community for that purpose, it was left for others to carry his beneficent designs into execution. In 1848 the Sisters of Mercy from Pittsburg founded a convent in the little Catholic village; a house was built for their reception, and a small portion of the land left by Dr. Gallitzin was made over to them upon certain conditions, one of which was that they should teach the girls' department of the parish school. A young ladies' academy was also opened, which they placed very appropriately under the invocation of St. Aloysius. The buildings were enlarged at different times, though after a preconceived plan, till the Sisters now have an academy which without presents a very attractive appearance, and within is well arranged for the purposes for which it is intended. It occupies a commanding position, and is surrounded by grounds neatly laid out and set with evergreens. The number of pupils has never been so large as that of St. Xavier's, nor is the course of studies so advanced. While the latter is adapted to the wants of those who by their circumstances are destined to move in the higher walks of life, the former is rather for the daughters of the middle class, those of limited means, who, while aiming to combine a useful with an accomplished education, give the preference to the former. Unfortunately, however, we find people of moderate means too often studying to ape the manners of persons of affluence, and the consequence is that the expense of their pretensions prevents them from ever attaining the reality. This is seen in many instances in the education of their daughters. Money is spent and time devoted to the acquiring of accomplishments, as they are called, which will be of no earthly use in after-life, and those who might by the same expenditure have acquired an education useful to themselves have little more at present than such as effectually unfits them for their station in life. It is hard to instil practical good sense into the minds of people in a land of shams like ours. And when educators would tell parents what is for the best, their advice is not acceptable.

St. Aloysius' has not in the past few years received the share of patronage to which it is entitled, but this is to be attributed to the depression of the times, and with the return of general prosperity the institution will flourish as in former years.

THE SISTERS OF ST. FRANCIS.

Three Sisters of this useful institute arrived from Buffalo, in November, 1865, and soon after opened St. Francis' Hospital on Forty-fourth Street, Pittsburg. When the orphan boys were transferred to the new asylum, in December, 1867, the Sisters purchased the house and grounds, on the South Side, the former of which became the mother-house of the Order in the diocese. A few years later they erected the present convent, which is a brick building perhaps 90 feet in length by 35 in width and three stories high, and placed it under the patronage of St. Joseph. In connection with it is the orphan asylum, of which mention will be made in its proper place. There are at present about fifty Sisters of the Order in the diocese, besides a large number of novices. The schools taught by the Sisters have already been referred to.

THE SISTERS OF ST. JOSEPH—MOUNT GALLITZIN SEMINARY, EBENSBURG.

The Sisters of St. Joseph were founded by Rev. Peter Medaille, at Puy, in France, in the year 1650. In 1836 a colony of six Sisters came to St. Louis, where they founded the first house of the Order in the United States. Twenty years later a house was established at Brooklyn, from which the foundation for the Diocese of Pittsburg was obtained by Rev. R. C. Christy, of Ebensburg, in the summer of 1869. Three Sisters arrived on the 2d of September, and opened a novitiate. They at the same time opened a boarding-school for small boys, which, in honor of the Apostle of the Alleghenies, they named "Mount Gallitzin Seminary." The building which was procured for their reception has since been considerably enlarged. The community is in a flourishing condition, although from its introduction into the diocese its members have had to struggle against many difficulties. The Sisters have houses at New Castle and Hollidaysburg in this diocese, as was stated in the history of the churches in those places, and at Columbus and Belaire in Ohio. The community numbers about thirty-five members, all of whom, with the exception of the Mother Superior, have been received in this diocese.

THE BENEDICTINE NUNS.

In the history of the Church at Carrolltown, a brief sketch was given of the introduction of the Benedictine Nuns into the diocese. St. Scholastica's convent in that village was the mother-house until the spring of 1879. But the difficulty of access to the place, the length and severity of the winter season, and other reasons induced the nuns to seek a more suitable locality. They accordingly purchased a large dwelling with a few acres of ground about eight miles south of Pittsburg, which is now the mother-house and novitiate. They have at present charge of all the German schools in Allegheny City.

THE URSULINE CONVENT AND YOUNG LADIES' ACADEMY, PITTSBURG.

We owe the presence of this Order among us to the disturbances created in France by the invasion of the German army in 1870. Eight of the French and English nuns in his diocese were authorized by the Cardinal Archbishop of Rouen to emigrate to the United States, and there seek the quiet and repose that it was no longer possible for them to enjoy in their native land. Upon their arrival in Pittsburg the same year they took possession of a house on Eighth Street, belonging to the diocese, where they remained until a more suitable home should be obtained. Leaving them for the present, we shall glance at the history of the Order.

The Ursuline Nuns were founded by St. Angela of Brescia, in 1537, for the virtuous education of young ladies. The first convent of the Order in the Western Continent was founded at Quebec, in 1639; the first in the United States, that at New Orleans, in 1727. The latter exists to the present time, and is the oldest convent of women in the country.

At the end of about a year the community of which I am now speaking purchased a very large brick dwelling on the cliff overlooking the Allegheny River, at a cost of $35,000. Additions were built for a like sum, and an academy for young ladies opened. The superior education, especially in the French language, afforded by the institution induced many of our leading citizens, irrespective of religious belief, to place their daughters under the care of the nuns. It need hardly be said, that, notwithstanding the short time the academy has been in existence, it has fully realized the expectations of its numerous patrons. In addition to its other claims it has that of being favored by the government with a charter which empowers it to graduate such of its pupils as go successfully through a complete course of studies. The present building, though spacious, is unable to accommodate all who apply for admission, and the nuns are looking forward to the time when they will have an academy where all the advantages of their system of education can be enjoyed by their pupils. With this end in view they purchased, in the summer of 1876, a property consisting of about thirteen acres of the most desirable ground at Oakland, which the owner, on account of his financial embarrassments, was obliged to sell at a sacrifice. It is within the city limits, and cost $35,000. The buildings, with the exception of a very large conservatory, are useless to the community; but it is the intention of the nuns to erect an academy and convent as soon as their circumstances will permit.

The community has had numerous acquisitions to its original number, and consists at present of about twenty-five professed nuns and a large number of novices, and it has every prospect of a flourishing career of usefulness.

The School Sisters of Notre Dame have been spoken of in the history of St. Philomena's Church, Pittsburg; the Sisters of St. Agnes, in St. Michael's Church, Hollidaysburg; and the Sisters of Divine Providence, in Sts. Peter and Paul's Church, Pittsburg. Those principally engaged in managing charitable institutions will next engage our attention.

CHAPTER XXIX.

CHARITABLE INSTITUTIONS—RELIGIOUS ORDERS OF WOMEN.

The Mercy Hospital, Pittsburg—St. Francis' Hospital, Pittsburg—Asylum of the Little Sisters of the Poor, Allegheny—St. Paul's R. C. Orphan Asylum, Pittsburg—St. Joseph's German Orphan Asylum, Allegheny—St. Michael's German Orphan Asylum, Pittsburg—House of the Good Shepherd, Allegheny—Conclusion.

THE MERCY HOSPITAL, PITTSBURG.

"THE poor you have always with you" is a prophecy applicable to the Church in all ages. But under certain circumstances it comes home with peculiar force. Ours, for example, is a population where objects of charity are at all times numerous. But although these are the first to enlist our sympathy and kindle the flame of Christian charity, there are others in better circumstances who, in time of sickness, long to be served by persons who have consecrated themselves by vow to works of mercy. Although Bishop O'Connor displayed the mind of a master in organizing the diocese over which he had been placed, yet he could not accomplish all things in a day; hence it was not until the beginning of 1847 that he saw the first Catholic hospital opened in Pittsburg. In January of that year the Sisters of Mercy rented a house and opened the Mercy Hospital for the reception of patients. With the return of spring arrangements were made for building a permanent institution. Large lots were secured on Boyd's Hill, about half a mile from the Cathedral, and a short distance from the summit of the bluff overlooking the Monongahela River. Work was commenced in August, and the new hospital was ready for the reception of patients in April, 1848. The building is brick, and although narrow, is about 125 feet in length and four stories high. Since its completion it has been under the care of the Sisters of Mercy, and it is the property of that community. The devotion of the good Sisters to the care of the sick, their skill, and the admirable order that reigns in every department of the hospital have secured for it a name and a patronage that show the superiority of Christian charity over much-vaunted philanthropy. But the very charitable character of the institution has made its existence a constant struggle; and this is perhaps the highest praise that could be bestowed upon it, that, not content with the good it is able to effect, it longs to extend its mercy yet further in behalf of suffering humanity. Not built with a view of making money nor under State patronage, the hospital has ever extended its charity to the poor as far as it was possible, trusting rather to the providence of God than to the rules of human prudence. Many pay, but not a few are received gratuitously.

During the first eighteen or twenty years the hospital was in some sense regarded as a diocesan institution, and an annual collection was taken up in the churches towards its support, for which in return certain privileges were granted to the sick of the congregations. But of late years it has become a private institution. The spiritual necessities of the patients were ministered to for many years by one of the priests attached to the Cathedral, but for the last ten or more years the institution enjoyed the advantages of a resident chaplain. Rev. M. J. Mitchell filled that position until early in December, 1879, when his health permitted him to take charge of a congregation, and the hospital was again made dependent upon the Cathedral.

ST. FRANCIS' GERMAN HOSPITAL, PITTSBURG.

In the month of November, 1865, three Sisters of St. Francis from Buffalo, N. Y., entered the Diocese of Pittsburg and were added to the other religious communities devoted to the cause of education and charity among us. Soon after their arrival they purchased four acres of ground on what is now Forty-fourth Street, and opened a hospital in the frame building situated on the grounds. The little community increased rapidly, and the mother-house was soon transferred to the South Side and permanently established at St. Joseph's, as we have seen. An attempt had once been made to purchase the property now occupied by the hospital as the site of the new St. Paul's Orphan Asylum, but the title was not then clear, and it was abandoned for the spot at present occupied by that institution. About half the original purchase was soon sold out in building lots, a transaction from which more was realized than the cost of the whole.

A small frame chapel was built by the Sisters soon after their arrival. But the hospital was ere long too small to afford accommodation to all who sought admittance, and it was determined to build a large one. Work was commenced on it in the spring of 1872, and it was completed in the fall of the same year and blessed by the Bishop September 26th. This hospital is one of the most substantial and best arranged buildings of its kind in the city. It is 150 feet in length by 40 in depth, four stories high, and has a wing extending back from the centre for a chapel. The interior arrangements are all that mechanical skill and Christian charity could devise for the relief and comfort of the inmates. The location, too, is superior to that of any other hospital in the city. The ground, which rises gradually from the river a distance of half a mile, places the institution so high that it enjoys a constant supply of fresh air, so desirable for invalids, and being in the northern part of the city it is free from the perennial cloud of smoke that hangs over Pittsburg. As if nothing should be wanting to enhance its attractions, the street in front of the hospital when opened was cut down from 10 to 20 feet, leaving the building on an elevation. The grounds between the hospital and the street have since been tastefully terraced. To the rear are the grove-like grounds of St. Mary's, and beyond those of the Allegheny cemeteries, with a fine country prospect. On the whole it is one of the most healthy and attractive locations that could have been selected. The old hospital is yet standing, and is used for patients afflicted with the more malignant contagious diseases. Mass is daily celebrated by one of the Capuchin fathers from St. Augustine's Church. St. Francis', though commonly regarded as a German hospital, is yet patronized by all classes of patients irrespective of nationality

THE ASYLUM OF THE LITTLE SISTERS OF THE POOR, ALLEGHENY CITY.

The need of an asylum for the aged poor had long been felt in our cities, not only that the corporal but much more the spiritual necessities of such as were thrown upon the public charity, or were in danger of being thrown upon it, might be properly ministered to at a time when they were on the eve of rendering an account of their lives. Moved at the sight of the destitution in which these unfortunate persons were placed, and conscious that but one effectual remedy existed, the Bishop applied to the mother-house of the Little Sisters of the Poor at Rennes, in France, for a foundation of the institute for his diocese. But other Bishops had already made similar requests, and he must await his turn. At length his request was granted, and, on the 24th of April, 1872, he had the happiness of welcoming a colony of seven Sisters into the diocese. They were received into a house on Eighth Street, the property of the diocese, which had previously been occupied by the Ursuline nuns, until such time as they should be able to secure a permanent home.

A brief sketch of this useful Order and the object to which it is devoted will no doubt be read with pleasure. It was at the little town of St. Servans, near St. Malo, in the north-west of France, that the foundation of the institute was laid. The parish priest of the town, the Abbé Le Pailleus, had long lamented the destitute condition of the aged poor, and had begged of God that He would raise up instruments for the amelioration of their condition. His prayers were heard, and God selected the pious priest himself for the good work. He felt interiorly moved first to select a poor girl of eighteen years, and later to associate with her another, an orphan of sixteen, to whom he gave a simple rule and whom he tried for two years before making known to them the work for which he was training them. This done, he committed an old blind woman to their keeping, and soon a poor woman living in an attic received them into her humble home. Here the foundation of the Order was laid October 15th, 1840. From this lowly beginning it grew to its present proportions. At first the aged inmates were permitted to beg; but the temptations to which they were sometimes exposed soon induced the Sisters to retain this humiliating occupation for themselves exclusively, and it has become one of their rules. In the beginning the house was called "The Good Women's Home," but at the end of four years the present familiar name was adopted. The Sisters follow the rules of St. Augustine, and add to the three customary vows that of hospitality. This requires them to give up their own beds if necessary, and to supply the aged with food before partaking of it themselves. It does not, however, mean, as some persons imagine, that the Sisters eat the fragments left from the old folks' table, but rather that if the supply of food is not sufficient for both, the Sisters and not the aged must fast. The "good Mother," as the superioress is called, told me with touching simplicity that Providence does not often demand this sacrifice at their hands. Think of that, you who discourse so eloquently of "philanthropy," "the cause of humanity," etc. Have you ever denied yourselves a meal or even a luxury for the sake of the poor? But here we have strangers coming among us to minister to our poor, who labor without any remuneration but their coarse clothes and coarser food, and who are at times actually in want of the sustenance upon which their laborious lives depend. Enthusiasm may sometimes carry away one or two in a nation, but here we have under our eyes a sustained effort, the extent of which is almost incredible. It is only in the Catholic Church that true charity is found.

The institute was approved by the Sovereign Pontiff July 9th, 1854, and it numbers at present about three hundred houses in different parts of the world. The first house established in the United States was that at Brooklyn in 1868.

The only conditions required of those who seek admission into the "homes" of the Sisters is that they should be at least sixty years of age and be willing to enter and remain. The poorest is as welcome as he who is able to pay his way.

To return to the Sisters among us. A suitable house was soon found on Washington Street, Allegheny, directly opposite the House of Industry of the Sisters of Mercy. It is a brick dwelling situated on a large lot 66 feet front by 300 feet deep, and which was purchased at a cost of $26,000. It was immediately fitted for their reception, and the Sisters moved into it with their charge Oct. 21st, 1872. Prior to that date two of the community had died. They had now eight aged persons in charge, but the number increased so rapidly that the new home was soon filled and additional accommodations were demanded. Strong in their trust in God, whom they were serving in the person of His poor, the Sisters in the summer of 1873 purchased the house and lot adjoining that which they occupied, at a cost of $28,000. The house is a brick dwelling, and the lot is 84 feet in front by 300 in depth. This house became the men's asylum, while the other was occupied by the women and the community. But it was not long before both houses were crowded, for the Sisters refuse no one so long as it is possible to receive him. As to food, they trust to Him who feeds the sparrows. There are at present ninety-one aged persons in the two houses, and little does the world know of the sacrifices demanded from the Sisters in providing and caring for this peculiar charge. Their sacrifices are heroic, and are a living proof of the truth of the religion that is capable of inspiring and sustaining them. But it is not in the home only that sacrifices are demanded; in their rounds soliciting aid the Sisters frequently meet with trials, although as a rule our citizens receive them kindly and appreciate the benefit they are conferring on humanity.

Such of the inmates as are able to work are not entertained in idleness. The women assist at the house work or sew for themselves, and the men keep the buildings and grounds in order.

It is the intention of the Sisters to build a large asylum when they are out of debt, but that cannot be for many years to come.

Mass is celebrated daily in the chapel by one of the Benedictine fathers from St. Mary's Church, by whom the other spiritual necessities of the community and inmates are also ministered to. There are at present eleven Sisters in the community.

ST. PAUL'S R. C. ORPHAN ASYLUM, PITTSBURG.

In a city like Pittsburg, which contains so great a laboring population depending principally on two or three branches of industry, there must necessarily be a large number of poor, for no species of manufactory continues for a long time without temporary cessations. Unfortunately for them there is also a delusion in the minds of many of those who work before the iron and glass furnaces that makes them imagine that the use of stimulants is necessary to sustain them in the heat to which they are exposed. Agriculture, too, has become so unpopular that our manufacturing centres are crowded with a class of persons who labor under the delusion that because they receive regular cash payments they must necessarily do well. Yet nothing is better demonstrated than the fact that high wages and regular cash payments foster extravagant habits and reduce many of those to ultimate poverty who receive them, unless they and especially their wives are well trained in the school of domestic economy. Unhappily this is not always the case. Many live up to their means, and if their income increases their outlay will keep pace with it. If there is a cessation of the weekly or monthly pay, they are in a little time reduced to the verge of want. Along with this is an unaccountable predilection for small houses with but one, or at most two, diminutive rooms but poorly provided with the means of ventilation, and of the use of even these scanty means the occupants appear to have no idea. An unwholesome atmosphere is generated which enervates the system and excites or increases an appetite for stimulants. Reform is necessarily difficult and slow, and as the greater part of these persons are Catholics, they leave, should death carry them off, a heavy burden on the Church to take care of their children. Half-orphans, or such as have been deprived of one of their parents, are often in equally destitute circumstances, and children both of whose parents are living are not unfrequently more to be pitied than orphans properly so called. They sometimes learn from a sad experience that "a man's enemies are those of his own household." I have had ample opportunities for collecting information regarding the condition of the destitute children in our cities. There are doubtless many poor children who have been reduced to that state without any fault of theirs or their parents, but if there were no others it would not be difficult to dispose of these.

That an asylum should be of a reformatory as well as protective character in a population like ours will be apparent to every one. But the successful imparting of such a character is one of the greatest difficulties to be met with in the management of indigent and neglected children. Vices and evil habits are contracted at so early an age and are so thoroughly rooted and grounded in the child by neglect and by the bad example of those who should have been its guardians and guides in virtue as to become in a short time a second nature, and it will only be after long years of patient and prudent discipline that they will at length be eradicated. But instead of being eradicated they will often be found to be only slumbering, and will be easily roused into activity when circumstances are favorable to them. It is terrible to think of the part that parents sometimes play in misleading and ruining their own children. Another difficulty which those have to contend against who undertake the reformation of this class of children is that a large proportion of those who receive children out of the asylum ignore to a great extent the obligation imposed on them of exercising care and vigilance over their moral and religious life. Under such circumstances the child's training must be perfected in the asylum, or, if not, in many cases it will never be perfected. The effect of past evil influence must be destroyed and the child must be armed against those of the future. For these reasons and for others of a less general character the proper management of the orphans and destitute children among us is a matter as difficult as it is necessary.

Recognizing the importance and necessity of caring for the small number of these children already depending upon

Catholic charity, Rev. John O'Reilly, then pastor of St. Paul's Church, took measures looking towards the opening of an asylum in 1838. On the 6th of July of that year he organized "St. Paul's Orphan Society," with himself as president, Joseph Armstrong vice-president, John Andoe treasurer, and Luke Taaffe secretary, and with a board of twelve managers selected from among the leading Catholic laymen of the city. To prevent confusion with a Protestant organization of the same name, the title was afterwards amended to that of "St. Paul's Roman Catholic Orphan Society." This society has existed to the present time, and according to the terms of the charter the board of managers must be selected from its members by an election held June 29th every year. But the society has long since dwindled into insignificance for want of being properly worked up.

A charter was obtained from the State Legislature April 3d, 1840, legally constituting St. Paul's R. C. Orphan Asylum, and authorizing it to receive, care for, and dispose of "any orphan child or children, and such other children as may be deprived of one parent."

Father O'Reilly soon after purchased lots on the corner of Webster Avenue and Chatham Street, those upon which St. Mary's Convent of Mercy now stands, and having erected a building opened an orphan asylum, which he placed under the care of the Sisters of Charity. When these Sisters withdrew from the diocese, about the year 1845, the asylum passed into the hands of the Sisters of Mercy, who have since had charge of it. But the care of the larger boys soon began to present difficulties. A solution was sought, which was, as we shall see, by no means successful. A farm of 247 acres situated in the north-western part of Lawrence County, near the State line, had been bequeathed to the Diocese of Pittsburg by a Mr. W. Murrin, on the conditions that an orphan asylum should be built upon it, and that a resident chaplain should be stationed there. Thinking that it might be made a home for the larger orphan boys, who might aid in supporting themselves by tilling the ground, a part of which was already cleared, a number of them were transferred to the farm and placed in charge of the Franciscan brothers about the year

1849. A brick asylum sufficient for their accommodation was also built, and the result of the experiment was anxiously awaited. But the distance from the city, the inconveniences of travel—for none of the railroads leading west from the city were then built—the expense of purchasing stock, utensils, etc., and sending them out, the impossibility of persons desiring to adopt boys going so far to make a selection, and a few other drawbacks, proved the project to be impracticable. But the use that was afterwards made of this circumstance as an argument against building the new asylum in the country was, to say the least of it, more ingenious than convincing. The children were withdrawn after a short time, and it was next proposed by some to open an ecclesiastical seminary on the farm. But that was not permitted by the terms of the bequest. There is so little disinterested charity in the world that bequests are sometimes so hedged in with conditions next to impossible as to make them a burden on the hands of those who receive them. In order to make the most of it the Bishop sold the farm to the Diocese of Cleveland for $3000, about the year 1851, and it still remains under the jurisdiction of the Bishop of that diocese. (See St. James' Church, New Bedford.)

The diocesan seminary in Birmingham had been closed, as we have seen, early in the summer of 1851, and it was not the intention of the Bishop to open it again in that place. He accordingly donated the frame building that had been used as a seminary, with 200 feet square of ground upon which it stood, to the board of managers, and the male orphan asylum was opened there in the latter part of 1851. Soon after a brick building was erected to serve in part for the orphans and in part as a convent for the Sisters in charge of them. The number of orphans naturally increased with the growth of the Catholic population, and at the close of that year there were seventy female children at the asylum on Webster Avenue, and twenty-four boys at that in Birmingham.

The proper training of the large boys was a matter that still puzzled both the Bishop and the managers, and another solution was attempted that was destined to be productive of as little practical result as that at New Bedford had been. In

February, 1861, a number of the larger boys were sent to the farm at Cameron Bottom, and placed under the care of the Franciscan brothers there. Here it was expected they should learn to work on a farm, and should in due time be indentured to the Catholic farmers in the surrounding country. For seven years there were from twenty to thirty boys with the brothers. But the experiment did not prove successful. Of those placed with the farmers in the vicinity, part have done well and part have not, while of those who left of their own choice the result is what might naturally be expected. I have said that one of the greatest difficulties to be met with in the management and disposal of orphans is to find persons to take them who will devote the proper care and attention to their religious training. But in justice to all it must be confessed that asylums, owing to defective management, are sometimes to be held accountable for a part in this unhappy state of affairs. But while the shortcomings of one may render the discharge of another's duty more arduous or difficult, it does not exculpate him for his own neglect.

The younger male orphans remained at the asylum in Birmingham. But the building besides being old was no longer capable of accommodating the number of children for whom the diocese was now forced to provide. It was also desirable to remove the female orpnans from the asylum on Webster Avenue; the house was now unsuited, and the Sisters wanted it to accommodate their growing community. It was therefore determined to build a new and magnificent institution, which should be a monument to the charity and zeal of the Catholics of the diocese, and the energy and enterprise of the managers. The resolution was also adopted of bringing all the English orphans of the diocese into one building. After considerable debating on the relative eligibility of different localities it was finally settled to erect it on the spot it now occupies on Tannehill Street, a little more than half a mile from the Cathedral and not far from Trinity Church. A lot about 300 feet square, with a street laid out through it, which it was believed would never be opened, was purchased at a cost of $9636.10, and work was commenced. In due time the foundations were ready for the laying of the corner-stone.

The ceremony was fixed for Sunday, June 10th, 1866, and preparations were made upon a grand scale. The Bishop, the clergy of the city and vicinity, and Catholic societies with banners and brass bands without number moved from the Cathedral to the grounds in the afternoon, and after appropriate discourses had been delivered by the Bishop and others the corner-stone was laid with the ceremonies prescribed by the ritual. The building progressed slowly owing to its vast proportions, but by the exertions of Father Hickey and the board of managers it was ready for occupation at the end of a year and a half. The Sisters and the orphan of both the male and the female departments took possession of it in the middle of December, 1867. The old boys' asylum was sold to the Sisters of St. Francis who had lately entered the diocese, and the girls' asylum to the Sisters of Mercy.

The lot upon which the new asylum stands is from ten to fifteen feet higher than the street it fronts on, and is supported by a massive stone wall of that height that runs the entire length. The building stands back about twenty feet, and is brick trimmed with cut stone. It is 200 feet in length by 40 in width, and has, besides the basement, three full stories and an attic finished with mansard roof. A wing 90 feet in length by 35 in width extends back from the centre, the lower story of which is used for the kitchen and refectory and the upper for the chapel. The asylum was estimated to cost the sum of $160,000. But the proportions of the building will strike the reader as not being the best that could have been adopted. And when it is added that a corridor nine feet wide runs the entire length of the building on each floor, including basement and attic, that no room can be more than fifteen feet wide, while some are from fifty to seventy-five feet long, and that no two rooms communicate with each other except by the corridor, the mistaken plan of the institution will be yet more apparent. The boys occupy one end of the building and the girls the other, and in all the corridors, the refectory, and the playgrounds, partitions separate the one department entirely from the other.

But however successfully a girls' asylum may be conducted in a city, it is not the place for a boys' asylum, unless some branch of useful industry be connected with it. As it is, the boys, even the largest, have no work, except such as properly falls to the lot of girls, and there is nothing to inspire and foster that spirit of Christian manliness and self-reliance without which life can be neither successfully nor honorably passed by the poor. Besides, if boys, especially the larger ones, are to be trained to a really useful career, it must be under the guidance of persons of their own sex. Sisters may teach the branches that usually enter into the ordinary school course—and there are few teachers better than our Sisters—but beyond this is the formation of character, and that is in a great measure out of their reach. It is much to be regretted that the two departments of the asylum should ever have been united, but it is more to be regretted that the boys' asylum should have been located in the city. So long as it is there it must necessarily be a failure, so far as the larger boys are concerned, unless some branch of industry be connected with it, and this seems impossible, at least at the present time. Had a small farm been purchased in some country place near the city, and the male asylum or industrial school been built upon it, the larger boys might have been properly prepared for the place they should hereafter fill in the world. And this could have been done under proper management with far less expense than has been incurred in the present asylum. Some of those who had the matter in hand were in favor of this, but the majority was against them, and objected that former attempts at a country asylum had not met with success. But while New Bedford and Cameron Bottom were at least sixty miles from the city, and it would require two days of exposure, fatigue, and expense to reach them, a place might have been secured without difficulty within less than an hour's ride of the city. It is now almost universally admitted by persons of experience that the country is the proper place to train boys; but wherever they are trained they must be taught to work. The action of many of the Bishops of this country confirms this view, and the success their experiments have met with proves the correctness of their theories, if anything so self-evident stood in need of confirmation. All the ends of a boy's asylum may be attained as well in the country as in the city, and some of them can be attained nowhere else but in the country. The religious and secular school training, being acquired in the institution, are independent of place. The health is built up more successfully in the country air. Boys have more ample opportunities of learning agriculture on a farm than on a small court paved with brick. Boys trained in a city asylum are of but little use to farmers, and hence it is that few farmers take them, and of those who do, but few are satisfied. Of what use is a boy to a farmer if he never saw a stalk of corn or a potato grow? But this is not the most important point. To teach children *how* to work is regarded by some persons as the leading duty of a protectory; but it is not. Why is it that a farmer's or a tradesman's son begins to work at a proper age, and sometimes before it, and does not complain? It is not, as some imagine, because he knows how, for the fact is he has yet to be taught, and his teaching is, after all, a small matter; but it is because the scenes in which he grew up were of such a character as to impress the great truth on his mind that labor is man's normal condition in this life. He knows that, as a matter of course, he must work when he is old enough. But train him in a city asylum in which there is no branch of useful industry, and where his only work will be to sweep and scrub the floors and take care of the children younger than himself —girls' work—and you have taught him, on the one hand, to be ashamed of the only work he ever did, and on the other to take as little even of that as possible. Let the system of training be such as to impress on the mind of a boy from infancy that he is born to work, and he will readily learn to work. It was my good fortune to be born of very poor parents, and to be obliged to begin work when but seven years of age; and this was continued on a farm or in public works, with the exception of three or four months of schooling during a part of the winter, for fourteen years. Even the summer vacations during my course in the seminary were given to hard labor. Hence, having labored from so early a period in life, and having been thrown among laborers as one of themselves, I had ample opportunities of learning what contributes to success and what does not. And I am convinced that the one point to which all should be directed is that of impressing upon the boy's mind, by the circumstances that surround him, that he is born to work. A system which aims at this will not fail to employ him usefully as soon as he arrives at the proper age.

Now, it is precisely in this that our new asylum is hopelessly defective. Boys' protectories have been made successful in other places, and near cities much smaller than ours, which had not a tithe of the industries of Pittsburg; yet ours, built at a time when Pittsburg was in the zenith of its prosperity, is deficient in the most essential point, because a mistaken idea of grandeur and not a sense of practical utility influenced those who controlled the destinies of the new institution. There is not an asylum or protectory in the United States capable of accommodating the same number that has cost so much and is so deeply in debt; yet, as was said, the city that is unparalleled on earth for the extent of its manufactories, as compared with the population, was then in its most flourishing condition.

A reformatory conducted on proper principles might have been able to receive a large number, if not all, of the Catholic boys who are sent to the Pennsylvania Reform School—House of Refuge—and, while making them contribute, in part at least, to their own support, would have trained them in accordance with Catholic principles. There are about eighty Catholic boys in this State institution, while there are only about half a dozen girls; and although they are permitted to hear Mass and go to confession, their opportunities are but meagre, and they are obliged to be present at all the heretical exercises conducted in the chapel of the institution by whatever preacher the authorities chance for the time to smile upon. Besides, they are constantly in the company of the worst boys in the State. Under such circumstances it is not to be wondered at that they should return from the institution, after the two years for which they are usually entered, with nearly all ideas of religion obliterated from their minds.

The lamented Bishop Domenec, while occupying the See of Pittsburg, frequently expressed to me his desire of leaving the present asylum to the girls, the small boys, and foundlings, and of building a reformatory somewhere near the city. But having been trained in a Catholic country, where everything was so different from what it is here, his ideas were not always the most practical, and, which is more to be regretted, he did not keep the affairs of the new asylum from the commencement sufficiently under his control.

A farm consisting of fifty-nine acres underlaid with coal and lying about five miles from Pittsburg was bequeathed to the asylum a few years ago, but the terms of the bequest are such that it will not be available for some time, and it is, besides, difficult of access. The asylum has always been maintained by voluntary contributions, such as collections in the churches of the diocese, by donations, fairs, etc., and by money paid by some persons for the maintenance of certain children. To obviate the difficulties arising from so precarious a means of support, the Orphan Society founded by Father O'Reilly in the beginning was revived in a slightly modified form under the title of "The Relief Association of St. Paul's R. C. Orphan Asylum," in May, 1878. This it was hoped would secure a permanent income, but it has only in part realized the expectation of those who revived it.

But notwithstanding every effort to meet the liabilities of the institution, it was sold by the sheriff for a debt due certain depositors about the beginning of December, 1878. But by a generous and united effort of the clergy and people, such as is seldom witnessed, much less in times like the present, $14,000 was immediately raised, and the institution was redeemed and set afloat to meet whatever other storms may be in store for it.

The largest number of orphans ever sheltered in the institution at once was about two hundred and eighty, but the average number is about two hundred and twenty-five. A priest usually resides in the asylum to minister to the spiritual necessities of the children; but at such times as one did not, they were attended from Trinity Church near by. The children usually spend the greater part of the day in school, but the larger girls do much of the sewing and housework. In better times they took in sewing. Little difficulty is found in disposing of the girls, for as soon as they are capable of taking care of a child they are usually wanted, and find a home for the most part in the city. But it is more difficult to dispose of the boys, for the reasons already given. The future of the asylum for many years will be a struggle for existence, and it cannot be known with certainty at present whether or not it is destined to be finally successful.

ST. JOSEPH'S GERMAN ORPHAN ASYLUM, ALLEGHENY CITY.

The German like the English orphan asylum took its rise near the parent church. In 1849 a colony of School Sisters of Notre Dame came to St. Philomena's Church from Baltimore and took charge of the female department of the school. A little later in the same year the new building, destined as a school for the children and a convent for the Sisters, was finished and occupied. There being as yet no German orphan asylum, the Sisters received the female orphans into the convent and cared for them. But the number increased, and their home, which was not meant to be permanent, was soon crowded. Measures were taken to provide a more suitable home, and one that would meet the future as well as the present wants of the destitute little ones. A very eligible lot of ground, containing about four acres, was purchased on Troy Hill in 1850, and the building of an asylum was soon after commenced under the supervision of the rector of St. Philomena's Church and a board of lay managers. The building was not finished for occupation until the spring of 1853. On the 1st of May of that year a number of Sisters from St. Philomena's with twenty-four orphans entered their new home. It was a neat and substantial brick building, sufficiently large to meet the wants of the inmates for many years, and it stood out prominently on the brow of the hill overlooking the Allegheny River and the western portion of Pittsburg. Being to the north-west of the cities it was not exposed to the smoke, while its elevated position secured a constant supply of fresh air and delightful scenery. But the Troy Hill of that day was not the Troy Hill of the present. The houses were few and of unpretending style. The place had yet to become celebrated for its beer-gardens and the boisterous Sunday gatherings that marked the period immediately preceding its incorporation into the city.

The opening of the asylum was a day of joy and festivity not only for the poor children, but also for the good German people. A grand picnic and open-air feast inaugurated the new institution and marked the anniversary for many years, until it was at length discontinued. But the Sisters and the children were not long in their new home before a calamity befell them which left them in a more destitute condition than they had been before. When the "dry summer" of 1854 had prepared the way for a conflagration by drying up wells and fountains, and when as yet the city did not supply water to the Troy Hill district, the asylum took fire July 25th, and was reduced to ashes without it being in the power of any one to stay the progress of the flames. The orphans had by this time increased to about thirty-five. The loss, beyond the amount covered by insurance, was $8000. A temporary home was prepared for the Sisters and children, and a new and much larger building was commenced on the site occupied by the former. Work was pushed forward with all speed, and the building was ready for occupation in an incredibly short space of time. The new orphanage is a splendid brick block 80 feet in length by about 40 in width, and three stories high besides the basement. It is one of the most prominent buildings on Troy Hill.

The German orphan asylum did not at first enjoy the advantages of a resident chaplain, but in the year 1853 Rev. John Fred. Wolf came to this country from Prussia and entered the Diocese of Pittsburg; and being too far advanced in years to enter on the mission—he was then about sixty-four—he was appointed chaplain of the asylum. For fourteen years he continued to reside in the institution and minister to the inmates, until he was called to his reward in a good old age, October 18th, 1867. His remains repose near the little mortuary chapel in the cemetery adjoining the asylum. Nothing is known of the life of Father Wolf beyond what is contained in the above lines. Upon the death of their chaplain the Sisters and orphans were again exposed to a season of spiritual privation, and were obliged for a time to go to the church of the Holy Name to hear Mass. But when an assistant was assigned to Father Mollinger of that church, Mass was celebrated regularly in the asylum. At length, in 1878, Rev. A. Roswogg was appointed resident chaplain, a position which he continued to fill until succeeded by Rev. J. Stillerich in July, 1879.

The number of orphans has gradually increased, and it is now about one hundred. Since the erection of the first asylum both the male and the female orphans have been kept in the institution. All the orphans attend school taught in the asylum during a certain portion of the day. The remaining hours are devoted by the larger boys to the care of the extensive garden, or to such other out-door work as may be assigned them, while the girls do the work of the house. Half-orphans as well as children deprived of both parents are received, and indeed, as in the English asylum, the former constitute the larger number. The children are disposed of in the same manner as those in the other asylum; but from the character of their training they give more general satisfaction. About the year 1870 an addition was built to the asylum.. A motion was also made about the same time to build a new asylum on the large farm owned by the institution not far from the eastern part of Pittsburg. But this was abandoned at least until such time as it could be done without entailing so heavy a debt. The asylum is in a flourishing condition, and is supported by a society similar to that established by Father O'Reilly for the support of St. Paul's, by collections taken up in the German churches of the two cities and of Allegheny County, by donations, and by the produce of the large garden attached to the institution. A German newspaper, *Der Republikaner*, was established for the benefit of the asylum many years ago, on the principle that all net proceeds, after paying a certain interest on the money invested, should go to the support of the institution. The money paid to the asylum from this source has been variously estimated, some persons placing it as high as $20,000. But for certain reasons nothing appears to have been paid for the last few years.

ST. MICHAEL'S GERMAN ORPHAN ASYLUM, PITTSBURG, SOUTH SIDE.

We remarked when sketching the history of St. Michael's Church, Pittsburg, that when the new convent of the Sisters of St. Francis was finished and occupied, in 1874, part of it was converted into an orphan asylum for the children of the congregation, where they have since been cared for and schooled by the Sisters. The number of orphans is necessarily small, since they are from but one parish, and will not perhaps exceed twelve or fifteen. But the foundation of the asylum besides being of advantage to the children is a further illustration of the energy that has characterized the congregation in every period of its history. It is not probable that the asylum will ever receive any other children than those of the parish, nor is it capable of accommodating many more than these.

THE HOUSE OF THE GOOD SHEPHERD, TROY HILL, ALLEGHENY CITY.

The institute of Our Lady of Charity of the Good Shepherd, or the Sisters of the Good Shepherd as the order is more commonly called, was established by Father Eudes, in France, in the early part of the seventeenth century. The object of the institute is the offering of an asylum to females whose virtue is exposed to danger, or the reclaiming of such as have fallen from virtue and are desirous of amending their lives. The rules are founded on the strictest principles of Christian charity, and no subject is received unless she is willing to enter; hence the asylum is in no sense a prison. The inmates are divided into two classes: the *penitents*, or those who have fallen from virtue, and in whose case, as a sanitary precaution, certain conditions are required, and the class of *perseverance*, or those who seek a refuge from the dangers to which they are exposed. But the two classes are wholly separated from each other, and are under the care of different members of the community. The better to shield from reproach those who are received into the house, the greatest secrecy is observed respecting their condition before entering; and no questions on this head are asked of the person that accompanies them. A still more ingenious invention of charity is that of giving the person received a fictitious name before she is introduced to the class of which she is to become a member. Hence not her condition only, but also her name, is unknown to all save the superioress.

The period for which persons are received is commonly two years, at the end of which time they are either returned to their friends, or the Sisters endeavor to find respectable situations for them. But if during her stay in the asylum any one has given entire satisfaction and is desirous of consecrating herself to a life of retirement from the world, she may remain. These are permitted to take a peculiar habit and make an act of consecration. A still higher grade are the Magdalenes. They are governed in many respects as the penitents are, but they also take the Carmelite habit with their rule and office, and are besides encouraged to practise certain corporal austerities not permitted the penitents. Magdalenes are not, however, found in every asylum, and as yet there are none in the one under consideration.

The founder of the Order met with serious opposition from many prudent and influential persons, who feared that the bringing together of women of such character, even for the sake of reform, would prove a dangerous experiment. But it was soon apparent that it was directed by the finger of God. The dictates of human prudence were not, however, disregarded. The selection of candidates for a mission so peculiar engaged special attention, and there is perhaps no other order in the Church so strict in this matter. The construction of the asylums received equal attention. They are separated from the convents to which they communicate by passages, the doors of which are always locked, and through which no one except the Sisters in charge of the inmates is permitted to pass. The Order itself is enclosed with the exception of the Sisters to whom the out-door business is confided, and who are for this reason called "the out-door Sisters."

From a knowledge of the object to which the Sisters of the Good Shepherd are devoted, it will readily be seen that few cities in the present state of society can well afford to be without one of their houses. More especially is this true of a city like Pittsburg, where so large a proportion of the Catholic population is poor; where many parents, owing to their indifference or their intemperate habits, are unfit to train up their children properly, and where they are obliged on account of their poverty to send their girls to live out without being careful, in all cases, to select proper places or to keep a vigilant watch over them. These and other causes made it desirable to have a house established in the city, and induced the Bishop to petition the community at Buffalo to give his diocese a foundation. His petition was granted, and six Sisters arrived at Pittsburg October 1st, 1872. They took possession of a house of the Sisters of Mercy, situated at the corner of Pride and Bluff streets, overlooking the Monongahela River and near the Mercy Hospital. It had for a few years previously been used by the Sisters of Mercy for a purpose somewhat similar, according to a special provision of their rules in cities where no House of the Good Shepherd exists. Here as many subjects were received as the limited accommodations would permit, which was never more than fourteen. But the occupation of this house was only meant to be temporary. Soon a spacious lot with a large brick dwelling on it was purchased on Troy Hill, Allegheny. It is situated at the brow of the cliff overlooking the Allegheny River and commands a good view of both cities and the surroundings, and being to the north of the cities is also free from smoke. A frame building 80 feet in length by 30 in width, and three stories high besides a basement, was erected as an asylum, while the dwelling should be used as a convent by the Sisters. This new asylum was taken possession of December 16th, 1874. The arrangement of the interior, which consists of school and work rooms, dormitories, etc., is admirably adapted to the purposes for which the building was erected.

The labors of the Sisters have generally been crowned with success; for, although hearts have been met with so callous as to resist every good impression, the number is small compared with those who have been reformed. It must not, however, be supposed that the girls—for unhappily the greater part of the subjects of such institutions are young—are maintained in idleness. The first, and among the natural means the most powerful for preserving or restoring virtue, is useful occupation, and this is a truth to which the Sisters attach due importance. The inmates are constantly employed, with the exception of the time set apart for necessary recreation. Under the direction of the Sisters who have charge of the several departments, they do the work of the house, the sewing of the community, and also take in sewing; and the younger girls devote a part of their time to study. But the strictest attention is paid to their religious and moral culture. Mass is daily celebrated in the chapel of the asylum; opportunities are offered for the frequent reception of the sacraments, an exercise to which the inmates are earnestly exhorted; pious reading is daily had for a suitable time in common, and nothing is omitted that could reclaim them from vice and establish them in virtue. There are at present about sixty inmates.

On the 5th and 6th of May, 1878, two or three attempts were made by one of the older inmates to set the asylum on fire, but she was at length discovered and handed over to the civil courts for punishment.

The community is in a flourishing condition, and from six members has increased to about double that number.

CONCLUSION.

In casting a retrospective glance over the period embraced within the present history, there is much to cheer, much to sadden the Christian heart. What a century ago was a forest, the habitation of savage beasts and yet more savage men, is now a flourishing portion of the Church of God. The little colony of six persons who first planted the standard of the Cross in Westmoreland County ninety years ago has, like the single mustard-seed to which the Church is compared by our divine Redeemer, multiplied until it will now number perhaps 140,000. At first its branches began to extend in different directions and here and there take root, spring up and flourish; and although many, alas! too many, souls have been lost to the faith for want of priests to minister to them, from lack of opportunities for seeing their religion presented with that attractive ceremonial with which it so well knows how to clothe itself, from indifference contracted in the pestilential atmosphere in which they were forced to move, and most of all from mixed marriages by which souls were led astray and families were multiplied and are still being multiplied, but not for God and the Church, the branches have still borne consoling fruit, and yet give cheering promise for the future. The colonies gradually spread and formed new ones. At first a priest would penetrate the wilderness and visit the scattered families, riding perhaps fifty, it may be a hundred miles, to visit and minister to a dozen souls—living, it might be said, on horseback and enduring hardships and exposing himself to dangers of which the world knows little, but which were appreciated by those in whose behalf he bore them. Settlements increased, the germs of congregations appeared, churches were built, parishes organized, and the Church gradually began to assume her proper form among us. But priests were as yet few, and one would be required to minister to two or three, perhaps to even a larger number of congregations. But the work of organization and subdivision went on until at present almost every church has its own pastor. Residences were then to be built, schools to be opened, and churches enlarged or replaced by others more commodious and substantial. Lastly, the schools were to be placed, as they have been in many instances, in the hands of religious. Colleges, academies, hospitals, and asylums were opened in their turn. The gradual steps by which these ends were attained have been traced in the course of the preceding pages. A study of these will afford a fair specimen of what takes place in every country but recently converted to the faith, or in which the faith is but recently planted. All cannot be accomplished in a moment, nor can that which is done be immediately brought to perfection. Man is prone to err, and the spirit of evil will not permit him to use the feeble powers with which he is endowed without molestation. If this malicious spirit cannot prevent a good work, he will study to render it in some way imperfect; if he cannot destroy, he will try at least to vitiate.

If then the reader should find something imperfect in the foregoing pages, let him not pass too severe a judgment until he has carefully considered all the circumstances, remembered the toil and labors of the few early missionaries, and the privations and exposure of the scattered faithful, and withal the imperfections of the narrative, and I doubt not he will find more for edification than for censure.

SUPPLEMENTARY CHAPTER.

ERRORS IN OUR EARLY CATHOLIC HISTORY.

"The old priest" mentioned by William Penn in 1686—The first priest to say Mass in Philadelphia—The first church in Philadelphia—Miss Elizabeth M'Gawley's Chapel near Nicetown.

THE lack of authentic records relating to our early history, and the want of critical examination of such as are extant, by early Catholic writers, have led to numerous errors. These having been frequently repeated by subsequent writers have come at length to be accepted as historical facts, and the author who would call them in question is regarded with suspicion. Having been led to believe that certain statements copied from standard authors in a previous chapter of this work (pp. 19-21) were errors of this kind, I began a careful investigation of the matter, and discovered the truth just in time to make the necessary correction before the electrotype plates were cast. Wishing to place the questions beyond further dispute—although they refer but incidentally to the present history—I have determined to add this supplementary chapter as the best means of discussing the errors in detail. The hold which they have on Catholic writers, and the desire of demonstrating the truth once for all, have induced me to accumulate evidence that would otherwise be superfluous. The most prominent of these errors are four in number: "The old priest" mentioned by William Penn in 1686; the priest who first celebrated Mass in Philadelphia; the first church built in Philadelphia; and the chapel said to have been built by Miss Elizabeth M'Gawley.

And first, of "The Old Priest:" Bernard U. Campbell, whose "Life and Times of Archbishop Carroll" was published in the *U. S. Catholic Magazine* (1844-1846), appears to have been the first to claim "the old priest" for a minister of the true faith. Quoting Mr. Watson,* he says—*U. S. Catholic Magazine*, 1845, p. 252—" As early as 1686, Wm. Penn mentions '*the old priest*' in Philadelphia." Here, then, is the unlucky quotation that has led all subsequent Catholic historians astray. Let us go back to Penn and to Mr. Watson, from whom Mr. Campbell copied the statement; for had he copied Penn's own words, there would have been no room for misunderstanding.

Penn's words are the following, as we find them in a letter written in the year 1686 from London to his steward James Harrison at Philadelphia. He requests Harrison to send certain rarities from the colony, " because people concerned ask much to see something of the place." Among other things he says: " Get also some smoked shad and beef. The old priest at Philadelphia had rare shad." † Mr. Watson says, speaking of the Roman Catholic churches in Philadelphia: "As early as 1686 I have recorded William Penn's letter to Harrison (his steward) wherein he tells him he may procure fine smoked shad of the *old priest* in Philadelphia. And in 1685 his letter spoke of Charles De la Noe, the French Minister, coming to settle among them with his servants as a Vigneron. These remarks may prove interesting inquiries to papists themselves among us, none of whom I am satisfied have any idea of any older chapel than the one now in Willing's alley, built in 1753, and now called the oldest." ‡ These extracts are the sole foundations for "the old priest" story. Let us examine them carefully. Penn's words give no clue whatever to the identity of the person mentioned; his reference is purely incidental. Writers who quote his words seem also to overlook the fact that this " old priest " must have been in Philadelphia not only in 1686, but at least as early as the beginning of 1684, since Penn, who sailed for Europe in May of that year, speaks of " the old priest " as well known to himself. Now, apart from the extreme improbability of a Catholic priest opening a fish-market at all, considered in itself, and apart from the little

---

* Annals of Philadelphia, vol. i. p. 454.
† Ibid., vol. ii. p. 411.
‡ Ibid., vol. i. p. 454.

custom he might expect from Quakers should he do so, can we suppose that Penn, who spoke of the most solemn act of Catholic worship as "the scandal of the Mass"—although he may not have done so out of pure bigotry—would permit a Catholic priest to live and traffic under his eyes in a colony of which he was sole proprietary?

Again, there were, as we shall see in the sequel, but two English-speaking priests in North America at that time; and it is beyond the reach of credibility that one of these should already be located and in business in a city laid out but two years before, when seventy-three years later, that is in 1757, there were only 397 Catholics, English and German, in and about Philadelphia.* And the more so as Catholic Maryland was sufficiently near, from which a priest could have visited the few Catholics if there had been any at that time in the city and vicinity, as they were afterwards visited. Besides, from the character of the immigrants it is fair to suppose that there were none whatever in the colony at that early day. No further mention is made of a priest until 1708, twenty-four years later, and it is certain he did not then reside in the city. There is no authentic record of a priest residing at Philadelphia until 1730 or 1732, that is at least forty-six years after "the old priest" was selling his "rare shad."

Mr. Watson, in the passage above quoted, is the first and only original authority for referring the words "the old priest" to a Catholic clergyman. But he, it is well to bear in mind, wrote about the year 1830, when reliable tradition had ceased to exist, and before historical criticism had investigated the matter so thoroughly as it has done at the present day. That Mr. Watson did not consider it a question deserving of careful investigation, and did not in fact investigate it, is clearly to be inferred from his own words: "These remarks may prove interesting inquiries for the papists themselves among us." But it is still more evident from his associating the name of Charles De la Noe with Penn's reference to "the old priest," by which he gives us to understand that he regarded De la Noe as a Catholic because he was a Frenchman, although he

* Colonial Record, vol. vii. p. 328.

proves in another part of his "Annals" (vol. ii. p. 112) that De la Noe was a Huguenot. Hence Mr. Watson, so far from adding weight to the words of Penn, only gives them a false interpretation and leads the reader astray.

Mr. Willis P. Hazard, who was employed to write a third volume of "Annals of Philadelphia," with a view, among other objects, of correcting, by the light of recent investigations, some of the errors into which Mr. Watson had fallen, when writing on the introduction of Catholicity into Philadelphia, altogether ignores the affair of "the old priest."* Again, Mr. Thompson Westcott, member of the Historical Society of Pennsylvania, whose " History of Philadelphia" Mr. Hazard in his "Annals" (preface) calls " that monument of perseverance, research, and historical acumen" which "will be quoted as long as the State exists," also ignores " the old priest " story when writing professedly of "the Catholic Church in Philadelphia before 1751." †

Whom then did Penn mean by "the old priest"? In the answer to this question we shall find additional proof of our position. Penn's letter, as I have said, affords no clue whatever to his identity; but it shows, when examined by the light of intrinsic evidence and history, that he could not have been a Catholic priest. There can be little doubt that Jacobus Fabricius, the German preacher of the Swedish Lutheran Church, was meant. He was in Philadelphia from 1677 to 1691, and although blind for a part of the time he had his agent Jacob Yung to look after his temporalities.‡

In addition to this accumulation of evidence, the Corresponding Secretary of the Historical Society of Pennsylvania, himself a Catholic, writes me : " In the entire lack of any evidence to the contrary I have no reason to doubt that the gentleman referred to was the Rev. Jacobus Fabricius, the Dutch pastor of the Swedish Lutheran congregation at Wicacoa, near Gloria Dei Protestant Episcopal Church in Philadephia.

---

* Annals of Philadelphia, vol. iii. p. 316.

† A History of Philadelphia from the Time of the First Settlement on the Delaware to the Consolidation of the City and District in 1854, chap. cxv. It was published in the *Sunday Dispatch*, but is to appear in book form.

‡ A History of New Sweden, etc., by Israel Acrelius, pp. 177-179.

The term 'priest' was applied to this person by his own sectaries, and was constantly used by William Penn and his fellow-Quakers in speaking of ministers of the Gospel, of whatever denomination of Christians." The same gentleman — to whom I acknowledge myself under special obligations in this matter — again writes : " As to the person indicated being Fabricius I feel the more confident to decide in consequence of my having made a special study of the early Swedish settlement on the Delaware."

When all available evidence has been brought to bear on the question, we are forced to conclude that "the old priest" was not and could not have been a Catholic clergyman, but that a degree of probability amounting almost to certainty points to Rev. Jacobus Fabricius as the person meant.

The second question to engage our attention is this: By whom was the first Mass—that of 1708—celebrated in Philadelphia? This question cannot, strictly speaking, be called an error of history, but it is a subject of useful and interesting inquiry, and the more so as those who have written professedly of the foundation of Catholicity in Philadelphia have devoted no attention to it.

Mr. Westcott* shall again be our guide. Having mentioned the Mass spoken of by Penn in 1708, he continues: " Beyond this mere reference, there is very little known in reference to the introduction of the Catholic religion in Philadelphia in 1708. But . . . certain facts have been derived from John Gilmary Shea of New York . . . which add very much to the interest attached to this subject. It has lately been discovered by investigation in England, by the Very Rev. Pamfilo da Magliano, Provincial of the Order of Franciscans in this country, that there were missionaries of that order in North America long before the Jesuits established the Catholic religion on a firm basis. This list of Franciscan missionaries is as follows :

" 1674. Polycarp Wicksted sent. He died before April, 1725.

" Basil Hobard, or Hubbard; died in Maryland, July, 1698.

---

* A History of Philadelphia, etc., chap. cxcii., note.

"Massey Massey; returned to England in 1677; died in England before October, 1702.

"Henry of St. Francis.

"1675. Edward Golding.

"1677. Henry Carew; died at sea about 1683.

"1700. James Haddock; died in Maryland on or before 1720.

"Bruno Taylor; returned on or before 1704.

"From this list," continues Mr. Westcott, "it seems probable that Polycarp Wicksted and James Haddock were in North America in 1708. In regard to Edward Golding and Henry St. Francis, there is nothing to establish when they died or left the country. Probability, therefore, points to Father Wicksted or to Father Haddock as being the celebrant of the Mass in Philadelphia in 1707-'8. In a letter from the Rev. John Talbot to George Keith . . . under date of Feb. 14th, 1708, he says: 'I saw Mr. Bradford in New York. He tells me that Mass is set up and read publicly in Philadelphia.'"

As regards the first church or chapel in Philadelphia, Mr. B. U. Campbell, in the work already quoted, has made another erroneous statement, in which subsequent historians have blindly followed him. Having cited the passage from Watson's "Annals of Philadelphia" referring to "the old priest," he adds: "Watson . . . says, 'This early mentioned Mass probably had its origin in the frame building on the north-west corner of Front and Walnut streets, which was the first chapel in Philadelphia.'" *

Mr. Westcott ignores this statement also, as he did that of "the old priest." Speaking of the early history of Catholicity, he says:† "The early records of the Catholic Church in Philadelphia are very meagre. . . . There were but few attractions for Catholics in the young colony. Hence the number of persons of that persuasion coming into Pennsylvania during the first twenty-five years after the settlement of Philadelphia must have been few. . . .

* Life and Times of Archbishop Carroll, *United States Catholic Magazine*, 1845, p. 252.

† A History of Philadelphia, etc., chap. cxv.

"The first notice that we have of the exercise of worship by the Catholics is contained in a letter from Penn to Logan, dated 29th, seventh mo., 1708:*

"'Here is a complaint against your government, that you suffer publick Mass in a scandalous manner. Pray send the matter of fact, for ill use is made of it against us here.' In another letter from Penn to a correspondent in Philadelphia, he says: 'It has become a reproach to me here with the officers of the crown that you have suffered the scandal of the Mass to be publickly celebrated.'" To this the historian adds: "This may seem somewhat intolerant; but it must not be considered as a voluntary protest of Penn in consequence of over-zeal. At the time at which these letters were written the 'hot church party' in Pennsylvania were exceedingly bitter against the proprietary government, and no effort was spared to prejudice the British Government against the provincial administration. A remonstrance, therefore, against Catholicism would seem to be a matter that would create a very strong impression in Great Britain, and help the project to have substituted a royal government for the proprietary government, established under the charter. Penn himself could not have refused to notice the subject, inasmuch as adverse action upon those complaints in England might have entirely prevented the exercise of religious liberty in the province, to secure which had been to him a labor of time, expense, and feeling."

The provincial government does not appear to have taken any action in the matter of the Mass referred to by Penn.

"At what precise place these religious exercises were held," continues Mr. Westcott, "is now unknown. Mr. Watson, in his 'Annals of Philadelphia,'† mentions three places in which, according to very vague and unreliable statements, Catholic worship might have been held. One of these, he says, was at the north-west corner of Front and Walnut streets, and he gives as an authority some statements made by persons who rested their belief upon hearsay." Having

---

* Penn and Logan Correspondence, vol. ii. p. 294.
† Vol. i. pp. 452, 453.

traced, from the city records, the ownership of the lot at the above place from its transfer by Penn to another Quaker, April 29th, 1683, to the present time, the historian remarks: "The special matter of interest connected with the history of this property from 1683 to the present period is that at no time during that long space of years has it been owned by any other person than a member of the Society of Friends. . . . It is impossible that, at any time previous to the death of Dickinson (one of the owners), in 1722, there could have been any Catholic worship in a house which was inhabited by Quakers." After carefully debating the case, he concludes: "It is possible that some tenant, between 1722 and 1732, may have permitted some occasional solemnization of the Mass there, but the occurrence must have been exceptional." That a chapel properly so called ever stood at the place is thus proven to be evidently false.

As to the second place spoken of as the site of a chapel, Mr. Westcott remarks: "Mr. Watson * mentions a statement by a lady who had heard it said that 'the house at the southeast corner of Second and Chestnut streets was built for a Papal chapel.' This statement also rests on hearsay, and is worthy of little credence." He then proceeds to prove that it cannot be regarded as true.

Which, then, and where was the first church in Philadelphia? There can be no doubt whatever that St. Joseph's Jesuit church was the first. Says Mr. Westcott: † "In the year 1730, or 1732 (accounts differ as to date), the Rev. Joseph Greaton, a member of the Society of Jesus, was sent from Maryland to Philadelphia. . . . Father Greaton must have found in the city a sufficient number of Catholics to justify the establishment of a church. He procured ground south of Walnut Street and east of Fourth Street, adjoining the Friends' Almshouse, under the shelter of which it is to be presumed he hoped for the protection which a more open position might not have insured. It is said that his original congregation consisted of eleven persons, and it is re-

---

* Annals of Philadelphia, vol. i. p. 453.

† A History of Philadelphia, chap. cxv. See also Watson's Annals, vol. iii. p. 318.

lated that Father Greaton was compelled to make his church very modest in appearance by including in it what seemed to be his dwelling-house. . . . The whole establishment (church and parsonage) must have been small, inasmuch as afterward, when it was enlarged, the building thus increased occupied a space of forty feet by forty feet. This little church was dedicated to St. Joseph. Although its opening did not probably attract immediate attention, it was not long used before the provincial authorities, anxious it is to be presumed to avoid difficulty with England, had their attention called to the circumstance. At a meeting of the Provincial Council, at which Thomas Penn, one of the proprietaries, was present, and Lieutenant-Governor Patrick Gordon presided, which was held on the 25th of July, 1734," the matter was presented to the Council, and it was asked if it was not contrary to the laws of England to permit " the publick exercise of that religion." At a meeting held on the 31st of the same month the matter was resumed. *

"Whether Governor Gordon wrote to England upon the subject," continues Mr. Westcott, " or whether he abandoned it, is unknown. It is certain, however, that there was no further attempt made to meddle with St. Joseph's Church, which went on slowly increasing in numbers without molestation. Kalm, the Swedish traveller, who wrote about the period 1748–'50, says, ' The Roman Catholics have in the south-west part of the town a great house, which is well adorned within, and has an organ.' " †

As regards the last error to be noticed, that relating to the chapel said to have been built by Miss M'Gawley, Mr. Campbell is the guide; and all, without exception, have followed more or less closely in his erratic footsteps. Taken together, the errors exposed in this chapter are fair specimens of the injury that is sometimes done to the cause of truth by repeating statements that have been advanced without sufficient grounds. After quoting Mr. Watson substantially as given below by Mr. Westcott, the author of the " Life and Times of

---

* Colonial Records, vol. iii. pp. 546, 563.
† A History of Philadelphia, etc., chap. cxv.

Archbishop Carroll," in the place already referred to, adds: "The testimony of Watson is conformable to the local tradition, although the inscription (on the tombstone) does not determine the priestly character of Brown."

Mr. Westcott in the work already cited states the question of the M'Gawley chapel, and disposes of it in the following manner: "Mr. Watson also says, 'There was a Roman chapel near the city of Philadelphia as early as the year 1729. At tnat time Elizabeth M'Gawley, an Irish lady, and single, brought over a number of tenantry, and with them settled on the land on the road leading from Nicetown to Frankford. Connected with her house she had the said chapel. Near the place, one eighth of a mile off, is a stone enclosure, in which is a large tombstone of marble inscribed with a cross and the name "John Michael Brown, ob. 15th December, A.D. 1750. R. I. P." He was a priest.'* Such research as the writer has been able to make in the records at Philadelphia has been insufficient to verify this statement exactly in the shape in which it has been made. No deed or grant to Elizabeth M'Gawley, or Gawley, or M'Cauley, has been found. There is no deed on record from this lady, nor is there any registry of her will or record of grant of letters of administration upon her estate. John Michael Brown, however, is not a myth; but he was no priest. On the 20th of Oct., 1742, John Michael Brown, 'Doctor in Physic,' bought . . . two hundred and ninety-three acres, situate upon the road leading from Frankford to Germantown. . . . On the 2d of May, 1747, Dr. John Michael Brown and Sarah, his wife, granted to Joseph Greaton, who was at that time the pastor of St. Joseph's Catholic Church in Philadelphia, seven and three quarter acres of this land, fronting on the road running from Frankford to Germantown. . . . The consideration was £46. . . . If there ever was any Roman Catholic chapel near Nicetown, it must have been built on this ground bought by Father Greaton, and after the year 1747. Mr. Watson* vouches for the statement by Deborah Logan (wife of Dr. George Logan, grandson of James

---

* Annals of Philadelphia, vol. i. p. 453.

Logan, proprietary-governor for William Penn) that she remembers the ruins of such a church when she was a girl. . . . Probably if such a chapel was erected it was not long maintained. . . . Dr. Brown was undoubtedly a Catholic. He describes himself as 'late of the West Indies, but now of Pennsylvania, a doctor of physic.' In the will is a bequest of £10, Irish, to Robert Kirwan, Bonnatopler, 'to be laid out in masses.' . . . Under these circumstances it seems most likely that Dr. Brown would have been buried in consecrated ground. If there had been any chapel and burial ground on his plantation he would have preferred that his body should there be interred. But in this particular his will is peculiar He orders 'my body to be interred in as private a manner as possible in the orchard on my plantation.'"† From these extracts one must necessarily conclude: First, that it is very doubtful whether there ever was a landowner by the name of Elizabeth M'Gawley; secondly, that it is almost certain there never was a chapel at all at the place mentioned, but if so, it could not have been earlier than 1747; thirdly, that John Michael Brown was not a priest, although it is very probable that Mass was sometimes said in his house, for in his will he mentions among his personal property "one church vestment, one chalice."

It is believed that a careful perusal of this chapter, and of the authorities adduced, all of which I have quoted from the originals, will set these vexed historical questions at rest forever.

* Annals of Philadelphia, vol. i., p. 453.
† A History of Philadelphia, etc., chap. cxv.